LANGUAGE FOR DAILY USE

Phoenix Edition

Gold

Phoenix Edition

LANGUAGE FOR DAILY USE

Harcourt Brace Jovanovich, Publishers

New York   Chicago   San Francisco   Atlanta   Dallas   and   London

ACKNOWLEDGMENTS

For permission to reprint copyrighted material, grateful acknowledgment is made to the following sources:

American Friends of the Hebrew University, Inc.: From *Einstein on Peace* edited by Otto Nathan and Heinz Norden. Copyright © 1960 by the Estate of Albert Einstein. Published by Simon and Schuster, Inc. Reprinted by permission of the Hebrew University in Jerusalem, Israel.

Chatto & Windus, Ltd.: "Pigeons" from *Differences* by Richard Kell. Published by Chatto & Windus, Ltd. Copyright © 1969 by Richard Kell.

Chilton Book Company, Radnor, PA.: Excerpt from *Dune* by Frank Herbert. Copyright © 1965 by Frank Herbert.

Thomas Y. Crowell, Publishers: "A Walk in the Forest" from *A Walk in the Forest: The Woodlands of North America* by Albert List, Jr., and Ilka List. Copyright © 1977 by Albert List, Jr., and Ilka List. "The Bells" by Edgar Allan Poe from *Poems of Edgar Allan Poe* selected by Dwight Macdonald. Copyright © 1965 by Dwight Macdonald.

Richard Curtis Associates, Inc.: "Dry Spell" by Bill Pronzini from *100 Great Science Fiction Short Stories*, edited by Bill Pronzini. Copyright © 1970 by Ultimate Publishing Co., Inc.

Doubleday & Company, Inc.: "The Sea Is Melancholy" by Agnes T. Pratt from *The Whispering Wind* edited by Terry Allen. Copyright © 1972 by the Institute of American Indian Arts. Excerpt from *The Story of My Life* by Helen Keller.

Farrar, Straus and Giroux, Inc.: Excerpt adapted from *Tuck Everlasting* by Natalie Babbitt. Copyright © 1975 by Natalie Babbitt.

Harcourt Brace Jovanovich, Inc.: Entries reprinted from *The HBJ School Dictionary*, copyright © 1977 by Harcourt Brace Jovanovich, Inc. "Feathered Friend" from *From the Ocean, From the Stars* by Arthur C. Clarke. Copyright 1953, © 1956, 1957, 1958 by Arthur C. Clarke. "maggie and milly and molly and may" by E. E. Cummings from his volume *Complete Poems 1913–1962*. Copyright © 1956 by E. E. Cummings. "Fog" from *Chicago Poems* by Carl Sandburg, copyright 1916 by Holt, Rinehart and Winston, Inc.; copyright 1944 by Carl Sandburg.

Harcourt Brace Jovanovich, Inc. and William Collins Sons and Co., Ltd.: Excerpt from a letter by C. S. Lewis from *Letters of C. S. Lewis* edited by W. H. Lewis, published in London in 1966. Copyright by W. H. Lewis and the Estate of C. S. Lewis.

Harper & Row, Publishers, Inc.: "Letter to Mr. Nadeau" from *Letters of E. B. White* by E.B. White. Collected and edited by Dorothy Lobrano Guth. Copyright © 1976 by E. B. White. Excerpt abridged from *Cheaper by the Dozen* by Frank B. Gilbreth (T. Y. Crowell). Copyright 1948, 1963 by Frank B. Gilbreth, Jr.

Holt, Rinehart and Winston, Publishers: "A Cloud Shadow" and "Two Tramps in Mud Time" from *The Poetry of Robert Frost* edited by Edward Connery Lathem. Copyright 1936, 1942 by Robert Frost. Copyright © 1964, 1970 by Lesley Frost Ballantine. Copyright © 1969 by Holt, Rinehart and Winston.

Houghton Mifflin Company: Entries reprinted from *Roget's II: The New Thesaurus*. Copyright © 1980 by Houghton Mifflin Company. Excerpt from *The Life and Letters of Emily Dickinson* by Martha Dickinson Bianchi. Copyright 1924 by Martha Dickinson Bianchi. Copyright renewed 1952 by Alfred Leete Hampson.

William Wayne Keeler: "Inaugural Address of the Chief of the Cherokees" by William Wayne Keeler from *Representative American Speeches: 1971–1972* edited by Waldo W. Braden. Copyright © 1972 by The H. W. Wilson Company.

Macmillan Publishing Co., Inc.: "Let It Be Forgotten" from *Collected Poems* by Sara Teasdale. Copyright 1920 by Macmillan Publishing Co., Inc., renewed 1948 by Mamie T. Wheless.

Harold Matson Company, Inc.: Excerpt from *Dandelion Wine* by Ray Bradbury. Copyright © 1953 by Ray Bradbury, © renewed 1981 by Ray Bradbury.

Norma Millay (Ellis): "Three Songs of Shattering I" (retitled "The First Rose on My Rose Tree") from *Collected Poems* by Edna St. Vincent Millay. Published by Harper & Row, Publishers, Inc. Copyright 1917, 1945 by Edna St. Vincent Millay.

National Geographic Society: Excerpt from *The Wondrous World of Fishes*. © National Geographic Society.

Plays, Inc., Publishers: "The Miraculous Eclipse" adapted by Joellen Bland from *Plays, The Drama Magazine for Young People*. Copyright © 1972 by Plays, Inc., Publishers. This play is for reading purposes only. For permission to produce this play, write to Plays, Inc., 8 Arlington St., Boston, MA 02116.

Random House, Inc.: "Broadcast Organization: Network Versus Spot" by Christopher Gilson from *Advertising: Concepts and Strategies* by Christopher Gilson and Harold W. Berkman. New York: Random House, 1980.

Simon & Schuster, a Division of Gulf & Western Corporation: "For the Light That Shone in This Country Was No Ordinary Light" by Jawaharlal Nehru from *A Treasury of the World's Great Speeches* edited by Houston Peterson. Copyright © 1954, 1965 by Simon & Schuster, Inc.

Larry Sternig Literary Agency and Edward D. Hoch: Adaptation of "Zoo" by Edward D. Hoch. Copyright © 1958 by King-Size Publications, Inc.

University of Nebraska Press: "Prairie Dawn" from *April Twilights* (1903) by Willa Cather, edited with an introduction by Bernice Slote, published by the University of Nebraska Press.

Viking Penguin, Inc.: "To Err Is Human" from *The Medusa and the Snail: More Notes of a Biology Watcher* by Lewis Thomas. Copyright © 1976 by Lewis Thomas. Originally published in the *New England Journal of Medicine*.

The H. W. Wilson Company: Entries reprinted from the *Readers' Guide to Periodical Literature* as follows: from 3/79–2/80 volume, copyright © 1979, 1980; from 5/10/81 issue, copyright © 1981 by The. H. W. Wilson Company.

Cover Photograph: John Iacono for *Sports Illustrated* © Time, Inc.

CONTENTS

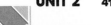

UNIT 6   199

UNIT 8 271

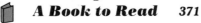

xiv

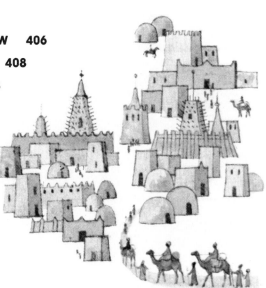

LANGUAGE
Learning About Sentences

STUDY SKILLS
Using the Dictionary

COMPOSITION
Writing Sentences

LITERATURE
Enjoying Poetry (1)

Effective writing requires the use of a variety of different kinds of sentences. In this unit you will learn about sentences that express different kinds of thoughts, that have different word order, and that include more than one subject and predicate. You will also learn to combine simple sentences in order to make them more interesting.

Another important element in effective writing is choosing one's words carefully. Using the dictionary, also covered in this unit, will be very helpful to you in selecting words and using them correctly. You will also be examining how new words are formed.

In poetry, word choice and word order are even more important than they are in prose. Lessons in this unit will cover rhyme, rhythm, and other sound devices that make poetry exciting.

At the end of the unit you will find a review of a book you may want to read. Look for this book, and other books that may be of interest to you, by using the card catalog in your school or local library.

LANGUAGE

Lesson 1: Understanding Kinds of Sentences

Melissa sent her cousin Jason this post card.

Dear Jason,

    I came home from vacation yesterday. What a great thing it was to see my friends again! What did you do at the beach all summer? Write soon.

Love,
Melissa

Think and Discuss

A group of words that expresses a complete thought is called a sentence. Compare these groups of words.

1. Melissa went to the mountains.
2. Had wonderful vacations.

Both word groups look like sentences. They begin with capital letters and end with periods, but both of them do not express complete thoughts. Which word group does express a complete thought? Group 2 does not express a complete thought. It is not a sentence. What words could you add to make the thought and the sentence complete?

There are four kinds of sentences. A **declarative sentence** makes a statement and ends with a period. An **interrogative sentence** asks a question and ends with a question mark. Which sentence in Melissa's postcard is interrogative?

A third kind of sentence gives a command or makes a request. This is an **imperative sentence,** and it also ends with a period. The subject of an imperative sentence is *you,* understood.

A fourth type of sentence expresses strong feeling or surprise. This is an **exclamatory sentence,** and it ends with an exclamation point. Which sentence in Melissa's message is imperative? Which sentence is exclamatory?

- A **sentence** is a group of words that expresses a complete thought. Every sentence begins with a capital letter and ends with a mark of punctuation.
- A **declarative sentence** makes a statement. It ends with a period.
- An **interrogative sentence** asks a question. It ends with a question mark.
- An **imperative sentence** gives a command or makes a request. It ends with a period.
- An **exclamatory sentence** expresses strong feeling or surprise. It ends with an exclamation point.

Practice

A. Decide which of these word groups are sentences. Copy only the sentences on your paper.

1. Camped in the mountains.
2. Melissa took her sleeping bag.
3. She camped out every night.
4. Millions of stars.
5. Everyone helped cook.
6. Hiked up the trail one day.
7. The sun was very hot.
8. Melissa fell in the water.
9. The icy brook.
10. It was too cold for a swim!

B. Copy these sentences. Then write *declarative, interrogative, imperative,* or *exclamatory* after each one.

11. Jason took his new mask and fins to the beach.
12. He couldn't wait to try them out!
13. Where is a safe place to dive?
14. How beautiful these fish are!
15. Come out for lunch, Jason.

Apply

C. 16.–25. Write ten sentences describing some place you have visited. Tell where you went, what you took, and who went with you. Use each of the four kinds of sentences.

Lesson 2: Understanding Complete Subjects and Predicates

Here are some sentences that Mark wrote about aviators.

1. The first licensed American woman pilot was Harriet Quimby.
2. She flew across the English Channel in 1912.
3. Blanche Stuart Scott and Bessica Raiche soloed in 1910.
4. Raiche and her husband built their plane together.

Think and Discuss

Mark has written his information in sentences. Each sentence has two parts. Both of these parts are necessary to express a complete thought.

One part of a sentence, called the **subject,** names someone or something. All the words that make up the subject are called the **complete subject.** In sentence 1 *The first licensed American woman pilot* is the complete subject.

The other part of a sentence is called the **predicate.** The predicate contains the verb, and it tells something about the subject. All the words that make up the predicate are called the **complete predicate.** In sentence 1 *was Harriet Quimby* is the complete predicate. What are the complete subjects in sentences 2, 3, and 4? What are the complete predicates?

> - The **subject** of a sentence is the part about which something is being said. All the words that make up the subject are called the **complete subject.**
> - The **predicate** of a sentence is the part that contains the verb and that says something about the subject. All the words that make up the predicate are called the **complete predicate.**

Practice

A. Copy these sentences. Draw one line under the complete subjects.

1. People all over the world loved flying exhibitions.
2. Ruth Law earned as much as nine thousand dollars a week for exhibition flights.
3. Bernetta Miller and Matilde Moisant were members of exhibition flying teams.
4. Moisant once left a plane crash with her clothes on fire.
5. The frightening experience did not stop her from flying.
6. Katherine Stinson flew exhibitions in Japan.
7. The Japanese women admired her skill and daring.

B. Copy these sentences. Draw two lines under the complete predicates.

8. Katherine and Marjorie Stinson founded a flying school.
9. Their brothers were aircraft designers.
10. Marjorie trained pilots for World War I.
11. Katherine applied to become a military pilot.
12. The military would not accept women pilots then.
13. Katherine flew the first airmail service instead.
14. She drove an ambulance in France later in the war.

C. Decide which of these word groups are sentences. Write the sentences. Draw one line under each complete subject and two lines under each complete predicate.

15. Katherine Stinson became a prize-winning architect.
16. Bessica Raiche became a doctor.
17. Amelia Earhart, the famous flyer.
18. More than a thousand women pilots flew during World War II.
19. Had excellent safety records.
20. Dr. Margaret Seddon is the first woman astronaut.

Apply

D. 21.–30. Imagine you are an exhibition flyer in an early plane. Write ten sentences describing the scene and what it feels like to fly. Draw one line under each complete subject and two lines under each complete predicate.

Lesson 3: Understanding Simple Subjects and Predicates

Read these sentences and name the complete subject and predicate in each.

1. My family likes to visit national parks.
2. We have visited Grand Canyon National Park twice.
3. The park is in Arizona.
4. President Theodore Roosevelt loved the Grand Canyon.
5. He made the canyon a National Monument in 1908.

Think and Discuss

The key word in the complete subject of a sentence is called the **simple subject.** The simple subject is usually a noun or a pronoun. It can have more than one word. In sentence 1 the complete subject is *My family*. The simple subject is *family*. What are the simple subjects in sentences 2–5? In which sentence is the simple subject more than one word?

The complete predicate also has a key word. The word is called the **simple predicate,** and it is always a verb. It can be more than one word. The complete predicate in sentence 1 is *likes to visit national parks*. The simple predicate is *likes*. What are the simple predicates in sentences 2–5? Which sentence has a simple predicate of more than one word?

> - The **simple subject** is the key word or group of words in the subject of a sentence. The simple subject is usually a noun or pronoun.
> - The **simple predicate** is the key word or group of words in the predicate of a sentence. The simple predicate is always a verb.

Practice

A. Copy these sentences. Draw one line under the simple subject in each sentence.

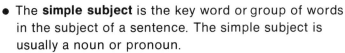

1. The Colorado River runs through the Grand Canyon.
2. At river level the canyon is 300 miles (480 kilometers) long.

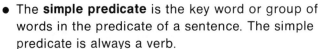

3. Rubber boats with motors take people into the canyon.

4. The Grand Canyon suffers from pollution.
5. Plans have been made to get rid of the motorboats.
6. Every year many people take boats through the canyon's rapids.
7. These boats have no motors.

B. Copy these sentences. Draw two lines under the simple predicate in each sentence.

8. Yellowstone National Park was the first national park in the United States.
9. This park is in Wyoming, Montana, and Idaho.
10. Many geysers can be found in Yellowstone.
11. The most famous has always been Old Faithful.
12. Old Faithful erupts regularly every 65 minutes.
13. People come to Yellowstone from all over the country.
14. The Teton Mountains rise south of Yellowstone National Park.

C. Copy these sentences. Draw one line under the simple subjects and two lines under the simple predicates.

15. Shenandoah National Park is in Virginia.
16. This park is located in the Blue Ridge Mountains.
17. Skyline Drive runs through the middle of the park.
18. This drive follows the ridge of the mountains through beautiful forests.
19. Breathtaking views of the Shenandoah Valley can be seen from Skyline Drive.
20. This park was a gift to the nation in 1935.

Apply

D. 21.–30. Write ten sentences about the animals in any park—city, state, or national—that you have visited or read about. Then draw one line under the simple subject and two lines under the simple predicate of each sentence.

A Challenge

Imagine that you are a visitor on a distant planet. Your host, a native of the planet, takes you on a guided tour of a park in a major city. In ten sentences describe the park. Draw one line under the simple subject and two lines under the simple predicate in each sentence.

Lesson 4: Understanding Word Order in Sentences

Read these sentences.

1. Simon climbed up.
2. Down came Simon.
3. Did anyone see it?
4. Get well soon. *(you)*

Think and Discuss

Most of the sentences you say, hear, read, and write follow the pattern of sentence 1. In this pattern the simple subject is followed by the simple predicate. This is called **natural word order.** Name the simple subject and the simple predicate in sentence 1 and tell which comes first.

Sometimes a sentence is more effective if we word it another way for emphasis. A sentence has **inverted word order** when the simple predicate comes before the simple subject instead of after it. Sentence 2 has inverted word order. The simple predicate *came* comes before the simple subject *Simon.*

Most interrogative sentences have inverted word order. If the simple predicate (verb) is made of two words, the simple subject comes between the two parts of the verb. What is the simple subject in sentence 3? Name the two parts of the simple predicate.

Sentence 4 is an imperative sentence. It has natural word order even though its simple subject does not appear. The subject of imperative sentences is always *you*—the person or persons to whom the command or request is given. Since *you* is only understood to be there, and is not actually written, the subject of imperative sentences is *you* (understood). Name the simple subject and the simple predicate of sentence 4.

Practice

A. Copy these sentences. In each sentence draw one line under the simple subject and two lines under the simple predicate. If the subject is *you* (understood), write *(you)* after the sentence.

1. Simon's family gathered the ladders, paint, and brushes.
2. Everyone in the family was excited.

3. Most excited of all was Wags.
4. Wags is Simon's puppy.
5. On the grass in the yard were the cans of paint.
6. Simon's mother stirred the paint carefully.
7. His father handed out the brushes to all the workers.
8. Where is Wags?
9. Has anybody seen him?
10. Stay away from the paint.

B. Copy these sentences. Next to each write *natural word order* or *inverted word order*.

11. Wags stepped in a can of bright blue paint.
12. Never had they seen a funnier sight.
13. Wags had been black and white.
14. Now he was black and white with blue legs.
15. Could anyone have a more colorful puppy?

Apply

C. 16.–25. Write ten sentences about painting a room. Write at least three sentences with inverted word order.

HOW OUR LANGUAGE GROWS

Writers have always been great inventors of words. Lewis Carroll, author of *Alice's Adventures in Wonderland,* suggested the use of *portmanteau* words. (A *portmanteau* is a suitcase.) He combined *miserable* with *flimsy* to make *mimsy,* and *slimy* with *lithe* to make *slithy.* Carroll also gave us the colorful word *gallumphing.*

Some of these words have been added to the language in this century. They have been invented by writers of advertisements, newspapers, and books. Can you tell what these words mean?

1. smog
2. motel
3. minibus
4. sitcom
5. gridlock
6. brunch
7. squawk
8. mo-ped

Lesson 5: Understanding Compound Subjects and Predicates

These sentences express complete thoughts, but they are not very interesting to read.

1. Anita visited the reservoir.
2. Miguel visited the reservoir.
3. Anita jumped from the bus.
4. Anita ran down the path.

Can you think of a way to make these sentences more interesting?

Think and Discuss

What is the complete predicate in sentences 1 and 2? The predicates are identical. You can make these sentences easier to understand and more interesting to read if you combine them.

5. Anita and Miguel visited the reservoir.

The new sentence has two simple subjects joined by the coordinating conjunction *and.* The new sentence has a **compound subject,** *Anita* and *Miguel.*

What is the simple subject in sentences 3 and 4? These sentences can be combined too.

6. Anita jumped from the bus and ran down the path.

The new sentence has one simple subject and two simple predicates—*jumped* and *ran.* A sentence that has two simple predicates has a **compound predicate.**

- A **compound subject** consists of two or more simple subjects that are joined by a coordinating conjunction such as *and, but, or, either . . . or, neither . . . nor, both . . . and, not only . . . but also.* Compound subjects have the same predicate.
- A **compound predicate** consists of two or more simple predicates (verbs) joined by a coordinating conjunction. Compound predicates have the same subject.

Practice

A. Copy these sentences. Draw one line under the compound subject or two lines under the compound predicate in each. Then write *compound subject* or *compound predicate* after each sentence.

1. This reservoir traps and holds millions of gallons after the spring rainfall.
2. Ferns and shrubs crowd its banks.
3. Swimming, fishing, and sailing are not allowed here.
4. Several picnickers skipped and ran along the shore.
5. They spread their blanket and opened their lunch.
6. They can eat here but not swim.
7. Miguel and Anita had made the salads.
8. Orange juice, apple juice, and milk were placed on the picnic blanket.
9. The juice and the sandwiches looked good and tasted even better.
10. The girls removed their shoes and ran through the grass.

B. Combine each pair of sentences to form a new sentence with a compound subject or a compound predicate. Then draw one line under the compound subjects and two lines under the compound predicates.

11. Miguel wanted to play softball.
    Anita wanted to play softball.
12. They looked for the ball.
    They found it in the picnic basket.
13. The bats were beside the bench.
    The bats were near the dugout.
14. Miguel called to his friends.
    He invited them to play.
15. His friends couldn't hear him.
    His friends didn't understand him.

Apply

C. 16.–25. Write ten sentences about a picnic. Use at least two compound subjects and two compound predicates. Draw one line under the compound subjects and two lines under the compound predicates.

Lesson 6: Understanding Compound Sentences

Read these sentences.

1. Gina brought the record player.
2. Marci brought the records.
3. Gina brought the record player, and Marci brought the records.

In which ways is sentence 3 different from sentences 1 and 2?

Think and Discuss

Sentences 1 and 2 each have one complete subject and one complete predicate. These are **simple sentences.**

Sentence 3 is made up of two simple sentences joined by the coordinating conjunction *and*. Sentence 3 is a **compound sentence.** Compound sentences are usually joined by coordinating conjunctions *or, and,* or *but*. A comma is always used before these conjunctions in a compound sentence.

How are the parts joined in this compound sentence?

4. They turned on the record player; nothing happened.

What two simple sentences have been combined in sentence 4?

Read this compound sentence. Notice that the first part has a compound subject, and the second has a compound predicate.

5. Gina and Marci called Charlotte, and she repaired and adjusted the record player.

- A **simple sentence** has only one complete subject and one complete predicate.
- A **compound sentence** is made up of two simple sentences joined by a comma and a coordinating conjunction or by a semicolon.

Practice

A. Copy these sentences. Write *simple sentence* or *compound sentence* after each one.

1. Gina had a record player, but it was broken.
2. Alan and Marci found another one.

3. It was old, and it looked awful.
4. They turned it on; it played beautifully.
5. Where are the rest of the records?

B. Copy these sentences. Draw one line under each complete subject and two lines under each complete predicate. Identify the simple sentence.

6. Adam made the decorations, and Karen put them up.
7. Charlotte invited everyone, but Kim couldn't come.
8. Kim and his family were out of town.
9. The food committee brought food; everyone was hungry.
10. Jim and John served the cookies, and Ann poured the juice.

C. Read these simple sentences. Think of another simple sentence to go with each one. Then write each pair as a compound sentence.

11. Alan wore a silly costume.
12. Marie wore a scary costume.
13. A prize was given for the best costume.
14. Matthew turned the record player up.
15. A dance contest was held.

Apply

D. 16.–25. Write ten compound sentences about working on a school newspaper. Draw one line under each complete subject and two lines under each complete predicate. Circle each comma and conjunction or semicolon.

To Memorize

The farther backward you can look, the farther forward you are likely to see.

Winston Churchill

What does Winston Churchill mean by "looking backward" and "looking forward"? How might you interpret this quotation in light of the saying that "history repeats itself"?

Lesson 7: Correcting Fragments and Run-on Sentences

Read these word groups.

1. We are studying the history of vaccination.
2. Our health class.
3. We all wrote reports the information was interesting.

Which word group is a sentence? Why are the other two word groups *not* sentences?

Think and Discuss

In order to express a complete thought, a sentence must have both a subject and a predicate. A word group that is missing either or both of these is called a **fragment.** To correct a fragment, supply the missing part or parts.

Word group 2 is a fragment. It tells *who* or *what* the subject is, but it does not tell what the subject *did.* What words would you add to correct this fragment?

A word group that expresses more than one complete thought without proper punctuation is called a **run-on sentence.** Word group 3 is a run-on sentence. What are the two complete thoughts in this word group? One way to correct a run-on sentence is to write the two parts as separate sentences. Another way to correct a run-on sentence is to make a compound sentence.

4. We all wrote reports. The information was interesting.
5. We all wrote reports, and the information was interesting.

A good way to detect run-on sentences is to read your paper aloud. Listen for the ends of sentences, and then check to see that you have punctuated the sentences correctly.

- A **fragment** is an incomplete sentence. It is missing either a subject or a predicate or both.
- A **run-on sentence** is two sentences that have been run together without the proper punctuation between them.

Practice

A. Copy these word groups. After each write *sentence, fragment,* or *run-on.*

1. Inoculation with a vaccine protects against disease.
2. Many years ago.
3. Has saved many people from getting smallpox.
4. Thousands of people used to die of it.
5. Smallpox broke out in New England in 1716 people were vaccinated.

B. Add words to these sentence fragments. Write the new sentences.

6. In 1716, a smallpox epidemic.
7. Hundreds of people.
8. Laughed at the vaccine.
9. Thought it wouldn't work.
10. Were vaccinated and lived.
11. Never got the disease.
12. The smallpox vaccine.
13. Made from cowpox virus.
14. Cowpox and smallpox.
15. Many diseases.

C. Correct these run-on sentences. Write the corrected sentences. Draw one line under the complete subjects and two lines under the complete predicates.

16. Lady Mary Montagu was the wife of the British ambassador to Turkey she lived during the eighteenth century.
17. Her family went to Turkey she saw smallpox vaccine being used there.
18. She became interested in it she believed that all doctors should know about the vaccine.
19. The family returned to London a smallpox epidemic broke out.
20. Lady Mary had her daughter vaccinated the daughter survived.

D. 21.–25. Copy the sentences that your teacher will now read aloud. Correct all run-on sentences.

Apply

E. 26.–35. Write ten sentences about a subject relating to health. Check each sentence to make sure it is not a fragment or a run-on sentence.

LANGUAGE REVIEW

Kinds of Sentences   pages 2–3

Copy these sentences, adding the correct capitalization and end punctuation. After each sentence write *declarative, interrogative, imperative,* or *exclamatory.*

1. where is all this smoke coming from
2. there could be a fire in that building across the street
3. what a terrible disaster this is
4. call the fire department

Complete Subjects and Predicates   pages 4–5

Copy these sentences. Draw one line under the complete subjects and two lines under the complete predicates.

5. We packed our suitcases.
6. Uncle Harry drove us to the station.
7. The woman in the booth sold us four tickets.
8. The train roared into the station.

Simple Subjects and Predicates   pages 6–7

Copy these sentences. Draw one line under the simple subjects and two lines under the simple predicates.

9. Much early literature came from minstrels and bards.
10. They chanted their tales to the melodies of the harp.
11. These storytellers often varied the details of a story.
12. Their long, heroic stories are called epics or sagas.

Word Order in Sentences   pages 8–9

Copy these sentences. Draw one line under the simple subjects and two lines under the simple predicates. After imperative sentences write (*you*). After each sentence write *natural word order* or *inverted word order.*

13. Listen to this experiment.
14. Through a pitch-dark room flew a bat.
15. From its throat came ultrasonic shrieks.
16. Echoes bounced off the walls to guide it.

Compound Subjects and Predicates   pages 10–11

Copy these sentences. Draw one line under the compound subjects and two lines under the compound predicates.

17. At daybreak the hikers made breakfast and packed the mules.
18. The rugged mountains loomed before them and cast giant shadows over the valley.
19. The streams and rivers were overflowing with heavy rains.
20. The weary hikers and their mules drank water from streams.

Compound Sentences   pages 12–13

Write a compound sentence for each of these word groups, using the conjunction or punctuation given in parentheses ( ).

21. Some people are afraid of bats. However, bats do little harm to people or animals. (;)
22. There are many species of bats in North America. Most bats live in the tropics. (but)
23. Several species eat large ground insects. Others eat insects from the surface of water. (and)

Fragments and Run-on Sentences   pages 14–15

Copy these groups of words. Write *complete sentence* after each complete sentence. Write *fragment* after sentence fragments. Write *run-on* after run-on sentences. Rewrite fragments and run-ons correctly.

24. Long ago in England people did not number houses or shops.
25. Displayed a sign instead.
26. The sign might show a fox, a bell, a stag, or perhaps a green dragon a barber's shop was designated by a pole.
27. Red and white spirals.

Applying Sentences

28.–40. Write 13 sentences about a visit to a science museum. Use inverted word order in 3 of the sentences, one of which should be interrogative. Include 2 compound sentences. Make 1 sentence exclamatory. Edit and proofread your sentences.

STUDY SKILLS

Lesson 8: Finding Words in a Dictionary

Leroy was considering going to see a movie. When he read a review of the film, however, he became confused. The critic said, "The plot is vacuous, the dialog inept, and the acting unbelievably dilettantish." Did the critic think the movie was good or bad?

Think and Discuss

When you come across an unfamiliar word, you can find its meaning by looking it up in a dictionary. The words in a dictionary are organized in alphabetical order. To find a word quickly, it helps to think first about the part of the dictionary in which it will appear. You can divide the dictionary into three major parts. The *front* contains all the words that begin with the letters A through G. The *middle* contains the words that begin with H through P. The *back* contains the words that begin with the letters Q through Z. In which part would you look to find *inept*?

Once you are sure you have the right part of the dictionary, look for the section that has words starting with the same letter as the word you are trying to find. For example, to find *inept,* you would look for the section of the dictionary that contains words beginning with *i.* Some dictionaries are thumb-indexed, so that you can turn quickly to the entries for each letter. If your dictionary is not thumb-indexed, find the right letter by looking at the *guide words,* which appear in dark type at the top of each page. They tell you the first word and the last word on that page. All the entries fall alphabetically between the two guide words.

Use the guide words to find the page with your word. For example, if you are looking up *inept,* begin by looking for guide words with the same first letter: *i.* Then look for guide words with the same first and second letters: *in.* If necessary, go on to other letters. When you have found the right page, scan it quickly to find your word. *Inept,* you will discover, means "clumsy and awkward."

Practice

A. Copy the following words in alphabetical order. Beside each word write the part of the dictionary in which it appears, *front, middle,* or *back.*

1. fount
2. digression
3. infielder
4. barracuda
5. affront
6. valiant
7. leer
8. truffle
9. sabotage
10. hangnail

B. Which words would you find on a dictionary page with the guide words *pulley-punctuate?* Write the words on your paper.

11. pulse
12. pug
13. pulp
14. pullet
15. pugilist
16. punctual
17. pump
18. pun
19. pulpit
20. punish
21. punch
22. pueblo
23. puma
24. punk
25. pumice

C. Copy the words that you would find on a dictionary page with the guide words *float–flour.* Then put them in alphabetical order.

26. flotilla
27. flourish
28. flirt
29. flounce
30. flitch
31. flit
32. floor
33. florist
34. flounder
35. flow

D. Write the following words in alphabetical order.

36. trick
37. trickster
38. tricked
39. tricksters
40. tricks
41. tricky
42. trickery
43. trickier
44. trickeries
45. trickiest

Apply

E. 46.–55. In your dictionary look up all the words listed in Practice A. Beside each write the page number on which the word appears and the guide words at the top of the page. Make a separate list of any words that are not in your dictionary and go to the library to look them up in a larger dictionary.

Look at the following dictionary entry.

> **cat·e·gor·i·cal** [kat′ə·gôr′i·kəl] *adj.* Positive
> and definite; without any question or condition:
> a *categorical* refusal **— cat′e·gor′i·cal·ly** *adv.*

How many different things can you learn about the word from
this entry? Name them.

Think and Discuss

A good dictionary will tell you many things about a word.
Here are some of them.

1. **Definition:** The entry will tell you all the possible meanings
   of the word. The sample word has the meaning "positive and
   definite."
2. **Syllabification:** The entry tells you how the word is divided
   into syllables. The sample word has five syllables:
   cat/e/gor/i/cal. If a word has to be hyphenated at the end of a
   printed or written line, it can be divided only between
   syllables.
3. **Pronunciation:** The entry tells you exactly how to pronounce
   the word. Marks used to indicate this are called **diacritical
   marks.** You should be familiar with the **macron** (¯), which
   marks a long vowel. Short vowels may have no markings at
   all, or they may be marked by the **breve** (˘). The **schwa** (ə)
   represents unaccented vowel sounds. **Accent marks** show
   which syllables receive the stress in pronunciation. The
   darker mark is the primary accent; the lighter one is the
   secondary accent. Which syllable receives the primary stress
   in the sample word?
4. **Part of speech:** The entry tells you how the word can be used
   in a sentence. The sample word is an adjective, so it can be
   used to modify a noun. There is even an example of its
   correct use as an adjective. What is the example?
5. **Spelling:** The entry word gives the correct spelling of the
   word. It shows where to use capital letters and apostrophes.
   You can also find out whether a compound word is spelled
   as one word, a hyphenated word, or two words with a space
   between them.

6. **Related forms:** An entry will tell you about related forms of a word. The sample entry tells the form of the word that can be used as an adverb. For irregular verbs the entry may show other tenses and other verb forms, such as the past and present participle. For nouns it will show unusual plurals. For adjectives that have degree, the entry will show all degrees.

Practice

A. Copy the following words. Look up the pronunciation. Copy the phonetic respelling on your paper.

1. clutch	2. rob	3. comic
4. dull	5. robe	6. cede
7. shake	8. magic	9. abbey
10. thin	11. key	12. wick
13. thing	14. grip	15. whine

B. Copy these words. Using your dictionary, divide them into syllables. Add primary and secondary accents. Tell the part of speech.

16. familiarize	17. unassuming
18. nutritious	19. womankind
20. prevaricate	21. hallucination
22. sensibility	23. fedora
24. stupidity	25. estuary

C. Look in your dictionary to see whether these words should be written as one word or two. Write the words correctly, adding hyphens and capitals as necessary.

26. iceberg	27. icecube	28. Iceland
29. icebox	30. icecream	31. icecold
32. icecap	33. icecreamcone	34. icehouse

Apply

D. 35. Look in the dictionary to see if you can find any words that are similar to your name or perhaps even spelled the same way. (Use either your first or last name.) Read the definition of the word and its history carefully. Write a paragraph to tell whether you think the word is or is not related to your name.

Lesson 10: Choosing the Correct Meaning

Read these sentences.

1. Can you sing a high note?
2. Who wrote this apology note?
3. I did note the date on the letter.

What is the meaning of the word *note* in each sentence?

Think and Discuss

Many words have more than one meaning. The meaning listed first in the dictionary is the **primary definition.** Less frequently used meanings are **secondary definitions.** Look carefully at all the entries given for a word. Sometimes there will be more than one entry if two words that are entirely different are spelled the same. These words, called **homographs,** may also have different pronunciations.

One way to make sure you choose the correct definition is to consider the **context.** How the word is used in the sentence or paragraph will give a clue to its meaning. Look at the definitions given for the entry *note.*

note [nōt] *n., v.* **not·ed, not·ing** **1** *n.* A brief record or jotting down of a word, sentence, fact, etc., that one wishes to remember: to make *notes* on a lecture. **2** *v.* To record or set down in writing: *Note* the date of his birthday. **3** *n.* Close attention; heed: What he said is worthy of *note.* **4** *v.* To pay careful attention to: *Note* how I do this. **5** *v.* To become aware of; observe: I *noted* her absence. **6** *v.* To mention. **7** *n.* A written comment, as at the bottom of a page or at the back of a book, explaining or adding more information to something: Shakespeare's plays have many *notes* to help the student. **8** *n.* A short letter. **9** *n.* A formal or official letter from one country or government to another. **10** *n.* In music, a symbol whose position on a staff indicates the pitch of the tone and whose form indicates its length. **11** *n.* Any more or less musical sound: the *notes* of a bird. **12** *n.* Any of the keys on a piano, etc. **13** *n.* A sign or quality: a *note* of winter in the air. **14** *n.* A piece of paper money issued by a government or a bank. **15** *n.* A written agreement to pay a sum of money at a certain time. **16** *n.* Importance; fame: He is a scientist of great *note.* —

Suppose you want to find the correct meaning for *note* as it is used in sentence 1. There are 11 meanings listed. Many of these can be ruled out immediately because they refer to something other than music. Which definition of *note* fits the context?

What example helped you choose the correct definition of *note*? In addition to examples, there may be drawings that help you understand the word's meaning. Also, if the dictionary tells the history or root of the word, you may have another clue to choosing the correct definition.

Practice

A. Read the dictionary definition for *ring.*²

ring² [ring] *n., v.* **ringed, ring·ing 1** *n.* A circle or round loop. **2** *n.* A narrow circle of metal, plastic, etc., worn on a finger as an ornament, used to hang curtains, etc. **3** *v.* To put or make a ring around; enclose: The crowd *ringed* the speaker. **4** *n.* A group of persons or things in a circle: a *ring* of houses. **5** *v.* To form a circle: The children *ringed* about the exhibit. **6** *n.* A group of persons, often organized for some unlawful or evil purpose: a *ring* of smugglers. **7** *n.* A space set apart for a contest or show: a circus *ring.* **8** *n. informal* The sport of prize fighting. **9** *v.* To put a ring in the nose of (a pig, bull, etc.). **10** *v.* In certain games, to throw a ring over (a peg or pin). — **run rings around** *informal* To do or be very much better than. — **ring′er** *n.*

Antique ring

Read the sentences below. After each sentence write the number of the definition of *ring* that applies.

1. A ring of cabins circled the lake.
2. She wore a gold ring on her left hand.
3. The fighters stepped into the ring.
4. A ring of shoplifters was caught.

B. In your dictionary look up the following words. Write the primary definition of each homograph.

5. colon
6. diet
7. fast
8. list
9. match
10. shed
11. size
12. top
13. wind

C. Each of the underlined words has more than one meaning. Copy the sentence, substituting one or more words from the appropriate definition in your dictionary.

14. Can I eat that <u>russet</u> without cooking it?
15. He put up only a <u>token</u> resistance.
16. The elephant took the peanuts with its <u>trunk</u>.
17. His entire composition was written in the passive <u>voice</u>.
18. She went to the library to look for an <u>abstract</u>.

Apply

D. **19.–22.** Choose from your dictionary a word that has at least four definitions. Write a short paragraph using all the meanings of the word.

COMPOSITION

Lesson 11: Combining Sentences

Read these sentences.

1. We must leave right now.
2. We will be late for the concert tonight.
3. We must leave right now, or we will be late for the concert tonight.

In what way is sentence 3 like sentences 1 and 2? In what way is it different?

Think and Discuss

In many cases you can write more mature and varied sentences by combining several short sentences into one longer sentence. The conjunctions *and, but,* and *or* are used to show relationships between sentence ideas. The conjunction *and* shows a similar or additional idea. A contrast between sentence ideas is shown with the conjunction *but.* The conjunction *or* indicates a choice of ideas. What choice is indicated in sentence 3?

How are two sentences joined in sentence 4?

4. We took the bus downtown; we walked the rest of the way to the concert hall.

In this sentence the semicolon takes the place of the comma and the conjunction *and.* Other words that are helpful when combining sentences are *therefore, however,* and *furthermore.* Study these sentences.

5. I did not like the first symphony.
6. It was not very well played.
7. I did not like the first symphony; furthermore, it was not very well played.
8. The second piece of the evening did not impress me much either.

9. I thought the third and last selection was great.
10. The second piece of the evening did not impress me either; however, I thought the last selection was great.

Sentences 7 and 10 were formed by combining two shorter sentences. In sentence 7 *furthermore* was used to indicate an additional reason. *However* is used in sentence 10 to show a contrast or exception. When *therefore* is used, it shows a conclusion or result. What punctuation marks are used with these words when joining two independent clauses?

Practice

A. Combine these sentences. Use the conjunctions *or, but,* or *and* with the correct punctuation, or use a semicolon to join the sentences.

1. He spoke loudly. He was not angry with the children.
2. The children did not hear. They chose to ignore him.
3. I tried to help. They did not listen to me.
4. The situation was difficult. It had always been so.
5. I become discouraged. I do not give up easily.

B. Combine these sentences with the words *however, therefore,* or *furthermore*. Correctly punctuate the new sentences.

6. The job is interesting. It pays well.
7. The company has a good reputation. Its policies and regulations must be sensible.
8. I will work there this summer. My friends will be working there too.
9. Last summer was very boring. I decided it would be a good idea to have a job for this summer.
10. I begin in two weeks. I am already as nervous as if tomorrow were my first day.

Apply

C. 11.–20. Write ten compound sentences describing a hobby or job you enjoy. Use all the methods of sentence combining presented in this lesson.

Lesson 12: Writing Effective Sentences

Read these sentences:

1. Lizzie Johnson was a cattle trader.
2. She was very successful.
3. She was called the Cattle Queen of Texas.

What do all three sentences have in common? Is there anything wrong with these sentences?

Think and Discuss

Sentences 1–3 are technically correct; each contains a complete subject and a complete predicate. Nevertheless, as a group the sentences are not very *effective.* They are monotonous and do not hold the reader's interest. Each follows a simple subject-verb-complement construction, each uses the same verb, and each contains only one fact. What do you suggest be done to make them more interesting?

As a general rule varying the form of the sentences will make your writing more effective. Here are some suggestions for ways to add variety to your sentences.

- Vary sentence order. A sentence in inverted word order can break up a series of natural-order sentences.

4. After the Civil War cattle were nearly worthless in the South.
5. Nobody got enough money for a herd to pay for its keep.
6. Then came the Chisholm Trail.

- Vary sentence structure. In addition to simple sentences, use compound sentences and sentences with compound subjects or predicates.

7. Lizzie Johnson rounded up strays in Texas and sold them for a fortune in St. Louis.
8. Cattle and the cattle business were quite familiar to her.
9. She had kept books for ranchers and taught bookkeeping in school.

> • Vary sentence length. A long, complicated sentence can be balanced with a short, simple statement.

10. When Lizzie was in St. Louis, she dressed like a wealthy lady and stayed in the best hotels to impress the bankers.
11. However, she preferred the company of cowhands.

> • Vary sentence types. An occasional question or exclamation will stand out in a series of declarative sentences.

12. Lizzie and her husband had a friendly rivalry.
13. They were both in the cattle business and shared the same foreman.
14. Sometimes they would steal from each other's herds!

Practice

A. Rewrite these short sentences by combining them into longer sentences.

1. a. Driving cattle on the Chisholm Trail was dangerous.
   b. The cattle could easily stampede.
   c. They could trample the drovers.
2. a. The cattle wanted to stop and rest.
   b. The drovers wanted to stop and rest too.
   c. There were no towns along the trail.
   d. There were few watering holes.
3. a. The trail ended in Kansas City.
   b. The railroad was there.
   c. It would take the cattle to St. Louis and points east.
4. a. The drive had to be carefully planned.
   b. There had to be enough grass for the cattle.
   c. There had to be enough water available for them.
   d. Then they would not lose too much weight.
5. a. Cattle driving was mostly done by men and boys.
   b. A few women and young girls made the drive too.

B. Rewrite at least four of these sentences. Change two sentences from natural to inverted word order and one from declarative to exclamatory. Combine short sentences to make long ones. Then copy the sentences into a single effective paragraph.

6. Two teenaged sisters lived in a boarding school in New Orleans in 1857.
7. They missed their mother.
8. **a.** She was in Mexico.
   b. She was buying horses to sell in the States.
9. Sally Skull rode up from the border with one hundred head of mustangs for New Orleans.
10. **a.** She wanted her daughters to have a good education.
    b. Now she could afford to pay for their schooling.

Apply

C. 11.–15. Use all of the rules in this lesson in writing a paragraph at least five sentences long.

Lesson 13: Editing Sentences

Vicki wrote a story. Read these sentences from that story and note how Vicki marked them.

1. A deep well stood in the village square.
2. Whole families were gathering at the well. Many people talked there in high, excited voices.
3. They were discussing something.

Editing Marks

☰ **capitalize**

⊙ **make a period**

∧ **add something**

⋏ **add a comma**

⌄⌄ **add quotation marks**

᧬ **take something away**

○ **spell correctly**

⌥ **indent the paragraph**

/ **make a lowercase letter**

∿ tr **transpose**

Think and Discuss

Most good authors of stories—or of any other kind of writing—do not let themselves be satisfied with the first version of what they have written. Instead, when they have finished the first version, or **draft,** they carefully reread their work and **edit** it. Editing includes correcting mistakes and rewriting material to make it better.

The box on this page shows ten editing marks that writers often use to mark corrections that they wish to make. Vicki used seven of these marks in sentences 1–3 to show how she wanted to improve the variety of the sentences. The marks in sentence 1, for example, indicate that Vicki will invert the word order. The marks in sentence 2 indicate that Vicki will combine two simple sentences into one compound sentence by using a semicolon. What do the marks in sentence 3 indicate?

Practice

A. 1.–3. Rewrite sentences 1–3, making all the changes that Vicki marked.

B. Copy these sentences; then use editing marks to improve their variety. You may change the word order, the type of sentence, or the sentence structure. Rewrite the edited sentences.

4. The mayor of the village soon appeared. He quieted the people.
5. He had dreadful news to tell them.
6. An invading army stood outside the village.
7. Would they attack in the morning? Would they allow the city to surrender?
8. These villagers were proud people. They would never surrender.
9. The mayor called for attention. He had a plan.
10. He cleared his throat. He quietly asked for a volunteer to spy on the enemy camp.
11. Young Rahim walked toward the mayor.
12. He saw his duty. He would sneak into the enemy camp and learn of their plans.
13. Rahim was a brave young man.

C. 14.–20. Close your books and take out a sheet of paper. Copy the sentences that your teacher will now read aloud. Make sure that you begin and end your sentences properly and that you punctuate compound sentences properly.

Apply

D. 21. Reread the sentences you wrote in Lesson 12. Can you improve their variety? Use the editing marks you have learned to make changes in the sentences. Then rewrite the sentences correctly.

MECHANICS PRACTICE

Beginning and Ending Sentences

- Begin the first word of every sentence with a capital letter.
- End declarative and imperative sentences with a period.
- End interrogative sentences with a question mark.
- End exclamatory sentences with an exclamation point.
- Separate the two parts of a compound sentence by a comma plus a conjunction or by a semicolon.

A. Copy these sentences, adding the proper capitalization and end punctuation.

1. did you ever read about Don Quixote, Yoshi
2. no; tell me something about him, Cora
3. Don Quixote, a Spaniard, believed that he was a knight errant
4. what does that mean
5. he traveled throughout the countryside with Sancho Panza, pretending to be a knight
6. how silly he must have seemed
7. please explain who Sancho Panza was
8. well, Yoshi, Sancho Panza was Don Quixote's squire and friend
9. Rosinante, an old horse, carried Don Quixote about the land
10. what unusual adventures he and Sancho Panza had

B. Rewrite each pair of sentences to make a compound sentence, using either a semicolon or a comma plus a conjunction.

11. Don Quixote and Sancho Panza traveled around the land. They had many unusual adventures together.
12. They came to a certain place. They saw several windmills there.
13. The windmills were real. To Don Quixote they looked like giants.
14. These were obviously evil creatures. He would have to destroy them.
15. He attacked one windmill. One of its blades scooped him up and then dumped him in a heap.

LITERATURE

Lesson 14: Understanding Rhyme Scheme and Rhythm in Poetry

Poetry expresses strong feelings and thoughts in a special way. Read this poem silently. Then listen carefully as it is read aloud.

The First Rose on My Rose Tree

The first rose on my rose tree
    Budded, bloomed, and shattered,
During sad days when to me
    Nothing mattered.

Grief of grief had drained me clean;
    Still it seems a pity
No one saw, — it must have been
    Very pretty.   *Edna St. Vincent Millay*

Think and Discuss

When words at the end of some lines in a poem have the same or similar sounds, they **rhyme.** Not all poems have rhymes. If a poem does rhyme, it follows a certain pattern or **rhyme scheme.** The rhyme scheme is shown with a letter of the alphabet at the end of each line. Lines that end with the same sound have the same letter. Read this poem.

Two Tramps in Mud-Time

The sun was warm and the wind was chill.	**a**
You know how it is with an April day:	**b**
When the sun is out and the wind is still,	**a**
You're one month on in the middle of May	**b**
But if you so much as dare to speak	**c**
A cloud comes over the sunlit arch,	**d**
A wind comes off a frozen peak,	**c**
And you're two months back in the middle of March.	**d**

Robert Frost

The stresses or beats in a line of poetry are the poem's **rhythm.** The rhythm of a poem is like the rhythm in music. The rhythm of the poem below is shown with accents (´). Read the poem aloud and stress the accented syllables.

A wórd is déad
When it´ is sáid,
Some sáy.
I sáy it júst
Begíns to líve
That dáy.

Emily Dickinson

How many strong beats do you hear in lines 3 and 6? How many strong beats do you hear in the other lines? The pattern of beats in a line of poetry is called **meter.**

Practice

A. **1.–8.** Copy the Edna St. Vincent Millay poem and write its rhyme scheme.

B. **9.–16.** Copy the Robert Frost poem and place accent marks on the stressed syllables.

C. **17.–27.** Edward Lear was one of the most famous writers of nonsense lyrics. He invented creatures and words just for the sake of rhyme. Copy the lyrics below and write the rhyme scheme.

There was an old person of Wilts
Who constantly walked upon stilts;
He wreathed them with lilies,
And daffy-down-dillies,
That elegant person of Wilts.

Find the nonsense word invented for the sake of rhyme. Make accent marks on the stressed syllables.

Apply

D. **28.–31.** Write a four-line humorous poem about an imaginary person. Mark the accents and rhyme scheme.

Lesson 15: Understanding Devices of Sound in Poetry

The sound of words together is more important in poetry than in any other kind of writing. Read this poem.

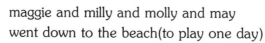

maggie and milly and molly and may

maggie and milly and molly and may
went down to the beach(to play one day)

and maggie discovered a shell that sang
so sweetly she couldn't remember her troubles,and

milly befriended a stranded star
whose rays five languid fingers were;

and molly was chased by a horrible thing
which raced sideways while blowing bubbles:and

may came home with a smooth round stone
as small as a world and as large as alone.

For whatever we lose(like a you or a me)
it's always ourselves we find in the sea

e.e. cummings

Think and Discuss

In the title and first line of the poem, the beginning /m/ sound is repeated four times. This sound device is called **alliteration.** Can you find other examples of this in lines 3 and 4?

Say the first line of the poem aloud again. What other sound is repeated in the line? The repetition of vowel sounds in several words in a line of poetry is called **assonance.** Find another example of assonance in line 4.

The repetition of consonant sounds in words is called

consonance. Read these lines from Edgar Allan Poe's "The Bells."

> Hear the sledges with the bells
>   Silver bells!

The use of words that sound like the things they name is called **onomatopoeia.** Here are examples from "The Bells."

> From the jingling and the tinkling of the bells

Both *jingling* and *tinkling* echo the sound they name.

Practice

A. Reread the poem "maggie and milly and molly and may" and answer these questions on your paper.

1. Find an example of alliteration in line 5.
2. Write two examples of onomatopoeia that would be appropriate for this poem.
3. Find an example of assonance in line 2.
4. Find an example of consonance in the last line.

B. 5.–12. Find two examples each of alliteration, assonance, consonance, and onomatopoeia in another poem or poems.

Apply

C. 13.–16. Write a four-line poem. Use two devices of sound.

A BOOK TO READ

Title: **The Kidnapping of Christina Lattimore**
Author: Joan Lowery Nixon
Publisher: Harcourt Brace Jovanovich

After the terror of kidnap, Christina Lattimore faces another nightmare. Her kidnappers swear that she was an accomplice, trying to extort money from her wealthy grandmother.

A startling climax concludes this exciting mystery story in which everyone comes under suspicion.

1 UNIT TEST

● **Kinds of Sentences**   pages 2–3

Number your paper from 1 to 8. Next to each number write the letter that tells you what kind of sentence each one is. Use this code.

a. declarative   **b.** interrogative   **c.** imperative   **d.** exclamatory

1. Have you seen this exhibit?
2. Look at the detail in this landscape.
3. How unusual it is!
4. What a good artist he is!
5. Please hand me a booklet.
6. This is my favorite painting, Nori.
7. Do not touch that frame.
8. Where has our guide gone?

● **Complete Subjects and Predicates**   pages 4–5

Copy these sentences. Draw one line under each complete subject and two lines under each complete predicate.

9. The glass harmonica was invented by Benjamin Franklin.
10. It consists of a series of bowl-shaped glasses with moistened rims.
11. The musician rubs the wet rims with a finger to produce a tone.
12. Marianna Kirchgessner popularized the glass harmonica in the late 1700's.
13. A quintet for the glass harmonica was composed by Mozart.

● **Simple Subjects and Predicates**   pages 6–7

14.–18. Copy the simple subjects and predicates from sentences 9–13.

● **Word Order in Sentences**   pages 8–9

Copy these sentences. Draw one line under each simple subject and two lines under each simple predicate. If the sentence is imperative, write (*you*) after it. Then write whether each sentence uses *natural word order* or *inverted word order*.

19. Please take this letter to the post office.
20. In my desk drawer is a book of stamps.
21. Have you found them yet?
22. Send the letter by registered mail.

● Compound Sentences   pages 12–13

Copy these sentences. Write whether each one is a *simple sentence* or a *compound sentence.*

23. Did you do your homework?
24. I did most of it, but I stopped for dinner.
25. Your research report is finished; it looks very good.
26. The footnotes and bibliography must be checked, though.

● Fragments and Run-ons   pages 14–15

Copy these groups of words. Write whether each one is a *complete sentence,* a *fragment,* or a *run-on.* Correct and rewrite the fragments and run-on sentences.

27. The sight of a glorious sunset.
28. Shades of violet and pink shot across the horizon.
29. The sun seemed to slip into the earth I had never seen such a vivid sight.
30. A navy blue, starless sky.

● Finding Words in a Dictionary   pages 18–19

Write in alphabetical order the words from this list that you would find on a dictionary page with the guide words *corrosion* and *cosy.*

1. cosmonaut   **2.** corral   **3.** corsage   **4.** counsel
5. cotillion   **6.** Costa Rica **7.** corsair   **8.** costume
9. corrugated   **10.** cosmic rays **11.** corps   **12.** Corsica

● Dictionary Entries   pages 20–21

Study this dictionary entry; then answer the questions that come after it.

ma·nip·u·la·tion [mə·nip′yə·lā′shən] *n.* **1** The act of manipulating. **2** The condition of being manipulated. **3** An instance or example of manipulating: a dishonest *manipulation* of the figures.

13. How many syllables are in the word?
14. How many schwas and how many macrons are in the word?
15. Which syllable has the secondary accent?
16. What part of speech is the word?

Correct Meanings   pages 22-23

Look up these words in your dictionary. Write the primary definition of each homograph.

17. lash   **18.** line   **19.** loom   **20.** lurch

Combining Sentences   pages 24-25

Combine these sentences by (1) using a comma and *or, but,* or *and;* (2) using a semicolon; or (3) using a semicolon and *however, furthermore,* or *therefore.*

1. Many people love flowering plants. Few people know how some of these plants are related.
2. Cinnamon and avocados are both members of the laurel family. Onions and daffodils both belong to the amaryllis family.
3. Wheat is related to corn and oats. Buckwheat is more closely related to rhubarb.
4. Could you guess that cashews are related to poison ivy? Did you already know that curious fact?
5. Peanuts, walnuts, almonds, and filberts belong to different families. Tea and coffee, two drinks that we often group together, also come from different families.

Effective Sentences   pages 26-28

Rewrite each of these sentences according to the directions in parentheses ( ).

6. The crowd grew quiet. The lifeguards grew quiet. (Make a compound subject.)
7. A doctor came forward. A doctor helped. (Make a compound predicate.)
8. An ambulance raced down the beach. (Invert the word order.)
9. Its siren was loud. It helped to clear a path. (Make a compound sentence.
10. I was very nervous. I was able to assist the paramedics. (Make a compound sentence.)

● Editing Sentences   pages 29–30

Copy these sentences, making the changes indicated by editing marks.

11. There are many Irish legends. *that* They tell of Finn Maccool.

12. Finn Maccool sat in the home of Finegas, learning poetry from him.

13. Finegas had caught the "salmon of knowledge." He asked Finn to cook it.

14. *When he turned the fish,* Finn burned his thumb and put it in his mouth.

15. From that moment on, Finn had only to put his thumb in his mouth, *and* He would receive special knowledge.

16. *What* That is a fish story!

● Beginning and Ending Sentences   page 31

Copy these sentences, adding the proper capitalization and end punctuation.

17. here's your grilled cheese sandwich, Bea
18. thanks; now please pass me some of those carrot sticks
19. isn't the sandwich I made delicious
20. how right you are, Jean

● Poetic Devices   pages 32–35

1. Copy this poem. Write in its rhyme scheme and use accent marks to show the stressed syllables.

A Cloud Shadow

> A breeze discovered my open book
> And began to flutter the leaves to look
> For a poem there used to be on Spring.
> I tried to tell her, "There's no such thing."
> For whom would a poem on Spring be by?
> The breeze disdained to make reply;
> And a cloud shadow crossed her face
> For fear I would make her miss the place.

Robert Frost

2. Name an example of onomatopoeia in line 2.
3. Find an example of consonance in line 4.

LANGUAGE
Learning About Paragraphs

COMPOSITION
Writing Paragraphs

STUDY SKILLS
Locating Information

LITERATURE
Enjoying Poetry (II)

If you have ever seen a bricklayer building a wall, you know how important organization can be. The bricklayer must have all the tools necessary for the job, plus a plan of action. The same things are true of writing paragraphs. In this unit you will study the function and placement of the topic sentence, which gives the main idea, and how to arrange in a logical order the sentences that give details or examples. You will also be learning to recognize material that does not belong in the paragraph you are writing.

Just as there is logic in the arrangement of sentences in a good paragraph, there is a logic to the arrangement of books on a library's shelves. When you use the card catalog to find the Dewey Decimal number of the book you want, you can readily find the place where that book is stored.

In this unit you will also learn about figurative language in poetry. You will see that you can use figurative language in your paragraph writing too.

LANGUAGE

Lesson 1: Understanding Paragraph Structure

Nell wrote this paragraph about women's clubs in the United States.

Most of the public libraries in the United States were founded by women's clubs. Women who met to share books with each other wanted to make reading available to their communities. At first they opened libraries in hotels, shops, courthouses, or anywhere else they could find space. In the 1890's and early 1900's, thousands of clubs raised the money to build permanent libraries for their towns.

Think and Discuss

The sentences about the way that women's clubs helped public libraries to grow form a **paragraph.** Notice that the first sentence in the paragraph is **indented.** A space has been left between the margin and the first word of the sentence.

- A **paragraph** is a group of sentences that develop a single topic.

The single topic is the **main idea** of the paragraph. The sentences all relate to this main idea.

The first sentence of Nell's paragraph states that most of the public libraries in the United States were founded by women's clubs. What sentences support this main idea?

The concluding sentence of a paragraph can do either of two things. It may simply add another detail to the paragraph, or it can sum up the idea presented. Does the concluding sentence of Nell's paragraph add the last detail or sum up the paragraph?

Practice

A. Answer the questions that follow this paragraph. Use complete sentences.

Club women have long made up mottoes for themselves. Since the 1890's, a national organization of black women has used the motto "Lifting As We Climb." Susan B. Anthony, who organized clubs to obtain voting rights for women, had the motto "Failure Is Impossible." With memorable phrases such as these, club women stated their attitudes and what they intended to accomplish.

1. What is the main idea of this paragraph?
2. What details in sentence 2 support this idea?
3. What details in sentence 3 support this idea?
4. In what way does the last sentence conclude the paragraph?

B. Arrange the following sentences in the proper order. Write the paragraph. Indent the first sentence. Put the sentence that states the main idea first, the sentences that add details next, and the sentence that sums up last.

5. They also cleaned up playgrounds and planted trees.
6. Before schools had PTA organizations, they had mothers' clubs.
7. Mothers' clubs had sanitary drinking fountains put in the schools so that children would not catch diseases by drinking from the same water dipper.
8. Because fathers wanted to help the schools too, the Federation of Mothers' Clubs became the Parent-Teacher Association.
9. They raised money to buy things such as playground equipment, library books, pianos, and record players.

Apply

C. 10. Select one of the following sentences as the main idea for a paragraph. Write the paragraph. Be sure to indent. Include at least four detail sentences. Your last sentence may sum up or add a final detail.

People form clubs for many different purposes.
Clubs often benefit others besides their members.
The library is an important institution in our community.
Most clubs have officers who help to run the meetings.

Lesson 2: Understanding Topic Sentences

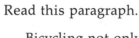

Read this paragraph.

Bicycling not only is fun; it's also good for your health. When you ride often and at top speed, bicycling helps to improve the efficiency of your circulatory system. The amount of oxygen distributed to the cells of your body is significantly increased. Bicycling also improves overall muscle tone, without straining any one muscle group. It helps to control weight gain in the lower body. Some people even maintain that bicycling is good for mental or emotional health. "When you are on your bike, you are at one with the environment and yourself," says one rider. "It feels really great!"

Which sentence tells you what the paragraph will be about? What happens to the paragraph if this sentence is omitted?

Think and Discuss

The sentence that expresses the main idea of a paragraph is the **topic sentence.** The topic sentence tells the reader what kind of information will be presented in the paragraph. In the paragraph that you have just read, the topic sentence says that the paragraph will be about the ways in which bicycling contributes to good health. What information does the paragraph provide on the topic?

Because it sets up expectations, the topic sentence is often the first sentence in the paragraph. Sometimes, however, the writer does not feel the need to set up expectations. He or she is more interested in "bringing readers around," so to speak. The object may be to make the readers realize something in the course of the paragraph, to lead them point by point to a conclusion, or even to surprise them. In such cases the topic sentence may appear later in the paragraph.

Read this paragraph.

People at the meeting said that riding bicycles helped them to lose weight and to firm their thigh muscles. Some said bicycling made them breathe more deeply and feel more peaceful. Some reported having fewer colds and coughs since they started bicycling instead of busing to school. In fact bicycling has been shown to have many beneficial effects on physical and mental health. It is especially valuable for people who work sitting at a desk all day and who seldom get physical exercise.

Which sentence expresses the main idea of this paragraph? Why do you suppose the writer chose to express the main idea in a topic sentence that was not the first sentence in the paragraph?

Practice

A. Copy these sentences. In each group write *topic sentence* next to the sentence that might function as the topic sentence for the others. Write *detail sentence* next to those that would develop the main idea.

1. **a.** Bicycle riding is one of the nation's fastest growing sports.
   b. More than 80 million bicycles are now on the road.
   c. Adult riders, especially senior citizens, are discovering bicycling in ever increasing numbers.
2. **a.** Bicycles are used for touring and camping.
   b. Bicycles are no longer used only for short commutes.
   c. Bicycles now compete in road and track races.
3. **a.** The new bicycles will be lighter and have more sophisticated gear systems.
   b. New kinds of bicycles will be built in the future.
   c. More bicycles will be custom made for a specific rider.

B. Supply a topic sentence for these paragraphs. Write the complete paragraph.

4. Accessories such as rear and front lights, reflectors, and reflecting tape are available for nighttime riding. Bells and horns are used by city riders. Racks, baskets, and packs of all kinds are used to increase the bicycles' carrying power.

5. Bicycles were popular in this country as early as the 1870's. At first no American models were available. Americans had to import their bicycles from England, which made the bicycles quite expensive. Bicycles experienced another surge of popularity in the 1890's and early 1900's. American models such as the Columbia and the American Rambler were popular "for ladies and gentlemen." Then the Model-T Ford came along, and the public lost interest in bicycles. A new wave of bicycling did not begin until the 1960's.

Apply

C. 6. Use the material in this lesson, as well as your own experience and knowledge, to write two paragraphs on bicycles. Choose one of these possibilities.

A paragraph that *begins* with the topic sentence, "Bicycles have a lot going for them."
A paragraph that *ends* with the topic sentence, "The popularity of bicycles seems to be constantly growing."

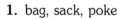

HOW OUR LANGUAGE GROWS

Do you eat *corn on the cob* or *roasting ears*? Do you turn on the *faucet* or the *spigot*? Do you wear *tennis shoes* or *sneakers*? The answer will depend on where you live. These words are examples of *regionalisms* or regional differences in speech. You may know all the words in those questions, but the one you use will probably be the one that you are used to hearing where you live. Regionalisms are beginning to disappear as mass communication, such as radio and TV, becomes more advanced. It is important to remember, however, that no regionalism is better or worse than another. Some things have many different names, all of them acceptable. Here are some things whose name varies regionally. Write the name that is used by your family or in your area.

1. bag, sack, poke
2. seesaw, teeter-totter, tilt
3. firefly, lightning bug
4. catch a cold, take a cold
5. dragonfly, darning needle, spindle

Lesson 3: Supporting the Main Idea

Maya was writing a paragraph for a report on the history of the space program. She had identified a main idea for her paragraph: "The first flight of the space shuttle *Columbia* did much to boost the morale of all Americans."

Here are five of Maya's detail sentences.

1. The space shuttle proved the effectiveness of our technology.
2. It offered examples of the bravery and skill of our astronauts.
3. It proved that we are still "Number One" in carrying out difficult space missions.
4. It cost 10 billion dollars—nearly twice what was originally estimated.
5. Those who watched the landing on television said, "It made me proud to be an American."

Which of Maya's sentences does not support her main idea? Should Maya include this sentence in her paragraph?

Think and Discuss

Sentences are grouped into a paragraph because they all refer to the same idea. The main idea is stated in the topic sentence, and all detail sentences in the paragraph must support, explain, or expand upon the main idea.

Maya decided that sentence number 4 did not really support her main idea. She omitted this sentence from her first draft. She found that her paragraph now had **unity;** that is, all the sentences were about the main idea. However, Maya was unhappy about omitting the reference to cost. It seemed important to her. For example, it represented sacrifice and commitment. If the space shuttle boosted morale, it did so *even though* most people knew it had cost a great deal. Maya rewrote her sentence on cost so that it would support the main idea and lead naturally to her conclusion.

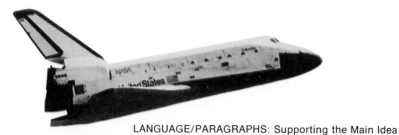

Notice how Maya changed the nature of the sentence from a negative statement to a positive one.

Although the shuttle cost 10 billion dollars, most Americans thought it was worth the expense.

Why does Maya's rewritten sentence on cost now support her main idea?

Detail sentences support, explain, or expand the main idea. They can also qualify or state reservations or limits that apply to the main idea. The important requirement is that they be clearly related and subordinated to the main idea as expressed in the topic sentence.

Practice

A. Copy each topic sentence. Under each write the sentences that support the topic sentence.

1. Many different clients are interested in renting cargo space on the shuttle.
   a. The first commercial bookings were obtained by NASA in 1976 — four years before launching.
   b. International telecommunications corporations are eager to rent space.
   c. Foreign governments are among the shuttle's clients.
   d. Medical research will be performed on future missions.
2. The spacelab on the shuttle will make possible a variety of scientific experiments never before performed.
   a. Scientists will be able to make exact observations about the sun and its energy output.
   b. Military advisers also hope that the shuttle will launch reconnaissance satellites.
   c. Physicists will be able to make sophisticated observations of high-energy and wavelike particles that do not ordinarily penetrate our atmosphere.
   d. They will be able to scan earth and ocean areas to detect minerals and other materials with economic importance.
3. The astronauts were middle-aged family men with similar backgrounds and experiences.
   a. Both had adolescent or young adult children.
   b. Both held degrees in aerospace engineering.

    c. Both had fighter pilot experience before becoming astronauts.

    d. Both were to fly in a craft that had not been previously tested.

B. In each pair copy the sentence that might be used in a paragraph in which the topic sentence was about the *success* of the space shuttle.

4. a. Many Americans thought that the money spent on the shuttle should have been used to solve social problems.

    b. Even those Americans who resented the high cost of the shuttle were swept along in the triumph of the landing.

5. a. The construction of the shuttle took about three years longer than had been anticipated.

    b. Although the construction of the shuttle took longer than anticipated, the technology was said to be "first rate."

6. a. Despite numerous last-minute setbacks, the countdown and lift-off went smoothly.

    b. Frayed wires and a leaky valve were discovered during the countdown.

Apply

C. 7. Write a paragraph about a major public event and the effect it had on you. Develop your own topic, or choose one of the following ideas.

The inauguration of a president
The first game of a World Series
An important speech by a public official
The opening night of a play or other performance in
    which you participated

A Challenge

    Imagine that you are an astronaut on the space shuttle. What would your duties be? How would you feel when you looked at Earth? Would you enjoy being weightless? How would you relax? Make the answer to *one* of these questions the topic sentence of a paragraph whose main idea will be supported by appropriate details.

LANGUAGE REVIEW

Paragraph Structure   pages 42–43

Read this paragraph, and then answer the questions that follow it.

The Hittites, who lived in Asia Minor more than 4,000 years ago, were a remarkable people in many ways. They invented a system for writing and had an intelligent code of laws. They were also skillful in working with stone. Their chief contribution to the world, however, was their knowledge of the practical uses of iron.

1. What is a paragraph?
2. What is the topic sentence of this paragraph?
3. Does the last sentence in the paragraph add a final detail, or does it sum up all of the other details?
4. How many detail sentences are there?
5. How do the detail sentences help the paragraph to make its point?
6. Express the main idea of the paragraph in your own words.

Topic Sentences   pages 44–46

Read these paragraphs. Copy the topic sentence from each one.

7. My little sister's lively nature is impossible to repress. One evening she appeared in the living room doorway just as Mom and Dad and their guests were about to go to dinner. Beth was wearing my pajamas, which were at least four sizes too large for her. The sleeves and legs flopped about over her hands and feet. Around her waist she had tied one of Dad's best silk ties. Behind her she dragged a damp towel to which was pinned her old Raggedy Ann doll. Her mischievous smile made it difficult to scold her.

8. A hundred balloons waved gently from the ceiling. Leaves of gold and crimson festooned the windows. The newly waxed floor sparkled. Our old gym had been transformed for our first party.

9. The first stages of learning to play the trumpet are torture to both the learner and the listener. The learner all too often cannot manage to make any noise at all, except for a depressing sputter of air. After a few lessons most beginners are able to produce a few loud blasts, which are usually off-key. Understandably, those who have to live with young trumpeters often banish them to some hideaway well out of earshot.

Supporting the Main Idea   pages 47–49

Read this paragraph and decide which sentence or sentences do not support the main idea. Then write the paragraph as it should be.

10.   My friend Rosa never liked sports until our school started allowing girls on the baseball team. On the first day of spring training, everyone had to try out for the team during gym. Rosa stepped up to the plate and swung lazily, just as she always does. To hit a ball properly, you must swing with energy and have a good follow-through. She hit the first pitch over the head of the left fielder. Rosa loves baseball now.

In this paragraph the writer starts out well but then goes off the track. Write the sentence in which you think the writer begins to wander from the topic. Then rewrite the paragraph so that it will have unity.

11.   There is nothing more peaceful and satisfying than fishing on a quiet lake. Few fish disturb your line, yet the line is always there to provide a sense of purpose. You keep a hold on it, occasionally you look at the hook, and now and then you apply a fresh worm. None of these movements will disturb your peace of mind. After all, isn't it peace of mind that we all seek? Our lives are too rushed, too full, too jumpy. It is not good for our mental health to be constantly agitated. Every person, young or old, needs periods of quiet meditation in order to lead a balanced, satisfied life.

Applying Paragraphs

12. Write a paragraph in which three detail sentences support a topic sentence. Choose one of these sentences as your topic sentence, or make up one of your own. You may place the topic sentence either at the beginning or at the end of the paragraph, but underline it where it appears in your finished paragraph.

The arrival of my baby sister (brother) changed my whole way of life.
The ancient necklace was an exquisite work of art.
Being short (tall) has its advantages.

STUDY SKILLS

Lesson 4: Learning About the Library

Your family is planning next year's vacation. You want to travel through Texas, but your sister and brother are not interested. Where would you find something about the history and geography of Texas that would persuade them to go there?

Think and Discuss

The library contains information about things that happened only yesterday and about the events that took place thousands of years ago. Although a library's collection consists mostly of books, it contains newspapers, magazines, and pamphlets as well. Some libraries may even have records and movies that you can borrow.

There are four main sections in most libraries: fiction, nonfiction, reference, and periodicals.

The category of **fiction** includes novels and short stories. In the fiction section of the library, books are arranged alphabetically by the last name of the author. If the same author has written several different novels, the books are arranged under his or her name, alphabetically by title.

Nonfiction books are those that contain factual information. This category includes books on science, engineering, music, art, religion, and history. It also includes poetry and plays. Nonfiction is arranged according to its subject. For example, all books about the fall of the Alamo will be grouped together, within a larger area that contains books about Texas history.

Biographies are a type of nonfiction that is sometimes put in a separate section of the library. Within the biography section books are arranged alphabetically by subject. If more than one author has written about the same person, books about the same subject are then arranged alphabetically by author.

Fiction and nonfiction usually *circulate* freely. If you have a library card, you may borrow any book in either section.

The books in the **reference section** usually do not circulate. You must use them inside the library. In the reference section you will find encyclopedias, almanacs, dictionaries, and atlases. This section may also contain specialized works, such as biographical dictionaries, books of quotations, and guidebooks.

In some libraries the reference section houses **periodicals**, but often they are given their own section. Here you will find current newspapers and magazines loose on the shelves. Back issues may be bound together in book form, or they may be stored on film. Pages reduced photographically are put on **microfilm.** Pages of microfilm may then be put together on a larger sheet of film called a **microfiche.** In the periodical section you will also find the **vertical file**, where pamphlets are stored, arranged in folders according to subject.

Practice

A. On your paper make four columns, one for each of the four major sections of the library. Copy each of the following library materials under the heading of the section in which you would find it in the library.

1. *The Return of Sherlock Holmes* by Arthur Conan Doyle
2. *The Life of A. Conan Doyle* by J. Dickson Carr
3. a mystery novel by John Dickson Carr
4. *Cassell's Spanish Dictionary*
5. a book on how to make quilts
6. the collected letters of Virginia Woolf
7. an article on lasers in *Science* magazine
8. a biography of Louis Armstrong
9. *Statistical Abstract of the United States*
10. a novel by V. S. Naipaul
11. the baseball scores from yesterday's paper
12. *The Quotation Dictionary*
13. *The Wizard of Oz* by L. Frank Baum
14. a book on houseplant care

15. an article from the *Daily News* on houseplant care
16. an article from *House & Garden* magazine on houseplant care
17. an article from *Encyclopaedia Britannica* on houseplant care
18. a science fiction novel about a houseplant from Mars

B. Copy these sentences and fill in the blanks.

19. Short stories are found in the _____ section.
20. Fiction is arranged _____ by author.
21. Books in the _____ section usually do not circulate.
22. Nonfiction is arranged according to _____.
23. The vertical file contains _____.
24. Many pages of microfilm can be put together on _____.
25. If you have a library card, you can borrow any book that _____.
26. Atlases are located in the _____ section.

C. Copy these fiction titles in the order in which they would be arranged on a library shelf.

27. *The Portrait of a Lady* by Henry James
28. *Portrait of the Artist as a Young Man* by James Joyce
29. *The Day of the Scorpion* by Paul Scott
30. *The Jewel in the Crown* by Paul Scott
31. *Emma* by Jane Austen
32. *Jane Eyre* by Charlotte Brontë

D. Copy the titles of these biographies in the order in which they would be arranged on the library shelf.

33. *Guido Cantelli* by Laurence Lewis
34. *James Wong Howe: Cinematographer* by Todd Rainsberger
35. *Joseph Conrad* by John Conrad
36. *Joseph Conrad* by Richard Curle
37. *Tops in Taps,* a biography of Ann Miller by Jim Connor
38. *Shoji Hamada: A Potter's Way and Work* by Susan Peterson

Apply

E. 39.–48. Visit the reference section of your school or local library. Make a list of ten books that might be helpful in doing a social studies assignment.

Lesson 5: Using the Card Catalog

You have recently acquired a German shepherd puppy that is very lively. Your parents have told you that you may keep the dog only if you train it to behave properly. You go to the library to look for a book on dog training. How would you locate the book on the shelf?

Think and Discuss

The **card catalog** is a tool that enables you to find any book in the library. It consists of thousands of cards, filed alphabetically in drawers. Here are examples of some cards that might be in the card catalog of your library.

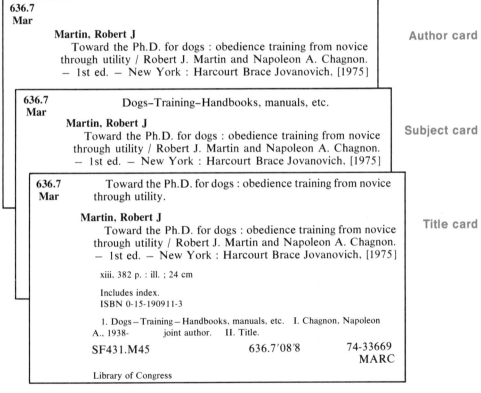

For every book the library owns, there are at least two different cards in the catalog. The **title card** lists the book by the first word of its title, and the **author card** lists it by the author's last name. If there are joint authors, there will be a card for each author.

For nonfiction books there is a third type of card in the catalog. The **subject card** lists the book by the subject about which it is written. A book may have more than one subject card to make it easier to locate. A book about Sojourner Truth, for instance, might have subject cards under *Sojourner Truth, Abolitionists,* and *Afro-American Biography.*

Each nonfiction book in the library has a **call number.** It appears on the upper left-hand corner of the card. It is based on the book's number under the **Dewey Decimal System** of classification. The call number tells the librarian where to find the book on the shelves. What is the call number of the book shown in the sample cards?

The cards also give other information about the book. Here are some of the things you can learn by looking carefully at a card: the city where the publisher is located; the publisher's name; the year the book was published; the number of pages in the book; and the special features such as illustrations, maps, indexes, or glossary.

In addition to the complete Dewey Decimal System number, the card gives the Library of Congress number of the book. The Library of Congress System and the Dewey Decimal System are alternate methods of classification.

In addition to the three cards shown, there will be at least one other card for the dog training manual in the card catalog. Under what will it be filed?

Practice

A. Copy the following sentences and fill in the blanks.

1. Librarians can locate any nonfiction book by using the
   _____.
2. Only nonfiction books have a _____ card.
3. For each nonfiction book there are _____ kinds of cards in the catalog.
4. For each fiction book there are _____ kinds of cards in the catalog.
5. All cards in the catalog are filed _____.
6. Call numbers are located in the _____ corner of the card.
7. Call numbers are based on the _____.
8. The Library of Congress System is _____.

B. Look at the title card shown on page 55. Answer these questions, using complete sentences.

9. What is the title of the book?
10. Who wrote the book?
11. When was the book published?
12. Is the book fiction or nonfiction?
13. What subject classification has been assigned to the book?
14. What is the complete Dewey Decimal System number of the book?
15. How many pages are in the book?
16. Is the book illustrated?
17. What special features does the book have?

C. Copy the following information. For each book write whether you would use the title, author, or subject card to find it in the library.

18. a book called *Energy and the Way We Live*
19. a novel by Agatha Christie
20. a book on colonial schooners
21. a book called *The Colonial Schooner, 1763–1775*
22. a book on whitewater canoeing
23. a book called *America's Working Women*
24. a play by Lorraine Hansberry
25. a book of Cochiti folktales
26. a book by Alfonso Ortiz
27. a book called *You're a Good Sport, Charlie Brown*
28. a field guide for identifying birds
29. a biography of Duke Ellington
30. a book called *Vietnamese Folk Poetry*

Apply

D. Go to your school or local library. Copy the author, title, and complete call number for each type of book below. Then find the books on the library shelves.

31. a book about cats
32. a book of poetry by Emily Dickinson
33. a biography of Pablo Picasso
34. a book on train travel

Lesson 6: Understanding the Dewey Decimal System

Our national library in Washington contains over 15 million books. Even your own school library probably contains thousands of books. Libraries use classification systems to help you find the book you want quickly and easily.

Think and Discuss

One system of classifying nonfiction books by subject was developed over 100 years ago by a librarian at Amherst College named Melvil Dewey. His system, now used by most libraries in the United States, is called the **Dewey Decimal System.**

The Dewey Decimal System begins with 10 major categories, expressed by a set of numbers.

000–999   General works (encyclopedias, periodicals, newspapers)
100–199   Philosophy (conduct, ethics, psychology)
200–299   Religion (world religions and creeds, ancient mythology)
300–399   Social science (customs, commerce, education, government, law, economics)
400–499   Language (dictionaries and languages)
500–599   Pure science (mathematics, astronomy, plants, animals, chemistry, physics)
600–699   Applied science (engineering, radio, aeronautics)
700–799   Arts and recreation (architecture, music, sports)
800–899   Literature
900–999   History (travel, geography, biography)

Each category can then be subdivided into 100 separate topics. For example, within the major category of science (500–599) there is the smaller unit of chemistry (540–549). Physical and theoretical chemistry is 541; laboratories and equipment is 542. With the use of **decimals** after the three-digit number, additional categories can be created as they are needed. Thus, physical chemistry is 541.3. Chemical solutions is 541.34. Photochemistry is 541.35. The use of decimals allows libraries to add categories for new information.

Note that literature (800–899) is in the nonfiction section even though it includes some fiction. Popular fiction, however, is not classified according to the Dewey Decimal System.

Practice

A. Copy and complete each sentence.

1. In the United States most libraries use the _____ System of classification.
2. Classification systems allow librarians to group nonfiction books by _____.
3. The Dewey Decimal System contains _____ major categories.
4. New categories can be added to the system by the use of _____.
5. The Dewey Decimal System is not used for books in the _____ section.

B. Copy the list of categories. Beside each one write the correct set of numbers for the category.

6. Religion
7. Literature
8. Applied science
9. Philosophy
10. Pure science
11. Arts and recreation
12. Language
13. Social science

C. Copy these topics. After each one write the category and the correct set of numbers.

14. a chemistry textbook
15. a book of poems by June Jordan
16. a history of Irish immigration to America
17. a biography of Henry Aaron
18. a book of instructions for building a radio
19. a newspaper article on Congressional ethics
20. a Swahili dictionary
21. a book explaining the problem of inflation
22. an automobile repair manual
23. a rule book for soccer
24. a collection of humorous essays by Robert Benchley
25. a book about Eskimo myths

Apply

D. 26.–35. Visit the nonfiction section of your school or local library. Draw a map that shows the location of each of the ten major categories.

COMPOSITION

Lesson 7: Developing a Paragraph with Examples

Li was writing a paragraph on the history of money. Read the first sentence of his paragraph.

Edible things have often been used as money.

What kind of information should Li give in the rest of his paragraph?

Think and Discuss

Li's topic sentence raises questions. On reading it, most people wonder *what* commodities were used as money. Li can answer this question by giving *examples* of these commodities in his detail sentences.

Read Li's paragraph.

> Edible things have often been used as money. Grain was used for payment in ancient Egypt. Salt was used to pay the soldiers of early Rome. Tea was circulated for centuries as the currency of the Far East. Most interesting in recent times was the Germans' use of coffee and sugar as mediums of exchange at the end of World War II when the official German currency became nearly worthless.

How many examples did Li give?

In many paragraphs the topic sentence makes a generalization or general statement. Examples that support this generalization are provided in the detail sentences. Only those examples that clearly support the generalization are cited. (Li did not include references to horns or items of clothing that have been used as money, because these would not have been examples of the edible kind of currency described in his topic sentence.)

In paragraphs where the topic sentence is supported by examples, it is sometimes effective to put the most important, interesting, or longest example last. In Li's paragraph the example from the historical period that is closest to the reader is given last. How do we know that Li considered this example most interesting?

Practice

A. 1. Li discovered that he had forgotten to mention cattle and other livestock—one of the earliest and most prevalent forms of money. Copy the original paragraph, adding this example where it belongs.

B. Copy these topic sentences. Under each one write the sentences that give examples to *support* the topic sentence.

2. Decorative items have often been used as money.
   a. Native Americans used attractive shells that had been made into tiny cylinders and strung on hemp.
   b. The teeth of dogs, tigers, and porpoises have served as money—and jewelry—in the South Sea Islands.
   c. Cattle were a medium of exchange for many centuries.

3. Commodities used as money are usually convenient to handle.
   a. The grain used by Biblical societies could be easily carried, divided, and stored.
   b. The inhabitants of Yap, an island in the Pacific, have for generations used large stones as a medium of exchange.
   c. When tea was used as money, it was often mixed with sawdust and baked into bricks for easy handling.

4. Today, many things fulfill the functions of money besides coins and paper currency.
   a. Credit cards are an accepted form of payment in many stores, restaurants, and ticket offices.
   b. Personal checks, technically a form of money, are widely circulated.
   c. A savings account is a measure of personal economic worth.

Apply

C. 5. Develop one of these topics by using appropriate examples.

Coins in the United States are stamped with symbols that have historical significance.
The portraits of famous Americans appear on our currency.

Lesson 8: Developing a Paragraph by Comparison/Contrast

Ray thinks that bears and raccoons have many things in common. Read his paragraph that compares them.

Bears and raccoons have some similarities in appearance, in habitat, and in behavior. Both are covered with thick fur, have a pointed snout and small ears, and have five-toed feet with sharp claws. Both are found in the United States and Canada, and both live in wild, wooded areas away from humans. Finally, both bears and raccoons are good swimmers, eat nearly everything they can find, and climb trees to rest or escape. They are believed to hibernate during the winter, but in fact both are known to leave their dens to search for food on mild winter days.

In what three major ways does Ray think bears and raccoons are similar?

Think and Discuss

Paragraphs that show how two things are *alike* are paragraphs of **comparison.** Paragraphs that show how two things are *different* are paragraphs of **contrast.** Both, however, are set up in much the same way.

Because you are dealing with a single paragraph in either case, you should limit yourself to a few qualities or characteristics. The qualities you use to compare or contrast your two subjects should be stated in the first sentence. Then, as you write your paragraph, you should deal with each quality *in the same order* in which you mentioned it in your topic sentence. This makes your paragraph logical and easy to follow.

Linda wrote a paragraph of contrast about bears and raccoons. She showed their *differences,* using the same qualities Ray had chosen to illustrate their similarities.

Bears and raccoons are quite different in appearance, in habitat, and in behavior. Bears grow from 3 to 8 feet long (.9 to 2.4 m) and weigh from 60 to 800 pounds (27 to 360 kg). Raccoons, however, are only 30 to 35 inches long (76 to 97 cm) and weigh between 12 and 25 pounds (5 to 11 kg). Bears are varicolored and have short, stumpy tails, whereas raccoons are usually gray with a black "mask" and have long, bushy tails. Bears most often live in caves, whereas raccoons live in trees, tall grass, or a hollow log or stump. Bears move slowly and clumsily except when hunting, and they live alone except during the mating season. Raccoons, on the other hand, move quickly and gracefully, and usually live in small family groups.

Why do you think both Ray and Linda always mentioned bears first in their paragraphs?

Practice

A. Copy these sentences. After each write *comparison* or *contrast,* depending on the way the paragraph should be developed.

1. A frog makes a better pet than an eel.
2. Both dogs and wolves belong to the same family.
3. Robins and pigeons have many things in common.
4. I prefer country life to city life.
5. The wide prairies and tall mountains of the American West are beautiful to see.

B. 6.–20. For each of the topics in Practice A, write three points of comparison or contrast.

Apply

C. 21. Choose one of the five topics in Practice B for which you wrote three points. Write a paragraph of comparison or contrast developing these points.

Lesson 9: Developing a Paragraph Using Time Order and Space Order

Stewart attended a concert of the Pottsville Symphony Orchestra with his class. He was asked to write a paragraph describing his observations. Read his paragraph.

> The Pottsville Symphony Orchestra was the largest gathering of musicians I had ever seen on one stage. My eyes were drawn toward the conductor, who stood on a raised podium at the front and center of the stage with her back to the audience. The first violins were to the conductor's left. The second violins, which play supporting violin parts, were slightly to the back of them. Opposite the violin section, on the conductor's right, were the cellos, and behind them were the violas. The large basses (or bass violins) could be seen at the back of the stage, to the right. The other instruments, mostly winds and brasses, were directly in front of the conductor. Small, higher-pitched instruments, such as the flute and clarinet, were toward the front. Larger, lower-pitched instruments, such as the bassoons, French horns, and trumpets, could be seen behind them. Finally, there was an active corner at the far left where the timpani, drums, chimes, and other percussion instruments contributed their special sounds. All in all, about 100 musicians were on stage.

This paragraph describes the spatial arrangement of a modern symphony orchestra. Which words help you to locate the different instrument groups?

Think and Discuss

The detail sentences in a paragraph are organized according to a definite plan. One kind of plan uses **space order.** The detail sentences tell where things exist in relation to one another. Why is this an effective plan for a paragraph describing a symphony orchestra?

Not all paragraphs can be developed by details that are organized spatially. Another student who attended the concert chose to describe a piece of music. Read her paragraph.

The most enjoyable piece on the program was Haydn's Symphony no. 94, which is called *Surprise*. The second movement opened with the theme played softly by the violins. The theme is played even more softly until, at the end of the repetition, a loud chord is heard. This is the famous surprise. After that, the original theme is heard in several entertaining variations. The final variation is full of tricky rhythms. It ends in crashing chords, followed by a coda (or end section) that creates suspense and fun. Even though you are not supposed to interrupt a performance of a symphony, the audience gave the second movement a long round of applause.

In this paragraph detail sentences describe an experience that takes place over time. The sentences are arranged according to time or chronology. The first detail sentence tells what happened first; the second tells what happened next, and so on. Why is **time order** effective in describing a piece of music?

Practice

A. Write these topic sentences. After each write *space order* or *time order,* depending on how the sentence would be best developed in a paragraph.

1. The opening *William Tell* Overture was followed by several longer works.
2. During the intermission the stage was rearranged to accommodate a piano soloist.
3. Symphony Hall is divided into different seating sections, each with its own ticket price.
4. The mural in the lobby showed scenes from the Romantic period of music.
5. Over the years the music director has tried to introduce his audiences to more modern musical works.

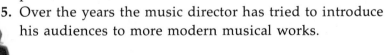

Apply

B. 6. Choose one of these topics. Write a topic sentence and develop it with detail sentences that are arranged according to space order.

The layout of an important building in your city or town

The location of your state in relation to other states

Your stage position in a chorus, musical, or dramatic performance in which you recently participated

The appearance of a room that is featured in a magazine advertisement

The arrangement of cups, plates, and glasses in your kitchen cupboard

C. Choose one of these topics. Write a topic sentence and develop it with detail sentences that are arranged according to time order.

The sports program at your school during the school year

A sequence of television or radio programs that you regularly watch or listen to

The sequence of birthdays and other personal holidays that are celebrated in your family

The steps involved in a scientific discovery or invention that you have studied

The events leading up to a significant occasion in American history

To Memorize

People themselves alter so much that there is something new to be observed in them forever.

Jane Austen

Jane Austen, an early nineteenth-century novelist, was a master at observing people and writing about the ways in which they changed. Can you pinpoint an important change — something new to be observed — in yourself that has occurred in the past year?

Lesson 10: Editing Paragraphs (I)

Read this paragraph that Rico wrote about famous left-handed people.

We left-handed people often have a hard time getting along in a right-handed world. *Some* Many people do not realize that ~~a great~~ many famous people have been left-handed. In the world of sports, *for example,* tennis star Jimmy Connors and *former* baseball pitcher Sandy Koufax are left-handed, as was baseball great Babe Ruth. In the political *arena* world, left-handedness has been historic. Roman emperor Tiberius and King George II of England were "lefties"; that trait *likewise* appeared in U. S. Presidents James A. Garfield, Harry S Truman, and Gerald Ford. ~~My uncle Fernando is left-handed too.~~ *In the world of art,* ~~Among artists,~~ you will find left-handed masters Michelangelo and Leonardo da Vinci; *similarly,* composers C. P. E. Bach and Cole Porter wrote with their left hand. In the movies you or your parents might have seen such noted performers as Charlie Chaplin, Harpo Marx, Betty Grable, or Judy Garland—all of whom were left-handed. *Yes, if you* ~~People who~~ have never known about "lefties" *you* have a lot to learn.

Editing Marks

- ☰ capitalize
- ⊙ make a period
- ∧ add something
- ⋏ add a comma
- ⌄ add quotation marks
- ⌇ take something away
- ○ spell correctly
- ⌟ indent the paragraph
- / make a lowercase letter
- ∿ tr transpose

What is the topic sentence of this paragraph? How is the paragraph developed?

Think and Discuss

When Rico studied the draft of his paragraph, he decided that it sounded choppy. It lacked **coherence**—a quality that paragraphs have when the sentences in them follow one another smoothly.

Rico used one method of achieving coherence in his draft— the repetition of key words and phrases. Notice that he often repeats the word *left-handed.* To avoid repeating himself too much, he also uses synonymous terms such as *lefties* and *wrote with their left hand.*

One way he improved the coherence of his draft was by using transitional words and phrases. Expressions such as *for example, likewise, similarly,* and *yes* help to tie ideas together. Which two expressions indicate an additional thought? Which one indicates a conclusion?

Rico also helped the coherence of his paragraph when he made the change from *people* to *you* in the last sentence. He found that making the point of view consistent improved his writing.

Notice that Rico made some changes so that each category was introduced by the words *in the.* Using parallel structure is a good way of connecting ideas coherently. Why do you think he changed *world* to *arena* in one of those introductions? Why did he omit the sentence about his uncle?

Practice

A. 1. Copy Rico's paragraph, making the changes that he marked.

B. Copy and complete these sentences.

2. Coherence is _____.
3. *In fact, likewise,* and *finally* are examples of _____.
4. "Most people do not know how you can relax properly" is an example of a sentence whose coherence could be improved by _____.
5. Two synonymous terms for the key word *poet* might be _____ and _____.
6. "Chuck wanted to own a car, to graduate from college, and to make 1 million dollars by his sixteenth birthday" is an example of a sentence whose coherence has been achieved by _____.

C. 7. Reread the paragraph you corrected in Practice A. Then close your book and write the paragraph as your teacher reads it aloud.

Apply

D. 8. Reread one of the paragraphs you wrote in Lessons 7–9. Could it be made more coherent? Make any changes that you feel are necessary; then rewrite it.

MECHANICS PRACTICE

Punctuating Names, Titles, and Abbreviations

- Capitalize names of people, including initials, titles, and abbreviations of titles.
- Do not capitalize nouns that show family relationships unless they are used as proper nouns.

    My grandmother made this sweater. There is Grandmother.

- Use a period after most abbreviations or titles.

    Sgt.   L.B.J.   Capt.   F.D.R.   Dr.

- Do not use a period in abbreviating names of organizations or agencies.

    IRS   NATO   NAACP   AFL-CIO

A. Rewrite these groups of words. Properly abbreviate the underlined part of each group.

1. Reginald Patterson, senior
2. John Fitzgerald Kennedy
3. Central Intelligence Agency
4. Mister Peter Alan Watkins
5. Francis Scott Fitzgerald
6. Doctor Maria Fernandez
7. Lieutenant Beth Ann Ralston
8. National Football League

B. Copy these sentences. Capitalize names of people and organizations. Properly abbreviate names of organizations and titles that precede names.

9. mom, dad, my sister kc, and I recently moved into a new apartment.
10. My mother introduced me to our superintendent, leonard j jordan.
11. superintendent jordan told us that emma x gould works for the federal bureau of investigation.
12. He went on to tell mom and me that mister juan alvarez is an artist for the american broadcasting company.
13. dr sandra k duprés, a veterinarian, has an office nearby.
14. dad asked superintendent jordan if he knew p r petrosko, an accountant for the american medical association.
15. mr jordan said that ms petrosko lived next door to captain david park.

LITERATURE

Lesson 11: Using Figurative Language in Poetry

Poets create descriptions with comparisons in interesting ways. These descriptions or word pictures appeal to the senses and imagination of the reader. Read this poem. What comparisons can you find?

Let It Be Forgotten

Let it be forgotten, as the flower is forgotten,
    Forgotten as a fire once was singing gold,
Let it be forgotten for ever and ever —
    Time is a kind friend, he will make us old.

If anyone asks, say it was forgotten
    Long and long ago —
As a flower, as a fire, as a hushed footfall
    In a long forgotten snow.

Sara Teasdale

Think and Discuss

In "Let It Be Forgotten" the word *as* is used in most of the comparisons. The poet, Sara Teasdale, says that the thing to be forgotten should be forgotten "as a flower," "as a fire," "as a hushed footfall/In a long forgotten snow" might be forgotten. Vivid word pictures that use the words *as* or *like* to make comparisons are called **similes.** To what senses does Sara Teasdale appeal in the similes she has used?

Is "Time is a kind friend" a simile? Although it is a word picture that makes a comparison, it does not use the words *as* or *like*. It is therefore an example of a **metaphor,** a vivid word picture that makes a comparison without using the words *as* or *like*. A metaphor is sometimes called an "implied comparison."

Now read this poem and look for comparisons.

Prairie Dawn

A crimson fire that vanquishes the stars;
A pungent odor from the dusky sage;
A sudden stirring of the huddled herds;
A breaking of the distant table-lands
Through purple mists ascending, and the flare
Of water ditches silver in the light;
A swift, bright lance hurled low across the world;
A sudden sickness for the hills of home.

Willa Cather

The poet, Willa Cather, uses vivid word pictures and comparisons to describe dawn on the prairie. The comparisons in "Prairie Dawn" are all metaphors; in fact, the entire poem consists of metaphors. One such metaphor can be found in the first line: "a crimson fire." Name three other metaphors in the poem.

When poets use similes and metaphors to make comparisons, they are said to be using **figurative language.** Similes and metaphors are called **figures of speech.**

Practice

A. Read this poem, and then answer the questions that come after it. Use complete sentences.

Fog

The fog comes
on little cat feet.
It sits looking
over harbor and city
on silent haunches
and then moves on.

Carl Sandburg

1. What two things are compared in this poem?
2. Is the comparison a simile or a metaphor?
3. The comparison begun in line 1 continues in line 2. To what do the "little cat feet" refer?
4. What do lines 3–5 mean?
5. What are two senses to which Carl Sandburg appeals in this poem?

B. Read this poem by Sir Walter Scott. Use complete sentences to answer the questions that come after it.

'Tis Merry in Greenwood

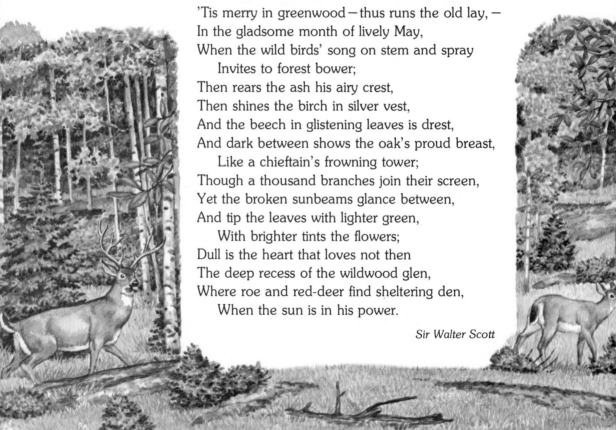

'Tis merry in greenwood—thus runs the old lay,—
In the gladsome month of lively May,
When the wild birds' song on stem and spray
    Invites to forest bower;
Then rears the ash his airy crest,
Then shines the birch in silver vest,
And the beech in glistening leaves is drest,
And dark between shows the oak's proud breast,
    Like a chieftain's frowning tower;
Though a thousand branches join their screen,
Yet the broken sunbeams glance between,
And tip the leaves with lighter green,
    With brighter tints the flowers;
Dull is the heart that loves not then
The deep recess of the wildwood glen,
Where roe and red-deer find sheltering den,
    When the sun is in his power.

Sir Walter Scott

6. Are the two comparisons in lines 5 and 6 similes or metaphors? How can you tell?
7. Express in your own words the metaphor in line 7.
8. List all of the similes in this poem.

9. In lines 10–13 the poet talks about the sunbeams "tipping" the leaves and flowers with color. To what kind of person is he comparing the sunbeams? Is such a comparison a simile or a metaphor?

C. Read these incomplete sentences. Use your imagination to complete each one. Write whether each of the comparisons is a *simile* or a *metaphor.*

10. A starless night is _____.
11. A cool lemonade on a hot summery day is like _____.
12. The sound of birds in early morning is as _____.
13. A young kitten is _____.
14. A full moon is like _____.

Apply

D. 15. Write a short poem about an event in nature. Use similes or metaphors to make comparisons. Identify each comparison as a *simile* or a *metaphor.*

A BOOK TO READ

Title: **The Whispering Wind: Poetry by Young American Indians**
Author: Terry Allen (editor)
Publisher: Doubleday

> "As sad and salt as tears,
> The sea is melancholy.
> It sings a song its mystic own,
> The minor, melancholy sea."

"The Sea Is Melancholy," by Agnes T. Pratt

In this collection of Native American poetry, written by students at the Institute of American Indian Arts, such diverse subjects as Native American folklore, nature, and loneliness are explored. The poems are lyrical and expressive. They are the voice of a unique American culture, but they are also universal, touching on themes that run through the lives of people in all cultures.

2 UNIT TEST

● **Paragraph Structure**   pages 42–43

Number your paper from 1 to 5. Read this paragraph, and then answer the questions that follow. Write the letter of the correct answer.

The famous book *Gulliver's Travels* is not a book of travel; the author, Jonathan Swift, wrote it as a biting criticism of his times. Political figures and ideas, attitudes and customs, as well as the English monarchy, were all held up to ridicule by Swift's acid wit. In this century *Gulliver's Travels* was adapted as a children's book because of the little folk and strange animals that are its characters. In the eighteenth century, however, Swift's book was recognized for what it was—a brilliant satire.

1. A paragraph contains: **a.** two or three main ideas. **b.** one main idea developed by a group of sentences. **c.** many unrelated sentences.
2. The topic sentence of this paragraph is: **a.** the third sentence. **b.** the first sentence. **c.** the fourth sentence.
3. The main idea of this paragraph is that: **a.** *Gulliver's Travels* was written in the eighteenth century. **b.** *Gulliver's Travels* has many funny and interesting characters. **c.** *Gulliver's Travels* was intended for adult readers.
4. A good example of a detail sentence is: **a.** the third sentence. **b.** the first sentence. **c.** the last sentence.
5. The last sentence expresses the main idea of the paragraph by:
   a. telling in what century *Gulliver's Travels* was written.
   b. mentioning the author's name again. **c.** summing up the topic sentence.

● **Topic Sentences**   pages 44–46

Read these paragraphs. Copy the topic sentence from each one.

6.   Mystic Seaport, Connecticut, is a great place to learn about this country's seafaring tradition. Visitors to Mystic Seaport find themselves in a whaling village of the 1800's. Residents of the village, dressed in period costume, explain what life was like in Mystic Seaport over a century ago. New England's last wooden whaling ship, the *Charles W. Morgan,* is in the harbor, and visitors may climb below decks and marvel at the discomforts of a whaler's existence. Every detail of this "living museum" is a pleasure to observe.

7. On May 20, 1927, Charles A. Lindbergh left Roosevelt Field and headed out over the Atlantic Ocean. Little did this modest young American suspect that he was about to become an international hero. Thousands of French people would greet him when he landed at Le Bourget Field, near Paris, after the first nonstop transatlantic flight. The newspapers would call him "the Lone Eagle" and "Lucky Lindy." He would be honored by parades and celebrations, and President Coolidge would award him the Congressional Medal of Honor and the first Distinguished Flying Cross in history.

8. A great military strategist, he led the warriors, women, and children more than 1600 kilometers (1,000 miles) across Idaho and Montana. He fought off the troops that tried to stop him because he believed that his people would be free in Canada. The government had taken his people's land, but he could not submit meekly to the injustice. In spite of his defeat in 1877, Chief Joseph of the Nez Percé is remembered as the "Indian Napoleon."

9. If you needed to travel by train a hundred years ago, you were in for a wearying adventure. The wooden benches were not long enough to lie on; in fact, most travelers brought boards and cushions to lay across the seats at bedtime. You might also find your slumber interrupted by the cries of a newsboy selling reading material. Furthermore, the stove that heated your car was used for cooking throughout the journey at mealtime.

● **Supporting the Main Idea**   pages 47–49

10. Read this paragraph and decide which sentences do not support the main idea. Then rewrite the paragraph as it should be.

Scientists have many questions about Jupiter, the largest planet in our solar system. I have often observed this planet through my telescope. One mystery is whether life exists on this great planet. I believe it does, but my science teacher disagrees. The *Pioneer* and *Voyager* probes have yielded tantalizing clues to the true nature of Jupiter. As space technology grows, many questions will undoubtedly be answered.

● **The Library**   pages 52–54

Copy these library materials and beside each write the section of the library where it would be found.

1. a vegetarian cookbook
2. a collection of letters written by Calamity Jane
3. a novel by Louisa May Alcott
4. a book of poems by Maya Angelou
5. a *Wall Street Journal* article on professional women
6. an encyclopedia article on Mary Church Terrell

The Card Catalog   pages 55–57

Copy this book information. For each item write whether you would use the *title*, *author*, or *subject* card to find the book in the card catalog.

7. a book called *Moving to Win*
8. a book of short stories by Stanislau Lem
9. a travel guide to Yugoslavia
10. a book about Hemingway's years in Paris
11. a book called *Hemingway's Paris*
12. an autobiography of Marian Anderson

The Dewey Decimal System   pages 58–59

Copy these titles. After each write the category in which the book belongs and the Dewey Decimal numbers of that section of the library.

13. *Famous First Facts and Records*
14. *The Collected Poems of Thomas Hardy*
15. *The Life of Florence Nightingale*
16. *How to Fix Your Bicycle*
17. *Baroque Music*
18. *Egyptian Mythology*
19. *Italian for Beginners*
20. *Great Moments in Baseball*

Paragraphs with Examples   pages 60–61

1. Write a paragraph using one of these topic sentences. Add details to support your main idea.

   Junk food is not good for you.
   Baseball is a very exciting (boring) sport.
   Voting is an important civic duty.
   My brother (sister) is always inventing something strange.

Paragraphs of Comparison/Contrast   pages 62–63

2. Choose a foreign country and write a report that compares or contrasts that country with the United States. Compare or contrast at least three points of the two countries.

Time Order and Space Order   pages 64–66

3. Write a short paragraph using either of these topics.

   The Street I Call Home (space order)
   My Favorite Season (time order)

● **Editing Paragraphs (I)**   pages 67–68

4. Choose any one of the paragraphs you wrote for exercises 1–3. Read it over carefully. Are the detail sentences clear? Does the order in which you present the details make sense? Use editing marks to make any changes that you feel are necessary to improve its coherence. Rewrite the paragraph.

● **Punctuating Names, Titles, and Abbreviations**   page 69

Rewrite these groups of words. Properly abbreviate the underlined part of each group.

5. Mister Luis Enrico Salcedo
6. Hubert Horatio Humphrey
7. Sergeant Andrew Lee Holt
8. American Federation of Teachers
9. Colonel Mary Choi
10. Henry Louis Mencken
11. Small Business Administration
12. Ralph Kelsey Phelps, junior
13. Joel Emerson, Registered Nurse
14. League of Women Voters
15. Doctor Lois Ruth Franklin
16. Gerald Rudolph Ford
17. Corporal Teresa Alvarez
18. Nancy Rogers Morrison
19. United Press International
20. Doctor of Philosophy
21. Thomas Stearns Eliot
22. Anne Morrow Lindbergh
23. Reverend Jim Ashe
24. Organization of American States
25. Senator Mary Haynes
26. National Football League
27. Carl Philipp Emanuel Bach
28. Admiral Ted Barnes
29. Strategic Air Command
30. Department of Transportation

● **Figurative Language in Poetry**   pages 70–73

1.–5. Identify the figures of speech in this poem. Write five sentences about the way the figures of speech add to the poet's description of pigeons.

Pigeons

They paddle with staccato feet
in powder-pools of sunlight,
small blue busybodies
strutting like fat gentlemen
with hands clasped
under their swallowtail coats;
and as they stump about,
their heads like tiny hammers
tap at imaginary nails
in non-existent walls.

Richard Kell

LANGUAGE
Learning About Nouns

STUDY SKILLS
Using Reference Materials

COMPOSITION
Writing Explanations

LITERATURE
Enjoying Myths

Look at the pictures on the opposite page. If you named all the things in the pictures, you could make use of common and proper nouns, singular and plural nouns, and possessive nouns. You will learn the special properties of each kind of noun in this unit, and you will also learn to use abbreviated nouns and nouns as appositives.

When you know the names of things, you can look them up in reference books. The encyclopedia, almanac, *Readers' Guide to Periodical Literature,* and other reference sources give particular kinds of information about their subjects. Some reference books will help you to find information about how to do things or why things happen, which you can use in writing how-to and expository paragraphs.

Many myths have been created to explain why and how things happen. In this unit you will read the myth of Daedalus and Icarus.

LANGUAGE

Lesson 1: Understanding Common and Proper Nouns

Read these sentences and name the nouns.

1. That giant redwood is also called a sequoia.
2. Many of these trees grow in Sequoia National Park.
3. David is filled with wonder when he sees sequoias.

Think and Discuss

Nouns are words that name people, places, things, and ideas A **common noun** names *any* person, place, thing, or idea. Common nouns are not capitalized. A **proper noun** names a *particular* person, place, thing, or idea. Proper nouns are always capitalized. What are the common nouns in sentences 1–3? What are the proper nouns? What do these nouns name — people, places, things, or ideas?

Another way to classify nouns is to tell whether or not what they name can be recognized by our senses. **Concrete nouns** name people, places, and things that can be recognized by our senses. **Abstract nouns** name things and ideas that cannot be recognized by our senses. *Redwood* in sentence 1 is a concrete noun. We can see and touch a redwood tree. What are the other concrete nouns in sentences 1–3? The word *wonder* is an abstract noun. It names something that cannot be seen, touched, smelled, heard, or tasted. Notice that a noun is common or proper and concrete or abstract. Is *wonder* a common or a proper noun?

- A **noun** is a word that names a person, place, thing, or idea.
- A **common noun** names any person, place, thing, or idea. Common nouns are not capitalized, unless they come at the beginning of a sentence.

> - A **proper noun** names a particular person, place, thing, or idea. Proper nouns are always capitalized.
> - A **concrete noun** names an object that can be recognized by at least one of the senses.
> - An **abstract noun** names a quality or an idea that cannot be recognized by the senses.

Practice

A. Copy these sentences. Draw one line under the common nouns and two lines under the proper nouns.

1. The frantic search for gold began when James Marshall discovered a small nugget in a sawmill at Coloma, California.
2. He was building the sawmill for John Sutter on the bank of the American River.
3. Marshall and Sutter ended their lives as poor men, but a man named Sam Brannan made a fortune.
4. He opened a store for the miners near the mill.
5. Then he dashed into San Francisco holding a container full of gold dust and shouted the news of the discovery.

B. Copy each noun and classify it as *common* or *proper* and *concrete* or *abstract.*

6. courage	7. ocean	8. mercy
9. John Adams	10. Asia	11. greyhound
12. key	13. girl	14. peninsula
15. halter	16. joy	17. sadness
18. Red Sea	19. Mars	20. Christia Adair

C. These words are common nouns. Copy each word and write a proper noun in the same category next to it. For example, *book* and *Johnny Tremain.*

21. town	22. car	23. person	24. ship	25. state
26. team	27. building	28. avenue	29. river	30. school

Apply

D. 31.–40. Using common and proper nouns, write ten sentences describing the town or city where you live or a place that you have visited.

Lesson 2: Understanding Singular and Plural Nouns

Read this paragraph and identify the nouns.

Jonelle, Ella, and Wanda had to write reports on wild animals. They went to the Museum of Natural History to study the displays. The first display showed several deer standing near a brook. A fox was hiding in some bushes, and two birds flew overhead. In the next window were several carabaos with their calves. The biggest carabao had the longest horns. The children took many notes.

Think and Discuss

Singular nouns name *one* person, place, thing, or idea. **Plural nouns** name more than one person, place, thing, or idea. In the paragraph above, which nouns are singular? Which are plural? Notice that all the plurals are not formed in the same way.

Forming the plurals of most nouns is not difficult if you follow these rules.

- Form the plurals of most nouns by adding *s.*
  report/reports, horn/horns, note/notes
- Add *es* to nouns ending in *s, ss, zz, x, sh,* or *ch.*
  dress/dresses, fox/foxes, bush/bushes,
- When nouns end in *y* preceded by a consonant, change the *y* to *i* and add *es.*
  sky/skies, country/countries

  If the *y* is preceded by a vowel, add only *s.*
  donkey/donkeys, turkey/turkeys
- Add *s* to some nouns ending in *o*; for others, add *es.*
  piano/pianos; echo/echoes, zero/zeroes
- To form the plurals of some nouns ending in *f* or *fe,* change the *f* to *v,* and add *s* or *es.*
  knife/knives, calf/calves, loaf/loaves
  (Some exceptions are: safe/safes, chief/chiefs, roof/roofs, muff/muffs)

- The plurals of some nouns are formed by a vowel change within the singular form or by an addition to the singular form.

    man/men, tooth/teeth, ox/oxen, child/children

- Some nouns have the same form for singular and plural.

    sheep, moose, salmon, elk, deer, fish

- To form the plural of a compound noun, make only the most important word plural.

    merry-go-round/merry-go-rounds

- A few nouns have only a plural form.

    news, scissors, trousers, measles

    Some of these nouns require a plural verb. Others are singular in meaning and require a singular verb.

    My trousers are ripped.   The news is good.

Practice

A. Copy these singular nouns. Then write the plural of each.

1. shoe	2. wife	3. hanger-on
4. woman	5. address	6. tomato
7. city	8. mouse	9. church
10. jack-o'-lantern	11. half	12. fish
13. foot	14. buzz	15. key

B. Copy these sentences. Use the plural form of each noun in parentheses ( ).

16. Ella saw a team of _____ in a farm display. (ox)
17. Some _____ were standing near the barn. (pony)
18. Two barn _____ were building a nest in the eaves. (swallow)
19. Three _____ were chasing the farmer. (goose)
20. Jonelle liked the exhibit with the family of _____. (moose)

Apply

C. 21.–30. Write five sentences using singular nouns from Practice A. Then write five sentences using plural nouns from the same list. Proofread your sentences to correct capitalization, punctuation, fragments, and run-on sentences.

Lesson 3: Understanding Collective Nouns

Read this poster.

> Be the first in your <u>class</u> to join the debate <u>team</u>! Become a member of the All-State Debate <u>Association</u>. The first debate will be judged by the <u>faculty</u>.

Which part of speech are the underlined words? What do these words have in common?

Think and Discuss

A *class*, a *team*, an *association*, and a *faculty* are made up of many people, but when they work as a group, we think of them as a single unit. Nouns that name such groups are called **collective nouns.** Some common collective nouns are *committee, jury, class, flock, club, team, family,* and *audience.*

Although they name a group, collective nouns are usually considered *singular.*

1. The faculty made <u>its</u> decision.
2. The <u>faculty</u> <u>has given</u> the award.

Sometimes, however, members of a group act as individuals. When they do, the collective noun is considered *plural.*

3. The <u>faculty</u> <u>were arguing</u> about the award.
4. The faculty prepared <u>their</u> reports.

The singular or plural idea is not expressed by the collective noun itself but by other words in the sentence. In sentence 1 the singular possessive pronoun *its* indicates that the faculty acted as a unit. How do you know that the collective noun in sentence 2 is singular? In sentence 3 you know that individual members were in disagreement because of the plural verb. How do you know that the collective noun in sentence 4 is plural?

Collective nouns can have plural forms.

5. The teams in our league play well.

Plural collective nouns are always used with plural verbs.

> - A **collective noun** names a group of persons or things.
> - A singular verb or singular possessive pronoun is used when the collective noun acts as a unit. A plural verb or plural possessive pronoun is used when there is individual action within the group.
> - Collective nouns have plural forms as well that are always used with plural verbs.
>
>   jury/juries   class/classes

Practice

A. Copy only the collective nouns from this list. Then use each collective noun in a sentence.

1. firm	**2.** automobiles	**3.** Congress
4. members	**5.** staff	**6.** students
7. trio	**8.** animals	**9.** association
10. orchestra	**11.** herd	**12.** offices
13. crew	**14.** women	**15.** crowd

B. Copy these sentences. Underline each collective noun and write *singular* or *plural* above it.

16. The administration announced a date for the concert.
17. The band will practice its music every day.
18. The chorus hopes to be in the program.
19. The quartet is very good.
20. The band will wear their new uniforms.

C. Complete each sentence with an appropriate collective noun.

21. The _____ hopes the new uniforms will fit.
22. The music _____ ordered the uniforms last month.
23. The trio practices every day, and the _____ does too.
24. The _____ will march into the auditorium.
25. The _____ will sing the school song.

Apply

D. 26.–35. Write 10 sentences using collective nouns from this lesson to tell about an event at your club or school. Use at least one collective noun in each sentence.

Lesson 4: Abbreviating Nouns

Mr. John Avery
709 E. Cedar St.
Chicago, IL 60611

Dr. Sarah Berman
2717 Wabash Ave.
Gary, IN 46404

What words on the envelope have been shortened?

Think and Discuss

Abbreviations are shortened forms of words. Most abbreviations stand for the titles of people and the names of days of the week, months, streets, states, geographical features, and radio and television stations. Abbreviations of days, months, streets, and states may be used in lists and on envelopes, but they are usually not appropriate in ordinary writing.

Since most abbreviations stand for proper nouns, you would not write, "The Dr. will see you now." Instead, you should write, "The doctor will see you now" or "Now Dr. Sarah Berman will see you."

When an abbreviation comes at the end of a sentence that ends with a period, use only one punctuation mark.

1. I had blood tests, X-rays, shots, etc.
2. Is my appointment at 9:30 A.M.?

Why does sentence 2 have a period and a question mark at the end?

> - Some abbreviations are formed from the first letters of the word to be shortened. Each abbreviation is followed by a period.
>   Mon., Feb., Ave. (Monday, February, Avenue)
> - Other abbreviations are formed from the first and last letters in theword.
>   Dr., Mr., Mt. (Doctor, Mister, Mount).

- Proper nouns made up of more than one word are usually abbreviated by using the first letter of each word.
  P.O., Gilford H.S. (Post Office, High School)
- Post office abbreviations for states are written with capital letters and no periods.
  WY, MO, KS (Wyoming, Missouri, Kansas)
- The abbreviations for some words have become so well known that they may be written like state abbreviations in capital letters and without periods.
  USA, TV, IBM (United States of America, television, International Business Machines)
- Some indications of time are always abbreviated when used with numbers.
  A.M., P.M. (ante meridiem, post meridiem)
- The Latin expression *et cetera*, which means *and so forth*, is almost always abbreviated.
  etc. (and so forth)

It is always a good idea to check with a dictionary if you are in doubt about how to abbreviate a word.

Practice

A. Copy these abbreviations. Next to each write the name or title it represents.

1. Blvd.	**2.** FBI	**3.** Mr.	**4.** Jan.	**5.** Fri.	**6.** Conn.
7. ME	**8.** Mt.	**9.** MA	**10.** Tues.	**11.** Oct.	**12.** IRS

B. Copy these proper nouns. Write the abbreviation for any word that can be shortened.

13. April	**14.** December	**15.** Florida
16. Senator Golden	**17.** Wednesday	**18.** Alaska
19. Professor Mattson	**20.** Doctor Rivera	**21.** Thursday
22. Westlawn Drive	**23.** Johnson Court	**24.** Apple River

Apply

C. 25.–34. Write ten sentences using the names of any states, days, or months. Write each full name in the sentence and write its abbreviation in parentheses after the sentence.

Lesson 5: Understanding Possessive Nouns

Read these sentences.

1. Rosa's new skates had red wheels.
2. Zak won the boys' skating contest.
3. An attendant watched the children's jackets.

What words show ownership or belonging in these sentences? What do Rosa, the boys, and the children "own" in these sentences?

Think and Discuss

A noun that shows ownership or possession is called a **possessive noun.** There are three rules for forming possessives.

> - Form the possessive of any singular noun by adding an apostrophe and *s.*
> - Form the possessive of plural nouns that end in *s* by adding an apostrophe only.
> - Form the possessive of plural nouns that do not end in *s* by adding an apostrophe and an *s.*

The possessive word in sentence 1 is singular. How is it formed? The possessive words in sentences 2 and 3 are plural. How are they formed? How do you know that the possessive word in sentence 2 is plural?

Apostrophes are used with nouns only when the nouns are possessive.

Practice

A. Copy these sentences. Underline each possessive noun. After each sentence write *singular possessive noun* or *plural possessive noun.*

1. Doris's parents own the skating rink.
2. It was her mother's idea to have the party there.
3. The parents' cars were used for transportation.
4. The parents enjoyed the children's excitement.
5. Some skaters' laces broke.

6. Ross's skates were lost in the confusion.
7. The owners' puppy ran onto the rink.
8. The puppy's paws slipped on the ice.
9. Ellen's records provided the music.
10. The parents' sandwiches were good.

B. Copy these sentences. Make each of the nouns in parentheses possessive. Be sure to notice whether the noun is singular or plural.

11. The Skaters in Wonderland theme was _____ idea. (Miguel)
12. _____ apron was a dish towel. (Alice)
13. The _____ costumes were interesting. (students)
14. The _____ ears were two carrots. (rabbit)
15. _____ silly grin was supposed to represent the Cheshire Cat. (James)

Apply

C. 16.–25. Write a paragraph about playing a game of your favorite sport. Use at least ten possessive nouns in the paragraph. Underline each one.

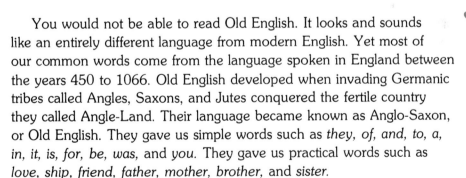

HOW OUR LANGUAGE GROWS

You would not be able to read Old English. It looks and sounds like an entirely different language from modern English. Yet most of our common words come from the language spoken in England between the years 450 to 1066. Old English developed when invading Germanic tribes called Angles, Saxons, and Jutes conquered the fertile country they called Angle-Land. Their language became known as Anglo-Saxon, or Old English. They gave us simple words such as *they, of, and, to, a, in, it, is, for, be, was,* and *you.* They gave us practical words such as *love, ship, friend, father, mother, brother,* and *sister.*

Use a collegiate or unabridged dictionary to find the original meaning of these words that have come to us from Old English.

1. daisy   2. clue   3. answer   4. road   5. quick
6. crib   7. nickname 8. bead   9. strike 10. knead

Lesson 6: Understanding Appositives

Read these sentences.

1. Johannes Kepler, <u>a German astronomer</u>, was the first person to describe accurately the motion of the planets.
2. The planetary orbits, <u>paths around the sun</u>, were not understood before his time.

Does the meaning of either sentence change if you read it without the underlined words? What do the underlined words do in these sentences?

Think and Discuss

The words *a German astronomer* tell who *Johannes Kepler* was, and the words *paths around the sun* define *orbits* in simpler words. These words give more information about the preceding nouns without changing the meanings of the sentences. Nouns or noun phrases that follow other nouns to explain them more fully are called **appositives**. (The word *apposition* means "placing side by side.")

> - An **appositive** is a noun or a noun phrase that is placed next to another noun in order to tell more about it.
> - Appositives are usually set off with commas unless the appositive is so closely related to the noun it explains that it appears to be part of that noun. Then no comma is used.

Read these sentences.

3. Isaac Newton, an English mathematician and physicist, showed that the laws of gravity control planetary motion.
4. Newton's work *Principia* was published in 1687.

What are the appositives in sentences 3 and 4? What punctuation is used?

Practice

A. Copy these sentences. Underline each appositive and circle the noun (or noun phrase) it explains.

1. The sun, a star, is a ball of brightly shining gas.
2. Mercury, Venus, Earth, Mars, Jupiter, Saturn, Uranus, Neptune, and Pluto, the nine major planets, orbit the sun.
3. The three planets farthest from the sun, Uranus, Neptune, and Pluto, were unknown in ancient times.
4. Uranus, the seventh planet, was discovered in 1781.
5. Uranus was discovered by Sir William Herschel, an English astronomer.
6. His sister Caroline discovered eight comets.
7. His son John was also an astronomer.
8. Most of the nine major planets have satellites, moons of varying sizes.
9. Thousands of minor planets, asteroids, orbit between Mars and Jupiter.
10. Ceres, the largest asteroid, was discovered in 1801.

B. Copy these sentences and complete them with appositives.

11. The stars, _____, have always fascinated people on Earth.
12. Imaginative people, _____, have produced much art and literature about outer space.
13. Some writers thought that Martians, _____, lived on the "Red Planet."
14. Others wrote about Venusians, who were believed to inhabit our nearest neighbor, _____.
15. Scientists proved that these beings, _____, could not exist.
16. *Star Wars*, _____, has shown us many "space" characters.
17. Space travel, _____, may eventually be possible for most people.
18. Some scientists believe that space colonies, _____, will become a reality before long.

Apply

C. 19.–30. Write twelve sentences about an aspect of science that you are interested in. Use an appositive in each sentence.

LANGUAGE REVIEW

Common and Proper Nouns   pages 80–81

Copy these sentences and underline all the nouns. Capitalize all proper nouns. Write whether each noun is *concrete* or *abstract*.

1. The declaration of independence is perhaps the most important of all American historical documents.
2. It announced the separation of the 13 colonies from great britain, and it stated that all people had certain rights.
3. On june 10, 1776, the second continental congress chose a committee to write the document.
4. The first draft was written by thomas jefferson.
5. Benjamin franklin and john adams made a few slight changes in it.
6. On july 2, 1776, the delegates in philadelphia began to debate the draft that jefferson had penned.
7. Some passages, such as one criticizing king george iii for his encouragement of slavery, were omitted.
8. The declaration of independence maintains that people are entitled to life, liberty, and the pursuit of happiness.
9. The document was read to the public on july 8, 1776.
10. The beautifully handwritten version—the one you will see if you visit the national archives in washington, d. c.—was not prepared and signed by the delegates until august 1776.

Singular and Plural Nouns   pages 82–83

Copy these singular nouns. Next to each write its plural form.

11. roof
12. radio
13. freshman
14. tax
15. editor-in-chief
16. noodle
17. memory
18. scissors
19. book
20. knife
21. gas
22. hero
23. tooth
24. sheep
25. donkey

Collective Nouns   pages 84–85

Copy these sentences. Underline each collective noun.

26. My family visited an old-fashioned farm last spring.
27. The farmer's herd of cows was grazing in a nearby meadow.

28. His team of horses shook their harnesses spiritedly.
29. Then the pair pulled the farmer's plow.
30. A litter of kittens was playing near the milking shed.

Abbreviating Nouns   pages 86–87

Copy these proper nouns. Next to each write its abbreviation.

31. Doctor Chan	32. Saturday	33. Reverend Smythe
34. Washington Boulevard	35. New Hampshire	36. Sutton Place
37. West Carlyle Street	38. March	39. Montana
40. Governor Price	41. New York City	42. Mount Sinai
43. Cross Junior High School	44. Tennessee	45. August

Possessive Nouns   pages 88–89

Copy these sentences, using the possessive form of the noun in
parentheses ( ) to make them complete.

46. _____ plan was to go fishing with her friends on her birthday. (Chris)
47. _____ fishing pole broke. (Juanita)
48. She borrowed _____ extra pole and caught three fish. (Laura)
49. The _____ scales glittered in the sun. (fish)
50. The _____ catch made a wonderful birthday dinner. (friends)

Appositives   pages 90–91

Copy these sentences. Underline the appositives and add commas
where needed.

51. I got my new dog a black Labrador retriever yesterday.
52. My sister Anne helped to pick him out.
53. Many retrievers are trained to hunt ducks and geese two kinds of waterfowl.
54. These dogs excellent hunters have a gentle disposition.
55. This breed was developed in Newfoundland an island off the eastern
    coast of Canada.

Applying Nouns

56.–65. Write ten sentences about your state. Use singular and plural
    nouns throughout. Use proper nouns in at least five sentences.
    Use at least one appositive, one possessive noun, one collective
    noun, and one abstract noun in your sentences.

STUDY SKILLS

Lesson 7: Using Encyclopedias and Almanacs

Which reference books would you use to find information on these topics?

1. a history of the colonization of Brazil
2. the name of South America's largest port
3. a biography of Chilean poet Pablo Neruda
4. the population of Peru

Think and Discuss

Two of the most valuable kinds of reference books are encyclopedias and almanacs. These two reference books contain different sorts of information.

An **encyclopedia** is a collection of articles on a wide variety of subjects. Each article is written by an expert who has summarized the general information on a topic. The subjects in an encyclopedia are arranged alphabetically, with guide words at the top of pages to help you find the article you want. Cross-references tell you where to find other information on a related subject. The index of an encyclopedia, usually found in the last volume of a set, tells you the volume, the page, and often the column of the article for which you are looking. The many illustrations contained in an encyclopedia are also listed in the index.

Sometimes you need a specific fact or statistic instead of a summary of general information on a topic. You sometimes may need information that is so recent that it has not yet been included in an encyclopedia. In those cases you will probably find an almanac more helpful than an encyclopedia.

An **almanac** is a single-volume reference work that is revised and published every year. An almanac consists mostly of statistics and charts. In an almanac, for example, you can find the latest sports records, award winners, and census figures. You will also find information on the political, economic, and social events of the past year, together with the names of the people and places involved in those events. Information in an almanac is arranged according to subject matter instead of alphabetically; you can consult the index of the almanac to find the particular information you want.

If you are looking for particular facts, especially current ones, you will probably find them quickly in an almanac. If you are looking for a discussion or explanation of facts or for articles on general topics, you should consult an encyclopedia.

Practice

A. Write whether you would use an encyclopedia or an almanac to locate these items of information.

1. the tallest mountain in South America
2. a description of the customs of the Nambikwara tribe
3. an explanation of volcanic activity in Ecuador
4. the capital and population of each South American country
5. the role of Argentina in World War II
6. the current oil production of Venezuela
7. the name of the American ambassador to Uruguay
8. a description of *pampas*
9. how the Patagonian Desert got its name
10. the significance of Spanish culture in modern Colombia

B. Answer these questions by consulting an encyclopedia or an almanac. Write the answer and the source you used.

11. What is the population of Mexico City?
12. What peoples have claimed Mexico City as their own?
13. Where are the floating gardens of Mexico City located?
14. How much does the Aztec Calendar Stone weigh?
15. In which part of Mexico is Mexico City located?

Apply

C. 16. Look up information about another city in South America, such as São Paulo or Buenos Aires. Use both an almanac and an encyclopedia in your research. Write a paragraph to summarize the kind of information available in each source.

Lesson 8: Using the Readers' Guide to Periodical Literature

Saito was preparing to write a report about politics in Japan. His teacher suggested that he use current magazine articles in his research, and she directed him to the *Readers' Guide to Periodical Literature* to aid him. Why might a magazine article be more helpful for research than an encyclopedia article?

Think and Discuss

The *Readers' Guide to Periodical Literature* is an index of articles from more than 200 different magazines. Like an encyclopedia, the *Readers' Guide* comes in many volumes, each of which is marked with the months and year covered by the articles listed inside. Within each volume, subjects are arranged alphabetically. Study these listings from the *Readers' Guide*.

History	Military policy
Photographs and photography	*See also*
Japanning of Japan; show at Japan House. J. Ashbery, il N Y 13:61-2 Ja 14 '80	Japan—Defenses
Industries	Politics and government
See also	Election that could turn Japan more hawkish. G. Ringwald, il por Bus W p 106 S 3 '79
Aerospace industries—Japan	Generalissimo in the darkness; K. Tanaka's comeback. E. Keerdoja and B. Krisher. il por Newsweek 94:12 S 10 '79
Airlines—Japan	
Automobile equipment industry—Japan	
Electronic industries—Japan	Japanese consensus, D. Kirk. New Leader 62:3 S 24 '79
Fish culture—Japan	
Fisheries—Japan	Japanese game. D. Kirk. New Leader 62:3-4 D 3 '79
Green Cross Corporation	
Hitachi Ltd.	*See also*
Mitsubishi Corporation	Elections—Japan
Motion picture industry—Japan	Political campaigns—Japan
Optical industry—Japan	Political parties—Japan
Photographic industry—Japan	
Shipbuilding—Japan	
Sony Corporation	
Steel industry—Japan	
Telephone companies—Japan	
Trading companies—Japan	

Each title in the center of a column is a subject heading under the general subject *Japan*. Centered titles in italics are further subheadings. Which heading has such a subheading? The *see also* headings are cross-references to additional information in related articles under other headings. A *see* reference would tell you that all the information on that topic is listed under another heading.

Notice that the information for each article is abbreviated. The information about the article entitled "Election That Could Turn Japan More Hawkish," for example, tells you that the author of the article is G. Ringwald; that it is illustrated; that it appeared in the September 3, 1979, issue of *Business Week;*

and that it was a one-page article, appearing on page 106 of that issue. The key for all of the abbreviations is located at the front of each volume of the *Readers' Guide*.

Practice

A. Use the sample section from the *Readers' Guide* in this lesson to answer these questions.

1. How many cross-references are listed under *Industries*?
2. What is the subheading under *History*?
3. What is the title of the first article from *New Leader* under the heading *Politics and government*?
4. Which magazine contains an article about K. Tanaka?
5. What are the volume number and issue date of the magazine in question 4?

B. Use a copy of the *Readers' Guide* to answer these questions.

6. What do these abbreviations mean: F, Spr, Ag, Je?
7. What are the abbreviations for these magazines: *Good Housekeeping, Car and Driver, Consumer Reports*?
8. In what city and state is *Natural History* published?

Apply

C. 9. In a current volume of the *Readers' Guide,* look up a subject that interests you. Find three articles that look promising. With your librarian's help, locate and read the three articles.

To Memorize

Only in growth, reform and change, paradoxically enough, is true security to be found.

Anne Morrow Lindbergh

A paradox is a statement that seems to contradict itself. In actuality, it expresses an important truth. Security usually means safety, firmness, and dependability, not growth, reform, and change. How would you explain this seemingly contradictory statement? Would you agree with it?

Lesson 9: Using Other Reference Sources

Books and periodicals are not the only sources of information. Suppose, for example, that you wanted to read a copy of *The New York Times* that was published on the day you were born, or hear Carl Sandburg reading his poems, or learn about daily life at West Point from a cadet's point of view. These kinds of information would not be available in the parts of the library in which you might first look. There are ways, however, for you to get such information.

Think and Discuss

A lot of valuable information can be found in **nonprint media**—sources of information that are not printed on paper. For example, newspapers and magazines that are more than a few years old are photographed in reduced form on rolls of film, called **microfilm,** or on cards, called **microfiche.** A machine in the library called a *reader* will allow you to study such material.

Records and **cassettes** are a good source of information if you are interested in musical compositions, dramatic readings of literature, speeches, recordings of stage performances, sound effects, or many other subjects. Many libraries have collections of such material.

If you want to study about your subject by viewing it, you may wish to look at **films, filmstrips,** or **slides,** which are available at many large libraries. If you want to study about stained glass, for example, you might learn a lot by viewing filmstrips or slides on the topic.

Television can also be a good source of information. You can take notes from helpful programs. In addition some programs offer **transcripts**—written reproductions of the program —or other materials for further study.

People can be excellent sources of first-hand information. You can sometimes gather information by attending and taking notes on a lecture. A similar method of gathering material is by conducting an **interview**. When you conduct an interview, remember these guidelines.

> **How to Conduct an Interview**
>
> 1. Make an appointment with the person you wish to interview. Be sure that he or she understands the nature of the interview. Arrange for enough time to cover all of your questions.
> 2. Prepare a list of relevant questions in advance.
> 3. Record what is said. Take careful, accurate notes, or use a tape recorder if possible.

Practice

A. Write the name of the reference source you could use in each of these situations.

1. You want to hear music that was popular during the Revolutionary War.
2. You want to review an interview you heard on TV.
3. You want to read about the 1980 Presidential election.
4. You want a record of your family's reactions upon visiting Los Angeles for the first time.
5. You want to see the contents of the tomb of Tutankhamen.

B. Imagine that you are interviewing the new basketball coach for your school newspaper. Read these questions and copy *only* those that would be relevant for such an interview.

6. In what area do you plan to work hardest with the team?
7. How much money do you make?
8. Do you like our team's uniforms?
9. Where did you go to college?
10. What do you think is the most important quality in a good basketball player?
11. What do you think of the school's plan for a girls' team?

Apply

C. 12. Imagine that you are responsible for preparing a new tourist attraction for your city or town—one that will tell about the history and current way of life there. Which of the sources discussed in this lesson would you use? What would you include in such a presentation?

COMPOSITION

Lesson 10: Writing Explanations (How-to Paragraphs)

Pete's parents were away on business for a week. Although his 21-year-old brother was in charge of the house, Pete decided that he would do most of the cooking himself. One night he made some delicious baked chicken. When his brother praised the meal and asked Pete how he had cooked the chicken, Pete gave him the directions in detail.

Think and Discuss

Writing a paragraph of **explanation** is a great deal like writing a recipe. The first thing to do is to list the materials or ingredients needed to complete the project you explain. After that you list each of the steps in the correct order and in as much detail as possible. Transitional expressions such as *first, then, next,* and *finally* make the directions easy to follow.

Read this paragraph of explanation that states the steps required to bake chicken.

Baking chicken is easy to do. You will need some fresh chicken parts, garlic salt, seasoned salt and pepper, half a stick of butter or margarine, and a baking dish. First, preheat the oven to 425 degrees Fahrenheit (218 degrees Centigrade). If you like a crispy crust, do not remove the chicken skin. Wash the chicken parts carefully and pat them dry with paper towels. Then sprinkle both sides with the seasonings. Next, place the chicken in the baking dish and dot each piece with a pat of butter or margarine. Finally, bake the chicken at 425 degrees Fahrenheit for about an hour. The chicken is done when you can pierce a meaty piece easily with a fork.

As Pete's older brother stated, Pete's baked chicken was delicious. What might have happened, however, if Pete had cooked the chicken first and put the butter and seasonings on *afterward?* Why is proper order important in paragraphs of explanation?

Practice

A. Put in order these steps on how to wash a load of laundry in a washing machine. Then rewrite the material as a paragraph of explanation. Remember to add a topic sentence that tells the reader what process you will explain.

1. Next, select the water level and temperature for the batch you are going to wash.
2. Finally, add detergent according to the instructions on the box or bottle.
3. First, divide the laundry into batches depending on the water temperature each will need. White clothes are usually washed in hot water, permanent press clothes in warm, and brightly-colored clothes in cold.
4. You will need a load of soiled laundry, a washing machine, and a box or bottle of detergent.
5. After this, turn the machine on so it can begin to fill.
6. When the washing machine has completed all the cycles, turn it off and remove the clean clothes.
7. Then, load the first batch into the machine, being sure not to pack the clothes too tightly.

B. 8–15. Complete this explanatory paragraph on using the clothes dryer.

Using a gas or electric clothes dryer _____. You will need _____. First, _____. _____, place them in the dryer so that it is only about half full. _____ turn the dial to select the number of minutes _____. _____, when the machine stops, _____.

Apply

C. 9. Write a paragraph of explanation in which you tell, in detail, how to build an imaginary machine. The *parts* of the machine may be imaginary too, but the explanation must be in a logical order.

Lesson 11: Developing Cause-and-Effect Paragraphs

Jeremy's mother recently took a job in a nearby town. This change affected the routines of the entire family, who now had to pitch in and perform tasks they had never done before. Read the paragraph that Jeremy wrote on this family situation.

My mom was recently made a vice-president of her company, and every day she takes the train to her new job in Megalopolis. Because of this, my sister Sue has to get the three of us up and off to school in the morning. Dad cooks most of the evening meals, and the rest of the family takes turns cleaning and doing the laundry. Not only are we all proud of Mom's promotion, but our new family schedule has made us much more aware of our duties and our responsibilities to one another.

Did Jeremy's paragraph show mainly *how* the family adapted or the *reasons* for the change?

Think and Discuss

A paragraph that gives the *reasons* for a certain situation or event is a **paragraph of cause.** A paragraph that lists a series of events that take place because of another happening is a **paragraph of effect.** Causes, in other words, tell *why* something happens. Effects tell *what* happens. Is Jeremy's paragraph one of cause or effect?

Notice that Jeremy began his paragraph by stating a cause. The major part of his writing, however, lists the results, or effects, of that cause. In the same way, a paragraph of cause often begins with an effect. The rest of the paragraph lists the reasons, or causes, for its occurrence. Read this paragraph of cause that Dorothy wrote.

I will always remember my trip to Italy. Because Italian is spoken in our home, I could understand almost everything I heard as I traveled. Moreover, the weather was perfect, with warm, sunny days and cool, moonlit nights. Parts of world history that I once thought dull came alive for me in Italy. The warmth and friendliness I found everywhere made me feel that I was really a part of a world community.

How many causes did Dorothy mention in her paragraph? What was her introductory effect?

Some paragraphs of cause and effect are actually an even mixture of the two. Read Lacey's paragraph about a frustrating day she recently had.

On the morning we were to leave for our camping trip, I was packed and ready nearly a half hour before Mr. Johnson and Cindy were due to arrive. As I learned later, however, Mr. Johnson had had trouble packing the camping gear, and as a result he was an hour late. By 11:00 we were on the road and making good time for Cooperstown. At 1:15 we stopped for lunch, but just as we placed our orders the grill broke down, and we had to wait for 40 minutes to eat. Back on the road at 2:30, we were caught in an enormous traffic jam and couldn't get off the highway for another two hours. There were other setbacks too, and the result of everything was that we didn't reach our camping site until 9:00 that night! Somehow I think that this was Mr. Johnson's last camp-out.

Nearly all of Lacey's sentences have both a cause and an effect. Although this type of paragraph is somewhat more difficult to write, it is very effective when you want to describe a series or a chain of events.

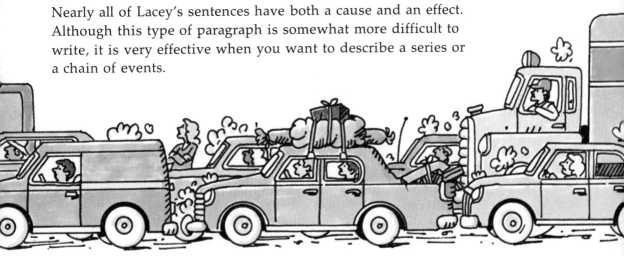

Practice

A. Copy these sentences. After each, write *cause* or *effect* depending on the kind of sentence it is.

1. A heavy rainstorm hit our town last week.
2. I accidentally threw a football through the Smith's open window.
3. Would you like to know how I got this scratch on my knee?
4. My dog Willis is the proud owner of a medal for heroism.
5. Yesterday I won five games of tennis in a row.
6. Marcia entered a homemade apple pie in a contest at the state fair.
7. Our school won first prize in the annual band contest.
8. Joe came to school wearing one brown sock and one blue sock.
9. This morning Al left his three-year-old cat alone with his eight-week-old kitten for the first time.
10. Jan cooked dinner for the family last night.

B. 11.–18. Copy one cause and one effect from the sentences in Practice A. For the *cause,* write four effects. For the *effect,* write four causes.

Apply

C. 19. Write a paragraph of cause *or* effect based on one of your choices from Practice B.

A Challenge

You are a teen-aged tuna fish. Explain to your younger sisters and brothers a few fishy facts.

Tell them in a paragraph of *cause* why there are so few fish in fish school this week.

or

Tell them in a paragraph of *effect* what happened the day that a clam clamped shut on your tail fin.

Lesson 12: Editing an Expository Paragraph

Study this paragraph that Archie edited.

> A ~~sever~~ *severe* thunderstorm struck the West Haven shore
> last night. The roaring wind ~~wipped~~ *whipped* the ~~bambo~~ *bamboo* blinds
> off our porch, and scattered pieces all along the
> beach. Power lines went down and we were without
> ~~eletrisity~~ *electricity* for hours. ~~Our two cats ran and played all~~
> ~~night as usual.~~ This morning at dawn the road was *back*
> flooded, and no traffic could get ~~thru~~ *through*. Thunder and
> lightning kept most of us awake until 4:00 A.M. *TR*

at midnight

What kind of paragraph had Archie written?

Editing Marks

- ≡ **capitalize**
- ⊙ **make a period**
- ∧ **add something**
- ∧ **add a comma**
- ᐁ **add quotation marks**
- ϱ **take something away**
- ○ **spell correctly**
- ⌡ **indent the paragraph**
- / **make a lowercase letter**
- ∼ tr **transpose**

Think and Discuss

Two of the most important things to check in editing **expository** paragraphs are *suitability* and *order*. Since the job of expository writing is to *explain,* the sense of an entire paragraph can be upset by errors in these areas. Archie's paragraph, for example, began with a cause, and it is clear that he meant his other sentences to be effects. He deleted sentence 4 because it was not *suitable*. What was wrong with it?

Notice that all of Archie's original sentences except one described the progress of the storm in good order. His last sentence, however, dealing with the end of the storm at 4:00 A.M., seemed to backtrack from the one before it. By transposing sentences in the paragraph, Archie restored logical order to his writing.

In addition to these major changes, Archie worked at making his paragraph more specific. By adding *at midnight* to his first sentence and stating a definite time period in the third and sixth sentences, Archie helped his reader to follow the storm's development as easily as he himself had done. How did Archie's addition of the word *beach* in sentence 5 make his explanation more specific?

Practice

A. Rewrite Archie's edited paragraph in correct form.

B. Anita edited her paragraph for grammar and punctuation but has not yet edited it for suitability and order. On a piece of scrap paper make the changes you think are necessary. Then copy Anita's paragraph as it should be.

¶Have you ever heard the saying, "No good deed goes unpunished?" Yesterday afternoon I ~~saw~~ *learned* the truth of that saying. I had (voluntered) *volunteered* to do the family shopping‸so after school I (stoped) *stopped* at Grocerama. I followed the shopping list closely‸ ~~and~~ and as a result I stayed within my budget.‸ The streets were wet when I (emergd) *emerged* from Grocerama‸ ~~because it had rained when I was~~ *inside,* ~~shopping in the store~~ Finally I reached home safely‸only to have my little (bother) *brother* grab the grocery bag from me at the front door. What a helpful child he is! (Balanceing) *Balancing* my groceries carefully, I avoided (steping) *stepping* into (pudles) *puddles* and (sliping) *slipping* on the wet curbs. (Triping) *Tripping* on the hall rug‸he fell and broke everything in that bag except for the loaf of bread and the canned goods.

C. Write the paragraph your teacher will dictate to you. Pay close attention to your spelling and punctuation.

Apply

D. Edit the paragraphs you wrote in Lessons 10 and 11. Concentrate on suitability and correct order but watch for errors in grammar and punctuation as well. Rewrite the edited paragraphs.

MECHANICS PRACTICE

Writing Place Names

- Capitalize the names of cities, states, countries, streets, avenues, monuments, and buildings as well as their abbreviations.

  Kansas City   West Germany   Park End Pl.
  Metropolitan Ave.   Twin Trade Towers

- Use a comma between the city and the state in an address; use a period after most abbreviations.

  San Francisco, CA   Ft. Sumter, SC

- When writing an address as part of a sentence, use commas between each element of the address.

  My cousin Jeannie lives at 810 Crescent Circle, Houston, Texas, in the United States of America.

Copy these sentences. Correctly capitalize and punctuate them.

1. For information on somalia, write the somalia national tourist agency box 553 nipagadishu somalia.
2. Have you ever been to florence alabama or to ft. dodge iowa?
3. How many people can fit into the empire state building at one time?
4. The home address of gov. f. v. collins is 18 whiteacre lane fergus falls minnesota.
5. Bruce's uncle works at the ecuador tourist commission p.o. box 2454 quito ecuador.
6. I wrote for information on australia to the chamber of commerce 288 edward st. brisbane queensland australia.
7. Janice's sister attends the university of illinois at edwardsville illinois, 47 miles from st. louis missouri.
8. In washington I visited the washington monument, the lincoln memorial, and the headquarters of the fbi.
9. We spent the summer with relatives at egg harbor wisconsin and at grosse isle michigan.
10. This letter is addressed to mr. and mrs. a. j. fieldstone 64 ocean trace road at augustine beach florida.

LITERATURE

Lesson 13: Reading a Myth

The inhabitants of the ancient world were puzzled by many of the things around them. Why did the sun rise in the east and set in the west? Why were the oceans salty and the rivers fresh water? Why were people always engaged in struggles for power? There were as yet no books of science or psychology to answer their questions, so these ancient people had to find the answers for themselves. They invented supernatural stories that would account for such happenings in nature and for the actions of human beings. What are these stories called?

Think and Discuss

The Greek word *mythos*, which means *tale*, gave the English-speaking world the word **myth.** Originally, before the invention of writing, myths were passed on by word of mouth. Later these stories of the supernatural were collected in books and preserved as part of each country's legendary history.

Myths generally fall into two categories: **nature myths** and **behavioral myths.** Nature myths attempt to explain the workings of the natural world. Behavioral myths, in contrast, try to interpret the thoughts, desires, drives, and actions of human beings. Because these myths often serve to teach people how they *should* act, behavioral myths are sometimes called **moral myths.**

Read this myth about a Greek architect named Daedalus and his young son Icarus.

Daedalus and Icarus

Among all those mortals who grew so wise that they learned the secret of the gods, none was more cunning than Daedalus.

He once built, for King Minos of Crete, a wonderful labyrinth of winding ways so cunningly tangled up and twisted around that, once inside, you could never find your way out again without a magic clue. But the king's favor veered with the wind, and one day he had his master architect imprisoned in a tower. Daedalus managed to escape from his cell; but it seemed impossible to leave the island, since every ship that came or went was well guarded by order of the king.

At length, watching the sea gulls in the air—the only creatures that were sure of liberty—he thought of a plan for himself and his young son Icarus, who was captive with him.

Little by little, he gathered a store of feathers great and small. He fastened these together with thread, molded them in with wax, and so fashioned two great wings like those of a bird. When they were done, Daedalus fitted them to his own shoulders, and after one or two efforts, he found that by waving his arms he could winnow the air and cleave it, as a swimmer does the sea. He held himself aloft, wavered this way and that with the wind, and at last, like a great fledgling, he learned to fly.

Without delay he fell to work on a pair of wings for the boy Icarus, and taught him carefully how to use them, bidding him to beware of rash adventures among the stars. "Remember," said the father, "never to fly very low or very high, for the fogs about the earth would weigh you down, but the blaze of the sun will surely melt your feathers apart if you go too near."

For Icarus these cautions went in at one ear and out by the other. Who could remember to be careful when he was to fly for the first time? Are birds careful? Not they! And not an idea remained in the boy's head but the one, joy of escape.

The day came, and the fair wind that was to set them free. The father put on his wings, and while the light urged them to be gone, he waited to see that all was well with Icarus, for the two could not fly hand in hand. Up they rose, the boy after his father. The hateful ground of Crete sank beneath them; and the country folk, who caught a glimpse of them when they were high above the treetops, took it for a vision of the gods—Apollo, perhaps, with Cupid after him.

At first there was a terror in the joy. The wide vacancy of the air dazed them—a glance downward made their brains reel. But when a great wind filled their wings, and Icarus felt himself sustained, like a halcyon-bird in the hollow of a wave, like a child uplifted by his mother, he forgot everything in the world but joy. He forgot Crete and the other islands that he had passed over:

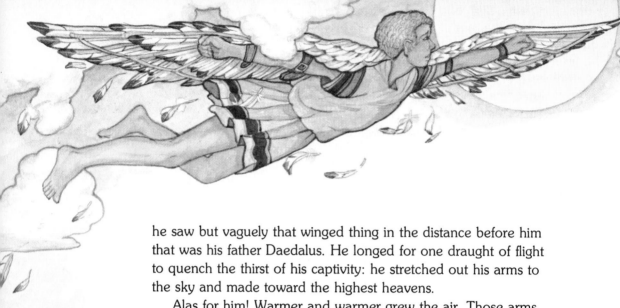

he saw but vaguely that winged thing in the distance before him that was his father Daedalus. He longed for one draught of flight to quench the thirst of his captivity: he stretched out his arms to the sky and made toward the highest heavens.

Alas for him! Warmer and warmer grew the air. Those arms, that had seemed to uphold him, relaxed. His wings wavered, drooped. He fluttered his young hands vainly—he was falling—and in that terror he remembered. The heat of the sun had melted the wax from his wings; the feathers were falling, one by one, like snowflakes; and there was none to help.

He fell like a leaf tossed down the wind, down, down, with one cry that overtook Daedalus far away. When he returned, and sought high and low for the poor boy, he saw nothing but the birdlike feathers afloat on the water, and he knew that Icarus was drowned.

The nearest island he named Icaria, in memory of the child; but he, in heavy grief, went to the temple of Apollo in Sicily, and there hung up his wings as an offering. Never again did he attempt to fly.

Practice

A. Copy and complete these sentences.

1. A _____ myth interprets human actions.
2. Myths are _____.
3. A _____ myth answers questions about the natural world.
4. "Daedalus and Icarus" is a _____ myth.
5. This myth attempts to explain _____.
6. Daedalus' advice to Icarus about flying was _____.
7. _____ was named after Icarus.
8. Myths were originally passed on by _____.

9. When myths were collected in books, these volumes became part of a country's _____.

10. Myths are considered supernatural stories because _____.

B. 11. Write the myth of Daedalus and Icarus in modern terms. Instead of trying to get away from King Minos' island, for example, Daedalus (give him another name) might be a city dweller longing to live in the country or a scientist who wants to go to the moon. Be sure to use all the elements of the original myth.

Apply

C. 12. Write a nature myth of your own, explaining *one* of these happenings:

why some trees change color in the fall
why clouds are white and the sky is blue
why fish live in water
why birds fly
why the moon's light is not as bright as the sun's

A BOOK TO READ

Title: **A Wizard of Earthsea**
Author: Ursula LeGuin
Publisher: Parnassus Press

In the group of islands known as Earthsea, there is a special island set aside for the study of wizardry, and it is there that Ged is learning to be a mage. But Ged is young and arrogant still, and in his need to prove himself superior to his classmates, he opens a door that should have stayed closed, and releases a creature so terrible that all who cross its path perish.

Ursula LeGuin has created a world where wizards reign and the line between life and death is shadowy and indistinct. Readers will sympathize with Ged, who must face the consequences of his dark deed and ultimately conquer the formless creature he has called up from beyond the locked door.

3 UNIT TEST

● **Kinds of Nouns**   pages 80–81

Number your paper from 1 to 8. Next to each number write the letter that tells you what kind of noun the underlined word is. Use this code.

a. common and concrete   **b.** common and abstract   **c.** proper and concrete

1. <u>Dr. Charles Drew</u> was an authority on blood plasma.
2. Before his time, there was no good way to store large quantities of blood plasma for <u>people</u> who might need it in emergencies.
3. Dr. Drew's <u>goal</u> was to find a method of preserving blood plasma.
4. His contributions saved the lives of many <u>soldiers</u> in World War II.
5. He also established the first <u>blood banks</u> in this country.
6. Dr. Drew was awarded the <u>Springarn Medal</u> for his efforts.
7. He became the head of <u>Freedmen's Hospital</u> in Washington, D.C.
8. His striving for <u>excellence</u> in all things will never be forgotten.

● **Singular and Plural Nouns**   pages 82–83

Each of these words can be used as a noun. Write the plural form of each one.

9. carriage	**10.** party	**11.** beach	**12.** moose
13. thief	**14.** echo	**15.** attorney-at-law	**16.** tray
17. sister-in-law	**18.** mumps	**19.** lullaby	**20.** chimpanzee

● **Collective Nouns**   pages 84–85

Copy these sentences and underline the collective nouns they contain.

21. A leader has been elected by the group.
22. The herd began to scatter in different directions.
23. Jocelyn's family is the largest in our area.
24. The verdict in this case is clear; why have the jury disagreed?
25. After an 8 to 3 victory, the softball team celebrated at a restaurant.

Abbreviating Nouns pages 86–87

Write the abbreviation for each of these nouns.

26. Wednesday
27. Georgia
28. United Mine Workers
29. April
30. Professor Hirami
31. Walnut Road
32. New Mexico
33. American Kennel Club
34. National Hot Rod Association
35. Gulf-to-Bay Boulevard

Possessive Nouns pages 88–89

Write the singular possessive and plural possessive forms of these nouns.

36. scholar   **37.** woman   **38.** butcher
39. trio   **40.** ox   **41.** child
42. baby   **43.** dentist **44.** puppy

Appositives pages 90–91

Copy these sentences. Underline each appositive and add commas where necessary.

45. Many women have been successful in new fields of endeavor areas once considered "man's territory."
46. In 1825 Rebecca Lukens the daughter of the owner of a failing ironworks took over the business and made it quite successful.
47. Nellie Bly a reporter for the *New York World* wrote popular stories about her 72-day trip around the world.
48. In 1908 57-year-old Annie Peck Smith became the first person to climb Peru's Mt. Huascarán a mountain then believed to be the highest in the western hemisphere.
49. At the age of 93, Helena Rubenstein the founder of a huge cosmetics empire was still running her business.
50. Sarah Caldwell one of the finest directors of opera became the first woman to conduct at the Metropolitan Opera House one of the most famous opera houses in the world.

Encyclopedias and Almanacs pages 94–95

Copy each line of information. Write whether an *encyclopedia* or an *almanac* would be the better source for that information.

1. a description of the way that photosynthesis works
2. the most recent population figures for Hong Kong
3. the major economic news from the past year
4. a biography of Ponce de León
5. the name of the head of the Liberian government

The *Readers' Guide to Periodical Literature*   pages 96–97

Answer the questions based on this excerpt from the *Readers' Guide.*

6. How long is the article in *Space World*? When did it appear?
7. Which entry has a subheading?
8. Is the article by D. Foster illustrated?
9. How would you find an article about Eastern Air Lines?
10. Who wrote the article about the 1860 solar eclipse?
11. Which magazine carried an article by G. Clifford?

> EAST, John P.
> It's still an uphill struggle but Senator John East persisted to become 'Helms on wheels.' G. Clifford, il pors People 15:47-8 Mr 2 '81*
>
> EASTERN, Air Lines, Inc.-Braniff Airways, Inc. merger. See Airlines—Acquisitions and mergers
>
> EASTPORT, Me.
> Economic tide turns in America's backwater [opposition to proposed Pittston refinery] D. Folster, il map Macleans 94:16 + F 23 '81
>
> EATING areas. See Dining alcoves, etc.
>
> EBERHART, Jonathan
> Solar system: blueprints for tomorrow, il Space World Q-12-204:4-7 D '80
>
> ECLIPSES, Solar
> History
> Getting to the 1860 solar eclipse. K. Bracher. il Sky & Tel 61:120-2 F '81

Other Reference Sources   pages 98–99

Answer these questions on your paper.

12. What is the name of the machine that enables you to view microfilm?
13. Name one topic for which a record would be a good source of information.
14. What is a transcript?
15. Write two appropriate questions to ask if you were interviewing the head librarian at your school.

Writing Explanations   pages 100–101

1. Imagine that you are trying to explain a supermarket to a girl or boy who is your age but who comes from a century in which people raised most of their own food. What details would you include? Write a paragraph that gives your explanation.

Developing Paragraphs of Cause and Effect   pages 102–104

2.–3. Choose one of these topics and write two paragraphs about it—one about what causes it and another about what its results are. Make up details if you must, but be sure to clearly distinguish between causes and effects.

    A Pet's Disobedience   Peace of Mind   Overeating

Editing an Expository Paragraph   pages 105–106

4. Choose one of the paragraphs you wrote for either of the two previous exercise. Edit your writing to make sure that all of your details are in the proper order and that all of them are suitable.

● Writing Place Names   page 107

Rewrite these addresses, adding the correct punctuation and capitalization where necessary.

5. Ms. Gisela Marcos
   16-57 verdugo lane
   el granada ca 94018
7. Dr. Marjorie Thurber
   104 redwood circle
   spartanburg sc 29301

6. Mr. and Mrs. C. A. Jefferson
   213½ jump hill rd
   levittown pa 19056
8. Mr. Peter Chun
   6430 hawthorne ave
   melrose park il 60164

● Myths   pages 108–111

Read this myth. Write a paragraph to explain its purpose or purposes.

Long ago there lived in the land of Egypt a poor farmer, Amenhotep by name, and his wife, Tefnut. Side by side they worked their small plot of land. The work was long and often difficult, but they never complained, for the love they felt for each other far outweighed any of the daily hardships that they had to endure.

Amenhotep and Tefnut honored both the gods and their neighbors. Every season they gave part of their harvest to the gods, and they were always ready to help people less fortunate than themselves. Even in times of famine they were willing to share some of their food with their less fortunate neighbors.

One day there was a terrible rainstorm. No one could remember ever having seen the water fall so hard or the Nile rise so quickly or so high. In trying to help save their neighbors, Amenhotep and Tefnut were lost. Their spirits came to stand before Osiris, the judge of all people who have died.

"Amenhotep and Tefnut," Osiris declared, "the love in your hearts shows itself clearly through the way you care for one another, through your devotion to the gods, and through your unselfish deeds toward your neighbors. Name a reward, and it shall be yours."

"If you please," Amenhotep said humbly, "farming is all that we know. If it is possible, we would like to remain farmers, help others—and stay together."

"So be it!" cried Osiris. "You shall be farmers forever. Amenhotep, the seeds that you sow will be the rain that I send to make the land green. Tefnut, you will reap the result—the rainbow, which I now give to gladden the hearts of people everywhere. All of humanity will call you blessed."

Even today you can see this loving couple at work—Amenhotep bringing the refreshing rain and Tefnut bringing the dazzling rainbow.

MAINTENANCE and REVIEW

Sentences   pages 2–3

Copy these sentences. After each write what kind of sentence it is.

1. What are Ben and Judy planning?
2. The two friends are planning a surprise party for Demetrios, and they have invited all his friends.
3. What a fantastic party it will be!
4. Judy invited the guests, and Ben ordered the food and supplies.
5. Can the party be only two weeks away?
6. Wear your best clothes to this celebration.
7. Nearer and nearer came the date of the party.
8. How surprised Demetrios will be, and how happy this surprise party will make him!
9. Do not tell Demetrios about our plans or give him any hints.
10. How many guests are invited?

Subjects and Predicates   pages 4–5, 6–7

11.–20. In sentences 1–10 draw one line under the complete subjects and two lines under the complete predicates. Circle the simple subjects and the simple predicates.

Compound Elements and Compound Sentences   pages 10–13

21.–25. Write all the sentences that have compound subjects or predicates in sentences 1–10. Draw one line under the compound subjects and two lines under the compound predicates. Then write all the compound sentences and underline each clause once.

Paragraphs   pages 42–43, 44–46, 47–49

Write this paragraph. Then follow the directions given after it.

Outside my window the chrysanthemums are in bloom. In the garden late tomatoes, beans, and squash are ripe and ready for harvesting. The maple trees that line our driveway are ablaze with red leaves, and the oaks at the lawn's edge are covered with gold. Sweet, spicy scents of apples drift down from the orchards. Far away, the mountaintops are crowned with a purple haze, and the harvest moon hangs huge and golden in the sky. How lovely is autumn in New England!

26. Underline the topic sentence of this paragraph.
27. How many detail sentences support the topic sentence?
28. How many detail sentences do not support the topic sentence? Write the numbers of these sentences.
29. How is this paragraph arranged?
30. Circle all the simple sentences in the paragraph. Then recopy any sentence that you think should be rewritten to offer better variety in the paragraph.

Nouns   pages 80–81, 90–91

Copy these sentences. Draw one line under all the common nouns and two lines under all the proper nouns. Circle all appositives.

31. Our classmate, Doug Reese, comes to school in a wheelchair.
32. His best friends, Marty and Eve, accompany him every day.
33. When Doug was seven years old, he was in an automobile accident.
34. Doug can no longer use his legs, but otherwise he is just like the rest of his classmates.
35. This bright, friendly boy is an example of bravery.
36. Doug plays the trumpet in our school band.
37. Last week Doug's trumpet had to be repaired, so Doug tried playing Steve's drums.
38. With a few lessons Doug could play the drums in a music group.
39. Next year when our class travels to New York, Doug will join us.
40. Doug, the president of our class, is a hard worker and a good friend.

Singular and Plural Nouns   pages 82–83

41.–47. List all the plural nouns in sentences 31–40.

Collective and Possessive Nouns   pages 84–85, 88–89

48.–55. List all the collective and possessive nouns in sentences 31–40 in the order in which they appear. Underline all collective nouns once and all possessive nouns twice.

Abbreviations   pages 86–87

Write the abbreviations for these proper nouns.

56. Governor
57. August
58. Senior
59. Avenue
60. Alabama
61. River
62. Ohio
63. Square
64. April
65. Doctor

LANGUAGE
Learning About Verbs

STUDY SKILLS
Vocabulary Building

COMPOSITION
Writing Narratives

LITERATURE
Enjoying Autobiographies

Choosing the right word for the job is a very important part of writing and speaking. Using the correct form of the verb will enable you to express not only the action taking place, but also something about who is doing the action and when it is done. You will also want to make the right choice among words that sound the same, look the same, or have similar meanings. A thesaurus will be very helpful for selecting exactly the word you need.

In this unit you will also learn to write and edit narrative paragraphs. An autobiography, which is a form of personal narrative, will be the literature selection. All the people pictured on the page opposite have written their autobiographies. The next time you go to the library, browse in the autobiography section to see whose story you might like to read.

LANGUAGE

Lesson 1: Understanding Transitive and Intransitive Verbs

Read these sentences and identify the verbs.

1. Frances wrote a recipe on the chalkboard.
2. John assembled the ingredients.
3. They prepared the batter.
4. The electric mixer hummed.

Think and Discuss

All the verbs in sentences 1–4 are **action verbs.** Action verbs such as *wrote, assembled,* and *prepared* express physical action, whereas action verbs such as *think, wish,* and *admire* express mental action.

Action verbs can be divided into two groups, depending on how they are used in sentences. When the action of a verb has a receiver, the verb is **transitive.** When there is no receiver of the action, the verb is **intransitive.**

In sentence 1 the action verb is *wrote.* Ask the question, "Frances wrote what?" The answer is *recipe.* Therefore, we can say that the word *recipe* receives the action of the verb *wrote.* In this sentence *wrote* is a transitive verb. What words receive the action of the verb in sentences 2 and 3?

In sentence 4 the action verb is *hummed.* The answer to the question, "The mixer hummed what?" is *nothing.* The mixer did not hum a tune; there is no receiver of the action of the verb. In this sentence *hummed* is an intransitive verb.

Many action verbs can be transitive or intransitive, depending on how they are used. Compare these two sentences.

5. Frances and John ate the cake.
6. They ate at the table.

What is the action verb in each sentence? What is the difference between these verbs?

> - A **verb** expresses action or a state of being.
> - An **action verb** expresses physical or mental action.
> - A **transitive verb** expresses action that is carried to a receiver of the action.
> - An **intransitive verb** does not have a receiver of the action.

Practice

A. Copy these sentences and draw two lines under the action verb in each one. Write *transitive* or *intransitive* to tell how the verb is used.

1. Berta and Nick made a loaf of bread.
2. The class watched.
3. First Berta heated the milk.
4. Then Nick added yeast and flour.
5. Nick kneaded the dough.
6. He kneaded for five minutes.
7. Everyone waited for the bread to bake.

B. Copy these sentences and draw two lines under the action verb in each one. After each sentence write either *transitive* or *intransitive*. Circle the receiver of the action of each transitive verb.

8. John stood behind the counter.
9. His friends sat at the table.
10. He measured the ingredients for cookies.
11. Then he broke two eggs into the bowl.
12. He stirred everything together.
13. The cookies browned in the oven.
14. His friends tasted the cookies.
15. The cookies disappeared quickly.

Apply

C. 16.–25. Write ten sentences telling how you prepare your favorite food. Use an action verb in each sentence. When you have finished, draw two lines under each action verb and write *transitive* or *intransitive* after each sentence.

Lesson 2: Understanding Linking Verbs

Read these sentences.

1. Tomatoes are the most popular garden plants.
2. The fruit of the tomato plant is green at first.
3. Later it becomes red or yellow.

Think and Discuss

Sentences 1–3 contain verbs, but these verbs do not express action. They "link" the subject of the sentence with a noun, a pronoun, or an adjective in the predicate that tells what the subject *is* or *is like*. These verbs are called **linking verbs.** All linking verbs are intransitive.

What are the verbs in sentences 1–3? What are the simple subjects? With what word or words in the predicate is each subject linked?

The most common linking verb is the verb *be* and its forms: *am, is, are, was, were, will be, has been, have been, had been, can be, could be, would be, might be, should be,* and *must be.* Sentences 1 and 2 use forms of the verb *be.*

Other common linking verbs are *seem, feel, become, grow, appear, look, sound, smell,* and *taste.* Some of these verbs can also be used as action verbs.

4. Miyoshi <u>smelled</u> the tomato.
5. The tomato <u>smelled</u> delicious.

Notice that in sentence 4 *smelled* is an action verb. In sentence 5 *smelled* is a linking verb. If you can replace the verb with a form of *be* without changing the meaning of the sentence, the verb is usually a linking verb.

>
> - A **linking verb** connects the subject of a sentence to a noun, a pronoun, or an adjective in the predicate. It does not show action.

Practice

A. Copy these sentences. Draw two lines under the verb in each sentence. Write whether it is an *action verb* or a *linking verb.*

1. The tomato is a member of the nightshade family.
2. Central American Indians grew the first tomatoes.
3. In Europe the tomato became a decorative plant.
4. People were superstitious about the tomato.
5. Most people called it the "love apple."
6. Some people feared the tomato.
7. Could it be poisonous?
8. Thomas Jefferson ate tomatoes.
9. They were a delicious American food.
10. Tomatoes did not become popular in the United States until a few years after the Civil War.

B. Copy these sentences. Draw two lines under the linking verbs. Then draw an arrow from the subject to the word to which it is joined by the verb.

11. Miyoshi is an enthusiastic gardener.
12. The fruit on her forty tomato plants is becoming ripe.
13. Miyoshi feels happy about her garden.
14. This must be the biggest tomato crop in town!
15. Miyoshi could be the best tomato farmer in the state.

C. Copy these sentences, completing them with predicate nouns, pronouns, or adjectives that could be joined with the subjects. Draw two lines under each linking verb.

16. Miyoshi felt _____ of her gardening skills.
17. She was _____, though.
18. Her crop was not _____ than California's.
19. California's crop was _____.
20. Next year, Miyoshi's crop will be _____.

Apply

D. 21.–30. Write ten sentences about a hobby of yours. Tell what made you choose this hobby. Use at least one linking verb in each sentence.

Lesson 3: Understanding Main Verbs and Helping Verbs

Read these sentences.

1. Communications satellites are artificial earth satellites.
2. These satellites are used to send radio, telephone, or television signals all over the world.
3. Satellites have been launched by giant rockets into orbit around Earth.

What are the verbs in sentences 1–3? Which verb consists of only one word? Which have two or more than two words?

Think and Discuss

Some simple predicates consist of more than one word. Such a predicate is called a **verb phrase.** Each verb in a verb phrase has its own separate function.

In sentence 2 the verb phrase is *are used. Used* is the **main verb** and *are* is the **helping verb.** Name the parts of the verb phrase in sentence 3. Notice that the main verb always comes last in the verb phrase and that the helping verb or verbs always come first. Read these sentences.

4. Communications satellites will be increasingly important in the future.
5. They will be beaming their signals to all parts of the solar system.

Name the verb phrases in sentences 4 and 5. Some verbs can be used as either main verbs or helping verbs. Note how *will be* is used in each of the sentences. In sentence 4 *will* is a helping verb and *be* is the main verb. In sentence 5 *will* and *be* are helping verbs. They show that *beaming* will take place in the future.

- A **verb phrase** is a verb that consists of more than one word.
- The **main verb** is the verb that expresses action or being.
- The **helping verb** is the verb that helps the main verb express action or being.

Practice

A. Copy these sentences. Draw two lines under the verb phrase, and circle the helping verb(s) in each one.

1. A communications satellite can be one of two kinds.
2. Passive communications satellites can reflect signals.
3. The United States has launched several passive communications satellites.
4. After eight years in orbit, *Echo I* was destroyed on reentry to the atmosphere.
5. *Echo II* has been orbiting the earth since 1964.
6. Signals to these large satellites must be very strong.
7. Radio waves will always weaken over great distances.
8. Active communications satellites can amplify signals from Earth.
9. These satellites have been transmitting since the 1960's.
10. Such satellites as *Telstar* have relayed television signals between the United States and Europe.

B. Complete these sentences by adding verb phrases. Draw two lines under each verb phrase, and circle the helping verbs.

11. The INTELSAT satellites _____ television broadcasts between the United States and Europe.
12. These satellites _____ service across the Atlantic and Pacific Oceans.
13. NASA _____ in the field of communications satellites
14. A single satellite _____ less than a third of Earth's surface at one time.
15. The sending and receiving stations _____ their antennas directly at a satellite.
16. Three of these stations _____ stations in any two parts of the world.

Apply

C. 17.–30. Write ten messages from other planets that might be relayed to Earth by satellites. Use helping verbs in each message.

Lesson 4: Understanding Principal Parts of Regular Verbs

Read these sentences. Note the underlined verbs.

1. Mercer and Brad compete in many track meets.
2. When the starting pistol fired, Mercer and Brad leaped from their places and raced down the track.
3. Both boys have earned and received trophies.

How are the verbs different in form from one another?

Think and Discuss

Each verb in English has three **principal parts** — three changes in form that help it to express time. This chart shows the principal parts of the verbs in sentences 1–3.

Present	Past	Past Participle
compete(s)	competed	(have, has, had) competed
fire(s)	fired	(have, has, had) fired
leap(s)	leaped	(have, has, had) leaped
race(s)	raced	(have, has, had) raced
earn(s)	earned	(have, has, had) earned
receive(s)	received	(have, has, had) received

What principal parts are used in sentences 1 and 2? Notice that both verbs in sentence 3 use the past participle form. When a compound predicate uses the past participle form and the verbs are close together in a sentence, the helping verb does not need to be repeated.

Each principal part helps to show when a particular action takes place. All other verb forms come from these principal parts. The six verbs on the chart are called **regular verbs.** The past and past participle forms of regular verbs come from the addition of *d* or *ed* to the present form. How would you form the past and past participle forms of the verb *jump*?

To form the past and past participle of regular verbs that end in a consonant followed by *y*, change the *y* to *i* and add *ed.*

Hurry, for example, becomes *hurried* in the past and past participle. Using the rule, how would you form the past and past participle of *carry*?

> - The three basic forms of a verb are its **principal parts.** These principal parts are the **present,** the **past,** and the **past participle.** The past and past participle of **regular verbs** are formed by adding *d* or *ed* to the present form. The past and past participle of regular verbs ending in a consonant followed by *y* are formed by changing the *y* to *i* and adding *ed.*

Practice

A. Write the principal parts of these verbs.

1. climb	2. work	3. tie
4. tidy	5. hurl	6. gain
7. play	8. pass	9. achieve
10. declare	11. accept	12. bury

B. Copy these sentences and draw two lines under the verb or verbs in each one. Write the name of the principal part over each verb; then write its other two forms after the sentences.

13. The announcer called over the PA system; the runners reported to the starting line.
14. Brad wished Mercer good luck.
15. Brad had tripped and sprained his ankle.
16. Now he watched Mercer from the sidelines.
17. When the whistle sounded, Mercer started quickly.
18. He has fixed his eyes on the finish line as he jogs along.
19. Now he has recovered from a stumble; he has pulled into the lead.
20. How proudly he smiles as the judges congratulate him!

Apply

C. 21.–35. Choose five verbs from Practice A or B. Use each verb in three sentences. Use a different principal part in each sentence.

Lesson 5: Understanding Principal Parts of Irregular Verbs (I)

The past and past participle of regular verbs are formed by adding *d* or *ed* to the present form. Study the verbs in these sentences. Which one does not follow that rule?

1. Lisa and Tom <u>live</u> in Chicago.
2. They often <u>attend</u> the games of the White Sox.
3. Lisa <u>has caught</u> a home run ball in the stands.

Think and Discuss

Verbs in which the past and past participle are not formed with *d* or *ed* are called **irregular verbs.** The principal parts of irregular verbs are formed in a variety of ways. Study this chart in which the verbs are listed in related groups.

	Present	Past	Past Participle
Group 1	come(s)	came	(have, has, had) come
	run(s)	ran	(have, has, had) run
Group 2	begin(s)	began	(have, has, had) begun
	drink(s)	drank	(have, has, had) drunk
	ring(s)	rang	(have, has, had) rung
	sing(s)	sang	(have, has, had) sung
	swim(s)	swam	(have, has, had) swum
Group 3	bring(s)	brought	(have, has, had) brought
	catch(es)	caught	(have, has, had) caught
	say(s)	said	(have, has, had) said
	sell(s)	sold	(have, has, had) sold
	think(s)	thought	(have, has, had) thought
Group 4	burst(s)	burst	(have, has, had) burst
	hit(s)	hit	(have, has, had) hit

In group 1 the present and the past participle are similar. The past form, however, has a changed vowel sound or is a completely different word. In group 2 the vowel *i* in the present changes to *a* in the past and *u* in the past participle. What patterns do you see in groups 3 and 4?

Practice

A. Copy these sentences. Draw two lines under the verb or verbs. Write which principal part was used in each sentence.

1. Tom and Lisa came to the baseball game.
2. Tom always buys the tickets and Lisa buys the refreshments.
3. Everybody sang the national anthem before the game began.
4. "The game has begun," said the announcer.
5. "We have come just in time," said Tom.
6. The shortstop caught the ball as the batter ran to first base.
7. "You have drunk all the root beer," said Lisa.
8. "Jackson has hit the ball over the wall," said Tom.
9. Jackson hits hard and runs fast, thought Lisa.
10. "I thought you brought more root beer," said Tom.

B. Write the principal parts of these verbs.

11. sing	**12.** burst	**13.** come	**14.** hit	**15.** think
16. swim	**17.** ring	**18.** run	**19.** sell	**20.** drink

Apply

C. 21.–35. Write fifteen sentences using each of the verbs from the word groups in Think and Discuss at least once.

HOW OUR LANGUAGE GROWS

The Native Americans—the first Americans—have contributed much to our country. They taught settlers from Europe how to plant, tend, and fertilize a plant called *maize*. They taught the settlers about the *pecan* and *hickory* trees; about animals such as the *caribou, muskrat, opossum,* and *chipmunk;* and about foods such as *hominy* and *succotash*. In doing so, they also enriched our language. The names of 26 of our states come from Native American languages. *Idaho,* for example, means "light on the mountain," and *Alabama* means "I clear the thicket."

1. What names of animals come from the Native American words *squunck, raugraoughcun,* and *otchuck*?
2. Name two other states whose names come from Native American languages.

Lesson 6: Understanding Principal Parts of Irregular Verbs (II)

Which verbs in these sentences follow the rules you have already learned about forming the principal parts of irregular verbs? Which of them do not follow these rules?

1. Laura Mathews <u>went</u> to Mexico last summer.
2. She <u>thought</u> she <u>had brought</u> her camera.
3. Instead, she <u>had taken</u> her radio.

Think and Discuss

The irregular verbs in this lesson all have one thing in common. All the past participles end in *n, en,* or *ne.* Study this chart.

	Present	Past	Past Participle
	do(es)	did	(have, has, had) done
	eat(s)	ate	(have, has, had) eaten
	give(s)	gave	(have, has, had) given
	go(es)	went	(have, has, had) gone
Group 5	grow(s)	grew	(have, has, had) grown
	know(s)	knew	(have, has, had) known
	ride(s)	rode	(have, has, had) ridden
	take(s)	took	(have, has, had) taken
	write(s)	wrote	(have, has, had) written
	break(s)	broke	(have, has, had) broken
	choose(s)	chose	(have, has, had) chosen
	fly(ies)	flew	(have, has, had) flown
Group 6	freeze(s)	froze	(have, has, had) frozen
	speak(s)	spoke	(have, has, had) spoken
	tear(s)	tore	(have, has, had) torn
	wear(s)	wore	(have, has, had) worn

In group 5 the present and the past participle are alike except for the past participle endings, whereas the past has a different vowel sound. In group 6, however, the past and past participle are similar and the present form is different. What are the three principal parts of the verb in sentence 3? To which group does it belong?

Practice

A. Copy these verbs. Next to each write whether it is in the *present, past,* or *past participle* form.

1. ate   2. have broken   3. froze   4. knows   5. rode
6. spoke   7. have taken   8. chooses   9. has flown 10. tore

B. Complete these sentences with the correct principal part of the verb in parentheses ( ).

11. Laura is glad she _____ to study Spanish. (choose, past)
12. Last summer Laura's family _____ a trip to Mexico. (take, past)
13. The family _____ directly to Mexico City. (fly, past)
14. Laura's father didn't _____ any Spanish, but her mother _____ a little. (speak, present; speak, past)
15. The family _____ a bus to the restaurant. (ride, past)
16. "I'm afraid I have _____ too much," said Laura's father. (eat, past participle)
17. The waiter _____ the family their check. (give, past)
18. Laura's father _____ many photographs. (take, past)
19. Laura _____ letters to everyone she _____. (write, past; know, present)
20. "I think I have _____ very fond of Mexico," Laura _____. (grow, past participle; write, past)

Apply

C. 21.–30. Write ten sentences about a trip you would like to take. In each sentence use at least one of the verbs from the word groups in Think and Discuss. After each sentence write which principal part you used.

Lesson 7: Understanding Verb Tenses

Read these sentences.

1. Edgar <u>writes</u> short stories.
2. Last week he <u>wrote</u> one about skaters.
3. He <u>will write</u> for a living someday.
4. Edgar <u>has written</u> more than 20 stories.
5. He <u>had written</u> six before his tenth birthday.
6. By the time he is 18, he probably <u>will have written</u> over 50 of them.

Which of Edgar's actions have taken place already? Which will take place in the future?

Think and Discuss

Verbs express time by means of forms called **tenses.** The verb *writes* in sentence 1 is in the **present tense** because it expresses an action that is happening *now,* in the present. *Wrote* in sentence 2 is in the **past tense.** The verb *will write* in sentence 3 expresses future time. It is in the **future tense.**

Has written is a verb in the **present perfect tense.** It shows an action that began in the past but is still going on. The present perfect tense is also used for actions that took place at some indefinite time in the past or took place from time to time and may still be taking place. *Had written* is in the **past perfect tense.** This tense indicates an action that took place in the past *before* some other past action. Finally, *will have written* is a verb in the **future perfect tense.** It indicates an action that will take place *in the future* but will be over before another future action occurs.

In sentence 4 *has written* indicates that Edgar's writing began during some indefinite past time. *Had written,* on the other hand, shows that this past action was over by the time another past action occurred—Edgar's tenth birthday. In sentence 6 both actions will take place in the future. Although the verb *is* by itself shows present time, the clause *by the time he is 18* indicates that the action has not yet taken place. However, the action expressed by the verb phrase *will have written* will already be over by the time the second action occurs—when Edgar is 18.

- The time expressed by a verb is its **tense.**
- The **present tense** expresses action that is taking place *now.*
- The **past tense** expresses action that took place at some *definite time in the past.*
- The **future tense** expresses action that will take place at some time in the *future.*
- The **present perfect tense** expresses action that took place at some *indefinite time* in the past or that began in the past and *is still going on.*
- The **past perfect tense** expresses action that took place in the past *before some other past action.*
- The **future perfect tense** expresses action that will take place in the future but that will be over *before some other future action.*

Each tense is formed in a different way. The present tense has the same form as the first principal part. The past tense has the same form as the second principal part. The future tense is formed from the first principal part plus the word *will.*

The word *have* or *has* added to the past participle forms the present perfect tense. The past participle plus *had* makes up the past perfect tense. Finally, the word *will* plus *have* plus the past participle will give you the future perfect tense. Study this chart, which shows the formation of these six tenses.

Present Tense

I write	we write
you write	you write
he, she, it writes	they write

Past Tense

I wrote	we wrote
you wrote	you wrote
he, she, it wrote	they wrote

Future Tense

I will write	we will write
you will write	you will write
he, she, it will write	they will write

Present Perfect Tense

I have written	we have written
you have written	you have written
he, she, it has written	they have written

Past Perfect Tense

I had written	we had written
you had written	you had written
he, she, it had written	they had written

Future Perfect Tense

I will have written	we will have written
you will have written	you will have written
he, she, it will have written	they will have written

The subject of a verb may be a noun or a pronoun. The pronouns used in the chart show the verb *write* in all its forms for each tense. Saying or writing all the forms of a certain verb is called **conjugating** it. What are the three principal parts of the verb *write*? How many forms of the verb are shown for each tense?

Practice

A. Copy these sentences and draw two lines under each verb. After each sentence write the name of the tense or tenses used.

1. Edgar has always liked short stories.
2. Once, when he was eight, he wrote a story himself.
3. His teacher, Mrs. Simmons, praised his work.
4. After that, Edgar read many stories and learned from them.
5. Now he writes stories that are almost professional.
6. When he reached the seventh grade, he had already written 15 of them.
7. Several children's magazines have included Edgar's earlier stories.
8. One story that he had written when he was 12 appeared in *Young Writers* magazine.
9. Mr. Hunt, Edgar's new teacher, predicts that Edgar will be a professional writer in a few years.
10. He will have written many more stories by then.

B. 11.–20. Copy this paragraph, adding the proper tense of each verb in parentheses ( ).

Isaac Asimov (write, present) a new book nearly every six weeks. Before he (start, past) writing science and science fiction books, he (write, past perfect) books on such topics as Shakespeare's plays. Before that, he (work, past perfect) as a professor. Asimov (begin, past) his full-time writing career in 1958, although by then he (finish, past perfect) some of his greatest work. People (say, present) that his books (give, present perfect) them good ideas about what (happen, future) in the future. By his sixty-fifth birthday, he (publish, future perfect) approximately 250 books.

Apply

C. 21.–30. Write a paragraph about a writer whose work you enjoy reading. Use at least five regular verbs and five irregular verbs in varying tenses in your paragraph. At the end of the paragraph, copy the verbs you used and write the tense of each one.

To Memorize

Shared joy is double joy and shared sorrow is half-sorrow.

Swedish proverb

Why does sharing your joy increase it and sharing your sorrow decrease it? State this proverb in your own words.

Lesson 8: Understanding Subject-Verb Agreement

Read these sentences.

1. The horse belongs to the rancher.
2. Those mules belong to him too.

Are the subjects of these sentences singular or plural? How do the verbs differ?

Think and Discuss

The subject and verb in a sentence must fit together grammatically. A singular subject, as in sentence 1, takes a singular verb. A plural subject, as in sentence 2, takes a plural verb. The characteristic of being singular or plural is called **number.**

- The subject and verb in a sentence must agree in **number.**

Some sentences present difficulties in selecting the correct verb form. Read these sentences and study the verb choices.

3. One of the horses (is, are) running across the corral.
4. From the horses (comes, come) a gentle whinny.
5. The pinto and the roan (helps, help) to herd the cattle.
6. Either the roan or the pinto (has, have) a new saddle.
7. The herd (follows, follow) its leader.
8. Thirty years (is, are) not an uncommon life span for a horse.

The simple subject of sentence 3 is the singular pronoun *one.* The phrase *of the horses* comes between the subject and the verb. Since *horses* is plural, you may be misled into using the plural verb *are.* Find the simple subject, *one,* and you will correctly choose the verb *is.*

Sentence 4 is written in inverted order. The subject comes *after* the verb in such sentences. The subject is the singular noun *whinny,* and it requires the use of the singular verb *comes.*

In sentence 5 the two parts of the compound subject are joined by the coordinating conjunction *and. Both* horses are the subject. Therefore, the plural verb *help* is used.

Sentence 6 also has a compound subject. But this compound subject is joined by the coordinating conjunction *or. Or* indicates that only *one* of the two horses is meant; therefore, use the singular verb *has.*

The subject of sentence 7 is the collective noun *herd.* As you studied in Lesson 3 of Unit 3, a collective noun can be singular or plural, depending on whether or not the group named by the collective noun acts as a unit. Here the herd is acting as a unit, not as individuals. Sentence 7 takes the singular verb *follows.*

A subject that is plural in form but singular in meaning takes a singular verb. The subject of sentence 8—*thirty years*—is singular in meaning, and it takes the singular verb *is.* You can verify that it is singular by seeing that *life span* is singular. The words *thirty years* and *life span* can be substituted for one another: *thirty years* is *life span; life span* is *thirty years.*

Practice

A. Copy these sentences. Choose the correct form of the verb in parentheses ( ).

1. A group of ranchers (studies, study) the horses.
2. Mr. Brown and Ms. Vale (is, are) neighbors.
3. Either he or she (is, are) interested in that quarter horse.
4. The price (seems, seem) too high to Mr. Brown.
5. Once, quarter horses (was, were) bred for quarter-mile races.

B. Rewrite each sentence using the correct present-tense form of the verb in parentheses ( ).

6. The mules _____ heavy loads. (carry)
7. One of the mules _____ stronger than the others. (seem)
8. _____ the horses working too? (be)
9. A team of horses _____ that wagon. (pull)
10. On the wagon _____ three bales of hay. (be)

Apply

C. 11.–20. Write ten sentences about a real or imaginary visit to a ranch or farm. Draw one line under each subject and two lines under each verb. Be sure that your subjects and verbs agree in number.

LANGUAGE REVIEW

Transitive and Intransitive Action Verbs   pages 120–121

Copy these sentences. Draw two lines under each action verb. After each sentence write whether the verb is *transitive* or *intransitive*.

1. The ancient land of Sumer lay between the Tigris and Euphrates Rivers.
2. Sumer had a harsh climate.
3. The land and weather were changing at that time.
4. In spite of the weather, people farmed the land.

Linking Verbs   pages 122–123

Copy these sentences. Draw two lines under the linking verb in each sentence. Draw an arrow from each subject to the word with which it is connected by the linking verb.

5. Sumerian farmers were very clever.

6. Sudden floods or long droughts could be calamities.

7. Dams and irrigation ditches became common on Sumerian farms.

8. These ancient farmers seem very modern to us.

Helping Verbs and Main Verbs   pages 124–125

Copy these sentences. Draw two lines under each verb phrase and circle the helping verb or verbs in each one.

9. Sumerians had developed the plow by 4000 B.C.
10. By that time oxen had been trained for farm work.
11. Sickles, axes, and hoes were used on Sumerian farms.
12. Barley and wheat must have been grown throughout Sumer.

Principal Parts of Regular Verbs   pages 126–127

Copy these sentences. After each write whether the underlined verb is in the *present, past,* or *past participle* form.

13. The Sumerians created a remarkable civilization.
14. Archeological evidence indicates the invention of a system of writing.
15. Archeologists have discovered symbols for whole words and sounds.
16. Sumerians recorded business transactions in this writing.

Principal Parts of Irregular Verbs   pages 128–129

Copy these sentences. Draw two lines under each verb and write which principal part was used. Sentences may have more than one verb.

17. Archeologists say that the Bronze Age began in Sumer.
18. Sumerians drank from bronze bowls.
19. Their metalworkers went beyond the copper tools of an earlier age.
20. Historians think that the Sumerians brought much to human history.

Principal Parts of Irregular Verbs (II)   pages 130–131

Copy these sentences. Draw two lines under each verb and write which principal part was used. Sentences may have more than one verb.

21. Sumerians wrote on clay tablets with a reed stylus, or *cunei*.
22. Time and weather have broken most of the cuneiform tablets.
23. Experts who have done research on the remaining tablets know their value.
24. These ancient records speak of achievements in many areas.

Verb Tenses   pages 132–135

25.–28. Complete this paragraph with appropriate verbs or verb phrases.
   Archeologists (present perfect) to us much about life in Sumer.
   Clay tablets (present) that Sumerians (past) much like people today.
   The tablets (present) us many facts about the Sumerians.

Subject/Verb Agreement   pages 136–137

Copy these sentences using the correct form of the verb in parentheses ( ).

29. The world's first schools (was begun, were begun) in Sumer.
30. These schools (is known, are known) to have been like ours.
31. A Sumerian school (was known, were known) as an *edubba.*
32. Sumerian students even (was assigned, were assigned) homework.

Applying Verbs

33.–42. Pretend that you are an archeologist of the future. Write ten sentences about life in the twentieth century, using at least five action verbs and two verb phrases.

STUDY SKILLS

Lesson 9: Understanding Homophones and Homographs

Notice the underlined words as you read these sentences.

1. The clown fought back a <u>tear</u> when he noticed a <u>tear</u> in his new costume.
2. The <u>band</u> uniform includes a bright <u>band</u> of gold cloth around the waist.
3. You can <u>hear</u> the concert better if you sit over <u>here</u>.

In which sentences are the underlined words spelled alike? In which sentences are they pronounced alike? In which sentence are they spelled and pronounced alike?

Think and Discuss

Some English words sound alike but are spelled differently and have different meanings. These words are called **homophones.** The words *flee* and *flea* are examples of homophones. They are pronounced alike, but they are spelled differently, and they have different meanings. In sentences 1–3 which words are homophones?

Some English words are spelled alike but have different meanings. These words are called **homographs.** The words *bass* (a kind of fish, pronounced bas) and *bass* (a deep singing voice, pronounced bās) are examples of homographs. Homographs sometimes have the same pronunciation. In sentences 1–3 which words are homographs? Homographs are indicated in most dictionaries with small raised numbers, called *superscripts,* following the entry: bat[1], bat[2].

> - **Homophones** are words that sound alike but have different meanings and spellings.
> - **Homographs** are words that are spelled alike but have different meanings and sometimes different pronunciations.

Practice

A. Copy these pairs of words. Write whether each pair is made of *homophones* or of *homographs.*

1. pain, pane
2. rode, road
3. course, coarse
4. horse, hoarse
5. fair, fare
6. wind, wind
7. lead, lead
8. bough, bow
9. bow, bow
10. night, knight
11. object, object
12. close, close
13. whole, hole
14. dear, deer
15. present, present

B. Complete each sentence with the correct homophone.

16. I can walk for (hours, ours) and watch the (sites, sights) at a county (fare, fair).
17. (It's, Its) (plain, plane) to me that (their, there, they're) is (know, no) better fun.
18. I walked (past, passed) the stall of a (burro, burrow) that was making loud noises.
19. The (sun, son) was beginning to grow (to, two, too) hot.
20. I began to (groan, grown) when my (feet, feat) grew tired.
21. (Eye, Aye, I) sat down with my Aunt Bette for a (hole, whole) hour.
22. She had made a good (prophet, profit) from the (currant, current) jelly that she had brought to (sell, cell).
23. The king and queen of the (fair, fare) will (reign, rain, rein) at a (great, grate) ball tonight.
24. (There, They're, Their) court will (wear, ware) fancy costumes.

C. 25.–30. Using your dictionary, write the correct pronunciation for each pair of homographs in Practice A.

D. 31.–39. Reread the sentences from Practice B. Then close your books and copy the sentences as your teacher reads them aloud.

Apply

E. 40. Imagine a situation in which a misunderstanding, based on a confusion of homophones, causes unexpected consequences. Write some dialog for a brief skit based on this situation. When you are finished, you may wish to dramatize your dialog with a partner.

Lesson 10: Understanding Synonyms and Antonyms

Study the underlined words in these sentences.

1. The beret in that window is quite expensive.
2. This green cap that I am wearing was cheap.

Which underlined words have similar meanings? Which have opposite meanings?

Think and Discuss

Because the English language has borrowed words from many other languages, it contains a number of words with similar meanings, such as *beret* and *cap*. Such words are called **synonyms.** Of course, two words rarely mean exactly the same thing. The slight differences in meaning between synonyms are called *shades of meaning.* For example, a beret, which is a round cloth head covering without a visor, often implies stylishness, European manners, or artistic ability; a cap, which is a more general term for a head covering, seems rather plain by comparison.

Expensive and *cheap* are examples of **antonyms,** words with opposite meanings. Antonyms are used to show great differences between words. Why would *expensive* and *moderate* not be good examples of antonyms? A word may have more than one antonym, depending on the definition of that word and the special shade of meaning that you wish to express. For example, an antonym for *cold* weather might be *hot,* but an antonym for a *cold* person might be *friendly.*

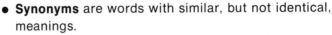

- **Synonyms** are words with similar, but not identical, meanings.
- **Antonyms** are words with opposite meanings.

Practice

A. Copy these pairs of words, and then write whether the words in each pair are *synonyms* or *antonyms*.

1. sweet, bitter	2. sweet, sour	3. sweet, dear
4. victory, defeat	5. unique, special	6. natural, artificial
7. right, correct	8. right, left	9. lofty, towering
10. honor, reverence	11. tender, gentle	12. bright, dark
13. bright, clever	14. spirit, courage	15. hero, coward

B. Write the words in the first column. Next to each word write its synonym from the second column. Then write its antonym from the third column.

16. guard	a. fortunate	aa. different
17. near	b. mature	bb. hinder
18. necessary	c. identical	cc. distant
19. ripe	d. defend	dd. tiny
20. help	e. assist	ee. order
21. same	f. mild	ff. spicy
22. enormous	g. close	gg. green
23. happy	h. riot	hh. attack
24. chaos	i. required	ii. unlucky
25. bland	j. huge	jj. forbidden

C. Rewrite each of these sentences, choosing from the words in parentheses ( ) the one that you think is most suitable. Be prepared to explain your choices.

26. Herman is my best (pal, acquaintance, chum, friend).
27. Herman and I went on a class (visit, excursion, tour, expedition) to a nearby amusement park.
28. Everyone (squinted at, peered at, stared at, surveyed) the clown with the floppy (sombrero, babushka, derby).
29. At noon we (ate, devoured, nibbled) our lunches quickly.

Apply

D. 30. Select a short poem that you have read and enjoyed. Make a "translation" of the poem by substituting as many synonyms as you can. Write a short paragraph discussing how the substitutions change the effect of the poem.

Lesson 11: Using the Thesaurus

Domingo was writing an editorial for his school newspaper.

If the school walkathon is to succeed, everyone must participate. A small turnout will mean failure for all.

"That's not very interesting," thought Domingo. "Maybe some synonyms would liven it up."

Think and Discuss

In Lesson 10 you learned that synonyms are words with similar meanings. A good knowledge of synonyms will enrich your writing. When you cannot think of an appropriate synonym, however, you can turn to a **thesaurus**, a collection of synonyms. Study the thesaurus entries.

---

failure   *noun*

1. The condition of not achieving the desired end: *the candidate's failure to win the election.*
2. One that fails completely: *The play was a failure. I am a failure as a writer.*

3. The condition or fact of being deficient.
4. A cessation of proper mechanical functions: *a power failure.*
5. Nonperformance of what ought to be done: *Failure to pay taxes can result in a stiff fine.*

1. **Syns:** insuccess, unsuccess, unsuccessfulness.
2. **Syns:** bomb (*Slang*), bust (*Slang*), dud (*Informal*), fiasco, flop (*Informal*), lemon (*Informal*), loser, washout.
3. SHORTAGE.
4. **Syns:** breakdown, outage.
5. **Syns:** default, delinquency, dereliction, neglect, nonfeasance (*Law*), omission.

student   *noun*

One who is being educated: *college students.*

Syns: educand, learner, pupil, scholar, scholastic (*Obs.*).

succeed   *verb*

1. To turn out well: *The lower crime rate indicates that the campaign to make the streets safer has succeeded.*
2. To gain wealth or fame: *sure to succeed as an architect.*

3. To occur after (another) in time.

1. **Syns:** click (*Slang*), come off, come through, go, go over, pan out (*Informal*), work out.
2. **Syns:** arrive, get ahead, get on, rise. —*Idioms* go far, go places, make good, make it.
3. FOLLOW.

Like a dictionary, this thesaurus lists words alphabetically, provides guide words, and gives a brief definition of the entries that it lists. It also names the part of speech for which each word can be used.

The right-hand column of the page lists synonyms for each definition in the left-hand column. Domingo's use of the word *failure* would be defined by the second definition. How many synonyms for that use of the word are given? *Shortage* and *follow,* the synonyms in small capital letters, are *cross-references,* guides to other synonyms.

These entries illustrate four special kinds of synonyms. *Informal synonyms* are used in conversation or in friendly letters. *Slang* refers to informal words that pass in and out of fashion. *Idioms* are commonly used expressions. Synonyms from special fields of knowledge, other languages or cultures, and earlier times are also listed. For example, the synonym *nonfeasance* is likely to be used only by lawyers. The synonym *scholastic* is *obsolete;* that is, it is a word once used with the meaning given but now no longer used in that way. Words listed as *archaic* are also old, but they are still used in specialized cases.

Practice

A. Look up these words in a thesaurus. Write three synonyms and one cross-reference for each word.

1. rough
2. cool
3. mobile
4. feat
5. isolate
6. typical

B. Use a thesaurus to find an idiom for each of these words.

7. poor
8. complete
9. lose
10. outrageous
11. clever
12. attentive
13. fortune
14. illusion
15. ugly

C. Look up these words in a thesaurus. For each word find a synonym that comes from a special field of knowledge, another language or culture, or an earlier time. Copy the synonym and indicate its source.

16. clear
17. pitying
18. swerve
19. jail
20. feature
21. elation
22. beautiful
23. illuminate
24. vindictive

Apply

D. 25.–30. Write six sentences about something that you recently accomplished in school. After you have written the sentences, use a thesaurus to help you determine whether you have used the best words. Change at least one word in each sentence. Write the new sentences.

COMPOSITION

Lesson 12: Writing Narrative Paragraphs

Arnold was asked to write a paragraph that told about an incident in his life. This is what he wrote.

> I never liked cats or cat lovers. I used to think cats were spooky and cat lovers odd. That is, I thought that way until one cold, damp day in March when I found Squeaky. I was hurrying home through the slush when I heard a tiny squeaking sound coming from an alley. I couldn't see anything, but then I felt something rubbing against my leg. It was a skinny, tan kitten, wet and covered with snow and shivering in the cold. I picked it up and put it inside my coat where it snuggled up against my body and soon stopped crying. Of course I had to take it home with me, just for the night—or so I thought at the time. It's been over two and a half years now, and Squeaky is still with me. So whenever I hear someone put down cats or cat lovers, I just smile. Then I think to myself, "You don't know Squeaky."

What kind of paragraph did Arnold write?

Think and Discuss

A paragraph that tells a story is a **narrative paragraph.** A short narrative paragraph, drawn from personal experience and written to entertain or enlighten, is called a **personal anecdote.** Like many other kinds of paragraphs, a personal anecdote has a definite plan of organization.

The *introduction,* or *beginning,* of an anecdote may do several things. It may set the scene for a story. It may introduce the characters in the story. It may provide other background information necessary to the story. At best it will do all three.

Which sentences in Arnold's paragraph make up the beginning of his personal anecdote? What do these sentences do?

The *body* of an anecdote tells what happens in the story. It includes only those details that are important to the story, and it tells them in recognizable order. Which sentences in Arnold's paragraph make up the body of the anecdote?

The final sentence or sentences in an anecdote form the *conclusion* of the story. The conclusion may summarize what happened in the story, comment on the significance of what happened, or bring the story back to the beginning. Which sentences in Arnold's anecdote make up the conclusion? How do these sentences bring the story to an end?

Practice

A. Arrange these sentences in order so that they tell a story. Then write the sentences in paragraph form. After the paragraph write which sentences belong to the introduction, the body, and the conclusion of the anecdote.

1. a. When I went to the audition, I made the mistake of taking along my dog Fetch.
    b. I wanted to get a part in that play more than anything else in the world.
    c. I could see that the director kept looking at Fetch during the audition.
    d. That is probably the closest I'll ever come to being in show business.
    e. *Annie* is a play about an orphan girl and her dog Sandy.
    f. When everything was over, Fetch had won the role of Sandy, and I had to settle for being the dog's trainer.

Apply

B. 2. Write a personal anecdote about an incident in your life or in the life of an imaginary character. Be sure it has an introduction, a body, and a conclusion.

A Challenge

Think of an inanimate object such as a doorknob or a stalk of celery. Write a "personal anecdote" from the point of view of the object.

Lesson 13: Editing a Personal Anecdote

Lisa had to write a personal anecdote for a class. This paragraph is her first version, or draft. As you read it, notice the changes she made in editing it.

(TR) *I'll never forget my thirteenth birthday. It started like a nightmare, but it ended like a dream!*

That morning
~~On the morning of my birthday~~ I was looking forward to being with my friends at school. The first ones I saw were Helen and Roberto. ~~They were~~ standing on the steps and whispering to each other. ~~But~~ when they saw me coming, they stopped ~~(wispering)~~ *whispering* and went ~~in~~ *into* the building. I had a funny feeling that they ~~were~~ *had been* talking about me. When I saw Helen in class, I asked her if she wanted to come over to my house after dinner. She *looked at me strangely.* ~~acted kind of strange.~~ Then Tony and Hal rushed by, without so much as saying hello. ~~Tony and Hal are brothers who live in the apartment building next to mine.~~ It seemed ~~like~~ *as though* all my friends were avoiding me. *Finally* ~~Then,~~ to top it off, Mr. Ellman asked me to stay after school and help him set up the learning ~~(centre)~~ *center* for ~~tomorrow's~~ *the next day's* class. By the time I ~~got~~ *arrived* home that evening, I was feeling ~~pretty~~ ~~(miserible)~~ *miserable.* ~~But~~ *however,* when I opened the door, I was greeted by all my friends, including Mr. Ellman, shouting, "Happy Birthday!"

What a surprise! No wonder I'll remember that day forever! *(TR)*

Think and Discuss

After Lisa had written the first draft of her anecdote, she read it over carefully. The story was told clearly and in order, but the introduction was weak. How did she make it stronger?

Lisa liked the surprise ending of her story. Now that she had a good introduction, however, she saw how she could make the conclusion even better. How did she improve it?

Reading the paragraph once more, Lisa noticed that one sentence was not really necessary. How did she indicate that she wanted to remove that sentence from the paragraph?

Lisa's other sentences needed minor corrections as well. Notice that she changed *on the morning of my birthday* to *that morning* so the sentence would flow smoothly from the introduction before it. The symbol *No ¶* means that since the sentence no longer begins the paragraph, it no longer has to be indented. Lisa also saw that *acted kind of strange* was a slangy expression, so she changed it to *looked at me strangely*. The phrase *at her answer* was added as a transitional expression.

To make her paragraph grammatically correct, *like* was changed to *as though*, and the transitional expression *however* replaced the conjunction *but*. Why did Lisa change *then* to *finally* and *tomorrow's* to *the next day's*?

Practice

A. 1. Rewrite Lisa's paragraph, making the changes she indicated on her first draft.

B. 2. Rewrite this paragraph, making all necessary changes.

Mom told me not to get my new cloths dirty on the first day of school. When Brad dared me to crawl through the large sewer pipe under the highway, I just couldn't back down. The highway goes from Smithtown to Pittsfield. So I crawled through the pipe. When I came out on the other side, my pants and shirt were filthy. I decided to wash them before Mom found out what happened. I guess I put too much soap in the washing machine. The next thing I knew soap suds were all over the basement. I was sitting on the top step, trying to think what to do, when I heard Mom come into the house.

Apply

C. 3. Reread the personal anecdote you wrote in Lesson 12. Check to see that the beginning and ending are strong, and that the middle is clear and in order. Edit your paragraph to make any changes you think are needed. Then rewrite the paragraph neatly on a separate sheet of paper.

MECHANICS PRACTICE

Writing Dialog

- Place quotation marks around the exact words of a direct quotation. If the quotation is divided into two parts by other words, place quotation marks around the quoted words only.

  "I hear you have a new puppy!" exclaimed Sue.
  "Yes, I do," answered Roger. "He's a beautiful rust red."

- Begin a direct quotation with a capital letter. If there are several sentences in the direct quotation, begin each sentence with a capital letter, but do not close the quotation until after the last sentence.

  "His coat is sleek and glossy. He is a perfect Irish setter pup," continued Roger.

- If the second part of a divided quotation is a new sentence, begin it with a capital letter. If the second part is a continuation of the same sentence, begin it with a small letter.

  "I never saw an Irish setter," said Dot. "May I see him?"
  "Come to my house," replied Roger, "this afternoon after school."

- Commas always go inside the quotation marks.

  "This is my dog, Eric the Red," said Roger.

- Periods always go inside the quotation marks. Question marks and exclamation points go inside the quotation marks if the quotation itself is a question or an exclamation.

  Roger continued, "We got him just the other day."
  "What a beautiful pup!" exclaimed Dot.
  "How old is he?" asked Sue.

- When a quotation occurs within another quotation, put standard quotation marks around the original quotation and single quotation marks around the added quotation.

  "About ten weeks," chuckled Roger. "The vet said, 'Eric will be a real handful in another month,' and I can see already that he's right."

- When you write dialog, begin a new paragraph every time the speaker changes.

"Why did you name him Eric the Red?" asked Dot.

"Well," said Roger, "he is a rusty red, and I thought that he might be adventurous like the historical Eric the Red."

"What a great idea!" exclaimed Sue.

A. Copy these sentences. Add the correct punctuation and capitalization.

1. this meeting will now come to order said June
2. Conrad raised his hand and asked why did you call this meeting today we're not supposed to meet until Friday
3. we have a problem June answered our treasury is out of money
4. but I thought interrupted Carol we had money left over from the pizza sale
5. we did answered June but we spent it all for Oscar's present
6. you spent it all shouted Greg I don't believe it
7. how much did the present cost Abby inquired
8. eight dollars sighed June and thirty-nine cents
9. so what do we do now asked Carol
10. i have an idea said Conrad we could have a street fair it would be fun and we could raise some money what do you think
11. i think that's a great idea cheered Abby

B. Read the following passage carefully. Then rewrite it correctly, capitalizing, punctuating, and indenting where necessary.

12. may I have your attention please said Harold we have to take a vote what are we voting on asked Arlene we are voting replied Harold on whether to have a food fair or a game fair all in favor of the food fair say aye aye shouted Alex, Trixy, and Zed three ayes for the food fair said Arlene, writing in a notebook now said Harold all in favor of the game fair say aye aye screamed Pete, Betty, and Arlene it's a tie said Arlene what do we do now asked Zed Harold hasn't voted yet remarked Trixy he has to break the tie how do you vote, Harold well said Harold since we're split evenly why don't we have both that's a great idea exclaimed Betty we'll have a food and game fair. hooray shouted everyone

LITERATURE

Lesson 14: Understanding Autobiographies

A **biography** is the story of one person's life written by another person. A biography usually begins with the subject's birth and ends with the last days or death of the subject. The author of a biography uses the **third-person point of view;** that is, the author consistently refers to the subject by name or with the pronoun *he* or *she.* What is one biography that you have read, heard about, or seen dramatized?

Think and Discuss

Life stories can also be written from the **first-person point of view.** Such is the case in an **autobiography,** in which the subject of the book writes his or her own life story. The writer uses the pronoun *I* instead of the subject's name or the pronoun *he* or *she.* In addition, an autobiography will relate the subject's life only up until the time that the book is written, unless someone other than the author finishes the book.

The writer of an autobiography has far greater freedom than the writer of a biography. The biographer records what he or she has learned about the subject through interviews or research. The autobiographer, on the other hand, can express personal likes and dislikes, give opinions about the people and events that were a part of his or her life, and relate anecdotes, the brief personal stories that greatly strengthen any autobiography.

Cheaper by the Dozen, by Frank B. Gilbreth, Jr., and Ernestine Gilbreth Carey, is an autobiographical look at an unusual family in the 1920's. Frank Gilbreth, Sr., and his wife, Lillian, were both industrial engineers and efficiency experts. They applied their studies to their home. As a result, the 12 Gilbreth children lived a life that was at times rather businesslike, but it was always a lot of fun. Read this selection from *Cheaper by the Dozen.*

On Friday nights, Dad and Mother often went to a lecture or a movie by themselves, holding hands as they went out to the barn to get the car.

But on Saturday nights, Mother stayed home with the babies, while Dad took the rest of us to the movies. We had early supper so that we could get to the theater by seven o'clock, in time for the first show.

"We're just going to stay through one show tonight," Dad told us on the way down. "None of this business about seeing the show through a second time. None of this eleven o'clock stuff. No use to beg me."

When the movie began, Dad became as absorbed as we, and noisier. He forgot all about us, and paid no attention when we nudged him and asked for nickels to put in the candy vendors on the back of the seats. He laughed so hard at the comedies that sometimes he embarrassed us and we tried to tell him that people were looking at him. When the feature was sad, he kept trumpeting his nose and wiping his eyes.

When the lights went on at the end of the first show, we always begged him to change his mind, and let us stay and see it again. He put on an act of stubborn resistance, but always yielded in the end.

"Well, you were less insolent than usual this week," he said. "But I hate to have you stay up until all hours of the night."

"If you think it's all right, Mother will think it's all right."

"Well, all right. We'll make an exception this time. Since your hearts are so set on it, I guess I can sit through it again."

Once, after a whispered message by Ernestine had passed along the line, we picked up our coats at the end of the first show and started to file out of the aisle.

"What are you up to?" Dad called after us in a hurt tone, and loud enough so that people stood up to see what was causing the disturbance. "Where do you think you're going? Do you want to walk home? Come back here and sit down."

We said he had told us on the way to the theater that we could just sit through one show that night.

"Well, don't you want to see it again? After all, you've been good as gold this week. If your hearts are set on it, I guess I could sit through it again. I don't mind, particularly."

We said that we were a little sleepy, that we didn't want to be all tired out tomorrow and that we didn't want Mother to be worried because we had stayed out late.

"Aw, come on," Dad begged. "Don't be spoil sports. I'll take care of your mother. Let's see it again. The evening's young. Tomorrow's Sunday. You can sleep late."

We filed smirking back to our seats.

"You little fiends," Dad whispered as we sat down. "You spend hours figuring out ways to gang up on me, don't you? I've got a good mind to leave you all home next week and come to the show by myself."

The picture that made the biggest impression on Dad was a twelve-reel epic entitled *Over the Hill to the Poor House,* or something like that. It was about a wispy widow lady who worked her poor old fingers to the bone for her children, only to end her days in the alms house after they turned against her.

For an hour and a half, while Dad manned the pumps with his handkerchief, the woman struggled to keep her family together. She washed huge vats of clothes. She ironed an endless procession of underwear. Time after time, single-handed and on her hands and knees, she emptied all the cuspidors and scrubbed down the lobby of Grand Central Station.

Her children were ashamed of her and complained because they didn't have store-bought clothes. When the children were grown up, they fought over having her come to live with them. Finally, when she was too old to help even with the housework, they turned her out into the street. There was a snowstorm going on, too.

The fade-out scene, the one that had Dad actually wringing out his handkerchief, showed the old woman, shivering in a worn and inadequate hug-me-tight, limping slowly up the hill to the poor house.

"I can see myself twenty years from now," he'd grumble when we asked him for advances on our allowances. "I can see myself, old, penniless, trudging up that hill. I wonder what kind of food they have at the poor house and whether they let you sleep late in the mornings?"

How can you tell that this selection is autobiographical?

Practice

A. Read these statements carefully. Copy the statements that are true. Rewrite the false statements to make them true.

1. A biography is written from the third-person point of view.
2. An autobiographer will refer to his or her subject by name.
3. Most autobiographies contain facts, opinions, and anecdotes.
4. *Cheaper by the Dozen* is a biography.
5. One fact stated in the selection is that Mother hated to go to the movies with Dad.
6. The anecdote in this selection describes the family's method of assigning special tasks around the house.
7. Dad's protesting against staying to see the show twice is a matter of the authors' opinion.
8. The movie that most impressed Father was *Over the Hill to the Poor House.*
9. Dad told the children that he would someday wind up in the poor house too.

Apply

B. 10. List some of the humorous incidents in your life. Write a brief account of one of those incidents. Remember to use both facts of the event and your opinions or impressions of it.

A BOOK TO READ

Title: **Barbara Jordan: A Self-Portrait**
Author: Barbara Jordan and Shelby Hearon
Publisher: Doubleday

Barbara Jordan grew up in the Southwest and, against all odds, went North to study at Boston University Law School. Her career took off when she was elected to the all-male, all-white Texas State Senate. From there she won a place in the U.S. Congress, and she went on to make her mark as a keynote speaker at the Democratic National Convention in 1976.

This story tells of a woman who has battled against prejudice all of her life and who, without fear or bitterness, has realized her dreams.

4 UNIT TEST

● **Transitive and Intransitive Action Verbs**   pages 120–121

Number your paper 1–6. Next to each number write the letter that tells you what kind of verb the underlined word is. Use this code: **a.** transitive **b.** intransitive

1. The Thespians' Club <u>produced</u> a play this year.
2. *The Emperor's New Clothes* <u>opened</u> May 1.
3. Everyone <u>loved</u> it.
4. It <u>ended</u> with a real bang too.
5. The stage manager <u>pulled</u> the wrong rope.
6. The curtain certainly <u>fell</u>, didn't it?

● **Linking Verbs**   pages 122–123

Copy these sentences. Draw two lines under the linking verb in each sentence.

7. *Macbeth* is a play by Shakespeare.
8. It could be our next production.
9. It looks awfully difficult, though.
10. Maybe another choice would be better for the Thespians.

● **Main Verbs and Helping Verbs**   pages 124–125

Copy these sentences. Draw two lines under the main verb and circle the helping verb or verbs in each sentence.

11. *Macbeth* has been performed before by actors our age.
12. We have also produced other plays by Shakespeare.
13. Inez has always wanted to play Lady Macbeth.
14. All right, we can read it together tomorrow.
15. She will certainly be excellent in the role.

● **Principal Parts of Regular Verbs**   pages 126–127

Copy these sentences. Then write whether each underlined verb uses the <u>present</u>, <u>past</u>, or <u>past participle</u> form.

16. You both <u>have tried</u> out for the same part.
17. <u>Have</u> you ever worked on a play <u>before</u>?

18. Yes, I <u>played</u> Bottom in *A Midsummer Night's Dream.*
19. The role of the Porter <u>needs</u> your comic talents.
20. Besides, George <u>has memorized</u> Banquo's lines already.

● Principal Parts of Irregular Verbs (I and II)   pages 128–131

Copy these sentences. Write the principal part of the verb indicated in parentheses ( ) to complete each sentence.

21. Shakespeare _____ this scene for King James I. (write, past)
22. He _____ the king was fascinated by the idea of witches. (know, past)
23. The witches _____ about the mischief they _____. (speak, present; do, past participle)
24. Then Macbeth _____ in on them. (burst, present)
25. Where _____ Benita _____? (go, past participle)
26. She _____ to get a cauldron for the witches' brew. (go, past)
27. Mai Li _____ one yesterday. (bring, past)
28. I _____ someone _____ it. (think, present; break, past participle)
29. Hurry, Benita, the rehearsal _____ five minutes ago. (begin, past)
30. I _____ all the way home and back on my bike. (ride, past)

● Verb Tenses   pages 132–135

Copy these sentences. Write the tense of the underlined verb after each sentence.

31. We <u>write</u> articles about all the plays for the school paper.
32. *Macbeth* <u>will have closed</u> before our next issue, however.
33. Roger <u>has written</u> a good press release.
34. He thought someone <u>had mailed</u> it yesterday.
35. I <u>sent</u> copies to the newspapers and radio stations this morning.

● Subject/Verb Agreement   pages 136–137

Copy these sentences. Choose the correct verb form to complete each one.

36. Four nights (is, are) not a long run for a play.
37. Everyone's parents (is, are) coming at least once to see it.
38. The cast (looks, look) like a good one.
39. Either Suzanne Smith or Benita Juarez (plays, play) the first witch.
40. David Washington and Bruce Elrod (plays, play) the part of Macbeth on alternate nights.

Homophones and Homographs   pages 140–141

Copy these sentences. Choose the correct homophones to finish each one.

1. Put some of that (vial, vile) brew in this (vial, vile).
2. (Wears, Where's) the nightgown Lady Macbeth (wears, where's) in the sleepwalking scene?
3. The school (principal, principle) says—this is the (principal, principle) show of the year.
4. Macbeth denied that Birnam (Wood, Would) (wood, would) come to Dunsinane.

Copy these sentences. After each one underline the pronunciation that would make the sentence correct.

5. Inez, are you content (kon′tent, kən·tent′) with your performance?
6. Yes, the Dinner Theater even offered me a contract (kon′tract, kən·tract′).
7. I recited my soliloquy in a contest (kon′test, kən·test′) for young actors.
8. Please don't desert (dez′ərt, di·zûrt′) us before the show closes!

Synonyms and Antonyms   pages 142–143

Copy these word pairs. After each pair write whether they are *synonyms* or *antonyms*.

9. foul/fair
10. sleep/slumber
11. skillful/cunning
12. perfect/whole
13. regard/gaze
14. constancy/faithfulness
15. counterfeit/true
16. woeful/glad
17. obscure/hidden

Using the Thesaurus   pages 144–145

Use this thesaurus entry to answer the questions that follow.

---

act   *noun*
1. The process of doing: *the act of thinking.*
2. Something done: *an act of bravery.*

3. The formal product of a legislative or judicial body.
4. *Informal.* A display of insincere behavior: *Her concern is just an act.*

5. A short theatrical piece within a larger production.
act   *verb*
1. To play the part of: *acted Juliet in summer stock.*

2. To produce on the stage.
3. To conduct oneself in a specified way: *always acts like a lady.*

1. **Syn:** action.
2. **Syns:** accomplishment, action, actus, deed, doing, thing.
3. LAW.
4. **Syns:** acting, dissemblance, masquerade, play-acting, pose, pretense, sham, show, simulation.
5. SKETCH *noun.*

1. **Syns:** do, enact, impersonate, perform, play-act, portray, represent.
2. STAGE *verb.*
3. **Syns:** acquit, bear, behave, carry, comport, demean[1], deport, disport, do, quit.

---

18. Which meaning of the word *act* would fit in the sentence, ''Banquo's ghost appears in *Act* IV.''

19. Which synonym of *act* would be appropriate in the sentence, ''When I finish drama school, I want to *act* for television.''

20. What part of speech is *act* in this sentence? ''*Act* like a hero, and you will be one.''

● Narrative Paragraphs   pages 146–147

1. Write a paragraph describing a night at the theater. It may be a description of something you have seen or something you have invented.

● Editing a Narrative Paragraph   pages 148–149

2. Edit the narrative paragraph you wrote in the activity above. Make sure your paragraph has an introduction, body, and conclusions. Use capital letters and punctuation marks correctly. Neatly rewrite your paragraph on a separate sheet of paper.

● Writing Dialog   pages 150–151

3. Rewrite this passage, adding proper capitalization and punctuation and indenting where necessary.

What a good performance Inez gave this evening! Mr. Garcia exclaimed. Don't you think so, Rosa? Mrs. Garcia smiled. Yes, dear, she *was* good. Now I am looking forward to seeing her play Cecily at the Dinner Theater remarked Mrs. Elrod. Just think, Rosa, she may be a famous actress one day. Maybe she will even win an Oscar. You may be rushing things there a bit, Jennie, said Mr. Elrod but I hope she will be a big success too.

● Autobiographies   pages 152–155

Copy these sentences from a student's autobiography. After each sentence write whether the student has expressed a *fact* or an *opinion*.

1. When I was tiny, I was given a job acting in a baby food commercial.

2. I think I must have been an awfully cute baby.

3. My baby pictures show that I had lots of curly hair and big eyes.

4. I lost the job right away, however, because I refused to eat the baby food.

5. I guess they thought it would be easier to find another baby than to change their product.

LANGUAGE
Learning About Adjectives and Adverbs
COMPOSITION
Writing Descriptions

STUDY SKILLS
Reasoning Correctly
LITERATURE
Enjoying Narrative Poetry

Look at the pictures on the opposite page and begin to describe them to yourself. You will quickly realize that nouns and verbs alone are not enough to make a good description. Adjectives and adverbs are needed to add sensory details and make comparisons. In this unit you will be using adjectives and adverbs to write descriptions, and you will also see them used in narrative poetry.

Two important reasoning tools are also dealt with in Unit 5: categorizing information and drawing analogies. Both skills are means of analyzing the relationships between similar pieces of information. You will sometimes use categorizing and analogies in writing descriptions, and you will also apply these skills to many other situations in your life.

LANGUAGE

Lesson 1: Understanding Common and Proper Adjectives

Notice how the underlined words give more information about other words in these sentences.

1. The <u>first</u> <u>flying</u> machine able to carry a person was built by <u>the</u> <u>Wright</u> brothers.
2. <u>Their</u> <u>first</u> flight was <u>short</u>.
3. It lasted <u>twelve</u> seconds.

Think and Discuss

The underlined words in sentences 1–3 modify nouns by adding information about them. Words that modify nouns or pronouns are called **adjectives.** Adjectives answer the questions *what kind, which one,* and *how many.* In sentence 1 *first* answers the question *which one* about the noun *machine.* In sentence 2 *short* tells *what kind* of flight it was. What question does *twelve* answer in sentence 3?

The words *a, an,* and *the* are called **articles,** and they are the most common adjectives. *The* is called a *definite article* because it refers to a *particular* person, place, or thing. The words *a* and *an* are *indefinite articles* because they refer to any one of a number of persons, places, or things.

The possessive pronouns, such as *your, her, his, its,* and *their,* are always used as adjectives to limit the meaning of a noun. *Their* is used as an adjective in sentence 2.

Sometimes nouns are used to modify other nouns. The word *Wright* is a noun when it stands alone. When it answers one of the three adjective questions, however, it is used as an adjective: *Wright brothers.*

Words that look like verbs are also used in adjectives. These verb forms are called **participles,** and they end in *ed* or *ing.* The participle *flying* in sentence 1 answers the question *what kind.* Therefore, *flying* is an adjective in sentence 1.

- An **adjective** is a word that modifies a noun or a pronoun.
- **Articles** are the most common adjectives. They are definite (*the*) or indefinite (*a, an*).
- A noun can be used as an adjective to modify another noun.
- A **participle** is a verb form ending in *ed* or *ing* that can be used as an adjective.

Sometimes adjectives come after a linking verb:

Their first flight was <u>short</u>.

When an adjective comes after a linking verb, it modifies the subject of the sentence.

Like nouns, adjectives are either common or proper. Common adjectives are not capitalized unless they begin a sentence. Proper adjectives are made from proper nouns and must always be capitalized. Identify the proper adjectives in sentences 1–3.

Practice

A. Copy these sentences. Underline each adjective and draw an arrow to the noun it modifies. Above each adjective write *common* or *proper*. Do not underline articles.

1. The glider flights of a German engineer interested the Wright brothers in aviation.
2. The excellent mechanics needed a handy place to work.
3. A repair shop for bicycles was available.
4. The excited brothers took turns on their first four flights.
5. They were great pioneers in American aviation.

B. Copy these nouns and modify each one with a common or proper adjective. Label the adjectives *common* or *proper*.

6. aircraft	7. equipment	8. biplane	9. jet
10. sky	11. weather	12. wing	13. factory
14. pilot	15. flight	16. speed	17. passenger
18. clouds	19. propeller	20. fuel	

Apply

C. 21.–30. Write ten sentences about taking a trip in an airplane. Use at least two adjectives (not counting articles) in each sentence.

Lesson 2: Comparing with Adjectives

Read these comparisons.

1. Greg wrote a <u>long</u> science report.
2. Juanita's report was <u>longer</u> than Greg's.
3. <u>Longest</u> of all was Adam's report.

What adjectives are used to compare the reports?

Think and Discuss

Comparison of adjectives is expressed in **degrees.** The underlined adjectives above show three degrees of length: *long, longer, longest.* The first adjective is in the **positive degree.** Positive degree is used when only one thing is being described, as in sentence 1. The **comparative degree** is used to compare two things. *Longer* compares Juanita's report to Greg's report. The **superlative degree** compares three or more things. The adjective *longest* is in the superlative degree.

- The **positive degree** is used to describe only one thing.
- The **comparative degree** is used to compare two things.
- The **superlative degree** is used to compare three or more things.

For most one- or two-syllable adjectives, the comparative degrees are formed by adding the endings *er* and *est.* All words of three or more syllables use *more* and *most* or *less* and *least* in the comparative and superlative degree. For some two-syllable adjectives, both forms are acceptable. The choice of form depends on the emphasis you wish to convey.

4. Eli is the <u>happiest</u> fellow in our class.
5. He is <u>most happy</u> after a test.

Positive	Comparative	Superlative
great	greater	greatest
heavy	heavier	heaviest
expensive	less expensive	least expensive
happy	happier *or* more happy	happiest *or* most happy

Some very common adjectives have *irregular* forms when they are compared. Study this chart.

Positive	Comparative	Superlative
good	better	best
bad	worse	worst
little	less, lesser	least
much, many	more	most
far	farther	farthest

Practice

A. Copy these adjectives. After each one write its degree of comparison.

1. less colorful
2. friendliest
3. smartest
4. most serious
5. farther
6. more comfortable

B. Write the comparative and superlative degrees for these adjectives. Use *er* and *est, more* and *most,* or *less* and *least.*

7. little
8. sweet
9. red
10. anxious
11. many
12. thoughtful
13. dirty
14. unusual
15. strong

C. Rewrite these sentences using the correct degree of comparison for each adjective in parentheses ( ).

16. Miyoshi is the _____ student in science class. (good)
17. Her notes are the _____ of all. (thorough)
18. Sheri looked at a _____ insect under the microscope. (small)
19. It was _____ than the one she had seen yesterday. (small)
20. Max put chemicals in the _____ beaker he could find. (big)
21. Max is _____ than he is graceful. (clumsy)
22. He dropped the _____ beaker of all. (expensive)
23. It was the _____ accident in class all year. (bad)
24. It was even _____ than when Bob burned the sulfur. (bad)
25. I have _____ homework in science than in music. (much)

Apply

D. 26.–35. Write ten sentences comparing different subjects in school. Use the three degrees of comparison, and label each adjective with the degree of comparison you used.

Lesson 3: Understanding Adverbs

Read this sentence.

1. Pilar sketched the horse.

What words could you use to tell when Pilar sketched the horse? What words would tell you how she sketched the horse, or how often she sketched the horse?

Think and Discuss

Today would tell when Pilar sketched. Such words as *eagerly* and *once* would tell how and how often she sketched. Words that tell *when, where, how, how often,* and *to what extent* are **adverbs.**

Adverbs modify verbs, adjectives, and other adverbs. Read sentences 2–4. The adverbs are underlined and the arrows show which word each adverb modifies.

2. Pilar quickly drew her outline.
3. Her sketches are quite good.
4. She used the charcoal very skillfully.

In sentence 2 the adverb *quickly* modifies the verb *drew.* In sentence 3 the adverb *quite* modifies the adjective *good.* In sentence 4 the adverb *very* modifies the adverb *skillfully.* What does *skillfully* modify?

Here are some words that are often used as adverbs. Notice the question each one answers.

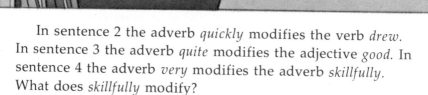

When?	yesterday	now	later	then	soon
Where?	here	there	outside	upstairs	back
How?	carefully	clearly	quickly	slowly	
How often?	often	always	never	frequently	
To what extent?	much	slightly	terribly		

The question *to what extent* is answered by a class of adverbs called *intensifiers*. Here are some other common intensifiers that can modify adjectives and other adverbs.

very	quite	almost	really	somewhat
not	least	more	rather	entirely
too	less	most	nearly	extremely

Which adverbs in sentences 2–4 are intensifiers?

- An **adverb** is a word used to modify a verb, adjective, or another adverb. Adverbs often answer the questions *where, when, how, how often,* and *to what extent.*

Practice

A. Copy these sentences. Underline each adverb and draw an arrow from it to the word it modifies. Some sentences have more than one adverb.

1. Pilar and her sister Layla go to art school regularly.
2. Pilar is quite serious about her work.
3. Frequently she sketches members of her family.
4. Layla is thinking seriously of becoming a professional artist.
5. Pilar and Layla work very diligently on their sketches.
6. They are both rather excited because they soon will have their own art show.
7. Pilar is almost ready because she draws more quickly than Layla.
8. Layla's finely drawn miniatures require many hours of hard work.

B. 9.–20. List each adverb in Practice A and write whether it tells *when, where, how, how often,* or *to what extent.*

Apply

C. 21.–30. Write a paragraph or two about your favorite hobby or activity. Use at least ten adverbs to modify verbs, adjectives, or other adverbs.

Lesson 4: Comparing with Adverbs

What are the adverbs in these sentences?

1. Helga practiced diligently for the Olympics.
2. Barbara practiced more diligently than Helga did.
3. Marie practiced most diligently of all.

Think and Discuss

Adverbs, like adjectives, have three degrees of comparison. The adverb *diligently* in sentence 1 is in the **positive degree,** for it describes only one person's method of practicing. In sentence 2 the adverbs *more diligently* are in the **comparative degree,** for they compare the method of practicing of two people. The adverbs *most diligently* in sentence 3 are in the **superlative degree,** for they indicate which of the three people is best at her method of practicing.

Most adverbs that end in *ly* in the positive degree are changed to the comparative and superlative degree by adding *more* and *most* or *less* and *least*. The comparative and superlative degrees of other adverbs are formed by adding *er* and *est*. Still others are irregular; their form is entirely different in the comparative and superlative degrees. Study this chart, which contains examples of each type.

Positive	Comparative	Superlative
busily	more/less busily	most/least busily
often	more/less often	most/least often
close	closer/less close	closest/least close
late	later	latest
well	better	best
badly	worse	worst

Practice

A. Copy these sentences and underline the adverbs that they contain. After each sentence write whether the adverb is in the *positive, comparative,* or *superlative* degree.

1. The Greek Olympic games were held regularly at Olympia.
2. Racing events were held earlier than any other event.
3. The one who ran most swiftly won a crown of olive leaves.

4. The modern Olympic games last longer than the ancient ones.

5. Today's winners stand most proudly when their national anthems are played.

B. Rewrite these sentences using the correct degree of comparison for each adverb in parentheses ( ).

6. Ginny swims _____ than Pam does. (smoothly)

7. Of all of the girls on the team, Pam learns _____. (quickly)

8. Pam stayed _____ than Ginny and worked on her kick. (late)

9. In a week Pam was swimming _____ than she had ever swum before. (well)

10. Of all the swimmers, Pam accepted her award _____. (proudly)

Apply

C. 11.–20. Turn to the sports page of a recent issue of a local newspaper. Carefully read the articles on that page and find ten sentences that contain adverbs that compare actions. Copy those sentences and underline the adverbs. Write whether each adverb is in the *positive, comparative,* or *superlative* degree.

HOW OUR LANGUAGE GROWS

An *acronym* is an abbreviated word invented by connecting the first letter or letters of a series of words. *Radar,* for example, is an acronym for "radio detecting and ranging," and *scuba* is an acronym for "self-contained underwater breathing apparatus." Many organizations, such as *NATO* and *UNESCO,* use acronyms to shorten their names.

An *initialism* is similar to an acronym except that each of its letters is pronounced. You are probably familiar with many of them: A.M., P.M. *TNT, ESP,* and *VIP.* Many Presidents, such as *F.D.R.* and *J.F.K.,* have been known by their initials.

Find the full form of these acronyms and initialisms: *NATO, NOW, TNT, ESP, VIP.*

Lesson 5: Using Adjectives and Adverbs Correctly

Read these sentences from advertisements.

1. Nothing satisfies your thirst as good as Pineapple Krush does.
2. Try Formula X-47 for the most fastest relief known.
3. Whose clothes are cleanest—yours or the ones washed in Snap?
4. You won't hardly believe how bright your teeth will be when you use Toothy.

Notice that each of these sentences contains an error in adjective and adverb usage.

Think and Discuss

Using adjectives and adverbs correctly can sometimes be tricky. Mistakes in the usage of adjectives and adverbs often occur in everyday speech and writing. It is helpful to remember that you use adjectives only when you want to describe a person, place, or thing. In order to describe an action or another modifier, you must use an adverb. In sentence 1 the adjective *good* should be an adverb. What word should take the place of *good* in sentence 1? Sentence 2 contains an example of double comparison: *most fastest*. The ending *est* already expresses comparison. There is no need to add the word *most*. In sentence 3 the superlative degree is used to compare only two things. How should sentence 3 be corrected? Sentence 4 contains a double negative, *won't hardly*. Do not use two negatives in the same sentence to express a negative statement. How would you write sentence 4 correctly?

The following adjectives and adverbs are frequently confused.

Real is always an adjective; *really* is always an adverb.

5. <u>Real</u> athletes eat Whammos.
6. They <u>really</u> give you energy in the morning.

Bad is always an adjective; *badly* is always an adverb.

7. This is a <u>bad</u> bruise.
8. Use Bliss Bandages when you bruise yourself <u>badly.</u>

Good is always an adjective; *well* is an adverb, except when it is used to mean "in good health."

9. Vigor Vitamins are <u>good.</u>
10. I know their products quite <u>well.</u>
11. I feel <u>well</u> because I take Vigor Vitamins.

Most is usually an adjective; when it means "very," however, it is an adverb. *Almost* is always an adverb.

12. <u>Most</u> people enjoy Krunchies at breakfast.
13. It is a <u>most</u> unusual cereal.
14. Krunchies <u>almost</u> explode in your mouth.

Practice

A. Copy these sentences, choosing the correct words from the modifiers in parentheses ( ).

1. Sean and his brother Pat wanted to win the Krunchies contest (bad, badly).
2. Sean bought the (biggest, most biggest) box of Krunchies in the supermarket.
3. Then he (couldn't scarcely, could scarcely) wait to get home and fill out his entry blank.
4. He mailed his entry blank (real, really) quickly.
5. Whose entry would arrive (soonest, sooner)—his or Pat's?

B. Rewrite these sentences, choosing the correct word in parentheses ( ). Circle the word that your choice modifies.

6. Pat was (real, really) angry when Sean won the contest.
7. In fact, he was (most, almost) ready to fight with Sean.
8. Then Sean felt (bad, badly).
9. He said that he would try to be a (good, well) brother.
10. They played (happy, happily) for the rest of the afternoon.

Apply

C. 11.–20. Invent two products and write five sentences to advertise each one. Be sure that each sentence contains a correctly used adjective or adverb.

LANGUAGE REVIEW

Adjectives   pages 162–163

Copy these sentences, adding adjectives to make them complete. Draw
an arrow from each adjective that you have chosen to the word it modifies.

1. My _____ family flew to California on a _____ jetliner.
2. We visited _____ and _____ Sequoia National Park.
3. My _____ sister and I went on a _____ hike on a _____ morning.
4. We stopped at several _____ places to admire the _____ trees.
5. Then we explored a (an) _____ cave.
6. We found a _____, _____ spot to eat our _____ lunch.
7. _____ clouds later moved into the area and threatened our _____ outing.

Comparison with Adjectives   pages 164–165

Rewrite these sentences, using the correct degree of comparison for
each adjective in parentheses ( ). After each sentence write whether
the adjective is in the *positive, comparative,* or *superlative* degree.

8. Which day was _____, yesterday or Monday? (cold)
9. This is the _____ spring I can remember. (rainy)
10. I am sure that there will be _____ sunshine this week than last. (little)
11. Sara is the _____ person I know. (cheerful)
12. Sara is _____ than usual because of the weather. (cheerful)
13. How I long for _____ weather than we have been having! (warm)
14. When the temperature rises, I will smile my _____ smile of all. (sunny)

Adverbs   pages 166–167

Copy these sentences. Underline each adverb and draw an arrow to
the word it modifies. After each sentence write whether the adverb
modifies a *verb,* an *adjective,* or another *adverb.*

15. Baking is a very enjoyable task.
16. Marta bakes her cakes more carefully than I do.
17. Scrub the baking pans thoroughly before you begin, Bill.
18. Measure all of the ingredients exactly.
19. Work carefully, or you certainly will ruin that cake.
20. My brother eats my successes quite hungrily and then smiles happily.
21. We have finished cleaning the kitchen; what should we bake now?

Comparison with Adverbs   pages 168–169

Rewrite these sentences, using the correct degree of comparison for each adverb in parentheses ( ). After each sentence write whether the adverb is in the *positive, comparative,* or *superlative* degree.

22. I _____ reread Ray Bradbury's novels. (frequently)
23. Bradbury describes people and things _____ than most writers. (vividly)
24. I think that *The Martian Chronicles* is the _____ written book I have ever read. (imaginatively)
25. I read each chapter _____ than the one before it. (eagerly)
26. I like to read each description _____ so that I may enjoy Bradbury's use of language. (carefully)
27. I cannot think of any book I can recommend _____. (enthusiastically)

Correct Use of Adjectives and Adverbs   pages 170–171

Rewrite these sentences, choosing the correct modifier in parentheses ( ). Draw an arrow from that word to the word that it modifies and write whether your choice is an adjective or an adverb.

28. Our mountain-climbing adventure (almost, most) wore us all out.
29. We climbed (almost, most) carefully, using safety lines all the way.
30. All of us had prepared ourselves (good, well) for the climb.
31. Zak boasted that he was in (good, well) shape, but he soon tired.
32. That is a (bad, badly) part of the trail.
33. When we reached the summit, we needed rest (bad, badly).
34. The climb was a (real, really) challenge to us.
35. It was well worth the effort, though, for the view from the top was (real, really) beautiful.

Applying Adjectives and Adverbs

36.–45. Write ten sentences about what life might have been like in colonial America. You may use your social studies textbook to help you with your research. Use adverbs and adjectives to compare that way of life with modern life. Be sure to use the three degrees of comparison correctly. Check your sentences to be sure that capitalization, punctuation, and subject/verb agreement are correct and that all of your adjectives and adverbs are used properly.

STUDY SKILLS

Look at these three words. What do they have in common?

iris, rose, violet

If you think for a moment, you will realize that these words have something in common besides being the names of flowers. What is it?

Think and Discuss

The ability to **classify** things—to sort things out into categories so that all the items in one category have something in common—is an important reasoning skill. As the example that you have just studied shows, classifying sometimes requires careful thinking about the different categories that are possible.

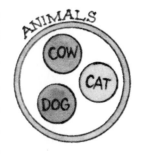

When you are classifying information, you may find it helpful to draw diagrams that will make your thought processes visual. Two kinds of diagrams are especially helpful. One is a *circle diagram.* Make a large circle for the general category. Draw smaller circles for each specific example inside the large circle, as in this example.

A second type of diagram used for classifying information is the *tree diagram.* Write the general category at the top of the tree. Then draw "branches" down from it to show the specific examples, as in this example. A tree diagram can be very helpful when your topic for classification will involve further branching of each example.

Whenever you are confused about relationships between the things that you are trying to classify, try putting them in diagram form.

Practice

A. Copy these lists of specific examples. Next to each list write the general category into which all of the items fit. Use a dictionary to find the meanings of unfamiliar words.

1. Nile, Amazon, Volga, Missouri
2. *Hamlet, Romeo and Juliet, King Lear, Macbeth*
3. Golden Gate, Brooklyn, Mackinac, Tacoma Narrows
4. stamps, baseball cards, toy soldiers, matchbooks
5. Andes, Appalachians, Rockies, Urals
6. dragon, unicorn, phoenix, chimera
7. Peru, Chile, Venezuela, Ecuador
8. conch, cowrie, scallop, nautilus
9. Arabian, Clydesdale, palomino, Appaloosa
10. Yellowstone, Everglades, Bryce Canyon, Glacier

B. Copy these general categories. Next to each category write four specific examples.

11. fish
12. holidays
13. school subjects
14. team sports
15. tools
16. states
17. novels
18. baked goods
19. house pets

C. Each of these lists of specific examples contains one item that does not belong with the others. Copy the *correct* items; then name the category in which they belong.

20. gold, emeralds, diamonds, sapphires
21. Jupiter, Mars, the moon, Venus
22. king, queen, prince, president
23. Sweden, Indonesia, Peru, Wyoming
24. blue, orange, dark, white
25. robins, collies, sparrows, cardinals
26. novel, biography, history, encyclopedia
27. bat, mitt, puck, shin guards
28. oak, acorn, maple, mahogany

Apply

D. 29.–38. Try to stump your classmates. Create ten lists of four items each that fall into the same category and see if they can guess the categories.

Lesson 7: Understanding Verbal Analogies

If you have an understanding of the degrees of comparison between adjectives and adverbs, you would understand if someone were to tell you that a certain state were *colder* or *warmer* than another. Suppose, though, that the comparison were expressed in this form.

MINNESOTA : COLD : : Arizona:
a. desert   **b.** hot   **c.** Phoenix   **d.** West

Think and Discuss

That second kind of comparison is known as a **verbal analogy.** The ability to understand and complete a verbal analogy involves good reasoning. That is why you will frequently find analogy questions on standardized tests. For example, the Scholastic Aptitude Test, which you will take if you are thinking about attending college, usually has a large section of analogy questions.

In the example that you have just read, you are asked to determine the relationship between *Minnesota* and *cold. Cold* weather is a characteristic of Minnesota living. Only one of the four choices will show the same relationship with Arizona. *Desert, Phoenix,* and *West* are all words that have something to do with Arizona, but none of them names a weather condition that is characteristic of Arizona living. *Hot,* however, is descriptive of Arizona's weather, so *b* is the correct answer.

Verbal analogies can describe many different kinds of relationships. As in the example that you have just studied, an analogy question can show the relationship between a subject and one of its important characteristics. It can show causes and effects, entire things and their parts, or many other relationships. Carefully think about the relationships between the words before you complete verbal analogies.

Practice

A. Copy these analogy questions. Underline the word that will correctly complete each one.

1. LOUISIANA : NEW ORLEANS : : Georgia :
   a. peaches   **b.** South   **c.** Atlanta   **d.** Kentucky
2. ORANGE : FRUIT : : potato :
   a. brown   **b.** vegetable   **c.** Idaho   **d.** baked
3. DECEMBER : WINTER : : March :
   a. soldier   **b.** windy   **c.** summer   **d.** spring
4. DOOR : KNOB : : suitcase :
   a. handle   **b.** traveler   **c.** briefcase   **d.** carry
5. MISSOURI : STATE : : St. Louis :
   a. St. Paul   **b.** city   **c.** arches   **d.** village
6. BONNET : HEAD : : boot :
   a. combat   **b.** walking   **c.** foot   **d.** leather
7. EYE : VISION : : nose :
   a. smell   **b.** running   **c.** touch   **d.** hearing
8. GOOSE : GOSLING : : cat :
   a. purr   **b.** dog   **c.** meow   **d.** kitten
9. SILVER : METAL : : diamond :
   a. oyster   **b.** clam   **c.** gem   **d.** white
10. AVOCADO : PIT : : tomato :
    a. pie   **b.** leaf   **c.** seeds   **d.** stem

B. Each of these lists of words will make an analogy if the words are put in the proper order. Write each analogy.

11. easy, nicer, nice, easier   12. depot, airport, train, jet
13. Brazil, Egypt, Nile, Amazon   14. match, cut, knife, burn

C. For each of these relationships, create an analogy.

15. sport : equipment used in the sport
16. name of animal : name of meat from animal
17. a male relative : a female relative
18. name of state : name of state capital

Apply

D. 19.–24. Create six more verbal analogies, based on relationships of your own choosing. Exchange your analogies with a classmate. Can you figure out each other's analogies?

COMPOSITION

Lesson 8: Combining Sentences with Adjectives and Adverbs

Rebecca wrote these sentences in a descriptive paragraph.

1. December 26 in New Orleans was warm.
2. It was also damp.

How might Rebecca combine these two short sentences into a single sentence?

Think and Discuss

You can combine short sentences in many ways to write longer, more varied sentences. Study these examples.

3. The happy crowd surged through the French Quarter. They were excited.
4. The excited, happy crowd surged through the French Quarter.
5. The crowd, excited and happy, surged through the French Quarter.

In sentence 4 both *excited* and *happy* modify *crowd*. They are placed *before* the noun they modify and are separated by a comma. The adjectives in sentence 5, on the other hand, are placed *after* the word *crowd* and are joined by the conjunction *and*. Notice that in each case the combined sentences are more interesting than the short sentences in sentence 3. Sentences 7 and 8 illustrate varied improvements over sentence 6.

6. Politely we watched the painters in Jackson Square. We were eager to watch them.
7. We watched the painters in Jackson Square politely but eagerly.
8. Politely but eagerly we watched the painters in Jackson Square.

How did Rebecca change the underlined words in sentence 6 before they could be combined?

Practice

A. Combine each of these groups of sentences to form new sentences.

1. Pam and I walked happily down Bourbon Street. We were cheerful.
2. We gazed into the sunny courtyards behind the houses. They looked inviting.
3. An old woman was slowly sweeping one courtyard. She was being careful.
4. Several patient customers were waiting in the courtyard at Brennan's Restaurant. They were waiting quietly.
5. I bought a silver ring in a nearby shop. The ring was bright and shiny.

B. Follow the directions for combining these sentences. Change word forms whenever necessary.

6. Later we ate fresh croissants at the Cafe du Monde. They were delicious. (Write a simple sentence with two adjectives joined by a comma.)
7. Then we strolled lazily along the levee. We were contented. (Use two adverbs joined by *and* in the middle of a simple sentence.)
8. The Mississippi River flowed slowly. It is a majestic river. (Write a simple sentence in inverted order introduced by two adverbs.)
9. We watched a Swedish ship dock safely. It seemed secure. (Write a complex sentence with an introductory dependent clause and two adverbs joined by *and* in the independent clause.)
10. Finally Pam's mom took us back to the motel. We were tired girls, but we were happy. (Write a compound sentence joined by a semicolon and with two adjectives joined by a comma in one of the clauses.)

Apply

C. 11.–20. Finish the story of Pam and Rebecca by describing the wintry weather they faced when they got back to Minneapolis on January 2. Write ten varied sentences by combining adjectives and adverbs.

Lesson 9: Writing Descriptive Paragraphs (Character Sketch)

Mr. Greenwald asked each student in his class to write a paragraph describing a person each knew well. Read Lillian's paragraph.

> My grandfather was a handsome man. He was not very tall, but he had bright blue eyes and a full head of white hair. He smiled a lot, especially while he was eating a plateful of my grandmother's beef ragoût or nibbling on a chunk of maple sugar from his family's farm in Quebec.

Mr. Greenwald told Lillian that her paragraph had some good points but that improvements could be made. What improvements would you suggest?

Think and Discuss

Descriptive paragraphs help readers to visualize, or see, whatever is being described. When you describe people, you should include both their *physical* characteristics and their *personality* traits. In that way your readers will be able to imagine not only what the person looks like, but also how the person acts and thinks. Such studies of people are called **character sketches.**

Lillian's character sketch of her grandfather started out well. By the time she had reached her third sentence, however, she had veered away from her topic and had begun discussing food. Lillian also realized that her character sketch was not vivid enough. Read Lillian's improved character sketch.

> My grandfather was a handsome man. The first thing most people noticed about him was his full head of snowy white hair. He always wore it parted in the middle, the way men did in the 1920's. When he smiled, which was often, his wrinkled face reminded me of a sheet of paper that someone had crushed and then smoothed out again.

What two physical characteristics and one personality trait did Lillian use in her sketch? What words or phrases helped you visualize her grandfather?

Practice

A. Read this character sketch. Answer the questions that follow. Use complete sentences.

Miss Anderson was a tall, sturdy, white-haired woman who ruled her classroom like a kingdom. The ice-blue eyes that looked out at us from behind her rimless glasses told us that she would stand for no nonsense. In spite of her sternness, however, she was always fair and sincerely interested in our progress.

1. Name five physical characteristics described here.
2. Name three of Miss Anderson's personality traits.
3. What adjectives and adverbs contribute to the writer's description of the teacher's personality?

B. Read these brief descriptions. For each person named, write two or three descriptive sentences that will indicate the person's appearance and personality.

4. Karin: 9 years old; tiny for her age; short dark hair; timid smile; warming up for her ballet class
5. Roberto: 12 years old; heavy-set, wearing a softball outfit and carrying a glove; running to the field
6. Aunt Colleen: 40 years old; freckled from the sun; curly red hair; quick to laugh

Apply

C. 7. Write a character sketch about someone you know well. Include both physical characteristics and personality traits.

To Memorize

Use what talents you possess: the woods would be very silent if no birds sang there except those that sang best.

Henry Van Dyke

Is Henry Van Dyke here talking about real birds in a real forest, or does his thought have a larger meaning? State his thought in your own words.

Lesson 10: Writing Descriptive Paragraphs (Place and Thing)

Read these paragraphs. They are from a book called *A Walk in the Forest: The Woodlands of North America.*

A forest feels very different from a city or a town or even from a big field on a cloudy day. When you walk into a forest you are suddenly shut away from the rest of the world. In summer the air in a forest is cooler and less dry than the air outside the forest. There is a leafy roof over your head, and under your feet the ground is soft. Your toes sink into it almost as if you were walking on a sponge.

You notice the air in a forest. It seems to have a shape, formed by the tall tree trunks growing close together. Tiny specks of dust drift in the golden streams of sunlight. The air curls under a fern frond and into the folds of a flower. It smells of leaf mold in one place, pine needles in another; here, some dusty ferns, and there, a mushroom that has been kicked over.

Albert List, Jr., and Ilka List

These paragraphs were written to tell what a forest feels like. Which adjectives help you to experience it?

Think and Discuss

Paragraphs that describe places and things require a different approach than character sketches. In describing scenes or objects, the five senses of touch, hearing, sight, taste, and smell are emphasized. The words that express such sense experiences are called **sensory words.**

Although most sensory words are adjectives and adverbs, nouns and verbs can also call to mind sights, smells, and feelings. Notice the verb *shut away* in the first paragraph. It gives a sense of apartness, of being closed in, of being alone. What other verbs in the two paragraphs call forth sensory experiences?

Sometimes phrases that compare a known with an unknown experience can help you to describe a scene or an object. **Figures of speech** such as similes or metaphors, which you encountered in Unit 2, can often be of use. Notice the simile *as if you were walking on a sponge* in paragraph 1. Since you know what a sponge would feel like if you had stepped on it, the simile makes you understand what the soft ground in the forest feels like.

As you attempt to describe sensory experiences in your descriptive paragraphs, use adjectives, adverbs, nouns, verbs, and figures of speech, but do not overdo it. Choose your words carefully, and keep a thesaurus handy to help you select the most appropriate words. Now read this paragraph that describes an object.

A seed that has just begun to sprout looks very much like a tiny, flat pebble with several small strings attached to it. The hard, outside covering called the seed coat ranges in color from greenish-gray to black. One surface has split open, and from within emerge the tiny wisps of tissue that are the beginnings of new roots. In the weeks and months that follow, the seed coat will wither and fall away, while the translucent root tendrils grow strong, anchoring the unfolding new plant to the nourishing soil.

This description lends itself most to the sense of sight. Which words in the paragraph help you to visualize the germinating seed?

Practice

A. Read these topic sentences. Copy the detail sentences that support each topic sentence and that might be included in a descriptive paragraph.

1. You feel very alone in the forest.
   a. The green canopy blocks all view of the road.
   b. The only sound is the shifting of the leaves and the whisper of your feet on the path.
   c. The smell of pine needles reminds you of winter.
2. The forest affects me like a mystery.
   a. The light is cool, green, and eerie.
   b. In the morning you can hear a joyful chorus of birds.
   c. Trees creak and twigs snap for no apparent reason.
   d. Animals scurry underfoot, unseen.
3. In winter the deciduous forest is gray and desolate.
   a. The trees stand gaunt and leafless against the sky.
   b. The ground is frozen hard and spotted with snow.
   c. Animals that in summer seemed to scurry into hiding at every step are coldly, absolutely silent.
   d. The snow sparkles like jewels.

Apply

B. 4. In a paragraph describe a natural setting that has a strong effect on you. In a second paragraph describe one aspect, or feature, of that setting. One of these suggestions may help.

Describe an ocean or beach you have visited. In a second paragraph describe the sand under your feet.

Describe a view seen from a high point in your area. In a second paragraph describe an object in that view.

Describe a river or other body of water with which you are familiar. In a second paragraph describe an obstruction in the water such as a clump of rocks or a fallen log.

A Challenge

Imagine that you are a young ant and that you have just attended your first picnic. You are eager to describe the smells, tastes, sights, and sounds of that event to your friends. Keeping an ant's-eye point of view, write a description of the great feast.

Lesson 11: Editing a Descriptive Paragraph

Jessie wrote this paragraph about a vacation cottage where she spends every summer. After reading the paragraph, she edited it to make her description more vivid.

Editing Marks

≡ capitalize

⊙ make a period

∧ add something

⋏ add a comma

⋎ add quotation marks

ℐ take something away

○ spell correctly

⌘ indent the paragraph

/ make a lowercase letter

∿ tr transpose

> What I like best about the cottage at Bridgewell is its closeness to the sea. There, at night, I can lie in bed and hear the *crash* sound of the *surf* water on the beach and the *grating sound* noise of pebbles being pulled out to sea by the *retreating* sea *smelling of bluefish, kelp, and wet sand* waves. Breezes *feel* cool against my sunburned skin. During the day I spend hours on the rocks by the shore watching the waves *break*. There, with the *strident cries* sounds of the sea gulls in my ears and the *rolling surf* waves at my feet, I am *content* happy.

Think and Discuss

When Jessie realized that her words were not vivid enough, she consulted her thesaurus for synonyms that would appeal to the senses. Whereas the words *sound, water,* and *noise* in sentence 2 were grammatically correct, the words *crash, surf,* and *grating sound* were superior from a descriptive point of view. Seeing that she had used the word *sound* again in sentence 5, Jessie looked through the thesaurus for words that would better describe the sea gulls' calls. The words *strident cries* were a major improvement over the original.

Just as she added vivid words to the paragraph, Jessie also looked for places to trim unnecessary words. Notice that in sentence 3 the phrase *feel cool against* was cut to be replaced by *cool* as a verb. Although removing the word *happy* from the same sentence did not shorten it, changing the word to *content* (with a slightly different shade of meaning) made it more exact.

To what sense do the added words in sentence 3 appeal? What other senses are evoked, or called up, by the paragraph?

Practice

A. **1.** Rewrite Jessie's paragraph, making the changes she indicated in her editing work.

B. Read these sentences from descriptive paragraphs. Make them more effective by adding specific details that appeal to the senses. (For example, instead of saying, "The house was very old," you might explain why it *looked* old or *smelled* old). If you wish, continue your description in one or more additional sentences.

    2. The house was very old.
    3. The doctor's waiting room was drab.
    4. It was a very modern theatre.
    5. This department store is very modern.
    6. The skyline was impressive.
    7. The disco is a noisy place.
    8. The hotel lobby is luxurious.
    9. The country road we chose was scenic.

Apply

C. **10.** Edit the paragraphs that you wrote in Lessons 9 and 10. Where appropriate, improve your sentences by adding specific details that appeal to the senses. Use editing marks to make all additions and corrections.

MECHANICS PRACTICE

Writing Days, Months, Holidays, and Historical Events

- Capitalize all proper nouns and adjectives, including the names of days, months, holidays, historical events, ethnic groups, and languages.

   World War I, New Year's Day, the Croatians, English

- In general, write out the names of centuries. If figures are used instead, add an apostrophe and an *s* after the date. Some special eras are capitalized.

   the eighteenth century, the 1500's, the Middle Ages

A. Capitalize and punctuate these sentences correctly.

1. Our history class meets on mondays and wednesdays.
2. Catullus was a poet of the golden age of rome.
3. The language of athens was greek; the language of rome was latin.
4. Some history books say that the dark ages extended from the fifth to the tenth centuries.
5. Other books list this period as the early middle ages.
6. The renaissance flowered in italy during the fourteenth and fifteenth centuries.
7. During this time the people did not think of themselves so much as italians, but rather as florentines or venetians.
8. The english, french, and german kingdoms grew strong during the sixteenth century.
9. Since 1789 the french have celebrated bastille day as a holiday.
10. The industrial revolution took place during the modern era, the 1800's.
11. In 1871 william I was crowned german kaiser in the french city of versailles.
12. At the united nations translators help french-speaking, chinese-speaking, and swedish-speaking diplomats to understand one another.

B. 13.–20.   Take out a sheet of paper and close your book. Copy the sentences that your teacher will now read aloud. Be especially careful to make your capitalization correct.

LITERATURE

Lesson 12: Reading a Narrative Poem

A poem can tell a story in a vivid and dramatic way. Read this first verse from "Lochinvar," a poem by Sir Walter Scott.

> O, young Lochinvar is come out of the west,
> Through all the wide Border his steed was the best;
> And, save his good broadsword, he weapons had none.
> He rode all unarmed, and he rode all alone.
> So faithful in love, and so dauntless in war,
> There never was knight like the young Lochinvar.

What is the rhyme scheme of this verse? What does this verse tell you about the personality of Lochinvar?

Think and Discuss

A poem that tells a story is called a **narrative poem.** The rhyme scheme in many narrative poems is strong. Is the rhythm of "Lochinvar" easy to recognize? Each line has four accented beats, each of which is separated by two unaccented beats. The rhythm, in fact, purposely imitates the galloping of a horse, for a dramatic escape on horseback is part of this narrative poem. Like "Lochinvar," many narrative poems also have a distinct rhythm.

Many narrative poems tell stories filled with heroic adventure and strong emotional themes such as love, justice, daring, charity, or patriotism. The first stanza of "Lochinvar" sets the scene for courageous, daring action that Lochinvar undertakes for the sake of his beloved Ellen.

These characteristics of narrative poetry—clear rhyme scheme and rhythm, heroic action, and strong emotional themes—have become so traditional, so expected, that some poets have used them to achieve a humorous effect. Read this poem.

Casey at the Bat

by Ernest Lawrence Thayer

The outlook wasn't brilliant for the Mudville nine that day;
The score stood four to two with but one inning more to play.
And then when Cooney died at first and Barrows did the same,
A sickly silence fell upon the patrons of the game.

A straggling few got up to go in deep despair. The rest
Clung to the hope which springs eternal in the human breast;
They thought if only Casey could but get a whack at that—
We'd put up even money now with Casey at the bat.

But Flynn preceded Casey, as did also Jimmy Blake,
And the former was a lulu and the latter was a cake;
So upon that stricken multitude grim melancholy sat,
For there seemed but little chance of Casey's getting to the bat.

But Flynn let drive a single, to the wonderment of all,
And Blake, the much despisèd, tore the cover off the ball;
And when the dust had lifted, and the men saw what had occurred,
There was Jimmy safe at second and Flynn a-hugging third.

Then from five thousand throats and more there rose a lusty yell;
It rumbled through the valley, it rattled in the dell;
It knocked upon the mountain and recoiled upon the flat,
For Casey, mighty Casey, was advancing to the bat.

There was ease in Casey's manner as he stepped into his place;
There was pride in Casey's bearing and a smile on Casey's face.
And when, responding to the cheers, he lightly doffed his hat,
No stranger in the crowd could doubt 'twas Casey at the bat.

Ten thousand eyes were on him as he rubbed his hands with dirt;
Five thousand tongues applauded when he wiped them on his shirt.
Then while the writhing pitcher ground the ball into his hip,
Defiance gleamed in Casey's eye, a sneer curled Casey's lip.

And now the leather-covered sphere came hurtling through the air,
And Casey stood a-watching it in haughty grandeur there.
Close by the sturdy batsman the ball unheeded sped—
"That ain't my style," said Casey. "Strike one," the umpire said.

From the benches, black with people, there went up a muffled roar,
Like the beating of the storm waves on a stern and distant shore.
"Kill him! Kill the umpire!" shouted someone on the stand;
And it's likely they'd have killed him had not Casey raised his hand.

With a smile of Christian charity great Casey's visage shone;
He stilled the rising tumult; he bade the game go on;
He signaled to the pitcher, and once more the spheroid flew;
But Casey still ignored it, and the umpire said, "Strike two."

"Fraud!" cried the maddened thousands, and the echo answered,
    "Fraud!"
But one scornful look from Casey and the audience was awed.
They saw his face grow stern and cold, they saw his muscles strain,
And they knew that Casey wouldn't let that ball go by again.

The sneer is gone from Casey's lip, his teeth are clenched in hate;
He pounds with cruel violence his bat upon the plate.
And now the pitcher holds the ball, and now he lets it go,
And now the air is shattered by the force of Casey's blow.

Oh, somewhere in this favored land the sun is shining bright;
The band is playing somewhere, and somewhere hearts are light,
And somewhere men are laughing, and somewhere children shout;
But there is no joy in Mudville—mighty Casey has struck out.

Pick any verse from this poem. What is its rhyme scheme?
Is the rhythm easy to find? What heroic action are you led to
expect? What are some strong emotional themes that you see
in "Casey at the Bat"?

Practice

A. Read these statements. Copy all of the true statements,
and correct the ones that are false.

1. The rhyme scheme and rhythm in many narrative poems
are very distinct.
2. All narrative poems are poems that tell stories.

3. All narrative poems are poems that tell stories of heroic adventure.
4. Courage is an example of a strong emotional theme that might appear in a narrative poem.
5. All narrative poems have the same rhythm.
6. Many narrative poems relate their events in a vivid, dramatic way.
7. "Casey at the Bat" tells the story of a much-respected baseball player.
8. "Casey at the Bat" fits the characteristics of a narrative poem.
9. Casey's home run saved the day for Mudville.

Apply

B. 10. Write a short narrative poem by telling the story of an adventure in verse. The rhyme scheme and rhythm should be clear, as should be the emotional theme or themes. You may wish to write a poem such as "Casey at the Bat" by making the reader expect one thing and then creating a humorous surprise ending.

A BOOK TO READ

Title: **Draw 50 Famous Cartoons**
Author: Lee J. Ames
Publisher: Doubleday

This is just one of a series of books designed to make an artist of anyone. No one can resist trying his or her hand at Mr. Ames's remarkable drawing books. Whether you like to sketch buildings, airplanes, spacecraft, animals, trucks, trains, dinosaurs, faces, or entire comic strips, you can learn to do a rather good job of drawing the very first time if you read and follow the artist's directions. What a way to illustrate that school report, create a personalized birthday card, design bulletin boards, or simply pass a few hours in rewarding relaxation! From the Empire State Building to the Taj Mahal, from a stegosaurus to a St. Bernard, from comics to canoes, this author, who once worked in the Walt Disney studios, leads you down a yellow-brick road to hours of sheer pleasure.

5 UNIT TEST

● **Common and Proper Adjectives** pages 162–163

Read this paragraph. Then copy the sentences that follow it, correctly completing each one.

For Maria winter was a painfully cruel season, seeping into her bones and settling into every crease and hollow of her aged body. At night the cold mercilessly invaded her room, whistling through the window cracks and screeching under her door, calling her by name. At these times she would lay shivering in her bed thinking forlornly of the cool Neapolitan nights she had known in her childhood. Why had she ever left the peaceful Italian hills where the air smelled of oranges and winter was only a short spell of rain?

1. There are: **a.** one **b.** two **c.** three proper adjectives in the paragraph.
2. The words: **a.** *cruel* and *crease* **b.** *painfully* and *aged* **c.** *cruel* and *aged* are examples of common adjectives in sentence 1.
3. In sentence 3 the adjective *cool* modifies the noun: **a.** *nights* **b.** *Neapolitan* **c.** *childhood*
4. There are: **a.** one **b.** two **c.** three common adjectives in sentence 4.
5. In sentence 2 a word that is usually used as a noun functions as a common descriptive adjective. That word is: **a.** *cold* **b.** *window* **c.** *door*.

● **Comparing with Adjectives** pages 164–165

Write the comparative and superlative degrees of these adjectives.

6. soft **7.** rich **8.** comfortable **9.** lonely **10.** trustworthy

● **Adverbs** pages 166–167

11.–15. Copy five adverbs from the paragraph about Maria. Next to each adverb write the word it modifies.

● **Comparing with Adverbs** pages 168–169

Copy these sentences, completing each with the correct form of the adverb in parentheses ( ).

16. _____ the snow began to fall. (slowly)
17. It fell _____ than had the rain. (silently)

18. Cars and people were covered _____ in areas where there was little protection. (fast)
19. Of our four pets my dog Frenchy _____ faced the snow. (bravely)
20. My mom drives _____ in the snow than my dad does. (confidently)

● **Using Adjectives and Adverbs**   pages 170–171

Copy these sentences. Indicate that you know whether the underlined word is an adjective or an adverb by drawing an arrow to the word it modifies.

21. Do you feel <u>well</u> enough to go out in the snow?
22. Donna had learned her lessons <u>well</u>.
23. It was <u>almost</u> dark by the time she returned.
24. "I feel wonderful," she said. "The cold air is <u>good</u> for me."
25. "I <u>really</u> like wintertime," she added.

● **Classifying Information**   pages 174–175

Copy these specific examples. Next to them write the category to which they belong.

1. perch, halibut, tuna, mackerel
2. Mars, Jupiter, Neptune, Pluto
3. Roosevelt, Harding, Madison, Jefferson
4. Atlantic, Pacific, Indian, Arctic
5. sonata, concerto, symphony, opera

Copy these general categories. Next to each write four examples.

6. poems   7. trees   8. rivers   9. flowers   10. islands

● **Verbal Analogies**   pages 176–177

Make each of these lists into an analogy using proper form.

11. children, golf, adults, hide-and-seek
12. anchor, tent, ship, peg
13. petal, tree, flower, leaf
14. skin, sound, touch, ear
15. Hartford, Texas, Austin, Connecticut

● **Combining Sentences**   pages 178–179

Combine each pair of short sentences into a longer, more varied sentence.

1. Winter in the Pacific Northwest is usually cold. It is often quite rainy too.
2. Clouds laden with moist air must rise to travel over the Cascade Mountains. The air is warm as well.
3. The clouds release their moisture as plentiful rain. This happens often.
4. Farther south in California it is rainy too. It is, however, much warmer.
5. The Great Plains lie open to blasts of Canadian air in winter. The air is freezing cold.

● Descriptive Paragraphs   pages 180–181, 182–184

Reread the descriptive paragraph about the old woman named Maria that appears at the top of page 192. Answer these questions.

6. Which words and phrases in the paragraph appeal to the sense of sight?
7. Which words and phrases appeal to the sense of hearing?
8. Which words and phrases appeal to the sense of touch?
9. Which words and phrases appeal to the sense of taste or smell?
10. What can you tell about Maria's personality based on this descriptive paragraph?

● Editing Descriptive Paragraphs   pages 185–186

11. Edit this descriptive paragraph to add sensory words.

The next morning I ran to my window to see how much snow had fallen during the night. Outside, the world was completely different. The hen house was almost completely covered with snow. Judging from the height of the hen house, nearly 3 feet of snow had fallen. Below my window I could see that Dad and Jimmy were already at work shoveling a path to the barn.

● Mechanics Practice   page 187

Capitalize and punctuate these sentences correctly.

14. Many people believe that winters were more severe during the 1300s and 1400s than they are now in the modern era.
15. Charles Dickens mentioned a particularly severe winter during the nineteenth century.
16. The ancient romans celebrated a special holiday called saturnalia during the wintertime.
17. In the canadian province of quebec, a special annual event takes place amid the snow and ice.
18. Both french and english residents of quebec celebrate what they call their winter festival.
19. It usually occurs during the month of january.
20. In the united states, february 2 1983 was celebrated as ground hog day.

Complete the statements that follow this narrative poem.

The Jumblies

They went to sea in a sieve, they did;
In a sieve they went to sea;
In spite of all their friends could say,
On a winter's morn, on a stormy day,
In a sieve they went to sea.
And when the sieve turned round and round,
And every one cried, "You'll all be drowned!"
They called aloud, "Our sieve ain't big;
But we don't care a button; we don't care a fig;
In a sieve we'll go to sea!"

The water it soon came in, it did;
The water it soon came in:
So, to keep them dry, they wrapped their feet
In a pinky paper all folded neat:
And they fastened it down with a pin.
And they passed the night in a crockery-jar;
And each of them said, "How wise we are!
Though the sky be dark, and the voyage be long,
Yet we never can think we were rash or wrong,
While round in our sieve we spin."

And in twenty years they all came back,—
In twenty years or more;
And every one said, "How tall they've grown!
For they've been to the Lakes, and the Torrible Zone,
And the hills of the Chankly Bore."
And they drank their health, and gave them a feast
Of dumplings made of beautiful yeast;
And every one said, "If we only live,
We, too, will go to sea in a sieve,
To the hills of the Chankly Bore."
Far and few, far and few,
Are the lands where the Jumblies live:
Their heads are green, and their hands are blue;
And they went to sea in a sieve.

Edward Lear

1. This poem tells the story of _____.
2. The _____ lines rhyme.

MAINTENANCE and REVIEW

Sentences   pages 2–3, 4–5, 6–7, 10–11, 12–13

Read these paragraphs. Then answer the questions that follow.

The Vikings, or Norsemen, were among the greatest shipbuilders of their time; in fact, they are well known for their invention of the *keel*. A long, narrow strip of wood attached to the underside of the ship, the keel reduced the rolling motion of the vessel. Thus it greatly improved the ship's speed and enabled it to go great distances without stopping for supplies. Most *knorrs,* or trading ships, sailed from Denmark, Norway, or Sweden to southern Europe with only the wind for power. On inland rivers, however, these huge ships were powered by as many as 15 pairs of oars.

Sailing in their magnificent ships, troops of Vikings traveled as far south as the Mediterranean Sea and as far west as Canada. Closer to their homeland, however, they made a number of attacks on England. Although the Viking warriors originally came to the island as invaders, many remained and settled there, strengthening the scattered tribes. William of Normandy, whose ancestors had been Vikings, finally united England in 1066. Of all the lands they reached, this small country in the North Atlantic felt the Vikings' influence most profoundly.

1. Copy the first paragraph. Draw one line under all complete subjects and two lines under all the complete predicates.
2. Copy the second paragraph. Draw one line under all simple or compound subjects and two lines under all simple or compound predicates.
3. Circle the only compound sentence in the selection.

Paragraphs   pages 42–43, 43–46, 47–49

4. Write the topic sentence of paragraph 1.
5. Write the topic sentence of paragraph 2.
6. Copy any sentence that does not support the main idea of the paragraph. If all sentences do support the main idea, write *correct*.

Nouns   pages 80–81, 82–83, 84–85, 88–89, 90–91

7. Copy the common nouns in paragraph 1. If a noun appears more than once, write it only the first time.
8. Copy *all* the proper nouns. If a noun appears more than once, write it only the first time.
9. Underline all the *plural* nouns in your answer to question 7.
10. Copy all the collective nouns in paragraphs 1 and 2.
11. Copy all the possessive nouns in paragraphs 1 and 2.
12. Copy all the appositives in paragraphs 1 and 2.

Verbs   pages 120–121, 122–123, 124–125, 126–127, 128–131

13. Copy all the action verbs in paragraph 2. Label each as *transitive* or *intransitive*.
14. Copy all the linking verbs in paragraph 1.
15. Copy all the verb phrases in paragraphs 1 and 2. Underline the main verb and circle the helping verb.

Write the principal parts of these verbs.

16. bring   17. run   18. hit   19. ride   20. help

Copy these sentences, completing each with the correct tense of the verb in parentheses ( ).

21. Carl Lorenson _____ (remember, present) his home in Sweden.
22. He _____ (come, past perfect) to the United States as a child of nine.
23. Carl _____ (sail, past perfect) on a large ship with hundreds of other passengers.
24. He _____ (say, present perfect) that he _____ (return, future) to Sweden someday.

Adjectives and Adverbs   pages 162–163, 164–165, 166–167, 168–169

25. Copy the adjectives, not including articles, in paragraph 1 on the Vikings. Write *positive, comparative,* or *superlative* after each adjective that can be compared.
26. Copy the adverbs in paragraph 1 on the Vikings. For each adverb that can be compared, write *positive, comparative,* or *superlative* after it.

LANGUAGE
Learning About
Complements

COMPOSITION
Writing to
Persuade

STUDY SKILLS
Word
Building

LITERATURE
Enjoying
Short Stories

When you studied verbs, you learned the word *transitive.*
This word comes from the Latin word *transire,* to go across.
A transitive verb "goes across" from a subject to an object,
which is a complement. In this unit you will learn about
different types of complements, including direct objects, indirect
objects, and predicate nominatives.

In Unit 6 you will discover how to build words with
prefixes, suffixes, and roots. Later in the unit you will write
a persuasive paragraph.

Often the plot of a short story involves persuasion. After
you read a short story, you may enjoy making up a story about
a person who is being persuasive and his or her effect on
others. Perhaps the pictures on the opposite page will give
you some ideas.

LANGUAGE

Lesson 1: Understanding Direct Objects

Read these sentences.

1. In the Dark Ages people needed.
2. The system of feudalism preserved.

What questions do sentences 1 and 2 leave unanswered?

Think and Discuss

Sentences 1 and 2 contain a subject and an action verb, but another sentence element is needed to complete the idea. You need to know what received the action named in the verbs. *Needed* and *preserved* are transitive verbs and they require a **complement**. A complement completes the thought begun by the subject and the verb. Transitive action verbs require a complement known as a **direct object**. Read these sentences.

3. In the Dark Ages people needed protection from their enemies.
4. The system of feudalism preserved order.

Sentences 3 and 4 answer the questions raised by sentences 1 and 2 because they contain direct objects. The word *protection* in sentence 3 answers the question, "What did the people need?" *Protection* is the direct object of the transitive verb *needed*. What is the direct object in sentence 4?

Read this sentence.

5. The Roman Empire had collapsed.

Sentence 5 does not contain a direct object. Why not?

- A **complement** completes the meaning begun by the subject and the verb.
- A **direct object** receives the action of a transitive verb or shows the result of the action.

Practice

A. Copy these sentences. Draw a line under each direct object. Some sentences contain more than one direct object.

1. The feudal contract was called a *fief.*
2. Under this contract a lord gave land and protection to a vassal.
3. The vassal, a fighting man, swore loyalty to his lord.
4. The vassals owed military service to the lord.
5. The vassal usually served the lord as a soldier for about 40 days a year.
6. The lord built castles and offered protection to the family of each vassal.
7. At this time bands of outlaws threatened the lives of unprotected people.

B. Copy these sentences. Draw two lines under each verb and write *transitive* or *intransitive* after each sentence. Circle each direct object. Not every sentence contains a direct object, and some may contain more than one.

8. An army of knights in shining armor fought very badly.
9. The knights lacked organization and a sense of military strategy.
10. At the sight of an enemy, they often charged ahead impetuously.
11. They seldom had a plan of attack.
12. They fought clumsily because of their heavy weapons and armor.
13. The knights of western Europe rarely obeyed orders.
14. The undisciplined knights often squabbled among themselves.
15. Better-organized enemies easily defeated them.

Apply

C. 16.–20. Imagine that you are a knight in feudal Europe. Write a paragraph about your life. Use a direct object in at least five sentences.

Lesson 2: Understanding Indirect Objects

Read these sentences.

1. Those cows give good milk.
2. Those cows give the farmer good milk.

What noun comes between the verb and the direct object in sentence 2?

Think and Discuss

The direct object in sentences 1 and 2 is *milk*. It tells what was given, and it is called a **direct object.**

The noun *farmer* in sentence 2 is an **indirect object.** It tells *to whom* the milk was given. Indirect objects are complements that tell *to whom, for whom, to what,* or *for what* the action of the sentence is performed.

It may be helpful to think of indirect objects as objects of the prepositions *to* or *for*. The preposition is not stated; it is understood. Thus, sentence 2 would be understood to read, ''Those cows give (to) the farmer good milk.''

An indirect object always appears before the direct object in a sentence. An indirect object can never appear in a sentence that does not contain a direct object.

A sentence can have more than one direct object or indirect object.

Read these sentences.

3. The farmer sold Jenny his old truck and car.
4. The farmer sold Jenny and Anne his old truck.
5. The farmer sold Jenny his old truck and Anne his car.

What are the direct objects in sentences 3–5? What are the indirect objects?

 • An **indirect object** tells to whom or for whom the action of the sentence is done.

Practice

A. Copy these sentences and draw two lines under each action verb. Then draw one line under each direct object and circle each indirect object. Not every sentence has an indirect object.

1. Jenny drove her truck to town.
2. She gave the grocer her order.
3. She bought Flip a bottle of dog shampoo.
4. Then she handed the clerk some money.
5. Later in the day, she gave the dog a bath.
6. The happily splashing dog gave Jenny a shower.
7. Meanwhile, Mike picked some apples.
8. Then he baked everyone an apple tart.
9. He offered the farmer one.
10. The farmer ate it quickly.

B. Copy and complete these sentences. Add a direct object if there is only one blank. Add an indirect object and a direct object if there are two blanks. (The objects may have modifiers.)

11. The farmer served _____ _____ every morning.
12. Then he fed _____ _____.
13. That hen lays _____ a week.
14. Mike plowed _____.
15. On hot days the farmer brought _____ _____.

Apply

C. **16.–25.** Write a paragraph about working at a real or an imaginary summer job away from home. Include an indirect object and a direct object in at least five of the sentences. Then underline the direct objects and circle the indirect objects.

A Challenge

Imagine that you are the manager of an intergalactic bazaar, where goods from hundreds of planets are bought and sold. Tell about an average day at your bazaar. Who bought what items, and for whom? You may make up nouns, but include indirect objects in some of your sentences.

Lesson 3: Understanding Predicate Nominatives

Read these sentences about a famous explorer.

1. Ferdinand Magellan offered the king of Spain his sailing skill.
2. Magellan discovered a famous strait.
3. He was a great explorer.

Which sentences have direct objects? Which sentence has an indirect object? What kind of verb is in sentence 3?

Think and Discuss

You have learned that a complement completes the meaning of a transitive action verb. *Offered* and *discovered* in sentences 1 and 2 are transitive action verbs. Sentence 1 has a direct object, *skill*, and an indirect object, *king*. Sentence 2 has a direct object, *strait*. The direct and indirect objects in these sentences complete the meaning of the verbs.

There is another kind of complement. It is called a **predicate nominative**. It is a noun that follows a linking verb and renames the subject of the sentence. The verb *was* in sentence 3 is a linking verb. Following the linking verb in the predicate is the noun *explorer*. *Explorer* refers to the same person as the subject of the sentence, *he*. The predicate nominative *explorer* is a complement that renames the subject and tells more about who or what *he* is.

Sentence 4 has a compound predicate nominative.

4. Originally, Magellan had been a Portuguese <u>sailor</u> and <u>navigator</u>.

Sailor and *navigator* follow the linking verb *had been* and rename the subject, *Magellan*.

>
> • A **predicate nominative** is a noun or pronoun that refers to the same person or thing as the subject of the sentence. The subject noun or pronoun and the predicate nominative are joined by a linking verb.

Practice

A. Copy these sentences. Draw one line under the subjects and predicate nominatives and circle the linking verbs.

1. Magellan's entire fleet was only five small ships.
2. Magellan's voyage across the Pacific was an important event in history.
3. The Pacific is the largest and deepest ocean.
4. The southern part of the Pacific is the South Seas.
5. Icebergs have never been a danger in the South Seas.
6. Many Pacific islands were volcanoes.
7. Others are low coral islands.
8. Today many of the islands have become tourist centers.
9. The deepest part of the Pacific is the Mariana Trench.
10. San Francisco has become a major port.

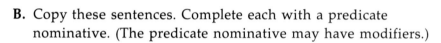

B. Copy these sentences. Complete each with a predicate nominative. (The predicate nominative may have modifiers.)

11. Ferdinand Magellan was _____.
12. *Victoria* and *Trinidad* were _____ of two of his ships.
13. The king of Spain became _____.
14. Magellan's voyage was _____.
15. The men on Magellan's crew were _____.

C. Read these sentences. Decide whether the underlined words are direct objects or predicate nominatives. Then write *direct object* or *predicate nominative* on your paper.

16. Charles I was the <u>king</u> of Spain.
17. Later he became <u>Holy Roman Emperor</u>.
18. He gave Magellan <u>ships</u> and <u>money</u>.
19. Magellan sailed his <u>ships</u> to the Pacific.
20. Magellan and his men became <u>heroes</u>.

Apply

D. 21.–30. Write a paragraph or two describing a real or imaginary voyage of discovery. Use linking verbs and predicate nominatives in ten of your sentences.

Lesson 4: Understanding Predicate Adjectives

Read these sentences.

1. Glenn was a guide.
2. Glenn was serious.

Which sentence has a predicate nominative? What is different about the other sentence?

Think and Discuss

The word *guide* in sentence 1 is a predicate nominative because it renames the subject, *Glenn.* The word *serious* in sentence 2 follows a linking verb and describes the subject. *Serious* is a **predicate adjective.**

Sentence 3 has a compound predicate adjective.

3. The bus looked <u>modern</u> and <u>clean</u>.

Modern and *clean* follow the linking verb *looked* and describe the subject, *bus.*

- A **predicate adjective** is an adjective that follows a linking verb and modifies the subject of the sentence.

All forms of *be* and the verbs *appear, seem, feel, become, look, sound, grow, smell,* and *taste* can be used as linking verbs with a predicate adjective. Remember that when verbs are used as linking verbs, they do not express action.

Practice

A. Copy these sentences. Draw one line under each subject and two lines under each linking verb. Circle each predicate adjective.

1. The ride to Bear Lake seemed endless.
2. Fortunately, the bus was comfortable and spotless.
3. The seats felt very soft.
4. The lunch stop was scenic.
5. The picnic area smelled woodsy.

6. Lunch tasted delicious to hungry sightseers.
7. Everyone was soon satisfied and happy.
8. The last part of the tour was especially interesting.
9. On our return the sky grew dark and gloomy.
10. The skyline looked threatening.

B. Copy these sentences. Complete them with predicate adjectives.

11. The guide was _____ .
12. Everyone felt _____ .
13. The captain seemed _____ .
14. The boat ride was _____ .
15. The air smelled _____ and _____ .

Apply

C. 16.–25. Write a paragraph or two about an imaginary trip with a group of people you do not know. Use at least ten linking verbs and predicate adjectives in your paragraphs.

HOW OUR LANGUAGE GROWS

One way in which language changes is by the creation of short words from longer ones. These short words are called *clipped words.* Sometimes both words remain in active use. *Attend,* for example, was shortened to *tend.* Both the clipped word and the longer word are used today, but they are not often thought of as being related. In other cases the longer word has disappeared as the clipped word has become more popular. *Cab* has come from *cabriolet* and *piano* from *pianoforte* in this way.

Some clipped words are at first considered to be slang terms. *Ad,* which once belonged to this group, is now considered by most people to be an acceptable short form of *advertisement.* Other clipped words, however, remain slang. While *professor* is considered conventional English, *prof* is not.

1. Look up these clipped words: *curio, bus, ruff, zoo.* From what longer word or words did each one come?
2. Can you think of any other shortened forms of words?

LANGUAGE REVIEW

Understanding Direct Objects   pages 200–201

Copy these sentences. Draw two lines under each action verb and one line under each direct object.

1. The Chinese played soccer in the third century B.C.
2. In 217 English soldiers celebrated a victory over Roman troops with a soccer game.
3. A picture shows a soccer game in Scotland in the seventeenth century.
4. The sport was called *football* for centuries.
5. The beginning of rugby football produced a great deal of confusion in names.
6. Finally the sport was named *soccer*.
7. In England a soccer player scored the fastest goal on record in 1958.
8. In 1964 another English soccer player matched that six-year-old record.
9. Each player scored a goal in only six seconds.
10. Brazilian player Pelé has scored as many as 139 goals in a single year.

Understanding Indirect Objects   pages 202–203

Copy these sentences. Draw two lines under each action verb and one line under each direct object. Circle the indirect objects.

11. Our neighbor baked Irene a birthday cake.
12. Two cousins brought her the ice cream.
13. Everyone gave Irene a silly gift.
14. Irene gave each guest a party hat.
15. My father sent her a surprise package.
16. The card with it wished Irene a happy year.
17. We sang her the birthday song.
18. Then the neighbor served everyone a slice of cake.
19. We handed her the empty plates.
20. After the party Irene sent her friends thank you notes.

Understanding Predicate Nominatives pages 204–205

Copy these sentences. Draw one line under the subjects and predicate nominatives. Draw two lines under the linking verbs.

21. Michelle is my best friend.
22. Last year she was the goalkeeper on our field hockey team.
23. She became captain yesterday.
24. My parents are team sponsors.
25. Everyone on our team is a good athlete.
26. Glenda is a fullback.
27. I am a forward.
28. Our coach was a college field-hockey star.
29. Our first game was a great success.
30. We will become champions.

Understanding Predicate Adjectives pages 206–207

Copy these sentences. Draw one line under each subject and two lines under each linking verb. Circle each predicate adjective.

31. The city was noisy and exciting.
32. Traffic noise sounded deafening.
33. The crowds of people seemed endless.
34. The stores looked inviting.
35. Smells from the bakeries were overpowering.
36. The street vendors were friendly.
37. The crowd at the street light grew restless.
38. Some people even became annoyed.
39. Others looked amused.
40. My visit to the city was memorable.

Applying Complements

41.–50. Write ten sentences about a real or imaginary camping trip. Use direct objects in five sentences and indirect objects in two of those sentences. Use predicate nominatives and predicate adjectives in the other five sentences. Proofread to be sure that capitalization, punctuation, and subject-verb agreement are correct.

STUDY SKILLS

Lesson 5: Using Prefixes

Notice the underlined words as you read this advertisement.

Bicycle race at noon today!
Bring your entry form or you will be
unable to compete.

Think and Discuss

Many English words are formed by adding syllables to the beginning of a base word. A **base word** is a complete word that has had no letter or syllables added to it. A syllable added to the beginning of a base word is known as a **prefix.**

> • A **prefix** is a syllable or syllables added to the beginning of a base word to change its meaning.

Study this chart of prefixes and their definitions. Notice how the prefixes give new meanings to the base words.

Prefix	Meaning	New Word
ante	before	**ante**room
anti	against, not	**anti**social
bi	two, twice	**bi**monthly
dis	undoing of, reverse of, not	**dis**honest
ex	former, out of	**ex**-governor, **ex**hale
extra	outside of	**extra**terrestrial
fore	before, in front	**fore**head
il	not (often before *l*)	**il**literate
im	not (often before *m*)	**im**mature, **im**polite
in	not	**in**active
ir	not (often before *r*)	**ir**responsible
inter	between, among, together	**inter**national
mis	wrong, bad	**mis**fortune
non	not	**non**fiction

Prefix	Meaning	New Word
over	too much, above, move lower	**over**heat, **over**throw
post	after	**post**war
pre	before	**pre**view
re	back, again	**re**call
semi	half, partly	**semi**circle
sub	under, below	**sub**way
tri	three	**tri**angle
un	not	**un**happy
uni	one	**uni**cellular

Notice that the prefix *ex* uses a hyphen when it means "former" but uses no hyphen when it means "out of."

Practice

A. Copy these words and circle their prefixes. Next to each word write its definition. Use the chart for help.

1. indefinite
2. illegal
3. rebuild
4. disappear
5. misbehave
6. nonsense
7. interact
8. subbasement
9. extraordinary
10. forearm
11. immobile
12. overflow
13. precooked
14. semiautomatic
15. postgraduate

B. Copy these sentences. Use a prefix from the chart to complete each one.

16. Elena had been the _____beaten bicycle champion for two years in a row.
17. She almost _____slept on the day of the race.
18. Anyone who was late would be _____qualified.
19. Her friend Lou was the _____president of the club.
20. He had the _____sight to call her before the race.
21. He _____minded her to wake up.
22. Some of the turns on the race course could be _____leading.
23. It would be _____possible, however, to miss the finish line.
24. The race was broadcast on the _____head speaker.
25. It would be _____broadcast on the radio that night.

Apply

C. 26.–35. Using a textbook, a newspaper, or a magazine, find ten words that use the prefixes listed in this lesson.

Lesson 6: Using Suffixes

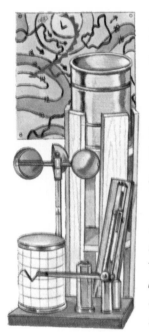

In the previous lesson you created new words by adding prefixes to the beginning of base words. You can also create words by adding syllables to the end of base words. Read these sentences and notice the underlined words.

1. Ira listened to the <u>dependable</u> weather reports.
2. He learned that the weather would be <u>cloudy</u>.

Name the base word in each underlined word. What syllable has been added to the end of each base word?

Think and Discuss

A syllable added to the end of a base word is called a **suffix.** A suffix usually changes the part of speech of a word and sometimes changes the word's meaning. For example, the base word *depend* in sentence 1 is a verb. The addition of the suffix *able* changes the word to an adjective. Name the part of speech of the word *cloud*. What part of speech does this word become after the suffix is added in sentence 2?

> • A **suffix** is a syllable or syllables added to the end of a base word. *Suffixes* change the way words are used as parts of speech.

Study this chart of common suffixes in which words have been grouped according to the new part of speech determined by the suffix.

	Suffix	New Word
	able, ible	break**able**, collaps**ible**
	en, n	gold**en**
	ful	power**ful**
Adjective-forming suffixes	ish	child**ish**
	ive	act**ive**
	less	hope**less**
	ous	joy**ous**
	y	ink**y**

Suffix	New Word

	Suffix	New Word
Noun-forming Suffixes	ance, ence	annoy**ance**, differ**ence**
	er, or	help**er**, conduct**or**
	ion, tion	act**ion**, reduc**tion**
	ism	hero**ism**
	ity, ty	authentic**ity**, certain**ty**
	ment	govern**ment**
	ness	rude**ness**
	self	her**self**
Verb-forming Suffixes	en, n	length**en**, whit**en**
	fy, ify	just**ify**
Adverb-forming Suffixes	ly	sad**ly**
	ward	back**ward**

How are words that end in *ment* often used in sentences? Notice that the suffixes *en* and *n* can form verbs and adjectives.

Practice

A. Copy these words and circle their suffixes. Next to each word write its part of speech. Use the chart for help.

1. modernize
2. kindness
3. bookkeeper
4. odorous
5. fashionable
6. rapidly
7. wooden
8. nullify
9. promotion
10. dependence
11. shorten
12. sideward
13. blameless
14. actor
15. useful

B. Copy these sentences. Complete them by using the suffixes on the chart in this lesson.

16. Ira gazed sky_____ for hours, it seemed.
17. He hoped that the storm_____ weather would soon pass.
18. How depressing this humid_____ was!
19. The broadcast_____ said that the rain would end short_____.
20. The peace seemed strange after the loud_____ of the storm.

Apply

C. 21.–30. Write ten sentences using at least one word from Practice A in each sentence.

What do the words in each group have in common?

1. microscope
   micrometer
   microfilm

2. autograph
   photograph
   telegraph

3. export
   import
   porter

Think and Discuss

You know that prefixes and suffixes can be added to base words to form new words. Another way to make new words is to combine word parts, called **roots.** A root is a part of a word that combines with prefixes, suffixes, and other roots to form a new word.

The word *microscope* in group 1 is an example of two roots being combined to form a new word. The root *micro* means "small," and the root *scope* means "see." *Microscope,* then, means "a device for seeing small things." The root *port* in group 3 means "carry," and the prefix *ex* means "out of." What does the word *export* mean? When the same root is combined with the noun-forming suffix *er,* the word *porter* is formed. What is a *porter?*

> • A **root** is a word part that can be combined with prefixes, suffixes, and other roots to form new words.

Study this chart of common roots and base words and the examples of new words that can be made from them.

Root	Meaning	New Word
aud, audio, audit	sound, hearing	**audit**orium
auto	self	**auto**graph
bio	life	**bio**graphy
dic, dict	say	**dict**ator
geo	earth	**geo**logy
gram, graph, grav	write	tele**gram, grav**en
kilo	thousand	**kilo**meter
log, logy	study	zoo**logy**
meter	measure	speedo**meter**
micro	small	**micro**wave

Root	Meaning	New Word
multi	many	**multi**colored
phone, phono	sound	**phono**logy
photo	light	**photo**graph
port	carry	**port**able
scope, scopy	see	micro**scope**
spec, spect	look	**spect**acle
tele	distant	**tele**gram
therm, thermo	heat	**thermo**meter
vis	face, see	**vis**age, **vis**ual
voc	call, voice	**voc**ation, **voc**al

Use this chart to give the definitions of all the words in groups 1 and 2 at the start of this lesson.

Practice

A. Copy these sentences. Underline all the words that contain roots listed on the chart. Then write the definition of each word that you underline.

1. Reporter Aretha Jones's telephone rang.
2. Aretha and the photographer rushed to their automobile.
3. They had to watch their speedometer as they raced to the blazing auditorium.
4. Aretha dictated her story after she interviewed some spectators.
5. She sent the story out on the teletypewriter that afternoon.

B. Copy these words and circle each root. Next to each word write another word containing the same root.

6. microwave
7. vocalize
8. inspection
9. predict
10. auditor
11. geophysics
12. archaeology
13. transport
14. photocopier
15. thermostat
16. vision
17. multinational
18. spectator
19. spectroscope
20. gravure

C. 21.–35. Study the words in Practice B. Take out a sheet of paper, and copy the words as your teacher reads them aloud.

Apply

D. 36.–45. Write ten sentences using words that contain the roots listed in this lesson.

Lesson 8: Using Compound Words

Notice the underlined words as you read these sentences.

1. Denise wanted to spend the summer <u>out-of-doors</u>.
2. She went to a ranch and slept in a <u>bunkhouse</u>.
3. A <u>crab apple</u> tree grew <u>outside</u> her <u>bedroom</u> window.

Think and Discuss

A word formed by combining two or more smaller words is called a **compound word.** The compound word *crab apple,* for example, is understood as a single word even though it is formed by combining two separate words. *Out-of-doors* and *bedroom* are examples of other compound words.

Different compound words are written in different ways. The words in an **open compound** are written as separate words. The words in a **hyphenated compound** are connected by hyphens. The words in a **closed compound** are written together. If you are not sure how to write a compound word, consult a dictionary.

> - A **compound word** consists of two or more words used as a single word.
> - An **open compound** is a compound word in which the words are written separately. (decimal point)
> - A **hyphenated compound** is a compound word connected by hyphens. (mother-in-law)
> - A **closed compound** is a compound word made of two words written together. (toothpaste)

Practice

A. Copy the compound words from these sentences. Write whether each one is an *open compound,* a *hyphenated compound,* or a *closed compound.*

1. Denise found that summertime was the perfect time to be in the countryside.
2. Everyone at the ranch hiked to the waterfall one afternoon.
3. One boy picked a bouquet of forget-me-nots and poison ivy.
4. Denise saw both a black widow and a daddy longlegs.
5. The hikers snacked on hard-boiled eggs and blueberries.

6. Denise ripped her knapsack on some barbed wire.
7. One of the ranch hands was a wonderful storyteller.
8. Everybody sat around the campfire to hear his tales.
9. He told the legend of the rattlesnake and the grizzly bear.
10. Denise sent a postcard to her sister and brother-in-law.

B. Match each word in the left-hand column with a word in the right-hand column to form a common closed compound.

11. grape	foot	
12. wind	vine	
13. up	dog	
14. corn	mother	
15. birth	day	
16. side	shield	
17. bare	writer	
18. type	field	
19. bull	walk	
20. grand	stairs	

Apply

C. Use each of these compound words in a sentence.

21. headlight	22. first-class	23. dial tone
24. spaceship	25. bull's-eye	26. high school
27. shoemaker	28. up-to-date	29. folk dance
30. beehive	31. attorney-at-law	32. ice cream
33. headquarters	34. run-down	35. ZIP code

To Memorize

If thou hast, of all the world's goods, but two loaves of bread remaining, sell one of them and buy hyacinths to feed thy soul.

Confucius

Confucius, a Chinese philosopher and teacher in the fifth and sixth centuries B.C., used the words *bread* and *hyacinths* to represent an important thought. What does it mean to "buy hyacinths to feed thy soul"?

COMPOSITION

Lesson 9: Writing a Persuasive Paragraph

Read this paragraph that Tamisha wrote about a problem in her town.

> I feel that the littering of our beaches must be stopped, for such littering has many undesirable consequences. Food scraps attract more birds and insects than would normally be at the beaches. Broken bottles pose a danger to people. The trash makes our beaches less attractive to the resort crowd, on whom our summer economy depends. If you have been on any beach lately, you know that littering is turning our town's biggest asset into a dump. We need to police our beaches and fine all litterers $50 or $100 — or whatever it takes to make them find a trash can.

What is Tamisha's purpose for this paragraph?

Think and Discuss

In some paragraphs the topic sentence expresses an opinion or states a position. The supporting sentences give reasons or evidence to support that opinion. The purpose of such a paragraph is to persuade the reader to think the way the writer does and possibly to take some action that the writer favors.

To be effective, a **persuasive paragraph** should end with a strong appeal to the reader. Therefore, when several reasons are given, the most important reason usually appears last. In Tamisha's paragraph the sentence about the economic effects of litter is the final reason given. Tamisha purposely placed it last, for she knew that most people would consider economic loss most important. The solution that she urges her readers to accept also involves economic loss. Tamisha knows that everyone will be concerned about the cost of a fine.

After Tamisha reread her paragraph, she decided to expand it by adding more details and giving each reason its own paragraph. As you read her revision, notice how she has supported her opinion. Her opinion and reasons are underlined.

Whether you are a resident of our town or a visitor, you cannot help but notice the large amount of litter on our beaches. This is a terrible situation. The littering of our beaches must be punished with a heavy fine, for such littering has many undesirable consequences.

For one thing, food scraps attract more birds and insects than would normally be at the beaches. Stroll down any beach and you will see swarms of wasps buzzing around discarded pieces of fruit and cans of soda. Sea gulls fight over half-eaten hot dogs. Many people complain about the numbers of birds and insects at the beaches, but few people connect the problem with their littering.

Broken bottles and rusty cans pose a danger too. People playing on the beaches, especially children, are liable to stumble over these dangerous objects. In fact the first-aid station at the main beach reported sending five people for tetanus shots and three people for stitches during this past summer as a result of such accidents.

Finally, the trash, which is especially heavy by the hotels, makes our beaches less attractive to the resort crowd. After all no one wants to pay for a vacation of walking through garbage and swatting flies. Our summer economy depends on these people, and it is important to keep them happy.

Littering is quickly turning our town's biggest asset into a dump. We need to police our beaches and fine all litterers $50 or $100 — or whatever it takes to make them find a trash can.

The sentence that expresses Tamisha's opinion contains a key word: *undesirable.* By showing in the next paragraphs just how littering made the beaches undesirable, she presented a good argument for imposing heavy fines on litterers. Notice that each reason was the topic sentence of a paragraph that supported Tamisha's opinion.

Practice

A. Copy these topic sentences for persuasive paragraphs. After each one write the *three* reasons that would best support it.

1. The police should take action against the double-parked cars in our neighborhood.
   a. Double-parked cars increase congestion in narrow streets.
   b. They make it unsafe for children to cross the street.
   c. A street full of such cars is ugly.
   d. Double-parked cars often block in the legally parked ones, producing loud horn-blowing and bad feelings.
2. You will benefit from the new cable TV company in town.
   a. The monthly subscription rate is not much more than that of going to a few movies.
   b. You will be able to see first-run movies before they come to TV.
   c. You will be able to watch stations from around the land.
   d. You will be able to see sports and specials that are not available on the networks.
3. You should finish high school even if it means temporarily sacrificing other goals.
   a. High school graduates find it easier to obtain a job than nongraduates do.
   b. Would you really want to miss your graduation ceremony?
   c. High school graduates are more quickly promoted than those who do not graduate.
   d. On the average, high school graduates earn significantly more money than nongraduates do.

Apply

B. 4. Write a persuasive paragraph on a topic about which you have a strong opinion, or choose one of the ideas in Practice A. Present three reasons to support your opinion.

Lesson 10: Editing a Persuasive Paragraph

Fletcher wanted to write an editorial for his school paper urging the school to offer first-aid courses. Read his opinion and the reasons he planned to give.

Opinion: Everyone should know basic first-aid techniques.

Reason 1: A person with knowledge of first aid can keep a victim calm before help arrives.

Reason 2: Knowledge of first aid can keep someone from having to pay for a visit to the doctor.

Reason 3: A person who knows first aid can save a victim's life.

Which of Fletcher's reasons is the strongest? Which of the reasons is the weakest?

Think and Discuss

Fletcher studied his outline and decided to replace his second reason before writing the first draft of his editorial. He knew that was not really incorrect, but he knew that he could find a more important reason to put in its place. Read the first draft of Fletcher's editorial. Notice what his three reasons are and which editing marks he has used to indicate other changes that he will make.

Editing Marks

≡ capitalize
⊙ make a period
∧ add something
⩟ add a comma
⩣ add quotation marks
℘ take something away
◯ spell correctly
¶ indent the paragraph
/ make a lowercase letter
∿ tr transpose

During this time of year∧the academic office
schedules after-school courses for the next year. I
believe that∧a course should be added: first aid.
Everyone∧should know∧first aid teckniques.
an important
, after all,   *basic*   *techniques*

A person with knowledge of first aid can keep a
victim calm∧before help arrives. Nervous movement can
make a victim's injuries worse.∧Someone with even
limited first aid knowledge close at hand will∧
reassure a victim and keep him or her still.
until professional
Having
help to

Second, someone with training can give immediate
aid
∧ help to ∧ an injured person. A trained person can often
a victim ⊙
                                                    more
keep an injury from becoming ∧ serious. For example, a
person who knows how to apply first aid to a burn can
prevent infection from setting in.

The most important reason for knowing first aid
techniques
(teckniques), however, ∧ is because that knowledge can save
a person's life. My family was (recently) eating at a
restaurant   TR
(restaraunt) when a man at a (near-by) table started
                                        nearby
choking. All around us people looked on ∧ not knowing
what to do. My Mother then jumped up, ran over to the
                            Heimlich maneuver
man, performed the (Himelick manuver), and saved his
                            the technique
life. She had learned ∧ it in a first aid class.
I hope that
∧ Hopefully the academic office will consider the
need for a first aid class after school next year.
The results could be a matter of life or death.

What reason has Fletcher added? Where in this editorial
has he placed his opinion? Each of Fletcher's three reasons
has become a topic sentence in this editorial, but one of them
is restated in his concluding paragraph. Why does he use the
phrase "life or death" at the end? Because of the revisions
he has made, Fletcher has an effective editorial that contains
three strong, well-supported reasons.

Practice

A. Copy Fletcher's editorial, making the changes that he has
marked.

Apply

B. Reread the persuasive paragraph that you wrote in Lesson 9.
Is it effective? Are all of your reasons strong, and is each
one well supported? Edit that paragraph to make any
changes that you feel are necessary, and then rewrite it.

MECHANICS PRACTICE

Writing Dates and Times of Day

- Capitalize the name of a month.

    May   June   December

- When you write a date, place a comma between the day and the year. Do *not* place a comma between the month and the day.

    April 1, 1983
    February 12, 1809, is Lincoln's birth date.
    She arrived on April 2.

- Place a colon between the hour and the minute in the time of day.

    8:00   3:15   11:32

- Use capital letters and periods in writing the abbreviations A.M. and P.M.

    6 A.M.   7:45 A.M.   12:03 P.M.

A. Write these dates and times correctly.

1. 1127 pm
2. 706 pm
3. august 22 1946 at 5 am
4. september 3 2007
5. december 22 1066
6. 313 am
7. 1201 am
8. july 4 1776
9. february 2 1961

B. Rewrite these sentences. Use capital letters, commas, and colons where necessary.

10. On may 30 1959 my grandmother received a party invitation.
11. The party would begin on june 4 1959 at exactly 1000.
12. On june 3 1959 at 230 pm, Grandmother had her hair cut.
13. At 11 am on june 4, she purchased a present for her nephew.
14. She reached her nephew's house at 958 pm, june 4 1959.
15. When her nephew opened the door, Grandmother's watch said exactly 1000.
16. Lamar just smiled. The party had ended at 1130 am.
17. Grandmother visited with her sister until 1230 am june 5 1959.
18. Her nephew, however, had to go to bed at 1030 pm.
19. On june 6 1959 Grandmother slept late.
20. She awoke at 1020 am.

LITERATURE

Lesson 11: Reading a Short Story

A short story is a work of fiction. There are several genres, or kinds, of short stories. In this lesson you will read two short stories, both of the science-fiction genre. One of the stories, "Dry Spell," is set in the present; the other, "Zoo," is a tale of the future.

Think and Discuss

Short stories share many of the features of novels. Both literary forms have introductions, complications, and resolutions. In the short story these parts must unfold quickly. The **introduction,** in which the characters and setting are presented, must be brief; the **complication,** which follows, reveals the problem to be solved; and the **resolution** must succinctly bring everything to a close.

Zoo

by Edward D. Hoch

The children were always good during the month of August, especially when it began to get near the twenty-third. It was on this day that the great silver spaceship carrying Professor Hugo's Interplanetary Zoo settled down for its annual six-hour visit to the Chicago area.

Before daybreak the crowds would form, long lines of children and adults both, each one clutching his or her dollar, and waiting with wonderment to see what race of strange creatures the Professor had brought this year.

In the past they had sometimes been treated to three-legged creatures from Venus, or tall, thin men from Mars, or even snake-like horrors from somewhere more distant. This year, as the great round ship settled slowly to Earth in the huge tri-city parking area just outside of Chicago, they watched with awe as the sides slowly slid up to reveal the familiar barred cages. In them were some wild breed of nightmare — small, horse-like animals that moved with quick, jerking motions and constantly chattered in a high-pitched tongue. The citizens of Earth clustered around as Professor Hugo's crew quickly collected the waiting dollars, and soon the good Professor himself made an appearance, wearing his many-colored cape and top hat. "Peoples of Earth," he called into his microphone.

The crowd's noise died down and he continued. "Peoples of Earth, this year you see a real treat for your single dollar — the little-known horse-spider people of Kaan — brought to you across a million miles of space at great expense. Gather around, see them, study them, listen to them, tell your friends about them. But hurry! My ship can remain here only six hours!

And the crowds slowly filed by, at once horrified and fascinated by these strange creatures that looked like horses but ran up the walls of their cages like spiders. "This is certainly worth a dollar," one man remarked, hurrying away. "I'm going home to get the wife."

All day long it went like that, until ten thousand people had filed by the barred cages set into the side of the spaceship. Then, as the six-hour limit ran out, Professor Hugo once more took microphone in hand. "We must go now, but we will return next year on this date. And if you enjoyed our zoo this year, phone your friends in other cities about it. We will land in New York tomorrow, and next week on to London, Paris, Rome, Hong Kong, and Tokyo. Then on to other worlds!"

He waved farewell to them, and as the ship rose from the ground the Earth peoples agreed that this had been the very best Zoo yet. . . .

Some two months and three planets later, the silver ship of Professor Hugo settled at last onto the familiar jagged rocks of Kaan, and the queer horse-spider creatures filed quickly out of their cages. Professor Hugo was there to say a few parting words, and then they scurried away in a hundred different directions, seeking their homes among the rocks.

In one, the she-creature was happy to see the return of her husband and offspring. She babbled a greeting in the strange tongue and hurried to embrace them. "It was a long time you were gone. Was it good?"

The he-creature nodded. "The little one enjoyed it especially. We visited eight worlds and saw many things."

The little one ran up the wall of the cave. "On the place called Earth it was the best. The creatures there wear garments over their skins, and they walk on two legs."

"Isn't it dangerous?" asked the she-creature.

"No," her mate answered. "There are bars to protect us from them. We remain right in the ship. Next time you must come with us. It is well worth the nineteen commocs it costs."

And the little one nodded. "It was the best Zoo ever. . . ."

In "Zoo" there is a surprising resolution. It shows the zoo exhibit as the alien sees it, from its point of view. What do you think the author is trying to say about the aliens?

Dry Spell

by Bill Pronzini

The bane of all writers, John Kensington thought glumly, *whether they be poor and struggling or whether they be rich and famous, is the protracted dry spell.*

He sat staring at the blank sheet of yellow foolscap in his typewriter. His mind was as blank as that paper. Not a single idea, not a single line of writing that even remotely reached coherency in almost three weeks.

Sighing, Kensington pushed back his chair and got on his feet. He went to the small refrigerator in the kitchenette, opened his last can of soda, and took it to the old Morris chair that reposed near his desk.

I've got to some up with something, he thought. *The rent's due in another week, and if I don't get something down on that grocery bill I can forget about eating for a while.*

He let his mind wander. It seemed, however, to be wandering in circles. Nothing. Not even . . .

Wait a minute.

Now wait just a minute here.

The germ of something touched a remote corner of his brain. It was a mere fragment, evanescent, but he seized it the way a man dying of thirst would seize a dipper of water.

Grimly, he hung on. The fragment remained. Slowly, inexorably, it began to blossom.

Kensington sat bolt upright in the chair, his eyes wide open now, the soda forgotten. His fingertips tingled with excitement. The coming of the idea was a catharsis, releasing the tension which had been building within him for the past three weeks.

It would be a science fiction/fantasy story, he thought, probably a novella if he worked it properly. He moistened his lips. *Now, let's see . . .*

Suppose there's this race of aliens plotting to take over Earth, because it is a strategic planet in some kind of inter-galactic war they're involved in. Okay, okay, so it's hackneyed. There are ways to get around that, ways to play that aspect down.

These aliens have infiltrated Earth and set up some kind of base of operations, maybe up in the mountains somewhere. They're assembling a kind of penultimate cybernetic machine which, when fully completed, will have the power to erase all rational thought from the minds of humans, turning them into obsequious zombies. Wait now. Suppose these aliens have a portion of this machine already completed. This portion would be capable of reading, simultaneously, the thoughts of *every* human on Earth, and of categorizing those thoughts for the aliens to study. That way, if any human somehow happened to blunder on the scheme in one way or another—mental blundering as well as physical would have to be considered, what with clairvoyance and the emanation into space of thought waves, and the like—then the extraterrestrials would immediately know about it. And what they would do would be to train the full strength of this completed portion of the machine on that particular human, and with it eradicate all those thoughts endangering their project, thus insuring its safety.

Kensington was sweating a bit now, his forehead crinkled in deep thought.

Sure, he thought, *it's a touch far out. But if I handle it right, who knows? At least it's a good, workable idea, which is a lot better than nothing at all. Now, how am I going to save Earth from this fate? It has to be in some way that is totally plausible, not too gimmicky, and . . .*

All at once the answer popped into his mind. *It's perfect!* Kensington thought. *There's not a flaw in it!* He grinned hugely. *Those aliens wouldn't stand a chance if I set it up this way.*

He stood abruptly and started for his typewriter. The progression of the story was already flowing, plotting itself firmly in Kensington's mind.

He sat at the typewriter, excitement coursing through him because he knew, he could feel, that the dry spell was at an end. His fingers poised over the keys.

Quite suddenly, quite inexplicably, his mind went blank.

He pressed his forehead against the cool surface of his typewriter.

Why, he moaned silently, *why, oh why can't I come up with just one little story idea?*

In what ways are the resolutions of these stories similar? In what ways do they differ?

Practice

A. Answer each of the following questions, using complete sentences.

1. How many settings are there in "Zoo"?
2. What problem does the introduction of "Dry Spell" concern?
3. What happens in resolution of "Dry Spell"?
4. Which of the alien civilizations in these stories seems friendlier?
5. In which parts of both stories do you learn how the aliens feel about humans?
6. In which parts of both stories do humans underestimate the intelligence of the aliens?
7. On what planet is "Dry Spell" set?
8. On what planet does the resolution of "Zoo" take place?
9. What must you assume about the aliens in "Dry Spell"?

Apply

B. 10. Write a science-fiction short story set on the planet Earth, with an alien as the main character. Write the story from the alien's point of view. Be sure to have an introduction, a complication, and a resolution.

A BOOK TO READ

Title: **Catch Me a Colubus**
Author: Gerald Durrell
Publisher: The Viking Press

What exactly *is* a colubus? If it is something about which Gerald Durrell is writing, you can be sure it is an animal of some kind.

The colubus monkey is just one of the peculiar animals to appear in this book, written while the author was involved in finding endangered species for his Jersey Wildlife Preservation Trust. Durrell, in a light and amusing style, details his trips to Africa and Mexico and tells of his run-ins with animals and humans, both friendly and not so friendly.

6 UNIT TEST

● **Direct Objects**   pages 200–201

Number your paper 1–7. Next to each number write the letter of the underlined word or word group that is the direct object of the sentence.

1. The Shoshoni taught Sacajawea her first language.
   a   b   c

2. But while she was young, enemy Indians captured her.
         a   b   c

3. These Indians sold her to become a French trader's slave.
        a   b   c

4. In her captivity Sacajawea learned many languages.
         a   b   c

5. Later she used her skills as an interpreter.
        a   b   c

6. She guided the Lewis and Clark Expedition to the Pacific and back.
               a   b   c

7. Her relatives found food and horses for the explorers.
      a   b   c

● **Indirect Objects**   pages 202–203

Copy these sentences and underline each indirect object.

8. Jani and Stefan gave Jolene a surprise party.
9. They had passed their friends invitations a week earlier.
10. Jolene gave the crowd a look of shock, and then she laughed.
11. Jani gave Jolene a chess set.
12. She and Stefan then served their guests refreshments.
13. Everyone wished the star of the party a happy birthday.

● **Predicate Nominatives**   pages 204–205

Copy these sentences and underline each predicate nominative. Circle the word to which each predicate nominative refers.

14. My best friend was a budding magician.
15. Toby's first attempts at magic, however, seemed complete failures.

16. The rabbit-in-the-hat trick appeared an impossible trick to learn.
17. More practice was a necessity.
18. Toby worked hard and became an expert in no time.
19. Now Toby is a professional sleight-of-hand artist.

● Predicate Adjectives   pages 206–207

Copy these sentences and underline each predicate adjective.

20. The expression "white elephant" sounds odd, but its history is quite interesting.
21. The expression, in fact, is Siamese in tradition.
22. Albino elephants were sacred to the emperor of Siam, and none could be destroyed without his permission.
23. When someone had been discourteous to the emperor, he or she would receive a white elephant.
24. Destroying the beast was, of course, illegal, and caring for it often caused the person to become penniless.
25. Today the term refers to any gift that is unwanted.

● Prefixes   pages 210–211

Copy these words and circle their prefixes. Define each word.

1. nonessential	2. mistake	3. interplanetary
4. prejudge	5. foretell	6. irrational
7. submarine	8. ex-senator	9. triangular

● Suffixes   pages 212–213

Copy these words and circle their suffixes. Next to each word write its part of speech.

10. contentment	11. powerless	12. restrictive
13. wonderful	14. commuter	15. fortify
16. sincerely	17. advantageous	18. pollution

● Roots   pages 214–215

Copy these words and circle the root or roots from which each was built. Then write a definition for each word without using a dictionary.

19. thermography	20. television	21. invocation
22. predictable	23. disrespectful	24. phonograph

Compound Words   pages 216–217

Copy these definitions. Then choose a word from the column A and a word from the column B that, when made into a compound, fits each definition. Write each compound correctly next to its definition.

		A	**B**
25.	high into the air	tight	fashioned
26.	a recording of a TV program	make	high
27.	without emotion	old	bass
28.	cosmetics	video	fish
29.	oysters, clams, mussels	funny	tape
30.	the largest stringed instrument	double	up
31.	a one-piece work garment	cold	wad
32.	a nerve at the elbow	sky	bone
33.	having to do with former times	shell	one
34.	a miser	some	blooded
35.	any particular person	cover	alls

Persuasive Paragraphs   pages 218–220

1. Write a paragraph that will persuade someone to perform one of these actions.

run for Student Council   bake a loaf of bread
visit Hawaii   read your favorite book

Editing a Persuasive Paragraph   pages 221–222

2. Copy this mythical advertisement, making the corrections shown. What is the topic sentence of this advertisement.

¶ Friends, do you have trouble heating your *cottage* home during the winter? Are these dark ages really dark? This is Thrifty Theodoric here to tell you that what you need is a dragon. That's right, folks! Dragons are (economickal) *economical*: They are happy with hay and only an occasional cow or two. They are *also* fuel-efficient; why, a full-grown dragon will put out *every day* enough flame to keep you and your neighbor warm and happy. The best is yet to come: Friends, dragons live forever. You will never need to have yours (replased) *replaced* or (serviced) *serviced*. Stop in and see me, Thrifty (Theordoric) *Theodoric* today. I will not be undersold!

Writing Dates and Times of Day   page 223

Write these dates and times of day correctly.

3. 1001 am
4. march 8 2016
5. september 4 1783
6. 334 pm
7. april 26 1970
8. 916 am
9. january 2 1863 at 820 am
10. june 30 1944 at 1139 pm
11. may 16 1901 at 530 pm
12. july 20 1969 at 421 pm
13. november 9 1803
14. 1201 Am
15. february 29 1888
16. january 1 2001
17. 915 pM
18. august 5 1695
19. 145 am
20. 245 PM
21. oct. 31 1982 at 1130 pm
22. dec. 24 1968 at 950 pm
23. june 18 1942 at 526 am
24. may 1 1842 at 315 am
25. 1159 am.
26. february 7 1964
27. 1050 aM
28. 857 Pm.
29. march 30 1754
30. 645 am

Short Stories   pages 224–229

These sentences are taken from "Feathered Friend," a short story by Arthur C. Clarke. Write whether each sentence would fit best into the *introduction,* the *complication,* or the *resolution* of the story. In what order would you place the sentences?

1. I had a nagging headache, and vague memories of fitful, disturbed dreams.
2. To the best of my knowledge, there's never been a regulation that forbids one to keep pets in a space station.
3. "Where's Sven?" I asked, not very much caring.
4. He slowly opened his hand, and there lay a tiny bundle of yellow feathers, with two clenched claws sticking pathetically up into the air.
5. Don't ask me why Sven wanted a pet, or why he chose the one he did.
6. To our delighted surprise, she revived at once.
7. She gave her series of "Come to the cookhouse, boys" trills—then promptly keeled over again.
8. "I don't get it," lamented Sven.
9. So now, if you visit any space station, don't be surprised if you hear an inexplicable snatch of bird song.
10. "Jim! There's something wrong with the air! That's why Claribel's passed out. I've just remembered that miners used to carry canaries down to warn them of gas."

LANGUAGE
Learning About Pronouns

STUDY SKILLS
Using the Parts of a Book

COMPOSITION
Writing a Book Report

LITERATURE
Reading an Essay of Opinion

Imagine how inconvenient it would be if every time you talked or wrote about someone named *Mary Margaret Smithers* you had to repeat the name *Mary Margaret Smithers* instead of using the pronouns *she, her, hers,* and *herself*. In this unit you will study the correct use of pronouns.

Then too, imagine how inconvenient it would be if you had to read a whole book before you could find out whether it contained some information you needed. By using the table of contents and the index, you can learn about what a book contains and where to find what you are looking for.

Book reviews can also be helpful in suggesting the right book for your interests. It helps, however, to realize that a reviewer's opinion may be different from your own. Reading an essay of opinion will introduce you to a new form of persuasive literature. The essay in this unit will demonstrate how a good writer can use words effectively to persuade others to share his or her beliefs.

LANGUAGE

Lesson 1: Understanding Pronouns

Compare the two versions of this paragraph from a mystery story.

Paragraph 1

The door slammed shut behind Tisa, and Tisa found Tisa locked in the room. Tisa twisted the doorknob. Then Tisa kicked the door, but the door wouldn't budge. There were two windows in the room, but the two windows were boarded shut. Tisa wondered how Tisa could get out in time to tell the police chief about Tisa's discovery.

Paragraph 2

The door slammed shut behind Tisa, and <u>she</u> found <u>herself</u> locked in the room. <u>She</u> twisted the doorknob. Then <u>she</u> kicked the door, but <u>it</u> wouldn't budge. There were two windows in the room, but <u>they</u> were boarded shut. Tisa wondered how <u>she</u> could get out in time to tell the police chief about <u>her</u> discovery.

What is the difference between the first paragraph and the second? What explains the awkwardness in the first paragraph?

Think and Discuss

The underlined words in paragraph 2 are pronouns. A **pronoun** is a word used in place of a noun. Pronouns helped the writer of paragraph 2 avoid the uninteresting repetition in paragraph 1. The noun to which a pronoun refers is called its **antecedent.**

The door slammed shut behind Tisa, and <u>she</u> found herself locked in the room.

Pronouns change form to show **number** (singular, plural) and **gender** (male, female, neuter). Pronouns also change form to show whether the noun they stand for is the person speaking (**first person**), the person spoken to (**second person**), or the person or thing spoken of (**third person**). Here are some common pronouns.

	Singular	Plural
First Person	I, me, my, mine, myself	we, us, our, ours, ourselves
Second Person	you, your, yours, yourself	you, your, yours, yourselves
Third Person	he, him, his, himself, she, her, hers, herself, it, its, itself	they, them, their, theirs, themselves

> - A **pronoun** is a word used in place of one or more nouns.
> - The **antecedent** of a pronoun is the word to which that pronoun refers.
> - Pronouns must agree with the noun they replace in **number, gender,** and **person.**

Practice

A. Copy these sentences. Underline the antecedents of the pronouns. Draw an arrow from each pronoun to its antecedent.

1. Mystery stories have been written for hundreds of years, and they are always popular.
2. Sir Arthur Conan Doyle wrote the Sherlock Holmes mysteries; he is one of the best known writers of detective fiction.
3. Sherlock Holmes and his friend Dr. Watson solve many baffling mysteries.
4. At one point in "The Speckled Band," Holmes knows that he is in great danger.
5. Later, Holmes and Watson discover that their would-be attacker is a snake.
6. The mystery "The Hound of the Baskervilles" takes Holmes and Watson to Scotland where they face danger on the moors.
7. Holmes often finds that he must make life-or-death decisions.

B. Copy these sentences, completing each with a pronoun that agrees in person, number, and gender with its antecedent.

8. Agatha Christie wrote detective fiction into which _____ wove many strange characters.

9. Christie was known for _____ use of complicated plots.

10. Sometimes innocent people fall into situations that make _____ look guilty.

11. At the end of Christie's stories, however, _____ innocent characters go free and _____ guilty characters are caught.

12. Edgar Allan Poe was an American writer with several mystery stories to _____ credit.

13. Poe's mysteries are called "ratiocinative" because _____ involve complicated reasoning.

14. In "The Purloined Letter" a man places a stolen letter where _____ is least likely to be found.

15. The detective, Auguste Dupin, finally finds the letter where _____ has been in plain sight all along.

Apply

C. 16.–25. Write ten sentences about a mystery story that you have enjoyed. Use at least one pronoun in each sentence, and draw an arrow from the pronoun to its antecedent.

HOW OUR LANGUAGE GROWS

English has borrowed words from many other languages. The foods we eat show our word borrowing. The Native Americans gave us *succotash*. The Spanish contributed *chili*. Trade with Italy gave us *spaghetti*. Thanks to German we have *sauerkraut* and *pickle*. African languages brought us *yam* and *banana*.

Using a standard dictionary, look up each of these food words and tell from which language it was borrowed.

1. waffle	2. pastry	3. chow mein	4. smorgasbord
5. sherbet	6. coleslaw	7. sarsaparilla	8. cookie
9. tea	10. pizza	11. yogurt	12. burrito

Lesson 2: Understanding Subject and Object Pronouns

Read these sentences.

1. The secretary gave the principal a message.
2. The secretary was Mr. Watson.
3. The principal gave the mail to Mr. Watson.

What are the functions of the underlined words in sentences 1–3?

Think and Discuss

The underlined words in sentences 1–3 can be replaced by either subject or object pronouns.

When pronouns are used in the place of subjects, they are called **subject pronouns.** Here is a list of subject pronouns.

Subject Pronouns

	Singular	*Plural*
First Person	I	we
Second Person	you	you
Third Person	he, she, it	they

Reread sentences 1–3. In sentence 1 the complete subject *The secretary* can be replaced by the subject pronoun *He.*

4. He gave the principal a message.

In sentence 2 *Mr. Watson* is a predicate nominative. *Mr. Watson* can be replaced by the pronoun *he.* Notice that a subject pronoun must be used when the noun being replaced is a predicate nominative.

5. The secretary was he.

The subject pronoun must be used when a sentence has been shortened, leaving the last part understood.

6. Mr. Watson is taller than I.

In this sentence the verb *am* is understood. The pronoun *I* is therefore the subject of the understood verb *am.*

Subject pronouns also can be used to form contractions with helping verbs.

7. <u>He will</u> write a hall pass. <u>We will</u> thank him.
8. <u>He'll</u> write a hall pass. <u>We'll</u> thank him.

Object pronouns are pronouns that are used as object nouns. Here is a list of object pronouns.

Object Pronouns

	Singular	*Plural*
First Person	me	us
Second Person	you	you
Third Person	him, her, it	them

Object pronouns can be used as direct objects. In sentence 3 *the mail* can be replaced by the object pronoun *it*.

9. The principal gave <u>it</u> to Mr. Watson.

Object pronouns can function as indirect objects.

10. John gave Mr. Watson the key.
11. John gave <u>him</u> the key.

In sentence 3 *Mr. Watson* is the object of a preposition. An object pronoun is used when the noun it replaces is the object of a preposition.

12. The principal gave the mail to <u>him</u>.

A pronoun can be part of a compound subject, a compound object, or a compound predicate nominative.

13. John and <u>she</u> are helping the principal.
14. Erica saw the principal and <u>me</u>.
15. The hall monitors are Steve and <u>I</u>.

Note that when a pronoun is part of a compound with a noun, it follows the noun and has the same function in the sentence that the noun has.

Practice

A. Rewrite each of these sentences, using pronouns to replace the underlined noun or noun phrase. If the noun you are replacing is the subject, write *subject* after the sentence; if the noun is a predicate nominative, write *predicate nominative*.

1. Our new principal is <u>Mrs. Garcia</u>.
2. <u>Erica and the band</u> welcomed her to the school.
3. <u>Erica</u> made a speech.
4. <u>The speech</u> was interesting and amusing.
5. The drum major was <u>Endo</u>.

B. Rewrite these sentences, selecting the correct pronoun in parentheses ( ). After each sentence write *subject pronoun* or *object pronoun.*

6. Jack and (I, me) help run the school library.
7. Our work keeps (we, us) after school.
8. The librarian gave Jack and (I, me) some new books to put on the shelves.
9. She asked if a book had been dropped by Jack or (I, me).
10. Jack said, "It was (I, me)."

Apply

C. 11.–29. Write ten sentences about buying a gift and mailing it to someone. Then replace the nouns in the sentences with pronouns.

To Memorize

My definition of a free society is a society where it is safe to be unpopular.

Adlai Stevenson

It is often difficult to have an opinion or belief that is not shared by most people one knows. Why is it important for a society to be safe for the unpopular?

Lesson 3: Understanding Possessive Pronouns

Look at the underlined words as you read these sentences.

1. These are <u>our</u> pets.
   This is <u>my</u> cat.
   That is <u>your</u> canary.

2. These pets are <u>ours</u>.
   <u>Mine</u> is a cat.
   That canary is <u>yours</u>.

Think and Discuss

Personal pronouns have possessive forms that show ownership. The possessive pronouns in the first set of sentences (*our, my, your*) are always used as adjectives. Which nouns do they modify? The possessive pronouns in the second set of sentences (*ours, mine, yours*) are subjects or complements.

Possessive Pronouns That Modify Nouns

	Singular	Plural
First Person	my	our
Second Person	your	your
Third Person	his, her, its	their

Possessive Pronouns That Are Subjects or Complements

	Singular	Plural
First Person	mine	ours
Second Person	yours	yours
Third Person	his, hers	theirs

Never use apostrophes with possessive pronouns. For example, do not confuse *its* with the contraction *it's*. Remember that *it's* always means *it is*.

3. <u>It's</u> fun to have a pet cat.   (contraction for *it is*)
4. <u>Its</u> fur is silky.   (possessive pronoun)

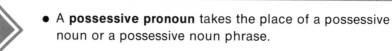

- A **possessive pronoun** takes the place of a possessive noun or a possessive noun phrase.

Practice

A. Rewrite these sentences. Substitute the correct form of the possessive pronoun for the underlined words.

1. That horse is <u>my horse</u>.
2. <u>The horse's</u> mane is pale gold.
3. The dog is <u>Jose's dog</u>.
4. The dog is <u>Jose's</u> favorite pet.
5. Alice's cat does not like <u>Pablo and Pilar's</u> cat.

B. Rewrite these sentences. Complete each one with a possessive pronoun.

6. Let's enter _____ pets in the pet show.
7. This entry form is _____.
8. _____ is on the table.
9. _____ boa constrictor is a sure winner.
10. _____ guinea pig won a prize last year.

C. Copy these sentences. Complete each one with the correct possessive pronoun or contraction.

11. The guinea pig licked (its, it's) paw.
12. (Its, It's) fur is brown and white.
13. The guinea pig was first imported from Guiana, but (its, it's) not really a pig.
14. (Your, You're) going to win a prize with that guinea pig.
15. (Your, You're) pet is the prettiest one I have seen.

D. 16.–25. Write the sentences that your teacher will now read aloud. Be sure to spell the possessive pronouns correctly.

Apply

E. 26.–35. Imagine that you and your friends have very unusual pets. Write ten sentences about your pets, using as many personal pronouns as you can. When you have finished, underline the personal pronouns.

A Challenge

Write a paragraph about an imaginary pet that might cause its owner some inconvenience. Use at least ten possessive pronouns in your paragraph.

Lesson 4: Using Reflexive, Intensive, and Demonstrative Pronouns

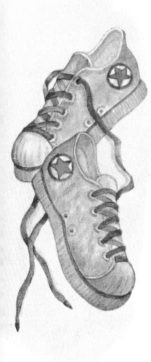

Read these sentences.

1. Lloyd prepared <u>himself</u> for the game.
2. <u>Those</u> are his favorite sneakers.

Think and Discuss

When *self* is added to some personal pronouns, **compound personal pronouns** are formed. Compound personal pronouns are called **reflexive pronouns** when they are used as direct objects, as indirect objects, and as objects of prepositions. They are called reflexive pronouns because they refer back to the subject. In sentence 1 the word *himself* is a reflexive pronoun that refers back to the subject *Lloyd*.

Compound personal pronouns are sometimes used for emphasis to intensify a noun or a pronoun. When they are used in this way, they are called **intensive pronouns.**

3. I <u>myself</u> scored the first points.

Compound Personal Pronouns

	Singular	*Plural*
First Person	myself	ourselves
Second Person	yourself	yourselves
Third Person	himself, herself, itself	themselves

Notice especially the words *himself* and *themselves*. Never say or write *hisself* or *theirselves*.

The pronouns *this, that, these,* and *those* point out particular people, places, or things. You will recall that these words can be used as adjectives in sentences such as these.

4. <u>This</u> game is exciting.
5. <u>These</u> seats are the best.

When they are used alone as in sentence 2, however, they are called **demonstrative pronouns.** The pronouns *this* and *these* point out things that are near. *That* and *those* point out things that are farther away.

6. <u>This</u> is my locker.
7. <u>That</u> is yours over there.

Never use the words *here* or *there* after a demonstrative pronoun.

> - A **reflexive pronoun** is a compound personal pronoun made with *self* that is used as a direct object, an indirect object, or an object of a preposition.
> - An **intensive pronoun** is a compound personal pronoun made with *self* that is used for emphasis to intensify a noun or a pronoun.
> - A **demonstrative pronoun** points out a particular person, place, or thing. The demonstrative pronouns are *this*, *that*, *these*, and *those*.

Practice

A. Copy these sentences. Complete each one with the correct reflexive pronoun. After each sentence identify the reflexive pronoun as a *direct object*, an *indirect object*, or an *object of a preposition*.

1. He hurt _____ when he fell.
2. We gave _____ a pep talk.
3. I gave _____ a last chance.
4. If the players try, they can help _____.
5. We were proud of _____.

B. Complete these sentences, using the correct reflexive, intensive, or demonstrative pronouns. Then write *reflexive, intensive,* or *demonstrative* after the sentence.

6. _____ is the biggest crowd we've ever had.
7. Libby congratulated _____ for selling all her tickets.
8. Coach Robins _____ threw out the first ball.
9. _____ in the next section are the noisiest fans in the gym.
10. We bought _____ some popcorn.

Apply

C. 11.–20. Write ten sentences about taking photos of a sports event. Use a reflexive, an intensive, or a demonstrative pronoun in each sentence. Underline the pronoun.

Lesson 5: Understanding Indefinite and Interrogative Pronouns

Read these sentences.

1. <u>Many</u> are coming to the camp picnic.
2. <u>Everyone</u> in our cabin is very excited.
3. <u>Who</u> is in charge of the food?

Think and Discuss

The words *many* and *everyone* in sentences 1 and 2 are called **indefinite pronouns** because they do not name a particular person or thing. Which indefinite pronoun is singular and which is plural? How can you tell?

Indefinite Pronouns

Singular			Plural	
all	everybody	none	all	many
another	everyone	no one	any	most
any	everything	one	both	several
anybody	most	some	few	some
each	neither	someone		
either	nobody	such		

When a singular individual pronoun is the subject of a sentence, use the singular form of the verb. When a plural indefinite pronoun is the subject, use the plural form of the verb.

The indefinite pronouns *all, any, most,* and *some* may be singular or plural, depending on the meaning of the sentence.

4. <u>All</u> of the food <u>is</u> gone. (singular)
5. <u>All</u> of the biscuits <u>were</u> good. (plural)

You know that a pronoun must agree with its antecedent in number and gender.

6. <u>Each</u> of the girls brought <u>her</u> canteen.

Sometimes you cannot be sure of the gender of the antecedent.

7. <u>Everybody</u> finished _____ work.

When the gender of the singular indefinite pronoun antecedent is unknown, use either *his or her* or change the antecedent to a plural and use the plural possessive pronoun *their.*

8. All of the people finished <u>their</u> work.

The *who* in sentence 3 is called an **interrogative pronoun** because it introduces a question. The words *who, whom, whose, what,* and *which* are interrogative pronouns when they introduce a question.

The pronoun *who* changes form according to its use. *Who* is used as the subject of a sentence. *Whom* is used as an object. The pronoun *who* is part of the contraction *who's,* which means *who is.* Do not confuse *who's* with the possessive pronoun *whose.*

> - An **indefinite pronoun** refers to any one or any number of people or things. It does not specify a particular person or thing.
> - The **interrogative pronouns** *who, whom, whose, what,* and *which* introduce questions.

Practice

A. Write these sentences, choosing the correct word in parentheses ( ).

1. Everyone at the picnic (like, likes) to eat.
2. Each of us carries (her, their) own lunch.
3. One of the tables (was, were) broken.
4. Some of the sandwiches (is, are) soggy.
5. The counselors asked (her, their) campers to clean up.

B. Write these sentences, choosing the correct interrogative pronoun in parentheses ( ).

6. By (who, whom) was the picnic announcement written?
7. (Who, Whom) said the picnic was going to be at the lake?
8. (Whose, Who's) going to go?
9. (Who, Whom) chose me to carry the firewood?
10. To (who, whom) did you give the matches?

Apply

C. 11.–15. Write ten sentences about a hike. Use five indefinite pronouns and five interrogative pronouns.

LANGUAGE REVIEW

Understanding Pronouns and Antecedents   pages 236–238

Complete these sentences using the correct pronoun in parentheses ( ).

1. Claudia gave (his, her, its) dog Ralph a bath late last Saturday afternoon.
2. Ralph was so unhappy about the bath that (he, she, it) howled the whole time.
3. The neighbors listened to (its, his, her) howls.
4. But (they, them, their) sympathy was with Claudia.
5. Claudia had (their, our, her) hands full.
6. (Them, They, Their) were full all right—full of Ralph and soap and fur!

Understanding Subject and Object Pronouns   pages 239–241

Write these sentences, selecting the correct pronoun in parentheses ( ).
After each sentence write *subject pronoun* or *object pronoun.*

7. Will you come skating with Paki and (I, me) at the new rink on Tremont Avenue?
8. Paki and (I, me) love to skate.
9. Who will help (they, them) clear the ice rink?
10. Please give Paki and (she, her) the shovels that are leaning against the wall over there.
11. (They, Them) will shovel the snow off the ice quickly.
12. Then (we, us) can skate all day.

Understanding Possessive Pronouns   pages 242–243

Write these sentences. Complete each one with a possessive pronoun. Use a different pronoun in each blank. After each sentence, tell whether the possessive pronoun is used as an *adjective,* a *subject,* or a *complement.*

13. Julia said that this costume is _____.
14. _____ is the one with the red skirt.
15. _____ costumes are finished.
16. _____ is almost ready.
17. Tia has the lead, and _____ costume, which was made by her father, is remarkably authentic.
18. I'm sure that everyone who sees it will find the play unforgettable because of _____ costumes!

Understanding Reflexive and Demonstrative Pronouns pages 244–245

Copy these sentences. Complete each one with the correct reflexive or demonstrative pronoun. Then write *reflexive* or *demonstrative* above the pronoun.

19. Jack, get _____ ready for some news.
20. Alma bought _____ a new bicycle.
21. Here, _____ is it!
22. _____ are the best wheels available.
23. She worked hard to earn the money by _____.
24. Her brother has promised _____ that he will buy a bicycle too.
25. He will have to get _____ a job.
26. _____ will not be easy to do.
27. Have you considered buying a new bicycle for _____?
28. _____ is a good idea!
29. I'll give _____ a present for my birthday.

Understanding Indefinite and Interrogative Pronouns pages 246–247

Rewrite these sentences, choosing the correct word in parentheses ( ). Then write *indefinite pronoun* or *interrogative pronoun.*

30. (Whose, Who's) the artist who painted this picture?
31. (No one, Many) seems to know.
32. (Someone, Both) is a good painter.
33. For (who, whom) was the picture painted?
34. (All, Any) of the students are trying to find out.
35. (Who, Whom) is the girl in the picture?
36. (Whose, Who's) interested in knowing that?
37. (One, Both) of us are sure of her identity.
38. It is Janet, and we know (who, whom) painted her.
39. Her sister Ellen is the artist (who, whom) we have been seeking.
40. Is there anyone (who's, whose) painting is better?

Applying Pronouns

41.–50. Imagine that you have just returned from another planet. Write ten sentences describing the people and places you have seen. Underline all the pronouns you use and tell what kind of pronoun each one is.

STUDY SKILLS

Lesson 6: Using the Front Matter

Tereza wanted to ask writers living in her state to read their works to the Poetry Society. In the reference section of the library, she located several books that listed writers.

One book was *Contemporary American Authors.* When Tereza looked at its copyright page, she saw that it had been published in 1940. She decided not to use it. Why?

Next she looked at *A Directory of American Poets and Fiction Writers.* It had a 1980 copyright. Its preface said it had been published "to help groups and individuals locate contemporary writers," and that it included "writers who perform their work." Where in the book would Tereza turn to see if writers are listed by state?

Think and Discuss

The pages numbered in small roman numerals are the **front matter** of a book. This includes the title page, copyright page, table of contents, and preface or foreword. It does not include the introduction, which is numbered as part of the main book.

- The **title page** gives the title, the author, the publisher, and the city or cities where the publisher is located.
- The **copyright page** always gives the name of the copyright holder, the copyright date, and the city where the book was printed. Usually it also gives an International Standard Book Number (ISBN, for ordering the book) and a Library of Congress Catalog Number.
- The **table of contents** lists the major features of the book such as chapters, unit divisions, maps, illustrations, and appendixes, with the page numbers on which they can be found.

- The **preface or foreword** explains things about the book such as how it came to be written or its value to the reader. The preface may be titled "Preface" or "To the Reader." In the preface the author often thanks those who helped him or her to create the book.

Open a book to the copyright page. You will notice that it is on the reverse of the title page. In addition to the basic information, it may give a facsimile catalog card, acknowledgment of previously published material included in the book, or the name of the printer. What is the difference between the printer and the publisher?

Practice

A. Use a book you have at your desk to answer the following questions. After each answer, tell where the information was or could be found: the title page, the copyright page, the preface, or the table of contents.

1. What is the title of the book?
2. What is the author's name (or the name of the editor)?
3. In what city does the publisher have its office?
4. Does the book contain maps?
5. How many chapters are in the book?
6. Are the chapters grouped into units?
7. What is the ISBN of the book?
8. What is the Library of Congress Catalog Number?
9. Who wrote the preface or foreword?
10. What is the title of the preface or foreword?
11. Does the author thank others for helping him or her?
12. Where was the book printed?

Apply

B. 13.–15. Choose three books from the library that are all on the same or similar subjects. Make a card for each book that gives the title, the author, the place where the publisher is located, the publisher's name, and the copyright date. Add to each card a brief description of the book, based only on reading the front matter.

Lesson 7: Using the Glossary and the Index

Lamont was reading a book about the Middle Ages for a school report. He wanted to find out whether the book had any information on the Bayeux Tapestry. First Lamont checked the table of contents. What do you think of his action?

Think and Discuss

Two places to look for specific information in a nonfiction book are the **index** and the **glossary** at the back of the book. The index lists nearly every piece of information in the book in alphabetical order. Following the index entry are the page numbers on which the information can be found and sometimes additional entries below it for illustrations or related topics. Look at this partial index page from Lamont's book.

Banners 65–68	**Bath, England** 105–107
decorative 65	commerce in 105
heraldry on (il) 67	history of (map) 106–107
of war 68	**Bayeux, France** 43–45
Barbarians 32–35	Bayeux Tapestry (il) 45
eastern 34–35	Norman invasion of . . 44–45
northern 32–34	William the Conqueror 43–44

According to this index, on what page will Lamont find information on the Bayeux Tapestry? What additional material will he find on the same page?

Like an index, a **glossary** is arranged in alphabetical order, but unlike the index, no page references are given. A glossary is a brief dictionary that contains words from the book that may not be familiar to the average reader. Each entry is listed in syllables often followed by a phonetic respelling, usually in parentheses. The part of speech and the various meanings of the word follow. Some glossaries also list the derivation, or language source, of each word. Look at this partial glossary.

sig·ni·fy (sig′ni fī), v. to be a sign of; to show or make
    known by a word, signal, or gesture.
sil·lock (si′lək), n. a kind of herring found in Scandinavian
    waters.
sin·is·ter (sin′əs tər), adj. left or left-handed (used during
    the Middle Ages); dishonest or underhanded; evil.
sire (sīr), n. a male parent; in earlier times, a man of rank or
    authority, especially the lord of a domain or realm.

Remember that a glossary is not a substitute for a dictionary
because of its limited number of entries.

Practice

A. Using the model index on page 252, answer these questions.

1. On what page can Lamont find information on the barbarian
   tribes of the eastern kingdoms?
2. What does the only map listed in the index show?
3. What other entries are listed under Bayeux besides the
   famous tapestry?
4. According to the listing for Bayeux, France, which of the
   related topics is discussed first in the text of the book?
5. On which page will Lamont find out what heraldry is?
6. Where would Lamont look for information on the tribes of
   Norway and Sweden?

B. Using the model glossary above, answer these questions.

7. What part of speech is the word *sillock*?
8. How many syllables are in the word *sire*?
9. Some glossary entries give the meanings of words as they
   are used in that particular book. Which words include
   special meanings not in current use?
10. How many meanings does the glossary give for the word
    signify?

Apply

C. 11. Using one of your textbooks, copy the first three entries
    from your first index page and the last two entries from
    your last glossary page. Then use the entry words in a
    humorous paragraph.

COMPOSITION

Lesson 8: Using Relative Pronouns to Combine Sentences

Read and compare these sentences.

1. About 400 years ago there was an African empire.
2. Its wealth and educational opportunities were remarkable.
3. About 400 years ago there was an African empire whose wealth and educational opportunities were remarkable.

As you can see, sentence 3 was formed by combining sentences 1 and 2. What word has been used to join them?

Think and Discuss

The word *whose* is a **relative pronoun.** A relative pronoun is used to introduce a group of words that refers to another noun or pronoun in the sentence. Such a group of words is known as a clause. The relative pronoun in sentence 3 is circled, and the clause that it introduces is underlined. The underlined clause is called an *adjective clause* because it modifies the word *empire;* it tells what kind of an empire it was.

Relative pronouns—the pronouns *that, which, who, whom,* and *whose*—are often used to combine sentences by introducing adjective clauses. Study the placement of the adjective clauses as you see how these sentences can be combined.

4. The Songhai Empire was a powerful trading state.
5. It stretched from Nigeria to the Atlantic Ocean.
6. The Songhai Empire, which stretched from Nigeria to the Atlantic Ocean, was a powerful trading state.
7. Askia the Great built Timbuktu, the capital.
8. He had been a general in the army of the empire's founder.
9. Askia the Great, who had been a general in the army of the empire's founder, built Timbuktu, the capital.

Where do the adjective clauses in these sentences appear?

Practice

A. Underline each adjective clause in these sentences. Circle the relative pronoun that introduces it and draw an arrow from the relative pronoun to the word it modifies.

1. Sonni Ali, who began as a common soldier, established the Songhai Empire in A.D. 1464.
2. Because he knew the importance of education, he took control of the University of Sankore, a center of study that was attended by students from Arabia and the Sudan.
3. The Songhai Empire, which covered more land than would Napoleon's someday, reached its peak under Askia Muhammad, who was called Askia the Great.
4. Askia was a leader whose early career had included service in Sonni Ali's army.
5. Askia unified his empire and expanded the trade that kept it alive.

B. Use a relative pronoun to combine each of these pairs of sentences. Be sure to punctuate your sentences properly.

6. Askia ruled a great empire. It was famous for its wealth.
7. In Timbuktu goods from North Africa were traded for goods from West Africa. Timbuktu became known as the "meeting point of camel and canoe."
8. Askia the Great was a generous, good-hearted ruler. He made his home in Timbuktu.
9. Abderrahaman Sadi el Timbuktu was a writer. His works describe the glory of that capital city.
10. Sadi's greatest work, the Tarishk el Sudan, describes a city. The city was filled with the coming and going of traders and students.

Apply

C. 11.–12. Write two paragraphs about the Songhai Empire. Your information may be based on research or on your own imagination. Include at least seven sentences that use relative pronouns.

Lesson 9: Writing a Book Report

Samantha wanted to tell her class about a book that she had read. Read the report that she wrote about it.

From the Mixed-up Files of Mrs. Basil E. Frankweiler

From the Mixed-up Files of Mrs. Basil E. Frankweiler was written and illustrated by E. L. Konigsburg. The novel tells the story of Claudia and Jamie, two suburban children who run away from home and hide in the Metropolitan Museum of Art in New York City. The children devise many clever strategies for living in the museum without getting caught by the guards, who are supposed to clear the museum of visitors every night.

One day they find a beautiful statue and attempt to trace its origin. Their search leads them to the home of Mrs. Basil E. Frankweiler, an 82-year-old art collector who is the former owner of the statue and the keeper of the mixed-up files named in the novel's title. She is a strong-minded woman who understands not only art but people. Mrs. Frankweiler helps Claudia and Jamie to answer their questions about the statue, but she also helps Claudia to answer some questions she had been asking about herself. The story is written from the point of view of Mrs. Frankweiler, as an account to her lawyer (who turns out to have a surprising relationship to the runaway children).

From the Mixed-up Files of Mrs. Basil E. Frankweiler deservedly won the John Newbery Medal, an annual award for a distinguished contribution to literature for young adult readers. It is a book that is full of humor, especially in its description of the relationship between the efficient and somewhat fussy Claudia and the penny-pinching Jamie. Their brother–sister relationship seems very realistic. The black-and-white drawings by the author add to the story's realism. The close calls of the two as they hide in bathrooms and under museum beds are both exciting and amusing. This novel, however, does have its serious side. Claudia comes to realize that she needs to learn from her experiences. How Claudia copes with this need is the main theme of the story. If you like humorous adventure stories that have a message, you will want to read <u>From the Mixed-up Files of Mrs. Basil E. Frankweiler</u>.

Think and Discuss

One way of sharing information about a book is to write a **book report.** A book report tells potential readers what the book is about, whether or not you liked the book, and why you have that opinion. By telling what kind of story it relates or what kind of information it develops, along with your opinion about how well it has been done, a book report will give potential readers the information they need to decide whether or not to read the book.

A book report can be divided into three sections. The first part names the author and title of the book and gives a summary of the book's plot. This section is called the **synopsis** of the book. If the book is fiction, the synopsis should include the setting, the main characters, and the nature of the action. The synopsis should not give the plot in detail; only a general account is necessary. Samantha's report tells what kind of adventure Claudia and Jamie had, but it does not tell everything that happened. If the book is nonfiction, the synopsis should tell what body of information is presented and the manner in which it is presented.

The **opinion** and **support** sections of a book report work closely together. State your opinion briefly. What is Samantha's opinion of the book she read? Then explain why you did or did not like the book. Try to make your reasons specific and to give examples from the book wherever possible. For example, "I thought that this was an amusing book" would not be a helpful comment; you should mention what is amusing about the book. What did Samantha mention as things that were amusing about her book? This last part of your book report may conclude with a brief restatement of your opinion.

Remember that when you are writing a book report you may note the elements of the book that did *not* satisfy you. If the events in an adventure story are not exciting, or if the subject of a biography does not come alive, you should say so and give reasons and examples to support your opinion.

Practice

A. Read this list of book titles and authors. For each book write two questions that you would want answered in a report about that book.

1. *A Wrinkle in Time* by Madeleine L'Engle
2. *The United States in World War II* by Don Lawson
3. *Kitty O'Neil: Daredevil Woman* by Karen Ireland
4. *The Cat Ate My Gymsuit* by Paula Danzinger
5. *My Friends the Wild Chimpanzees* by Jane van Lawick-Goodall

B. Copy these sentences. Next to each sentence write whether it would be part of the *synopsis,* the *opinion,* or the *support* section of a book report.

6. *Black Hawk* is the autobiography of a man who led the Sauk people some 150 years ago.
7. I found *A Face for Me* to be inspiring.
8. These dramatic moments add to the excitement of the book.
9. This book was illustrated by Garth Williams.
10. The science experiments were impossible to follow.
11. I doubt that you will find a more interesting book on Australia than this one.
12. What a warm and witty story this is!
13. Even though the characters in this novel have some fantastic adventures, they all remain quite believable.
14. This mystery was published in 1977.

Apply

C. 15. Write a book report about a fiction or nonfiction book that you have read recently. Make sure that your report contains all three sections, and try to use examples from the book itself as you write.

Lesson 10: Editing a Book Report

Hernando wrote a report on a book he had read. Read the first draft of his book report and note the changes that he has marked.

Nisei Daughter

Nisei Daughter is ~~a book by~~ *the autobiography of* Monica Sone, a Japanese-American. She is herself a nisei daughter—the daughter of Japanese ~~emigrants~~ *immigrants*, but born and educated in America. *In fact,* Monica thought of herself as an American until she was six years old. Then one evening her mother made an announcement. Since Monica (or Kazuko, as she was called as a child) was Japanese, she would have to attend a Japanese school. Kazuko was shocked. As she said, "I didn't see how I could be a Yankee and Japanese at the same time."

Kazuko's ~~battle~~ *struggle* to keep her Japanese heritage in her American ~~birthplace~~ *homeland* forms the theme of Nisei Daughter. We see Kazuko *grow older and* gradually learn that many people outside the Japanese community are suspicious of her, and we ~~feel~~ *share* her pain in realizing that to some people, being different is being dangerous. Kazuko, now out of high school, attends ~~scretarial~~ *secretarial* school, but her plans for working ~~are~~ *must be* put aside when she becomes ill. At a sanitarium she becomes friends with patients who make her feel proud to be a nisei. At the end of her stay, she says, "nothing could possibly go wrong now."

On December 7, 1941, something ~~went~~ *did go* wrong. After the start of World War II, Japanese throughout the West Coast were seen as a threat. Kazuko and her family find themselves among the thousands shipped off to

---

Editing Marks

≡ capitalize

⊙ make a period

∧ add something

⩓ add a comma

⩗ add quotation marks

℘ take something away

◯ spell correctly

¶ indent the paragraph

/ make a lowercase letter

∼ transpose
tr

Camp Minidoka. *which* ~~It~~ was one of the many relocation
camps set up *in the United States* for the Japanese. During her year there
Kazuko shows time and time again that she is proud to
have two heritages. When she leaves Minidoka to go to
work and then to college in the Midwest, she says, "
now I felt more like a whole person instead of a
sadly split personality. The Japanese and the American
parts of me were blended into one. "

It ~~The book~~ is full of humorous moments, such as *Kazuko* her
experiences at the Japanese school and later as a
dental assistant. It has some sadness in it too, as
when the family says good-by to their grandfather in
Japan. Monica Sone, however, blends the funny and sad
moments well; her style is easy to read.

TR (I heartily recommend Nisei Daughter.) TR

(A Nisei Daughter is a warm, inspiring book.)

Think and Discuss

Hernando's first draft included the synopsis and support
sections of a book report, but he failed to state his opinion
clearly. He added his opinion to the final paragraph. What mark
did he use to show the direct quotations from *Nisei Daughter*?
How many times did Hernando mark places to combine
sentences by using relative pronouns? In which paragraphs does
this kind of change appear?

Practice

A. Copy Hernando's report, making the changes that he
   indicated with editing marks.

Apply

B. Reread the book report you wrote for Lesson 9. Is it in the
   proper form? Mark any changes you wish to make, and then
   rewrite it.

MECHANICS PRACTICE

Writing Titles

- Capitalize the first word and all other important words in a title.

  ''This Land Is Your Land''   <u>Battle Beyond the Stars</u>

- Place quotation marks around titles of songs, articles, short stories, TV shows, chapters in books, and short poems.

  ''Hail and Farewell''   ''Stopping by Woods on a Snowy Evening''

- Underline titles of books, plays, newspapers, magazines, movies, records, works of art, musical compositions, and long poems.

  <u>The King and I</u>   <u>Dynamite</u>   <u>American Gothic</u>

A. Imagine that you are from a future time and are part of an archeological dig at a ruined library. Copy these sentences. Add capitalization, quotation marks, and underlining where needed.

1. The first room contained works of music and art; we found prints of whistler's mother, return of the hunters, and the sleeping gypsy, along with a photograph of Michelangelo's david, a statue that is now lost.
2. We found a record album, still intact, that contained Moussorgsky's pictures at an exhibition and Suppé's light cavalry overture.
3. I found the sheet music to the song take me home, country roads.
4. My brother found a book that contained Beowulf, an epic poem.
5. Then my father uncovered the periodicals room; he waved undamaged copies of better homes and gardens, time, and newsweek triumphantly.
6. As we paged through good housekeeping and gourmet, we saw articles such as 100 uses for turnips.
7. After we had opened the main reading room, I found a copy of great american poems and sat down to read paul revere's ride and fog.
8. In the vertical file my mother found scripts from the TV series star trek, the play the sound of music, and the movie superman.
9. We packed the novels moby dick and the pearl into a box.
10. We also packed a book that had such short stories as the open window and the necklace.

B. 11.–15. Write the sentences that your teacher will now read aloud.

LITERATURE

Lesson 11: Reading an Essay of Opinion

You know that a composition or an essay must have a recognizable introduction, body, and conclusion. What kind of information should be included in each section?

Think and Discuss

This essay comes from a book called *The Medusa and the Snail: More Notes of a Biology Watcher* by Lewis Thomas. Dr. Thomas delights in observing trends in science and relating them to human behavior. His essay "To Err Is Human" points out the positive side of our human ability to make mistakes.

To Err Is Human

Everyone must have had at least one personal experience with a computer error by this time. Bank balances are suddenly reported to have jumped from $379 into the millions, appeals for charitable contributions are mailed over and over to people with crazy-sounding names at your address, department stores send the wrong bills, utility companies write that they're turning everything off, that sort of thing. If you manage to get in touch with someone and complain, you then get instantaneously typed, guilty letters from the same computer, saying "Our computer was in error, and an adjustment is being made in your account."

These are supposed to be the sheerest, blindest accidents. Mistakes are not believed to be part of the normal behavior of a good machine. If things go wrong, it must be a personal, human error, the result of fingering, tampering, a button getting stuck, someone hitting the wrong key. The computer, at its normal best, is infallible.

Mistakes are at the very base of human thought. If we were not provided with the knack of being wrong, we could never get anything useful done. We think our way along by choosing between right and wrong alternatives, and the wrong choices have to be made as frequently as the right ones. We get along in life this way. We are built to make mistakes, coded for error.

A good laboratory, like a good bank or a corporation or government, has to run like a computer. Almost everything is done flawlessly, by the book, and all the numbers add up to the predicted sums. The days go by. And then, if it is a lucky day, and a lucky laboratory, somebody makes a mistake: the wrong buffer, something in one of the blanks, a decimal misplaced in reading counts, the warm room off by a degree and a half, a mouse out of his box, or just a misreading of the day's protocol. Whatever, when the results come in, something is obviously in error and then the action can begin.

The misreading is not the important error; it opens the way. The next step is the crucial one. If the investigator can bring himself to say, "But even so, look at that!" then the new finding, whatever it is, is ready for snatching. What is needed, for progress to be made, is the move based on the error. The capacity to leap across mountains of information to land lightly on the wrong side represents the highest of human endowments.

It may be that this is a uniquely human gift, perhaps even stipulated in our genetic instructions. Other creatures do not seem to have DNA sequences for making mistakes as a routine part of daily living, certainly not for programmed error as a guide for action.

We are at our human finest, dancing with our minds, when there are more choices than two. Sometimes there are ten, even twenty different ways to go, all but one bound to be wrong, and the richness of selection in such situations can lift us onto totally new ground. This process is called exploration and is based on human fallibility. If we had only a single center in our brains, capable of responding only when a correct decision was to be made, instead of the jumble of different, credulous, easily conned clusters of neurones that provide for being flung off into blind alleys, up trees, down dead ends, out into blue sky, along wrong turnings, around bends, we could only stay the way we are today, stuck fast.

We should have this in mind as we become dependent on more complex computers for the arrangement of our affairs. Give the computers their heads, I say; let them go their way. Think of what we could gain from the near infinity of precise, machine-made miscomputation which is now so easily within our grasp. We could begin the solving of some of our hardest problems. How, for instance, should we go about organizing ourselves for social living on a planetary scale, now that we have become, as a plain fact of life, a single community? We can assume, as a working hypothesis, that all the right ways of doing this are unworkable. What we need, then, for moving ahead, is a set of wrong alternatives much longer and more interesting than the short list of mistaken courses that any of us can think up right now. We need, in fact, an infinite list, and when it is printed out we need the computer to turn on itself and select, at random, the next way to go. If it is a big enough mistake, we could find ourselves on a new level, stunned, out in the clear, ready to move again.

Like all good essays, "To Err Is Human" can be divided into three recognizable parts. Where does each section begin and end?

An **essay of opinion** sets forth the writers ideas on a specific topic. Although its basic function is to *inform,* the element of *persuasion* is often present as well and it can be identified by key words such as *ought, must,* and *should.* In which part of this essay does Dr. Thomas try to persuade you to think as he does? What is it that he wants you to believe?

Formal writing, of which the serious essay is an example, is usually made up of a variety of sentences, many long and some short. Note how well this is done in the fourth paragraph by comparing the length of sentences 3 and 4.

Formal writing also lends itself to figures of speech. Notice the poetic use of *personification* in "dancing with our minds" in the seventh paragraph. Look, too, at the beautiful *repetition* of six prepositional phrases just a few sentences later. In the last paragraph notice the smooth *alliteration* of "complex computers" and "machine-made miscomputation." All these devices make the complicated sentences of the essay somehow smoother and easier to follow. What other examples of such figures of speech can you find?

Practice

A. Answer these questions in complete sentences.

1. With what observation does Dr. Thomas begin his essay?
2. What points are made in the body of the essay that refute, or disagree with, the belief that human errors are bad and present the writer's own ideas?
3. What conclusion does Dr. Thomas draw from these points?
4. What point does Dr. Thomas make about the difference between humans and animals?
5. What is your reaction to Dr. Thomas's conclusion? Explain why you feel that way.

Apply

B. 6. Choose a topic about which you have a strong belief. Do any research that may be necessary, and then organize and write an outline similar to the thought process followed by Dr. Thomas. Then write the essay.

A BOOK TO READ

Title: **Johnny Tremain**
Author: Esther Forbes
Publisher: Houghton Mifflin

In 1773 Johnny Tremain was a 14-year-old apprentice to a Boston silversmith. He was talented and gifted, and his future seemed especially bright when Paul Revere, the most famous silversmith in Boston, started to become interested in his work.

Then one day disaster struck! A crucible of molten silver broke, and Johnny's hand became so burned that it became useless.

After a long period of anguish, Johnny finally became a dispatch rider for the Committee of Public Safety. He became involved with the dramatic events that would soon lead to the Revolutionary War.

A dramatic battlefield discovery brings this exciting book to its happy and satisfying conclusion.

7 UNIT TEST

● **Pronouns**   pages 236–238

Number your paper 1 to 8. Next to each number write the letter of the answer for the pronoun that will correctly complete each sentence.

1. When Dorothea Dix visited a Massachusetts house of correction in 1841, _____ was shocked.
   a. they   **b.** her   **c.** she   **d.** me
2. Criminals and the mentally ill were treated shamefully, and little distinction was made between _____.
   a. him   **b.** them   **c.** ourselves   **d.** us
3. She could not let _____ forget what she had seen there.
   a. me   **b.** yourselves   **c.** her   **d.** herself
4. _____ set out to improve conditions for those people.
   a. They   **b.** She   **c.** His   **d.** We
5. She worked until she was 80 to see _____ dream come true.
   a. her   **b.** their   **c.** it   **d.** myself
6. Although Dorothea Dix improved conditions in prisons, _____ think that her greatest work was done for the mentally ill.
   a. me   **b.** yours   **c.** I   **d.** he
7. She inspected asylums and reported _____ abuses to the government.
   a. its   **b.** them   **c.** you   **d.** their
8. _____ must agree that Dorothea Dix was a remarkable woman.
   a. Her   **b.** You   **c.** My   **d.** Us

● **Subject and Object Pronouns**   pages 239–241

Copy these sentences. Next to each one write whether the underlined pronoun is being used as a *subject*, a *direct object*, or an *indirect object*.

9. Golf developed in Scotland about 900 years ago, where the Romans had once played it in another form.
10. They had called their game *paganica*.
11. Paganica gave them the opportunity to knock a feather-stuffed leather ball around the countryside with a bent stick.
12. The first known written report of golf comes from 1457, when King James II of Scotland banned it.

266   TEST: Unit 7

13. He did not want golf to replace archery, upon which James believed the defense of the country depended.

● **Possessive Pronouns**   pages 242–243

14.–21. Copy this paragraph. Replace each underlined word or group of words with the appropriate possessive pronoun.

Ming Liang Chong and her brother Chung Sook checked Ming Liang and Chung Sook's pockets again. Where was the house key? "I gave Chung Sook's key to you," Chung Sook said. Ming Liang answered, "I took Chung Sook's and put it with Ming Liang's, but what did I do with them then?" Ming Liang searched Ming Liang's memory and recalled that she had left them on the dresser. "We will have to ask Mr. Stamos if we can borrow Mr. Stamos's key. Dad gave it to him for emergencies." They said to him, "We cannot find Ming Liang's and Chung Sook's keys. May we borrow Mr. Stamos's?"

● **Reflexive and Demonstrative Pronouns**   pages 244–245

22.–29. Write eight sentences about a hobby or a game you enjoy. Use a reflexive or a demonstrative pronoun in each sentence.

● **Indefinite and Interrogative Pronouns**   pages 246–247

Copy these sentences. Underline each indefinite pronoun and circle each interrogative pronoun.

30. Someone at our picnic likes chicken very much.
31. Whose bottle of apple juice is this, Marion?
32. Has anyone noticed that some of this celery is a bit soggy?
33. Which of these delicious-looking bananas is for me?
34. What has everybody brought for dessert?
35. All of us will clean up the area before leaving.

● **Using the Front Matter**   pages 250–251

Turn to the front of this book and answer these questions. Write *title page, copyright page,* or *table of contents* to indicate where you found the answer.

1. How many units are there in this book?
2. Who was the consultant for Curriculum and Instruction?
3. Where was the book printed?
4. On what page does Unit 3 begin?
5. How long is each Unit Test?
6. Who published this book?
7. On what pages will you find a lesson entitled "Understanding Gerunds"?

Using the Glossary and the Index   pages 252–253

Turn to the back of this book and answer these questions. Write whether you found each answer in the *glossary* (the Review Handbook) or the *index*.

8. On what page is there a discussion of syllabication?
9. What is an infinitive?
10. What is the definition of a *transitive verb*?
11. On which pages do the "To Memorize" features in this book appear?
12. How many poems are presented in this book?
13. How many uses does an apostrophe have?
14. On what pages will you find a discussion of the characteristics of a novel?
15. When should you use a colon?

Combining Sentences with Relative Pronouns   pages 254–255

Combine each group of sentences by using a relative pronoun.

1. Krakatoa lies near Java and Sumatra. It is a volcanic island.
2. In 1883 its volcano had an eruption. The eruption was one of the largest in modern times.
3. The island trembled in the grip of an earthquake. The island was partially blown up in the explosion.
4. The resulting tidal wave killed some 36,000 people. The people lived on nearby islands. Such a tidal wave is called a *tsunami* in that part of the world.
5. New islands were formed from ashes and lava. These ashes and lava came from Krakatoa.

Writing a Book Report   pages 256–258

6. Imagine that you have found the first book ever written. Write a two-paragraph book report about it. Give a brief synopsis of the plot or information in the book, your opinion, and support for your opinion.

Editing a Book Report   pages 259–260

7. Edit the book report that you wrote for the previous exercise. Make sure that it contains all three parts, clearly stated. Make any changes that you find necessary, and then rewrite it.

Writing Titles   page 261

Copy these titles, adding capitalization, quotation marks, or underlining where needed.

8. reflections on a gift of watermelon pickle   (poem)
9. the bride comes to yellow sky   (short story)

10. greatest hits of the violin   (record)
11. the bridge over the river kwai   (movie)
12. the roar of the greasepaint, the smell of the crowd   (play)
13. plain talk from the plains   (magazine article)
14. samson and delilah   (opera)
15. make room for daddy   (TV series)

● **An Essay of Opinion**   pages 262–265

Read this essay of opinion. Then answer the questions that follow.

Of all the beings on all the planets in the Galaxy Arcturus, I find the creatures on planet #5 the strangest of all. At first sight they appear civilized, but upon studying them for any length of time one cannot help but conclude that they are unquestionably barbaric.

First of all, the creatures are ugly beyond belief. Their bodies consist of an elongated fleshy stalk with a pair of tentacles emerging from either end, rather like a starship with a double set of landing pods. A globular mass protruding from the top of the stalks seems to serve as a communications center.

Second, when two of these creatures desire to communicate, they wave their tentacles in a most disgusting manner, moving them up and down while simultaneously emitting grunts and growls from an opening in the globular mass. It's absurd!

To take nourishment, the beings adopt a strange gesture, bending their stalks almost double and poising themselves atop objects that seem to relieve the pressure on their lower tentacles. The nourishment itself comes in various forms, all so disgusting in appearance and in smell that a being of our order is moved to misery. The nourishment is ingested in a most disagreeable way, shoved a little at a time into the same orifice that emits the garbled gurglings they call language.

I could continue for some time to describe these creatures, but my lack of a suitably strong constitution makes it impossible. I can only add that I am convinced such primitive beings can never be numbered among the civilized inhabitants of our sphere. I strongly recommend that they be left to their own devices on the home planet they so quaintly call *Earth*.

1. With what statement of opinion does the writer begin the essay?
2. What points does the writer make to support this opinion?
3. With what conclusion does the writer end the essay?
4. What devices of language can you find in the essay? Note the paragraph in which each example occurs.
5. Describe the personality of the author of this essay. Give reasons for your opinion.

8

LANGUAGE
Learning About Prepositions, Interjections, and Conjunctions
COMPOSITION
Writing a Research Report

STUDY SKILLS
Organizing Information
LITERATURE
Enjoying Plays

In Unit 8 you will be writing a research report. This is a very important skill that you may find yourself using throughout your life—gathering information, organizing it, and writing it in a clear and interesting manner for others.

When writing a research report, you will need to build sentences. Prepositions will help you to express complex thoughts clearly. Conjunctions will also be valuable in combining information in interesting ways and helping you to express your thoughts fluently.

One part of speech you will rarely use in a research report is the interjection. Interjections carry almost no information except the feelings of the speaker. They will be useful in writing a play, however. As you look at the scenes from plays on the opposite page, write some dialog for the characters.

LANGUAGE

Lesson 1: Understanding Prepositions and Prepositional Phrases

Read these sentences.

1. The archeologist sifted <u>through</u> the soil.
2. Ann Wilson worked <u>beside</u> him.

What is the function of the underlined words?

Think and Discuss

The words *through* and *beside* are called **prepositions.** In sentence 1 the preposition *through* shows the relationship between the noun *soil* and the verb *sifted.* What relationship is shown by the preposition in sentence 2?

A group of words that begins with a preposition and ends with a noun or a pronoun is called a **prepositional phrase.** The noun or pronoun that follows the preposition is called the **object of the preposition.** If the object of a preposition is a pronoun, it must be an object pronoun. Read this list of prepositions.

about	around	between	in	out	under
above	at	beyond	inside	outside	until
across	before	by	into	over	up
after	behind	down	near	past	upon
against	below	during	of	through	with
along	beneath	for	off	to	within
among	beside	from	on	toward	without

> - A **preposition** is a word that shows the relationship between a noun or a pronoun that follows it and another word in the sentence.
> - A **prepositional phrase** is a group of words that begins with a preposition and ends with a noun or a pronoun called the **object of the preposition.**

Some prepositions can cause problems. Study each pair of words to be sure that you know when to use each one.

Among refers to three or more things.
Between refers to two things only.

3. The five archeologists divided the equipment among themselves.
4. Dr. Markley and I set up an umbrella between us.

At shows that someone or something is already in place.
To shows movement toward someone or something.

5. The professor is at the dig.
6. Ann Wilson is walking to the dig.

In means "within" or "inside."
Into shows movement from the outside to the inside.

7. We found these articles in the soil.
8. Everything is put into a bag and labeled.

Practice

A. Copy these sentences. Underline each preposition and draw an arrow from it to its object.

1. The dig is near Centerville.
2. Every morning we meet at the hotel.
3. We climb into the jeep.
4. Then Dr. Markley drives us across the rough terrain.
5. The leaders stand around the tent and plan the day's work.

B. Complete each sentence with the correct preposition.

6. Everyone wanted to work (at, to) the dig.
7. Dr. Markley chose (among, between) all the best students.
8. Just (among, between) you and me, I was afraid that I wouldn't be selected.
9. The chosen students went (at, to) a photographer.
10. That picture has a special place (in, into) my photo album.

Apply

C. 11.–20. Write ten sentences about a science activity you enjoy. Use a prepositional phrase in each sentence.

Lesson 2: Using Prepositional Phrases as Adjectives and Adverbs

Read these sentences.

1. The people in the line waited impatiently.
2. The boy behind me dropped his money.
3. The money fell through a grate.

Name the prepositional phrase in each sentence.

Think and Discuss

Prepositional phrases can be used as modifiers just as individual adjectives and adverbs can. In sentence 1, for example, the prepositional phrase *in the line* modifies the noun *people* by answering the question *which ones.* Because it modifies a noun, the entire phrase is used as an adjective. In sentence 2 *behind me* modifies the noun *boy* by telling *which* boy; therefore the prepositional phrase is used as an adjective. What question does *through a grate* answer in sentence 3? What word does it modify? How is it used?

Do not be confused if a word is used sometimes as an adverb and sometimes as a preposition. Whenever the word is a preposition, it is followed by the rest of a prepositional phrase. Whenever the word is an adverb, it stands alone. How is the underlined word in each of these sentences used?

4. Gina looked <u>down</u> the aisle.
5. Then she sat <u>down</u>.

Practice

A. Copy these sentences. Underline each prepositional phrase, and draw an arrow from it to the word it modifies.

1. The sign above the theater door was brightly lighted.
2. The girl with the sad expression lost her ticket.
3. Estelle likes a seat near the aisle.
4. The people behind us are making too much noise.
5. The popcorn in this box is stale.
6. The movie was filmed on location.
7. The film crew arrived before the actors.

8. The sun grew hotter during the morning.
9. The director stopped shooting at noon.
10. She sat under an umbrella.

B. Copy these sentences and underline the prepositional phrases. After each write whether it is used as an *adjective* or as an *adverb*.

11. The star of the film is Ruby Wayne.
12. Ruby is from Missouri.
13. Her family is proud of her success.
14. Screenings are held in a special theater.
15. The building beside the theater contains the studio offices.
16. A certain friend of mine knows Ruby Wayne personally.
17. Once I attended a screening of a new film with this friend.
18. After the screening I met the actress and the parents of the actress as well.
19. They were all very gracious to me.
20. It was the most exciting event of my life!

Apply

C. 21.–30. Write ten sentences about a movie or TV show you have seen recently. Use prepositional phrases as adjectives in half of the sentences and as adverbs in the other half.

To Memorize

Our whole life is but one great school; from the cradle to the grave we are all learners; nor will our education be finished until we die.

Ann Plato

Ann Plato was one of the earliest black women to teach school in the United States. She published these words in Hartford, Connecticut, in 1841. She knew that most of her people in this country still lived in slavery and were not permitted to learn how to read and write. How does that knowledge make her words more meaningful? What kinds of learning are there in life besides formal schooling?

Lesson 3: Understanding Interjections

Cora and Pauline were hanging posters in their room. This is part of their conversation.

1. Oops, I dropped a thumb tack.
2. Ouch! I stepped on it.
3. Oh dear! I'm sorry.

What do the word that introduce each sentence express?

Think and Discuss

Words and brief expressions such as *oops, ouch,* and *oh dear* that are used only to express feelings are called **interjections.** The word *interjection* comes from a Latin word that means "to throw into." Interjections are thrown into a sentence to show feeling and to make dialog more lively.

Some interjections express strong feelings, and some express mild feelings. Others can be used either way, depending on the meaning the writer wishes to convey. Interjections that express strong feelings are followed by an exclamation point. Those that express mild feelings are followed by a comma. Do the interjections in sentences 1-3 express strong or mild feelings?

Here is a list of some common interjections.

ah	dear me	my	oh dear	oho	well
aha	hey	my goodness	oh my	oops	whew
alas	hurrah	oh	oh no	ouch	wow

> • An **interjection** is a word or a brief expression that is used to express feeling.

Practice

A. Copy these sentences. Underline the interjections and the punctuation that accompanies them.

1. Oh no, I have misplaced one of our posters.
2. Aha! Here it is.
3. Hurrah! You found it.
4. Hey! I have an idea. Let's hang that one here.
5. My, it looks nice over the desk.

B. Copy these sentences, inserting commas and exclamation points where needed. Remember to capitalize words that follow exclamation points.

6. Ah what a pretty scene on this poster.
7. Hey that's where we went on vacation last year.
8. My goodness you're right.
9. My what a difference these posters make.
10. Whew I'm glad we're finished.

Apply

C. 11.–20. Write ten sentences about decorating your room at home or at school. Use an interjection in each sentence and be sure to punctuate the sentence correctly.

HOW OUR LANGUAGE GROWS

The alphabet took thousands of years to invent. The earliest form of writing is called *picture writing*. There were no letters, words, or sentences in picture writing.

The next stage in the development of writing can be seen in the Egyptian *hieroglyphics*. Pictures were used as symbols for actions and ideas. *Water* was represented by a wavy line instead of a picture. This wavy line slowly evolved into our letter *m*.

The ancient Chinese developed a similar system of writing, parts of which are still in use today. A picture of a woman along with a picture of a child meant "good." *Sun* plus *tree* meant "east." *Sun* plus *moon* meant "light."

Alphabets made of letters to represent sounds were developed by the Hebrews, passed on to the Phoenicians, and then passed on to the Greeks. Each culture changed and adapted the shapes of the letters to their own needs. The Romans borrowed the Greek alphabet and changed it once again. Today our alphabet is based on the letters used by the Romans two thousand years ago.

1. Using your dictionary, tell how the word *alphabet* came to be.
2. Later scholars added *j* to the Roman alphabet. What other letter was added as well?

Lesson 4: Understanding Conjunctions

Read these sentences.

1. Flowers have often represented ideas <u>and</u> emotions.
2. <u>Both</u> the Greeks <u>and</u> the Romans had flower languages.

What is the function of the underlined words in these sentences?

Think and Discuss

Words that join other words or groups of words in a sentence are called **conjunctions.** Individual words, phrases, and simple sentences are joined by **coordinating conjunctions.** The most common coordinating conjunctions are *and, but, or, so, yet,* and *for.* Note that coordinating conjunctions join words or word groups that have equal value in a sentence. Remember that a comma precedes a conjunction that joins two sentences.

3. Victors in the Greek games joyfully <u>yet</u> modestly wore crowns of wild olive.
4. Roman generals prized oak leaves, <u>for</u> they were a symbol of victory in battle.
5. The lotus was a sacred symbol in Egypt <u>and</u> in India.
6. The chrysanthemum was native to Asia, <u>so</u> it became the national flower of Japan.

Which kind of words or word groups have been joined by the coordinating conjunctions in sentences 3-6?

Conjunctions that are used in pairs are called **correlative conjunctions.** The most common correlative conjunctions are *either . . . or, neither . . . nor, both . . . and, not only . . . but (also),* and *whether . . . or.* These conjunctions are always separated by other words or word groups in a sentence. When correlative conjunctions are used in a sentence, they must be placed as close as possible to the words they join.

7. Nobles in fourteenth century England wore <u>either</u> a red <u>or</u> a white rose to show their allegiances to the House of Lancaster or the House of York.
8. The Wars of the Roses were <u>not only</u> long <u>but also</u> pointless.
9. <u>Neither</u> the House of Lancaster <u>nor</u> the House of York won a clear victory.

You will learn about a third type of conjunction, the subordinating conjunction, in Unit 9.

> - A **conjunction** is a word that joins words or groups of words.
> - A **coordinating conjunction** joins words or groups of words of equal importance in a sentence.
> - **Correlative conjunctions** are used in pairs to join words or groups of words in a sentence.

Practice

A. Copy these sentences. Circle the conjunctions and write whether they are *coordinating* or *correlative*.

1. China had a complete floral alphabet, but it was not understood outside of China.
2. In the West flower language was common in both art and literature.
3. In Shakespeare's *Hamlet* Ophelia speaks of flowers in a way that is not only sad but also strange.
4. English poets claimed that the bloom of the amaranth could neither fade nor die.
5. Flower language was popular during the reign of Queen Victoria, for it was a sentimental era.
6. To Victorians the dogrose symbolized either pleasure or pain.
7. Foxglove was a symbol of insincerity, so it was not a favorite flower for bouquets.

B. 8.–14. Using the sentences in Practice A, draw a line under the words or word groups joined by the conjunctions. Identify the kinds of words or word groups you have underlined.

Apply

C. 15.–20. Write a paragraph about some imaginary flowers or plants. Describe the flowers or plants and tell what they symbolize. Use at least six different coordinating or correlative conjunctions in your paragraph. Be sure that the words or word groups have equal value in the sentence.

LANGUAGE REVIEW

Prepositions and Prepositional Phrases   pages 272–273

Copy these sentences, completing each with a suitable preposition. Then underline each prepositional phrase.

1. Early _____ the morning, Rhonda goes _____ her sister's room.
2. When both are dressed, they walk _____ the stairs and _____ the kitchen _____ breakfast.
3. _____ work, their dad prepares breakfast _____ them.
4. Then he walks _____ the train station _____ the center _____ town.
5. _____ breakfast, Rita and Rhonda wash the dishes.

Prepositional Phrases Used as Adjectives and Adverbs   pages 274–275

Copy these sentences, underlining each prepositional phrase. Tell if each phrase is used as an *adjective* or as an *adverb*.

6. The girls' mother works at a factory that makes computer parts.
7. Mrs. Tyler knows a great deal about computers and uses her knowledge to advantage.
8. Mr. Tyler teaches in a school for handicapped people.
9. One of the things he teaches them is how they can live on their own.
10. Rhonda and Rita are proud of their parents.

Interjections   pages 276–277

Copy these sentences, capitalizing and punctuating properly.

11. Hey don't drop that saucer, Rita.
12. Oops it almost slipped out of my hand.
13. Sssh don't wake Mom; she just got to bed.
14. Oh my, I certainly hope she didn't hear me.
15. Well you really weren't too noisy.

Conjunctions   pages 278–279

Copy these sentences. Draw one line under coordinating conjunctions and two lines under correlative conjunctions.

16. You and I should go to the bakery and to the supermarket, but where should we go first?
17. Both the bakery and the supermarket open at eight.

18. I will go to the supermarket, and you can go to the bakery.
19. We'll get to the supermarket about eight o'clock, for the bus ride takes about half an hour.
20. Let's walk home from the supermarket and buy an ice cream cone on the way.

Copy these sentences, adding an appropriate conjunction to each. After each sentence, write whether you have used *coordinating* or *correlative* conjunctions.

21. Rhonda is the mathematics expert, _____ Rita is better in English and science.
22. Rhonda may decide to work with _____ computers _____ some other electronic equipment.
23. Rita has not made a career decision, _____ she is still very young.
24. _____ Rita _____ Rhonda will work in the city this summer.
25. Rhonda always pictures Rita in a laboratory _____ in a science museum.
26. One summer Rhonda attended a computer camp _____ Rita helped out at the zoo.
27. Rita learned _____ to clean animals' cages _____ to feed the smaller animals.
28. At first she was not allowed to work by herself, _____ then the keeper realized that she was competent.
29. Rita likes to work at the zoo, _____ the keeper likes her work.
30. Rhonda wants to attend another computer camp, _____ Rita will do volunteer work at a hospital.

Applying Prepositions, Interjections, and Conjunctions

31.–40. Write ten sentences about a career in math or science. Use at least five prepositional phrases, two interjections, five coordinating conjunctions, and five correlative conjunctions. If you can work more than the stated number of parts of speech into your sentences, so much the better. In doing this, however, do not allow your sentences to become awkward.

STUDY SKILLS

Lesson 5: Choosing and Limiting a Topic

Velma and Cleo were assigned to write a ten-paragraph report for their science class. They chose the topic *ants*. When they looked up *Ant* in the encyclopedia, however, they found information on the importance of ants, ants' bodies, life in an ant colony, how ants protect themselves, and how they communicate with one another, as well as details about a few of the ten thousand known species of ant. Even this one article had more information than they could use, and they had been told to consult at least four sources. What should they do?

Think and Discuss

Velma and Cleo realized that their topic was too broad. They decided they were most interested in how ants communicate, and they asked their teacher if they could limit their report to that. He agreed that their decision was a good one.

How to Select a Topic for a Research Report

1. **Make sure your topic fits the subject area assigned. If you are not sure, consult your teacher before you begin.**
2. **Choose a topic that interests you. A good research report requires much reading, taking of notes, and writing about the subject. Starting with a subject that interests you will help your concentration.**
3. **Check to be sure the information you need will be available. Look for cards under your topic in the card catalog, listings in *The Readers' Guide to Periodical Literature*, and entries in the encyclopedia and more specialized reference books.**
4. **Most important, limit your topic. Trying to pack too much information into a brief report will be confusing and will keep you from having enough space to explain your facts.**

Practice

A. Here are some proposed titles for research reports. Copy each group with its entries arranged from the broadest to the narrowest topic.

1. **a.** The History of Mathematics
   b. The Origins of Geometry
   c. Pythagoras's Triangles
2. **a.** Famous Songs of the American Civil War
   b. Famous American Songs
   c. The Origins of "Dixie" and "The Battle Hymn of the Republic"
3. **a.** Recent Trends in Modern Dance
   b. Modern Dance in the Twentieth Century
   c. Twyla Tharp's Influence on Dance in the 1970's
4. **a.** The Red Cross
   b. Clara Barton and the Founding of the American Red Cross
   c. The History of the Red Cross

B. Copy the topics that would be appropriate for a research report approximately ten paragraphs long.

5. Wild Animals
6. Pests That Attack Tomato Plants
7. The Development of the Railroad Dining Car
8. Edible Wild Plants of Indiana
9. Vegetable Gardening
10. The History of Hawaii

C. Copy each of these broad topics. Below each write two related, narrower topics that might be dealt with in a report of ten or fewer paragraphs.

11. Computers   12. Physical Fitness
13. Pigeons   14. Women in Medicine
15. Vice-Presidents of the United States

Apply

D. 16. Choose a broad topic that you might like to research for a report. Use your interests to narrow the topic. Go to the library and compile a list of references on the subject. Try to find at least four sources.

Lesson 6: Taking Notes Efficiently

When Velma and Cleo got to the library, they agreed to divide up the sources they had found and take down the important information.

"I'm just going to put my books on the photocopy machine and copy all the pages that have information we might use," said Cleo.

"Don't do that," said Velma. "It will cost extra for the copies, and you will still have to take notes."

Why would it be necessary for Cleo to take notes?

Think and Discuss

Taking notes is not just a means of preserving information; it is also the first step in writing your report. Through taking notes, you begin selecting and categorizing the information you will use. Here are some guidelines for effective note-taking.

How to Take Notes

1. Make a card for each source you consult, giving the title, author, publisher, place of publication, and date or volume number. This information will be necessary for your bibliography.
2. Put each topic from each source on a separate card or slip of paper. Then you can easily arrange your information in accordance with your outline.
3. Identify the topic and the source on each card. Be sure to record the page number(s).
4. Take notes in your own words, using abbreviations to save time and space.
5. Information you intend to quote exactly should not be abbreviated and should appear in quotation marks. Be sure to write the name of the author or speaker you are quoting.
6. Check each card carefully to avoid errors.

When you have finished taking notes, you should have all the information you need for your report, in a form that is ready to use. Why is it important to note the exact source of each fact?

Practice

A. Examine these note cards Sherry made for her report on soccer organizations. Write your answers to the questions, using complete sentences.

<table>
<tr>
<td>

(International)
Federation Internationale
de Football
Association (FIFA) governs
all soccer assocs. in world
--140+ natl. assocs.
Sets int'l rules.
<u>World Book Encyclopedia</u>
1980   p. 448 d

</td>
<td>

(International)
FIFA formed 1940.
"... membership is larger
than that of the United
Nations."
<u>The New Columbia
Encyclopedia</u>
1975   p. 2548

</td>
</tr>
<tr>
<td>

(England)
London Football Assoc.
formed 1863 to help public
distinguish "football" from
rugby. Name <u>soccer</u> comes
from abbreviation of word
association.
<u>New Columbia Encyclopedia</u>
      p. 2548

</td>
<td>

(U.S.)
U.S. Soccer Football Assoc.
formed 1913.
Governs both prof. and
amateur orgs.
<u>New Columbia Encyclopedia</u>
      p. 2548

</td>
</tr>
</table>

1. Why is the word in parentheses written at the top of each card?
2. Why did Sherry use abbreviations in her notes?
3. What is the number in the lower right corner of each card?
4. How many sources did Sherry consult?
5. Why did she put a passage in quotation marks?
6. Why is the information on cards one and two on separate cards instead of the same card?
7. Why is the information on cards two, three, and four on separate cards, not the same card?
8. How is Sherry planning to organize her report?

Apply

B. 9. Choose a single subject to research and take down at least six items of information on it.

Lesson 7: Making a Topic Outline

Angelica was preparing a report on strange creatures of the sea. First, she consulted several sources and made notes.

She noticed that each creature lived in one of three kinds of habitat—around the reefs, in the open sea, or in the vicinity of the deep sea vents. She divided her cards into those categories and gave each pile of cards a roman numeral in her outline. However, two piles still had too much information for single paragraphs. What should she do?

Think and Discuss

An outline provides a framework for a report; it establishes the basic organization of ideas. Here is Angelica's outline.

Strange Creatures of the Sea

I. Introduction
II. Creatures of the coral reef
   A. Fish that are poisonous
      1. Stonefish
      2. Demon stinger
      3. Sargassum fish
      4. Lionfish
   B. Fish that are not poisonous
      1. Trunkfish
      2. Triggerfish
      3. Parrot fish
III. Creatures of the Midwaters and Depths
   A. Fish that can be dangerous
      1. Electric ray
      2. Stargazer
   B. Fish that are odd but not dangerous
      1. Lantern fish
      2. Hatchetfish
      3. Angler fish
      4. Windowpane
      5. Walking fish
IV. Creatures of the vents
V. Conclusion

Angelica's report turned out to be seven paragraphs long. Which points in her outline represent paragraph topics? Notice that each level of subdivision is indented from the one above it. The first level is indicated with roman numerals, the second with capital letters, the third with arabic numerals. If she needed further subdivisions, Angelica could have used lowercase letters. Notice that she never uses an /A/ without a /B/ or a /1/ without a /2/.

Angelica's outline is especially well-organized because it makes use of *parallel structure*. The points on each level of an outline must be in the same form as those on similar levels. In other words, all the capital letters must refer to items expressed by the same type of phrase or sentence. Another parallel involves the arrangement of ideas in the outline. These are also parallel in Angelica's outline. Besides the Introduction and Conclusion, all the roman numerals refer to creatures in their habitats. What is the similarity between A and B under II and A and B under III? What is the similarity between the points numbered with arabic numerals?

Practice

A. Write this mixed-up outline in proper form.

3. Add fennel, thyme, tarragon, or dill to the whole fish for flavor. 3. Cover the pieces with bread crumbs or corn meal. B. Prepare the fish pieces. 1. Oil the skin of the entire fish. C. Fry the fish pieces in hot oil for three to five minutes. Methods of Cooking Fish D. Baste the fish with oil as it cooks. B. Oil the grill. 2. Dip them in a mixture of beaten egg and water. II. Deep Frying (fish pieces) A. Prepare a bed of coals. C. Prepare the whole fish. 1. Dust the pieces with flour. I. Grilling (a whole fish) A. Heat oil or shortening to 375° Fahrenheit in the fryer. 2. Rub salt, pepper, and lemon juice on the inside of the fish.

Apply

B. In preparation for writing a research report, talk over possible subjects with your teacher. Be sure your subject is appropriately narrow. When you have decided on a subject, do some research and take notes. Then write a preliminary outline in correct form.

Lesson 8: Preparing a Bibliography

Angelica showed her report on strange sea creatures to her Aunt Sofia.

"Oh, Angie," said Sofia. "How did you know all these things? We never catch fish like that on any of our trips!"

"Look at this last page of my report," said Angelica. "That's my bibliography. It lists the books and articles I read. I made notes, and then wrote about the creatures in my own words."

"Show me a picture of this ugly hagfish," said Sofia.

"One of the books listed in the bibliography has a picture of it," said Angelica, looking down the list. "Here it is. I remember seeing a hagfish in *Wondrous World of Fishes.* Tomorrow I'll check it out of the library for you."

Why did Angelica include a bibliography with her report?

Think and Discuss

A **bibliography** is valuable to the readers of a book, report, or article. It tells them where to find further information, indicates how much research was done, and shows what kinds of sources were used and how recent the information is.

The bibliography card you made for each source should contain all the information you need for an entry. There are many kinds of bibliography entries. These are the most common.

Book { Allyn, Rube. Dictionary of Fishes. St. Petersburg, Fla.: The Great Outdoors Publishing Co., 1953.

Article in a magazine or newspaper { Ballard, Robert D., and Grassle, J. Frederick. "Incredible World of the Deep-sea Rifts." National Geographic, November 1979, pp. 68–73.

Book with an editor instead of an author { Grosvenor, Melville Bell, ed. Wondrous World of Fishes. Washington, D.C.: National Geographic Society, 1965.

Encyclopedia article { Smith, C. Lavett. "Fish." The World Book Encyclopedia, vol. 7, pp. 138–152. Chicago: World Book-Childcraft International, Inc., 1980.

Your bibliography will be alphabetized by author's last name. How do you write the authors' names when there are two authors?

Practice

A. Each of the following bibliography listings contains one or more errors. Copy them in correct order, making the necessary corrections. After each listing write whether it is a *book*, a *magazine article*, or an *encyclopedia article.*

1. 1980. Bringle, Mary Beth. "Charlotte Perkins Stetson Gilman." American Women Writers, vol. 2, pp. 131–133. New York: Frederick Ungar Publishing Co.
2. Texas Women: A Celebration of History, by Mary Beth Rogers. Austin, Tex.: Texas Foundation for Women's Resources, 1981.
3. Norton, Mary Beth. American Heritage, April/May 1980, pp. 102–107: "The Philadelphia Ladies Association."
4. "Woman," in The World Book Encyclopedia, volume 21, pages 316–321. By Cynthia Fuchs Epstein. World Book-Childcraft International, Inc., 1980. Chicago.
5. Ann Firor Scott, The Southern Lady: From Pedestal to Politics, *1830–1930,* Chicago, University of Chicago Press, 1970.
6. Lerner, Gerda. Black Women in White America: A Documentary History (New York: Random House, 1973).

Apply

B. 7. If you have not already made bibliography cards for your research report, make them now. Be sure you have all the information you need on each card. Then write the bibliography section of your report in correct form.

A Challenge

You have just written a best-selling nonfiction book called *How to Be Healthy and Happy 365 Days a Year.* Your book has been so successful that an important magazine ran an article on several of the ideas you presented. After that an article on you and your book appeared in a prominent encyclopedia. Make up three bibliographical entries in correct form—one for your book with you as author, one for the magazine article with a different author, and one for the encyclopedia article. Feel free to invent names, dates, and pages as necessary.

COMPOSITION

Lesson 9: Working from an Outline

Having taken some excellent notes and having finished her outline for "Strange Creatures of the Sea," Angelica was ready to begin the first draft of her report. What are some of the things Angelica should keep in mind as she writes?

Think and Discuss

Angelica realized that the research she had done gave her more than enough material to work with. Her biggest job in writing the first draft of her report would be to keep it *organized.* So when she started, she put her outline on one side of her work and her note cards, in order, on the other side.

To catch her readers' interest at the beginning, Angelica chose one of the most outlandish fish in her whole collection for her **introduction.** The hagfish, a primitive saltwater fish without eyes, bones, scales, jaws, or limbs, would have her audience so interested, she hoped, that they would not be able to put her report down. From that point her strange creatures, each one so interesting and so different from all the others, would hold her readers' attention to the end.

As Angelica wrote the **body** of her report, she followed her outline step by step. In one of her paragraphs on creatures of the midwaters and depths, she wanted very much to add a sentence or two on the ratfish and the channel rockfish. She resisted the temptation, however, telling herself that nothing could go into the report that was not on her outline. What other good reasons can you give for agreeing with Angelica's decision?

Reaching her **concluding paragraph,** Angelica decided that it should sum up what she had said in paragraphs 2 through 6. She chose the moray eel, another strange and often frightening creature, to bring her report to a close. Reading the paper over afterward, she noticed several things that needed changing and a few sentences that would have to be rephrased. Basically, however, it was a good, sound first draft, and she was pleased.

Practice

A. Look back at Angelica's outline in Lesson 7. Then answer these questions.

1. What should be the main idea of paragraph 4?
2. Into what paragraph would the demon stinger go?
3. What single basic concern did Angelica have to keep in mind as she wrote her first draft?
4. What do the stonefish, the demon stinger, the sargassum fish, and the lionfish have in common?
5. In which paragraph would Angelica mention that not all strange-looking fish are dangerous?

B. Imagine that you are writing a research report on sleep and dreaming. Read this partial outline. Then answer the questions that follow it.

III. Kinds of dreams
A. Wishful dreams
B. Remembering dreams
   1. Childhood memories
   2. Recent remembrances
C. Nightmares

6. From which part of the research report does this paragraph or section come?
7. In writing the first draft of this report, you mention dreams of the future as a form of wishful dreams. Under which heading or in which part of the section must you place it?
8. What would make a good introduction for this research report?
9. How might you conclude a research report on sleep and dreams?
10. You want to include some material on hallucinations in this section of your report. Where would you place it according to your outline?

Apply

C. 11. Write one or two paragraphs based on the partial outline given in Practice B. Follow the instructions given in this lesson on page 290.

Lesson 10: Writing a Research Report

According to her outline, Angelica planned her report to be seven paragraphs long. Why did her teacher agree that it was an acceptable length?

Think and Discuss

Here in its entirety is a copy of Angelica's report.

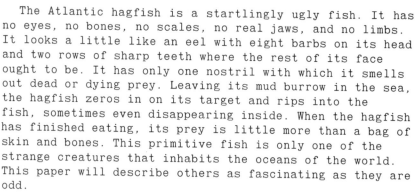

Strange Creatures of the Sea

The Atlantic hagfish is a startlingly ugly fish. It has no eyes, no bones, no scales, no real jaws, and no limbs. It looks a little like an eel with eight barbs on its head and two rows of sharp teeth where the rest of its face ought to be. It has only one nostril with which it smells out dead or dying prey. Leaving its mud burrow in the sea, the hagfish zeros in on its target and rips into the fish, sometimes even disappearing inside. When the hagfish has finished eating, its prey is little more than a bag of skin and bones. This primitive fish is only one of the strange creatures that inhabits the oceans of the world. This paper will describe others as fascinating as they are odd.

The most dangerous fish along the coral reefs is not the shark. It is a shapeless mass of flesh called the stonefish, whose spines are so poisonous that the venom can kill a human being in minutes. The demon stinger and the sargassum fish are also covered with poisonous spines. The first hides itself on the sea bottom where it resembles a strangely shaped rock or shell, whereas the second hides in the multicolored sargassum weed that gives it its name. Because both blend into their surroundings, they are extremely dangerous to swimmers and skin divers. The beautiful lionfish, in contrast, swims in open water, waving its fins that look like delicate feathers. Each of the fins, however, is as sharp as a needle and gives off a deadly poison. Other fish and unwary swimmers alike are often targets for the lionfish.

In contrast to their spiny neighbors, the trunkfish, the triggerfish, and the parrot fish are not dangerous to humans. Trunkfish got their name because they look like boxes or trunks made of bony scales that encase them, exposing only their eyes, lips, tail, and shaving-brush fins. The triggerfish has one sharp spine on its back and a softer one behind it which it sets like the trigger of a gun. When an unsuspecting small fish swims too near, the trigger is released and the spine pierces the victim, which becomes the triggerfish's lunch. The stoplight parrot fish, so called because of its red, yellow, and green spots, is the only fish that wears a nightgown to bed. From special glands in its gill chambers, the parrot fish secretes a mucus in which it envelops itself while it sleeps. Scientists think that this "nightgown" protects the parrot fish when it would otherwise be helpless.

The electric ray and the stargazer do not live in tropical waters. They are dangerous mostly to other fish and to swimmers in the Atlantic and Pacific oceans. The electric ray looks like a large gray pancake on the ocean floor. It moves slowly, has flabby muscles, small teeth, and weak eyes, but it packs 75 volts of electricity in its body. The stargazer lies on its stomach in the sand exposing only its upturned eyes and open mouth to its victims. When a likely meal swims by, however, the optic nerves of the stargazer generate 50 volts of electricity to stun its prey.

Most of the fish that live in the midwaters and in the depths, that is, 600 or more feet (180 meters) below the surface, are merely odd. The lantern fish, for example, has tiny pearllike organs along its sides that give off light in the dimness of the deep sea. The tiny hatchetfish, too, emits light from photophores that glow like embers on the underside of its body. Angler fish are strange creatures that wear built-in "bait" on their heads. Dangling these fleshy lures in front of them, anglers actually fish for other fish. The curious windowpane, which resembles a flounder, has both eyes on the same side of its head. It lies on the sandy ocean bottom on the side without eyes and looks upward with the pair on the other side. Like a chameleon, the windowpane blends in perfectly with its surroundings—so well, in fact, that the viewer seems to be looking through a window at the ocean floor beneath. The walking fish is so called because instead of lying on the sand, it struts along on its pectoral fins, which serve as legs. One variety called the mudskipper actually walks on the mud flats when the tide goes out.

Vents in the ocean floor are openings through which hot seawater from deep in the earth jets upward like a geyser into the colder surrounding water. Near these mineral-laden vents dwell strange red worms that live in clumps of waving tubes attached to coral formations. These tube worms have no eyes, no mouths, and no intestines at all. Only their "heads" protrude from the tubes, absorbing molecules of food through their bright red skins. Red blood pigment called hemoglobin accounts for their color and apparently helps to distribute food throughout their bodies. Fields of footlong blood-red clams live nearby, attached to the coral in clusters. Because of the minerals

in the vent water, these giant clams grow 500 times as fast as the ordinary variety. Although their shells are white, the blood—red flesh inside is colored with hemoglobin like that of the tube worms. Neither creature is found anywhere in the ocean except near the deep—water vents.

So many strange fish live in the sea that this paper could never describe them all. Perhaps the moray eel, 6 feet (1.8 meters) long, is typical of most of them. Although it is larger than many, its protective coloration helps it to blend in with its surroundings. Then, when a likely meal swims by, it attacks with lightning speed. With only two narrow fins down the entire length of its body, and its head only 1/9 of its total size, this eel is certainly as strange as all the other animals in this paper. Readers who would like to learn more about the curious life in the seas might like to read Wondrous World of Fishes, published by the National Geographic Society. Perhaps you will be as fascinated as I was with the variety of underwater life.

As she intended, Angelica's report was seven paragraphs long, each paragraph full of material to fascinate and delight her readers. In general, she restricted herself to a physical description of each creature. It was an outstanding feature that made each one *strange,* as her title indicated. Whenever she discussed food-catching or some other interesting characteristic, she mentioned it only as a quality associated in some way with the creature's appearance. Why did Angelica limit herself in this way? How did Angelica keep the body of her report flowing smoothly along?

Practice

A. Write the first draft of paragraph 1 for a research report based on the outline you made for Apply in Lesson 7.

Apply

B. Write your own research report based on a topic and outline approved by your teacher.

Lesson 11: Editing a Research Report

As you learned in Lesson 9, the most important part of writing a research report is keeping it *organized*. What points, then, will you check most carefully when you edit?

Think and Discuss

Here is paragraph 4 of the first draft of Angelica's research report. It includes some information that remained until the final copy was typed as well as some errors she corrected. Study this edited manuscript.

> The electric ray and the stargazer do not don't live in tropical waters, as the others do. They are dangerous mostly to other fish and to swimmers in the Atlantic and Pacific Oceans. The electric ray looks like a large gray pancake. It moves slowly, has flabby muscles muscles, small teeth, and weak eyes, but it packs 75 volts of electricity in its body. It is about as dangerous as its cousin, the electric eel, except that its body type is quite different. However, When a likely meal swims by the stargazer, the its optic nerves of the stargazer generate 50 volts of electricity to jolt his prey stun its prey. Otherwise the stargazer lies on its stomach in the sand, showing exposing only its eyes and his upturned its open mouth to his its victims.

The biggest change in organization in this paragraph involves making the last sentence the second to last sentence. Angelica made the change when she realized that *describing* the stargazer was more important than explaining how the creature gets its food. For this reason she felt that the description should be given first. What other changes did this necessitate?

Notice that Angelica added the vivid simile *like a large gray pancake on the ocean floor* to describe the electric ray. How does this improve the paragraph? Why did she change the word *his* to the word *its* in three places?

While she was writing the first draft of her report, Angelica had considered adding the anableps and the paddlefish to the section on fish of the midwaters and depths. She was sorry

that she had to eliminate these interesting fish from her final report. Here is her paragraph on these two strange creatures.

> The anableps of Central America is often called the four-eyed fish. The upper part of each lens is like that of a human to focus in air. Because it scans the water for enemies and the surface for food, the anableps has eyes that can focus both in air and in water. The lower part is rounded like that of a fish for water vision. The paddlefish is found in the Mississippi River of the United States. As it swims around with its great toothless mouth wide open, it scoops in only tiny shellfish and plants. It has a broad beak which measures one-third the length of its body, and its jaws open in a way that seems impossible. Hunting for food, the paddlefish drops the lower half of its head like an elevator, thereby opening its mouth.

Which two sentences in the paragraph are clearly out of order? How should they be rearranged?

Practice

A. Rewrite Angelica's edited paragraph from the first page of this lesson. It will *not* be the same as her final edited version in Lesson 10.

B. Copy Angelica's paragraph on the anableps and the paddlefish. Then use editing marks to show where each of the new sentences should be.

C. Angelica wrote the conclusion of her report as a summary of what she had written in the body. However, she used the moray eel as an example to stand for the characteristics of all the other fish she had described. Write another conclusion for Angelica's paper. It may be a different kind of summary, or it may end the paper in some other suitable way. When you have finished, edit your conclusion for organization and correct order.

Apply

D. Edit your own research report. Check especially for good organization in the entire report and for proper order within each paragraph. Use editing marks to make any changes you may need. Finally, recopy or retype your report in finished form, and give both versions to your teacher.

MECHANICS PRACTICE

Using Commas and Semicolons

- Place commas after every element but the last in a series.

  The ratfish, the trumpetfish, and the channel rockfish all live in salt water.

- Use commas to set off names in direct address and after the introductory word *yes* or *no*.

  Do you know, Miriam, what the puffer fish does? Yes, it inflates its body so that other fish cannot swallow it.

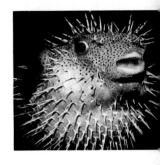

- Use a comma to set off transitional expressions and other "interrupters" in a sentence.

  Moreover, the puffer fish has spines covering its whole body. Would you, perhaps, like to meet a puffer fish?

- Use commas after two introductory prepositional phrases and to set off appositives.

  In the middle of the night, the hagfish swam out of its mud burrow. The hagfish, a primitive fish, was looking for a meal.

- Use semicolons to separate items in a series in which commas have already been used.

  Nonpoisonous fish such as the trunkfish, major general, and parrot fish; dangerous fish such as the electric eel and the stargazer; and odd fish such as the hatchetfish, the angler fish, and the lantern fish all live in tropical waters.

A. Punctuate these sentences correctly.

1. What was your research paper about Tony?
2. After many hours of research I decided to write about oil.
3. Oil which is in the news so much these days seemed interesting.
4. Did you know for example that plastic jugs are made with oil?
5. No I didn't know that.
6. Detergent bottles fruit juice bottles and milk bottles trash bags garbage bags and storage bags and cups glasses and mugs are all made out of petroleum-based plastic.

B. 7.–12. Reread the sentences from Practice A. Then close your book and write the sentences as your teacher reads them aloud.

LITERATURE

Lesson 12: Reading a One-Act Play

You have already read a short story and are about to read a one-act play. What do you think might be the most important difference between these two types of literature?

Think and Discuss

The **one-act play** is very much like a short story. Both contain few characters and cover short periods of time. The action, called the *plot* in a play, is divided into three main parts—the **introduction,** the **body** or conflict, and the **resolution.**

The characters and setting are revealed in the introduction. The chief character, the **protagonist,** deals with the **antagonist,** his or her opponent, in the body of the play. The conflict between them is revealed through **dialog,** which is what the characters say, and **plot,** which is what the characters do. The conflict reaches its high point in the **climax** of the play. The climax is the moment in which the action reaches a turning point. The resolution, also called the **dénouement,** is all the action that results from the climax. In the resolution the problem in the conflict is solved, and all the "loose ends" of the plot are tied together.

As you read this play, try to identify its main parts.

The Miraculous Eclipse

From *A Connecticut Yankee in King Arthur's Court* by Mark Twain
Adapted by Joellen Bland

Characters

Old Hank, as an old man   **Merlin** the Magician
Boy   **Four Guards**
Hank Morgan, a young man   **Courtiers**
Sir Kay, a knight of the Round Table   **Knights**
Clarence, a page boy   **Servants**
King Arthur

<h2 style="text-align:center">Scene 1</h2>

BEFORE RISE: *A street in Hartford, Connecticut, in 1879. A barrel stands center.* **Old Hank Morgan** *enters slowly from right, followed by* **Boy.**

Boy: Excuse me, Mr. Morgan? Some of the boys have been telling me that . . . well, that you can sure tell a whale of a story! The boys dared me to ask you to tell your version of King Arthur and his knights of the Round Table.

Old Hank: They did, eh? Well, son, I can tell you anything you want to know about King Arthur, because I knew him well when I was a young man. I knew all the folks at Camelot, including that cagey old humbug, Merlin.

Boy: But he lived in the sixth century! Well, sir, if you've got some time, I'd sure like to hear your story.

Old Hank: I've got all the time in the world. You see, I was born and brought up right here in Hartford, Connecticut, so I am a Yankee of the Yankees, and very practical. As a young man, I went to work as a blacksmith. One day a big fellow knocked me down with a crusher to my head that made everything crack! My world just went out in total darkness, and when I came to, I wasn't in Hartford any more. *(Both go off left, Lights dim to indicate shift of scene to a country road in England. Lights come on full again on* **Young Hank,** *who enters from right, his hand on his head, as if in pain.)*

Young Hank: Oh, my aching head! *(Looks around)* Where am I? This doesn't look like any place I've seen around Hartford. *(***Sir Kay** *bounds in from left with drawn sword and takes threatening position in front of him.)*

Sir Kay *(Holding swordpoint to* **Hank's** *chest):* My name is Sir Kay. In the name of the King, I take you captive! You are now my property and must come with me at once! *(Starts off by pushing* **Hank** *in front of him with sword.)*

Hank: Uh, by the way, Sir Kay, how far are we from Hartford?

Sir Kay: I have never heard of the place. We're headed for Camelot.

Hank: Camelot? There isn't any town by that name in Connecticut!

Sir Kay: You are not in Connecticut.

Hank *(Stopping again):* Well, where in the world am I?

Sir Kay: England! *(***Hank's** *mouth drops open in astonishment, as* **Sir Kay** *pushes him off stage left.)*

*   *   *

Time: *England, in the year 528.*

Setting: *A courtyard in Camelot. At center is a platform with a throne on it.*

At Rise: **Courtiers, Knights, Guards** *and* **Servants** *move busily back and forth.* **Sir Kay** *and* **Hank** *enter from left. At the sight of* **Hank,** *all stop to stare and point at him.*

Sir Kay *(Poking* **Hank** *with sword):* I warn you, don't try to escape. *(***Hank** *looks around, puzzled, as* **Clarence,** *a page boy, steps out in front of him, smiling and looking him over from head to foot.)* My page, Clarence *(Pointing to him),* will keep you in charge until I come back for you. *(Exits right.)*

Hank: Page, did he say? Go on! A boy your size can't be much more than a paragraph!

Clarence: You have an unusual way of speaking, sir, but you are welcome! I hope you will find me to be your true friend.

Hank: Well, my boy, if you're really my friend, you can tell me where I am. That escapee from a circus who brought me here said this was England, but he's obviously not in his right mind and ———

Clarence: Nay, sir, my master, Sir Kay, spoke the truth. You are in England. This is Camelot, the court of King Arthur.

Hank *(Hesitantly):* And — ah — what year is it?

Clarence: The nineteenth of June, in the year five hundred twenty-eight.

Hank *(Repeating words mechanically):* Five twenty-eight? *(Turns away dazedly)* Five twenty-eight. *(Looks at* **Courtiers,** *then at himself)* I'm sure it was 1839 when I got up this morning. I look like 1839, but all these people look like . . . five twenty-eight. *(Pacing)* Five twenty-eight . . . that was the year when a total eclipse of the sun occurred . . . on June 21st at three minutes past noon. Just two days from now.

Clarence: King Arthur is coming now. *(***Herald** *enters right, holding trumpet, and walks to center.)*

Sir Kay *(Bowing low):* My lord King, most noble knights and ladies of the realm! Behold this curious captive I have conquered!

King Arthur: And where did you find this strange creature, Sir Kay?

Sir Kay: I came upon this horrible ogre, my liege, in a far land of barbarians called Connecticut. I killed his thirteen attending knights in a three hours' battle and took him prisoner! Behold this menacing barbarian while you may, good people, for at noon on the twenty-first he shall die!

Hank *(Jumping up):* What? What have I done to deserve death? I haven't even been in this century more than half an hour!

Sir Kay: You have suffered defeat at my hands. You must die! To the dungeon with him!

King Arthur: A cheer for Sir Kay, truly a brave knight of the Round Table! **(Hank** *is dragged out left by* **Guards,** *as* **Courtiers** *cheer* **Sir Kay.** *Curtain.)*

*   *   *

Before Rise: A dungeon cell. There are a pile of straw and a low stool to one side. **Clarence** *sits on stool, watching* **Hank,** *who lies sleeping on straw.* **Hank** *stirs, stretches, his eyes still closed.*

Hank *(Not seeing* **Clarence***):* What an astonishing dream I have just had! King Arthur's Court! What nonsense! *(Turns over, opens his eyes sleepily, sees* **Clarence,** *and sits up abruptly)* What! Are you still here? Go away with the rest of the dream! Scat!

Clarence *(Laughing):* Dream? What dream? *(Stands up)*

Hank *(Jumps up):* I'm still in the dungeon! This dream is more serious than I thought. Clarence, my boy, you're the only friend I've got. Help me think of a way to escape from this place.

Clarence *(Looking around fearfully, then speaking close to* **Hank's** *ear):* Merlin, that terrible and mighty magician, has woven wicked spells about this dungeon. *(Nervously)* No man can escape it and live!

Hank *(Laughing):* Merlin has cast a few spells, has he? That cheap old humbug? Bosh! His magic doesn't amount to shucks compared to mine. Now, look here, Clarence, I'll be your friend, and you must be mine.

Clarence: I am your friend, I assure you!

Hank: Good. Now you get word to the King that I am the world's mightiest and grandest magician, and that if any harm comes to me I will quietly arrange a little calamity that will make the fur fly in these realms.

Clarence *(Terrified):* Yes, yes, at once! *(Backs off right, then turns and runs out.)*

Hank: That should get me off the hook pretty quick. *(Struts back and forth confidently for a moment, then suddenly stops.)* Ah! What a blunder I've made! I sent Clarence off to alarm the King

with the threat of a calamity I haven't thought of yet! These sixth-century people are childish and superstitious. They believe in miracles. Suppose the King asks me to name my calamity? (**Hank** *sinks down onto stool, chin in hands, as lights fade out. In a moment, lights come up again. He remains on stool in same position.*) I've got to stall for time. I can't think of anything. I . . . what's that? (*Looks off right.*) Here's Clarence. I have to look confident. (**Clarence** *enters from right, dejectedly.*) Well?

Clarence: I took your message to my liege the King, and he was very much afraid. He was ready to order your release, but Merlin was there and spoiled everything. He persuaded the King that you are crazy, and that your threat is nothing but foolishness because you have not named your calamity. Oh, my friend, be wise and name it, or you may still be doomed! (**Hank,** *deep in thought, frowns, and then smiles.*)

Hank: Ah! I have it! Just in time, too. (*Turns to* **Clarence** *and draws himself up haughtily*) How long have I been shut up in here?

Clarence: Since yesterday evening.

Hank: Then today is the twentieth of June?

Clarence: Yes.

Hank: And I am to be burned tomorrow. At what time?

Clarence (*Shuddering*): At high noon.

Hank: Listen carefully. I will tell you what to say to the King. (*In deep, measured tones*) Tell him that at high noon tomorrow I will smother the entire world in the dead blackness of midnight!

Clarence (*Falling to his knees*): Oh, have mercy!

Hank: I will blot out the sun, and it will never shine again! Go! Tell the King! (**Clarence** *staggers to his feet and backs off right in terror.*)

Hank: Ha! The eclipse will be sure to save me, and make me the greatest man in the kingdom besides! (*Lights fade out for a moment to indicate brief passage of time, then come up again.* **Hank** *remains seated.*) Of course, if they want to compromise, I'll listen, but I'll have to stand my ground and play my hand for all it's worth. (*Looks off right*) Ah, that must be Clarence coming back now. (**1st** *and* **2nd Guards** *enter right.*)

Hank (*He is seized by* **Guards.**): Wait a minute! The execution is tomorrow!

2nd Guard: The order has been changed and set forward a day. Come! (*Speechless,* **Hank** *is dragged out right. Curtain*).

* * *

Setting: *The Courtyard in Camelot. There is a stake center, with bundles of wood stacked around it.*

At Rise: **Courtiers, King Arthur,** and **Merlin** *stand right and left, as* **Hank** *is dragged in right by* **1st** *and* **2nd Guards.**

Merlin *(Approaching* **Hank,** *waving his arms and sneering):* You call yourself a magician? Then stop the devouring flames if you can! I defy you! *(Beckons to* **Guard** *who comes forward with torch.* **Hank** *throws up his arms in an attitude of despair, and suddenly lights begin to dim. All gasp and look up.)*

Courtiers *(Ad lib):* Look! The sun is disappearing! It's getting dark, and it's only noon! *(Etc.)*

Hank *(Looking up in surprise):* The eclipse! It's starting! I don't know where it came from, or how it happened, but I'd better make the most of it, or I'm done for! *(Strikes grand attitude, pointing upward)*

Merlin *(Frantically):* Apply the torch!

King Arthur: I forbid it! *(***Merlin** *snatches torch from* **Guard** *and starts toward the stake.)*

Hank: Stay where you are! If any man moves I will blast him with thunder and lightning! *(***Merlin** *backs away.)*

King Arthur: Name your terms, reverend Sir, even to the half of my kingdom! But banish this calamity!

Hank *(Looking up):* Well . . . I must have some time to consider.

King Arthur: But it grows darker every moment!

Hank: Nevertheless, I must think! *(Looks up as lights continue to dim to almost complete darkness)* What is this? How am I to tell whether this is the sixth century or not with this eclipse coming a day early? *(Pulls the sleeve of* **3rd Guard**) What day of the month is this?

3rd Guard *(Stepping back, terrified):* The twenty-first, sir.

Hank: The twenty-first! *(To himself)* That featherheaded Clarence told me today was the twentieth! Sir King, whether or not I blot out the sun forever, or restore it, is up to you. You must appoint me your perpetual minister, and give me one percent of all increases in revenue that I may create for the state.

King Arthur: It shall be done! Away with his bonds! Do him homage, all of you, for he is now at my right hand and clothed with power and authority! Now, sweep away this darkness and bring the light again. *(***Guards** *untie* **Hank.**)*

Hank *(To himself):* I wish I knew how long this eclipse is supposed

to last! *(To **King**)* Let it be known that I shall be called The Boss, and all who do as I say and don't get in my way will be spared any further calamities.

King Arthur: Everything shall be as you say, Sir Boss, only bring back the sun!

Hank *(To himself)*: I hope it's time. *(Solemnly lifts his arms and gazes upward)* Let the enchantment dissolve and pass harmless away! *(Darkness continues. The people stir uneasily. He waves his arms in grand flourish. Still it remains dark. He makes more flourishes, and slowly the lights begin to come up, gradually becoming brighter and brighter. **Courtiers** shout for joy.)*

Clarence: Oh, thank you, Sir Boss! You have worked a wondrous miracle, but I beg you, never do it again!

Hank: Don't worry, Clarence, I won't do this particular miracle again. *(Starts off left with his arm around **Clarence's** shoulders, then suddenly stops, scratching his head.)* A Connecticut Yankee in King Arthur's Court! You know, a situation like this has all kinds of possibilities! And if I ever get back to Hartford, what a story I'll have to tell! *(Goes out left with **Clarence** as **Courtiers** bow to him and curtain falls.)*

The End

Practice

A. On a separate sheet write the answers to these questions. Use complete sentences.

1. Who is the protagonist of this play?
2. Who is the antagonist?
3. What is the climax of the play?
4. What are the two settings?
5. Why is the protagonist able to save his life?

B. **6.–10.** Write five sentences to describe Hank Morgan's personality.

Apply

C. **11.** Write a paragraph or two to summarize the plot of this play.

A BOOK TO READ

Title: **A Gathering of Days**
Author: Joan W. Blos
Publisher: Charles Scribner's Sons

In the year 1830, on a small farm in New Hampshire, Catherine Hall began to keep a journal. For a year and a half, she faithfully recorded the events that took place, from the everyday quilting, berrypicking, and sugaring, to the dramatic plight of a runaway slave and the tragic death of Catherine's best friend.

In this story of early America, Joan Blos shows both the rigors and the joys of Catherine's existence. Through Catherine's eyes, the reader gets a sense of life in a different time and place.

UNIT TEST 8

● **Prepositions and Prepositional Phrases** pages 272–273

Read each of these model sentences. Then copy each sentence that follows, completing it correctly.

1. *How many sides are there in an octagon?* The prepositional phrase begins with the word **a.** *are,* **b.** *in,* **c.** *octagon.*
2. *In my book of elementary geometry, there are two pages of pictures showing plane figures.* The number of prepositional phrases in this sentence is **a.** one, **b.** two, **c.** three.
3. *The picture of the octagon shows eight sides.* This sentence contains **a.** a prepositional phrase used as an adjective, **b.** a prepositional phrase used as an adverb, **c.** no prepositional phrase.
4. *I have seen this book before, and I like it.* This sentence contains **a.** a prepositional phrase used as an adjective, **b.** a prepositional phrase used as an adverb, **c.** no prepositional phrase.
5. *I will take it home with me tonight.* This sentence contains **a.** a prepositional phrase used as an adjective, **b.** a prepositional phrase used as an adverb, **c.** no prepositional phrase.

● **Interjections** pages 276–277

Copy these sentences. Punctuate each interjection.

6. Aha a light bulb just went on in my head.
7. Well how did that happen?
8. Wow I just realized that *octa* means *eight* and *gon* means *angle.*

● **Conjunctions** pages 278–279

Copy these sentences. Draw one line under coordinating conjunctions and two lines under correlative conjunctions.

9. A polygon is a plane figure, and it has many angles.
10. You may be a smart person, but you don't know how many angles are in a hexagon.
11. You're wrong, Zuni, for I know that a hexagon has six angles.
12. Not only did I look it up in a dictionary, but also I looked in a textbook.

Choosing and Limiting a Topic   pages 282–283

Copy the topics that would be suitable for a seven- to ten-paragraph research report. If any topic is too broad or too narrow, write in a suitably narrowed topic on the same subject.

1. The History of Algebra
2. Using Mathematics at the Supermarket
3. How Cats and Dogs Communicate with Humans and with One Another
4. The Solar System
5. Training Dolphins at Sea World
6. Economics
7. Simple Ways to Save Money
8. Architecture Through the Ages

Note Taking   pages 286–287

9. Read these paragraphs from *Wondrous World of Fishes* published by the National Geographic Society in Washington, D.C. Then take a brief set of notes on the material it contains.

> Most fishes have eyes set wide apart, one on each side of the head, and that is the way the flounder and halibut start life. But before they grow an inch long their eyes wander curiously. One eye, in the halibut usually the left, begins migrating to the other side of the head. At the same time the fish, which had been swimming upright, begins to lean. The eye continues moving, and the fish continues leaning. In a few days the roving eye has moved nearly 120 degrees to join the other one, and the fish swims with his eyeless side parallel to the bottom.
>
> Most fish hear acutely, in spite of the absence of external ears. Because sound travels much better in water than in air, a fish does not need humanlike ears to collect sound waves, nor does it need ear drums to pass them along. Instead, sound waves strike the flesh and bone of the head. These relay the sounds to inner ears which pass the message to the brain.

Outlining　pages 286–287

10.–20. Write this mixed-up outline in correct form.

A. Use of protractor 3. Read measurement of angle where other side crosses scale of protractor. The Geometry of Angles C. Obtuse angle 1. Place center of protractor at vertex, or point of angle. B. Interpretation of symbols for angles A. Right angle II. Measurement of angles 2. Place base line of protractor along one side of angle. B. Acute angle I. Types of angles

Bibliographies　pages 288–289

Write these bibliographical entries in the correct form.

18. (This entry is for a *book*.) 1963 Algebra and Trigonometry Harper & Row, Inc. Abraham P. Hillman and Gerald L. Alexander New York
19. (This entry is for a *magazine article*.) Scientific American July, 1968 "Standards of Measurements" Allen V. Astin pp. 50–62
20. (This entry is for an *encyclopedia article*.) "Mathematics as a Calculatory Science" Vol. 11 Chicago Fern Moss Encyclopaedia Britannica pp. 671–696 1974 Encyclopaedia Britannica, Inc.

The Research Report　pages 290–291, 292–294

1. Study this outline for one paragraph of a research report on mathematics in ship navigation. Then write the first draft of the paragraph that comes from the *body* of the paper.

I. Ancient navigation
  A. Begun by Greeks
  B. Aided by invention of astrolabe
    1. Helped determine location
    2. Used position of the sun or stars to do this
II. Modern navigation
  A. Aided by invention of sextant
    1. Measures angles
    2. Uses the sun or a known star for one point
    3. Uses the horizon as second point
  B. Modernized further by electronics

Editing a Research Report　pages 295–296

2. Edit the paragraph you wrote about mathematics in ship navigation. Use editing marks to indicate changes. Edit for correct capitalization and punctuation as well as for *order*.

Copy and punctuate these sentences correctly.

3. Did you know Leroy that an obtuse angle measures more than 90 degrees?
4. Yes Leta in the far reaches of my memory I seem to recall that fact.
5. Tell me then how many degrees are there in an acute angle?
6. An angle two rays with the same endpoint is not cute or ugly Leta.
7. You know of course that an acute angle may have 20 degrees.
8. Mathematics as you may know has a fascinating history Leroy.
9. Yes I have heard you mention it.
10. Think of the contributions of Euclid Archimedes and René Descartes!
11. Al-Khuwarizmi a famous Arabian mathematician organized the study of algebra.
12. It was of course the Greeks who first recognized irrational numbers.
13. Your fascination with mathematics Leta seems a bit irrational to me.
14. You Leroy strike me as being somewhat illogical.
15. Here in the park on a spring afternoon I would rather talk about baseball Leta.
16. Well Leroy the distance between home plate and the pitcher's mound between the pitcher's mound and the bases and between first second third and home plate are all precise mathematical relationships.
17. Somehow Leta you have taken all the fun out of discussing baseball.
18. Statistics an important part of baseball records is a branch of mathematics Leroy.
19. My favorite branch of mathematics though is calculus an important advance that marked the beginning of modern mathematics.
20. My favorite branch of baseball Leta is called the St. Louis Cardinals a team that is better than the Los Angeles Dodgers the Chicago Cubs and the San Francisco Giants all rolled into one.

● **A One-Act Play**   pages 297–305

Answer these questions in complete sentences.

1. As a type of literature, how is a one-act play like a short story?
2. What are the words spoken by the characters called?
3. What name is given to the *action* of the play?
4. Into what three main parts is the play's action divided?
5. What name is given to the main character of the play?
6. What name is given to the character who opposes the main character?
7. What name is given to the high point of the action?
8. What occurs in the dénouement of the play?

MAINTENANCE and REVIEW

Read and then copy these paragraphs.

Glass is common and everyday to us, but glass objects once were items of great value. The first glass vessels were made about 3,500 years ago in Mesopotamia and Egypt. The making of glass at that time was difficult and quite expensive; as a result, few people could afford glass items. Rulers bought themselves glass jewelry, jars, and boxes. For example, from the tomb of King Tutankhamun comes a beautiful earring of gold and blue glass. In his time the glass was probably as expensive as the gold. Merchants bought glass containers for wine and oil. Cities and towns along the eastern Mediterranean supplied glass objects for the wealthy.

The market for glass changed considerably around 30 B.C. with the invention of an important glassmaking tool—the blowpipe. No one knows the inventor of the blowpipe, but his or her invention made glass available to practically everyone. During the next 400 years, glassmaking flourished. Artists produced painted or gilded blown glass. They also made vases of layered glass and produced raised designs on them by cutting away parts of the outer layers. In the British Museum sits the Portland Vase, an example of this layering technique. New techniques made glassware more ornate—and less costly to produce. Glassmakers reached a high point in their craft during this era, and the availability of glass to all produced glass-manufacturing centers throughout the Roman Empire.

Sentences and Paragraphs   pages 6–7, 10–13, 44–49

1. Draw one line under each simple subject in paragraph 2 and two lines under each simple or compound predicate.
2. Which sentence in paragraph 1 contains a compound subject?
3. How many compound sentences are there in paragraph 1?
4. Underline the topic sentence in each paragraph.
5. How do the details in paragraph 2 support the main idea?

Nouns   pages 80–81, 82–83

6. Name five proper nouns that appear in this passage.
7. Circle ten common nouns that appear in paragraph 1. Which of the ten are singular, and which are plural?

8. Name two abstract nouns that appear in this passage.

9. How many appositives are there in this passage? What are they?

Verbs pages 120–135

10. Which verbs in paragraph 1 are action verbs? Which are linking verbs?

11. Which of the action verbs in paragraph 1 are transitive?

12. Write the three principal parts of these verbs.

buy   afford   supply   produce   come   reach

Which of these verbs are irregular?

13. What tense is used most often in this passage? What other tense is used occasionally?

Adjectives and Adverbs pages 162–163, 166–167, 170–171

14. Name eight adjectives and two adverbs that appear in these paragraphs. Name the word or words that each one modifies.

Complements and Pronouns pages 200–207, 236–247

15. Name a direct object, an indirect object, a predicate nominative, and a predicate adjective that appear in this passage.

16. Write whether each of these pronouns that appear in the passage is a *subject, object, possessive, reflexive,* or *indefinite* pronoun.

all   few   her   his   no one
their   them   themselves   they   us

Prepositions and Conjunctions pages 272–275, 278–279

17. List ten prepositional phrases that appear in paragraph 2.

18. List four prepositional phrases that act like adjectives and two that act like adverbs in paragraph 1. What word or words does each one modify?

19. What three coordinating conjunctions appear in this passage? Name two examples of the use of each one.

20. How many correlative conjunctions are there in this passage?

9

LANGUAGE
Building
Sentences

COMPOSITION
Writing a
News Article

STUDY SKILLS
Preparing
for Tests

LITERATURE
Enjoying
Novels

What do writing a news story and preparing for a test have in common? In both cases it is essential to get the facts straight. In addition, it is often important to get the material as quickly as possible. In this unit you will practice skimming and scanning, preparing for tests, gathering and checking facts, and writing and editing a news story. You will also learn about clauses and how they work together to produce interesting, varied sentences. As you read a selection from *Dandelion Wine,* a novel by Ray Bradbury, you will see the importance of presenting even fictional information in an entertaining way.

Study the pictures on the opposite page. If you were in charge of a newspaper, which pictures would you use? Imagine a headline that would be appropriate for each picture. You may wish to make note of your ideas for use in your own news story later in this unit.

LANGUAGE

Lesson 1: Understanding Clauses

Read these sentences:

1. Marty works at the recycling center on Saturdays.
2. He separates glass bottles, and his sister Kim separates aluminum cans.

What kind of sentence is sentence 2? Find two groups of words with a subject and a verb in sentence 2.

Think and Discuss

A group of words that contains a subject and verb is called a **clause.** A clause that can stand alone as a simple sentence when it has proper capitalization and end punctuation is called an **independent clause.**
Read this sentence.

3. <u>The glass bottles are crushed</u> <u>after they are separated.</u>

Sentence 3 has two clauses connected by a conjunction. What is that conjunction? Conjunctions like *after* are called **subordinating conjunctions.** A subordinating conjunction becomes part of the clause that follows it and turns that clause into a **dependent clause.** A dependent clause cannot stand alone as a sentence. It must be joined to an independent clause in order to make sense. A sentence that contains one independent clause and one or more dependent clauses is a **complex sentence.**

If a sentence contains a dependent clause and more than one independent clause, it is called a **compound-complex sentence.** Read this sentence.

4. Kim gave a speech on recycling, and many people wanted to help after they learned about recycling.

Which clauses in sentence 5 are independent? What is the dependent clause?

- A **clause** is a group of words that contains a subject and a verb.
- An **independent clause** is a group of words that contains a subject and a verb and can stand by itself as a sentence.
- A **dependent clause** contains a subject and a verb but cannot stand alone because it does not express a complete thought.
- A **complex sentence** contains one independent clause and one or more dependent clauses.
- A **subordinating conjunction** is a conjunction used to introduce some type of dependent clause. It becomes part of the clause and makes it a dependent clause.
- A **compound-complex sentence** has more than one independent clause and at least one dependent clause.

Practice

A. Copy these sentences. Circle each coordinating conjunction and underline each subordinating conjunction. Write whether each sentence is *simple, compound, complex,* or *compound-complex.*

1. Marty and Kim ride their bikes or walk to the recycling center.
2. Kim usually wears old jeans, but Marty wears overalls.
3. Although the glass-crushing machine is small, it is very noisy, and Marty must wear earplugs.
4. After Marty gathers up the bottles, he separates them by color.
5. The crushed glass is put into cartons; they are picked up during the week.
6. When she begins her work, Kim puts on a pair of gloves.

Apply

B. 7.–10. Use a social studies or science textbook to find an example of each type of sentence discussed in this lesson. Write each sentence and label it *simple, compound, complex,* or *compound-complex.*

Lesson 2: Understanding Adverb Clauses

Read these sentences.

1. Jennifer drew a map before she hid the treasure.
2. After she gives the signal, we will look for the treasure.

What kind of sentences are sentences 1 and 2? What is the dependent clause in each one? What question does each clause answer?

Think and Discuss

In all of the complex sentences you have read so far, the dependent clauses have been **adverb clauses.** An adverb clause is a dependent clause that begins with a subordinating conjunction and is used in the same way as an adverb is used. In sentence 1, the dependent clause, *before she hid the treasure*, is an adverb clause. It answers the questions *when.* Which word in the independent clause does this clause modify? Which word in the independent clause does the adverb clause in sentence 2 modify?

Which subordinating conjunction is used to introduce the adverb clause in sentence 1? in sentence 2? Here is a list of some common subordinating conjunctions used to introduce adverb clauses.

Subordinating Conjunctions

after	if	when
although	since	whenever
as	that	where
as if	though	wherever
because	unless	whether
before	until	while

Subordinating conjunctions help you to join ideas so that you can express just the meaning you want. Notice how the meaning of the following sentence differs with each conjunction.

Jennifer hid the treasure $\left.\begin{array}{l}\text{after}\\\text{before}\\\text{while}\end{array}\right\}$ she drew a map.

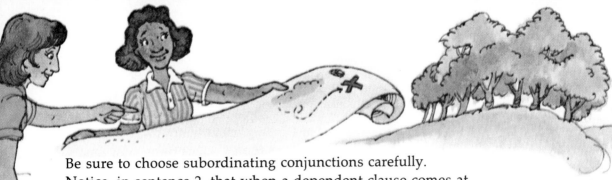

Be sure to choose subordinating conjunctions carefully.

Notice, in sentence 2, that when a dependent clause comes at the beginning of a sentence, it is separated from the independent clause by a comma. When it comes at the end, as in sentence 1, it is usually not separated from the main clause. If a dependent clause appears in the middle of a sentence, dividing an independent clause, it is set off with commas.

> - An **adverb clause** is a dependent clause that begins with a subordinating conjunction and is used in the same way as an adverb is used.

Practice

A. Copy these sentences. Underline the adverb clause in each one and tell what word in the independent clause it modifies.

1. Everyone cheered when Cleo walked in with the treasure.
2. She carried the bottle as if it were made of gold.
3. Because she likes riddles, Jennifer had put a message in it.
4. Before she could get her prize, Cleo read the message.
5. All the guests listened while Cleo read the poem.

B. Add an adverb clause to each of these independent clauses.

6. Jennifer's parents were making lemonade _____.
7. Craig and Garnetta did not have a map _____.
8. We all had to wait _____.
9. Cleo almost missed the treasure _____.
10. Everyone laughed _____.

Apply

C. 11–20. Plan a treasure hunt for your friends. Write ten sentences about the treasure map and the rules of the hunt. Use an adverb clause in each sentence.

Lesson 3: Understanding Adjective Clauses

Read the following sentences.

1. The boy who did the magic tricks is my cousin.
2. His magic hat, which he found, is his prize possession.

The underlined words are dependent clauses. What are the independent clauses in sentences 1 and 2? What words in sentences 1 and 2 do the dependent clauses modify?

Think and Discuss

In addition to being used as adverbs, dependent clauses may also be used as adjectives, to modify nouns. These are called **adjective clauses.** In sentence 1, the dependent clause, *who did the magic tricks,* modifies *boy,* the subject of the independent clause. Notice that this clause begins with the pronoun *who.* *Who* joins or *relates* the adjective clause to the noun it modifies. *Who* is a relative pronoun that refers to the antecedent *boy.*

The **relative pronouns** are *who, whose, which,* and *that.* Relative pronouns act in the way that nouns and pronouns do in the clauses they introduce. In sentence 1, *who* is the subject of the adjective clause *who did the magic tricks.* What is the function of the relative pronoun in the adjective clause in sentence 2?

Adjective clauses are **restrictive** or **nonrestrictive.** Restrictive clauses *identify* the noun they modify; therefore, they do not require commas. Nonrestrictive clauses merely give more information about the noun they modify. That information is not necessary for identification or clarity of meaning. Therefore, nonrestrictive adjective clauses are set off with commas. You can read a sentence leaving out a nonrestrictive clause without describing the basic meaning of the sentence.

3. The magic tricks that I like best involve sleight-of-hand. (restrictive)
4. Card tricks, which can be quite difficult, have always fascinated me. (nonrestrictive)

- An **adjective clause** is a dependent clause that begins with a relative pronoun and modifies a noun or pronoun.
- A **relative pronoun** introduces an adjective clause and relates it to the noun the clause modifies. An antecedent is the noun referred to by the relative pronoun.
- A **restrictive adjective clause** identifies the person or thing it modifies and is not set off by commas.
- A **nonrestrictive adjective clause** tells more about the noun it modifies and is set off by commas.

Practice

A. Copy these sentences. Underline each adjective clause and circle the relative pronoun that introduces it. Draw an arrow to the noun modified.

1. I know the people who came to the magic show.
2. The ones whom you invited are my friends.
3. My cousin is the one whose magic made him famous.
4. This is the trick that I like least.
5. His best trick, which is last on the program, is my favorite.

B. Complete these sentences, filling in each blank with the correct relative pronoun. After each sentence, write whether the clause is restrictive or nonrestrictive.

6. The table _____ is in the center has a false top.
7. The tablecloth, _____ I made, is purple with gold stars.
8. The person _____ is sitting in the corner will be asked to assist.
9. Please seat the late-comers, _____ are standing by the door.
10. The girl _____ guessed the right hat won the prize.

Apply

C. 11.–20. Imagine that you are an amateur magician. Write ten sentences about your first magic show. Use an adjective clause in each sentence.

Lesson 4: Understanding Noun Clauses

Read these sentences.

1. The driver must be careful.
2. Whoever is driving must be careful.

Which group of words acts as the complete subject of sentence 1? Which group of words acts as the complete subject of the second sentence?

Think and Discuss

A dependent clause that is used in the same way as a noun is used in a sentence is called a **noun clause.** A noun clause may be used in any of the following ways.

As Subject: *What you say about the roads* worries me.
As Direct Object: I know *how slippery icy roads can be.*
As Predicate Nominative: That is *why I am so concerned.*
As Object of Preposition: I will give this scraper *to whoever needs it.*

Words that introduce noun clauses include *who, whose, whom, which, what, whoever, whichever, that, when, where, why, how, whether,* and *if.*

- A **noun clause** is a dependent clause that is used in the same way that a noun is used in a sentence.

Practice

A. Copy these sentences. Underline the noun clause in each one. After each sentence, write whether the clause is used as *subject, direct object, object of a preposition,* or *predicate nominative.*

1. The fact is that all the roads for miles around are very dangerous.
2. The weather report states that there will be six inches of snow by morning.
3. I wonder whether the snow plows are out clearing the major highways yet.
4. There are cots prepared for whoever gets through to town.
5. What I want is a cup of hot cocoa.
6. I don't remember where we put the snow shovel.
7. They should give a prize to whoever built that snow sculpture.
8. What our dog likes best is romping in the snow.
9. The radio stations have regular reports on what the condition of the roads is.
10. Do you suppose that school will be closed tomorrow?

B. Use the following noun clauses in sentences.

11. where the snow has fallen
12. whoever needs tire chains
13. how high the snowdrifts are
14. that icicles are forming
15. what the next news report says
16. where my ice skates are
17. whether the pond has frozen
18. that the bird feeder has been filled with birdseed
19. how the sun sparkles on the newly fallen snow
20. what I like best about snow

C. 21.–30. Tell how you used each noun clause in the sentences you wrote for Practice B.

Apply

D. 31.–35. Write five sentences about a winter you remember. Include a noun clause in each one.

Lesson 5: Correcting Misplaced Modifiers

Read this sentence.

1. Lia saw beautiful fish looking through her underwater camera.

According to this sentence, who or what is looking through the camera?

Think and Discuss

A modifier—a word, phrase, or clause that adds to or changes the meaning of other words—should be placed as close as possible to the word it modifies. Otherwise, it may appear to be modifying the wrong word. The phrase *looking through her underwater camera* should refer to Lia, but its placement in the sentence makes it seem to refer to the fish. It is a **misplaced modifier.** To correct the misplaced modifier in sentence 1, place the modifying phrase at the beginning of the sentence, closer to the word it modifies: *Looking through her underwater camera, Lia saw beautiful fish.*

Now study this sentence.

2. My mask was lost by another diver with safety glass.

According to this sentence, it is another diver, not the mask, that has safety glass. To correct this misplaced modifier, the writer should place the phrase *with safety glass* after *mask,* the word it modifies.

Sentences 1 and 2 are difficult, but not impossible, to understand. With a little rereading, a reader can usually figure out what the writer of a sentence with a misplaced modifier intended. That, however, is not a fair burden to put on the reader. When you write, keep your modifiers as close as possible to the words they modify.

Practice

A. Correct the misplaced modifiers as you rewrite these sentences.

1. We saw a beautiful coral formation swimming over the reef.
2. Rochelle wore a belt around her waist that was weighted.

3. A shirt was worn by the guide that was tattered.
4. Finally the beach was located by our guide covered with multicolored shells.
5. Lia saw a sea turtle laying its eggs on the way to a noontime picnic.
6. Rochelle walked over to the picnic table dripping with seaweed.
7. We saw dolphins swimming from our hammocks on the beach.
8. One tourist was burned by the sun without a hat.
9. Our guide told us stories of the shipwrecked sailors he had saved when he had nothing better to do.
10. We listened to every tale the guide told us without saying a word.

Apply

B. 11.–20. Write ten sentences about a snorkeling trip. Use a modifying phrase or clause in each sentence. Make sure that your modifiers are properly placed.

HOW OUR LANGUAGE GROWS

Have you ever heard someone or something described as *gargantuan, puckish,* or *quixotic*? These are examples of words that come from the names of characters in literature. *Gargantuan,* for example, means huge; it comes from the name of a giant king in a novel by Rabelais. *Puckish,* or impish, comes from *Puck,* a mischievous sprite in Shakespeare's *A Midsummer Night's Dream. Don Quixote,* the title character in a novel by Cervantes, was an impractical idealist; those who think as he did are called *quixotic.*

Here are some names of literary characters. What kind of person does each one describe?

1. Scrooge
2. Galahad
3. Chicken Little
4. Pied Piper
5. Cinderella
6. Ugly Duckling

LANGUAGE REVIEW

Clauses   pages 314–315

Copy these sentences. Draw one line under each independent clause.

1. Jewel's roof had a leak in it, and her friends had promised to fix it.
2. Dark, heavy clouds scudded across the sky; it looked like rain.
3. Then Marini came along, and the work began to go more quickly.
4. She crawled onto the roof but could not reach the chimney.
5. The skies grew darker, and we hurried to finish the job before the next rainstorm.
6. Gail found the loose shingles and replaced them.
7. Am I mistaken, or is the basement filling with water now?

Adverb Clauses   pages 316–317

Copy these sentences. Underline each adverb clause and circle the subordinating conjunction that introduces it.

8. Angela cannot go outside until she finishes her lab experiment.
9. Because she wants a good grade, she will work until it is finished.
10. While Angela works on her experiment, Evita is writing a book report for English class.
11. When their homework is finished, Angela and Evita go out and visit with their friends.
12. Although Evita enjoys English, she hopes to be a scientist someday.
13. She reads science magazines as she walks to school every morning.

Adjective Clauses   pages 318–319

Copy these sentences. Underline each adjective clause and circle the relative pronoun that introduces it. After each, write whether the clause is *restrictive* or *nonrestrictive*.

14. Alfred Nobel was a man who experimented with nitroglycerin in his father's factory in Sweden.
15. He wanted to make nitroglycerin, which was a dangerous substance, into a safe and useful explosive.
16. In 1865 he invented a safe blasting gelatin, which later was called dynamite.
17. Nobel, who strongly believed in peace, had reservations about his own invention.

18. He established a fund that contained a portion of the profits from the invention.
14. The fund, which supplies the money for Nobel Prizes, is still in existence.
20. The Nobel Prize has been given to hundreds of people who have performed outstanding services for humanity.

Noun Clauses   pages 320–321

Copy these sentences. Underline each noun clause. After each sentence write whether the clause is used as *subject, direct object, object of a preposition,* or *predicate nominative.*

21. Manaba asked whether the Native American Culture Club was meeting on Wednesday.
22. The answer was that the meeting will be held on Thursday.
23. The club will give an award to whoever does the best research on Native American games.
24. Kulya, Paco, and Namid will evaluate whatever the club members find.
25. What Kimama is hoping is that she will win.
26. She has discovered that Native Americans played the familiar shell game with moccasins long before the arrival of the Europeans.

Misplaced Modifiers   pages 322–323

Correct the misplaced modifiers as you rewrite these sentences.

27. Bibi found a paramecium looking through her microscope.
28. The beaker was carried by a student that was cracked.
29. The net was repaired by the coach with a big hole in it.
30. A poem was read by the actor that is more than 500 years old.

Applying Sentence Building

31.–40. Write ten sentences trying to persuade two friends to go on a bus trip with you. You may wish to write the sentences in dialog form. At least five of the sentences should be complex, and one should be compound-complex. Use at least one noun clause, one adjective clause, and one adverb clause in your sentences. Check to see that none of your sentences contain misplaced modifiers.

STUDY SKILLS

Lesson 6: Skimming and Scanning

When you are studying, you want to make good use of your time. You can make every minute count if you learn to read efficiently.

Think and Discuss

One type of quick reading is called **scanning.** When you scan, your eyes run quickly down the page, looking for certain words or phrases. You are scanning when you use the table of contents and the index of a book to find a specific kind of information. By scanning you will quickly be able to determine which pages of a book contain the information that you want.

Once you have found the appropriate section of the book, you can start to skim. **Skimming** means reading to find the main idea and key points. Sometimes skimming is all you need to do; you can quickly jot down the information you need and go on to something else. You may sometimes decide to reread certain paragraphs more carefully. Many students start their assigned reading by skimming. When they go back to read the passage in detail, they will have a clearer idea of how the material that they are reading fits together.

Here are some tips to help you skim a passage effectively.

How to Skim a Passage

1. Check the first sentence of each paragraph, which often mentions the topic.
2. Check the last sentence of each paragraph, which often is a summary.
3. Look for key words and phrases.
4. Take special note of words that are printed in italics or boldface.
5. Pay special attention to topic headings.
6. Look for charts and lists.

Practice

A. Read this list of questions; then read the paragraph that comes after it. Answer the questions and write whether you used *skimming* or *scanning* to get the answer.

1. What is the main idea of this paragraph?
2. What is a network?
3. To what does the word *spot* refer?
4. What two kinds of TV and radio stations are mentioned?
5. Name a key word in this paragraph.

While radio and television stations are different in many ways, they are organized similarly. Some stations belong to a nationwide system of programming, or network, whereas others are independent local producers and buyers of their own shows. This distinction is important to advertisers, who may buy either network or "spot" — that is, local — broadcast time, or both.

Apply

B. 6. Select any book from your school or local public library. Scan the book for no longer than five minutes. Then write a two-paragraph report on what you learned about the contents of the book and its usefulness.

A Challenge

It is the year 3080, and you are head librarian at Interstellar Library #465. You have made a rare find. It is a manual written for visitors to Mars. Excited by your find, you scan the book. You find several sections on manners at meals such as "What to Do When You Attend a SQUANO and Find an XPLG in Your EMPILN." Another chapter, dealing with the problem of introductions, is entitled "Protective Clothing to Wear When Introducing a GRANUSLATER to a MONUBLASH." Later, you skim both chapters and note the key words QUASHKELL, UNGOT, and MOLENC in the first one describing dinners difficult to consume neatly. In the second chapter you find UNHELC and QUISHING the JABBULATOR as phrases *not* to mention in making introductions. Armed with this information, write paragraphs for either or both of these chapters for the *Martian Manual of Manners*. Add other creatures, dishes, and introduction rituals whenever you need them.

"We have a science test at the end of next week," Tomás said to his friend Pat. "I am nervous about it."

"Really?" Pat answered. "I'm not nervous; I have been preparing for it all along. Let me tell you what I do."

Think and Discuss

One reason that some people become nervous about taking tests is that they do not do any studying until the night before the test. You will feel more confident if you constantly review what you cover in class—and you will remember the material better too. Part of this review should include going over notes you have made on your reading assignments, homework, and reports you have done. Set up a regular schedule for review, and stick to it.

Your most important study materials are your textbook and your class notes. As you carefully read your class notes, check for any that seem incomplete. When you find incomplete notes, reread the material on which they are based. Carefully reread only those parts of the text that you need to review; skim through the rest of the material. Note points that you do not understand, and raise them in class or privately with your teacher.

Use all of your study materials to make a rough outline; then use the outline to make up a test on the material. If you cannot answer some of the question, go back and find the answers.

Study in a quiet, comfortable area with good lighting and no distractions, if possible. Get plenty of sleep the night before the test so that you will be alert.

When you take a test, keep these points in mind.

How to Take a Test

1. **Plan your time. Do not spend more time than you should on any one question.**
2. **Be sure that you read each question carefully and that you understand all directions. If you are not sure what a certain question is asking from you, do not guess. Ask your teacher.**
3. **Be sure to number each item correctly if you are answering questions on a separate sheet of paper.**
4. **If there are several questions that require essay answers, read all of them over quickly before you answer any of them.**
5. **Unless you are required to answer the questions in order, answer the easy ones first and then the hard ones.**
6. **If you are not sure of an answer, make an intelligent guess.**
7. **Save a few minutes at the end of the test period to proofread your answers.**

Practice

A. Here are some things that Tomás told Pat he had done to prepare for previous tests. Copy the statements that show good study and test-taking methods. Correct the unhelpful statements.

1. I read my science assignment just before I go to bed.
2. If I do not understand something I have read, I ask questions about it at the next class.
3. I never save my homework.
4. Before an exam I reread all of the material carefully.
5. Since I study so hard the night before, I get little sleep.
6. When I take a test, I read all the questions carefully.
7. I always answer the questions in the order they are given.

Apply

B. 8. Start preparing for your next test now. Set up a schedule of review, and use your study materials to make up a test on which you can judge your knowledge of the material.

COMPOSITION

Lesson 8: Writing a News Story

Read these paragraphs.

Odette Turner, a 68-year-old art major in her sophomore year at Whitman University, has been awarded the Alma Johnson Scholarship. Mrs. Turner is 1 of 12 students to receive the prize, and she is the only winner from Clearview. The scholarship, which is given annually by the Professional Staff Conference of the University, will pay $1,000 of Mrs. Turner's tuition per semester for the rest of her undergraduate career.

At a ceremony on April 12, Mrs. Turner was commended for her "outstanding example to the student body." She accepted her first check in the company of her husband Ralph, her daughter Margaret, and her grandson Cleon. Cleon is a political science major in his junior year at Whitman.

After the ceremony, Mrs. Turner said, "I plan to use this scholarship to finance some courses in secondary education and to continue my study of advanced watercolor technique. I am very proud of this honor."

Think and Discuss

These paragraphs form a **news story.** The purpose of a news story is to tell readers in a brief, factual, and interesting way about something that has happened.

Notice the questions answered in this article.

Who?	Odette Turner, a 68-year-old art major
What?	was awarded the Alma Johnson Scholarship
Where?	Whitman University
When?	April 12
Why?	She was an "outstanding example to the student body."
How?	in a ceremony

Which of the questions are answered in the first paragraph? Which are answered in the second paragraph? The first paragraph of a news story contains the most essential information. It is sometimes called the *lead,* for it presents the leading information. For this story about Mrs. Turner, the leading information answers the questions *who, what,* and *where.* In other stories the answers to other questions might be considered leading information.

The paragraph or paragraphs that follow the lead give supporting details. These details are arranged in the order of their importance, with the most important details placed in the earlier paragraphs. Material that is optional is placed near the end of the story. In that way, if the story has to be shortened to make room for something of more importance, all the writer or editor has to do is to cut as much as is necessary from the bottom. The quotation from Mrs. Turner is considered optional information to this story, so it appears at the end. The information in the second paragraph gives supporting details that could also be omitted if the need arose.

The last part of a news story to be written is usually the *headline.* The headline relates, in abbreviated form, the main ideas of the lead. The headline for the story about Mrs. Turner could be "Turner Wins Scholarship" or "Clearview Woman Awarded Scholarship." Because Mrs. Turner's age is unusual and therefore an attention getter, another possibility is "Clearview Woman, 68, Wins College Scholarship." The actual headline chosen will depend in part on the amount of space that is available on the newspaper page.

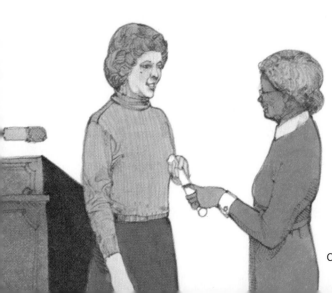

Practice

A. Read these facts that a reporter has gathered for a news story. Copy those facts that belong in the lead paragraph.

1. A new clinic has been established for diagnosis and treatment of people with high blood pressure.
2. The clinic is at Mercy Hospital.
3. All diagnostic tests will be performed free of charge.
4. The clinic will open on Monday, September 13.
5. The clinic will be directed by Dr. Miriam Shapiro.
6. Dr. Shapiro is a cardiologist who has written several books on high blood pressure, as well as a popular book on stress in the workplace.
7. "High blood pressure is a major health concern of many people in our community," said Dr. Shapiro.
8. Further information on the clinic can be obtained by calling 650-7100, Monday through Friday, from 10:00 A.M. to 4:30 P.M.

B. 9. Use the information in Practice A to write a news story. Try to answer all six questions in your article, and put the information that you consider most important first.

Apply

C. 10. Write a news story on an event that has occurred in your classroom or school during the past month. If your school has its own newspaper, you may wish to submit your story for publication.

To Memorize

Injustice anywhere is a threat to justice everywhere.

Martin Luther King, Jr.

The idea expressed by Martin Luther King, Jr., is not a new one. Seneca, a Roman philosopher born almost 2,000 years ago, said, "A kingdom founded on injustice never lasts." How might injustice, or the violation of some people's rights, be a threat to the rights of everyone?

Lesson 9: Editing a News Story

Read this first draft of a news story that Pamla wrote.

≡	capitalize
⊙	make a period
∧	add something
⋏	add a comma
⌄"	add quotation marks
⤶	take something away
○	spell correctly
¶	indent the paragraph
/	make a lowercase letter
∾ tr	transpose

Local Pig ~~Gets~~ *Wins* Caribbean Cruise
In Cereal Contest

When a ~~letter~~ *telegram* addressed to Julius C. Gundersen *from Merry-Go-Round Foods* arrived at the Gundersen household, *Tuesday afternoon* Cyrel Gundersen read it to his wife, Grete. The ~~letter~~ *telegram* said that Julius had won *a Caribbean cruise,* the first prize in the "Why I Love Carousel Crunchies" essay contest. Cyrel and Grete then read the ~~letter~~ *telegram* to Julius. Julius, who ~~can not~~ *cannot* read, is four years old. He is also a pig.

Julius Caesar Gundersen is the ~~four-year-old~~ 410-pound Yorkshire hog who is the Gundersens' pet. Interviewed at their farm, located on Thorndyke ~~Lane~~ *Road* near Route 522, the Gundersens explained. "He was the runt of a neighbor's litter, but he was a real little fighter. We offered to take care of him, and we named him Julius Caesar," Mrs. Gundersen said. "He *just* loves Carousel Crunchies," Mr. Gundersen added. "When I heard about the contest, I knew that I had to send in an entry for him, just as a joke. I never figured that he *actually would* win."

The *two-week* cruise will take Julius Caesar and his "parents" to Jamaica, ~~Hiati~~ *Haiti,* *Puerto Rico,* and Barbados. "If you think we're surprised," Mr. Gundersen said, "Wait until you see the face of the ship's captain when we bring Julius on board."

Does the edited first draft of Pamla's news story answer all six questions?

Think and Discuss

The information that Pamla added to the first paragraph of her news story helps to answer two questions. It completes the answer to the question *what* by giving the name of the cereal company, and it answers the question *when* by adding *Tuesday afternoon* to the first sentence.

Pamla has also edited her news story for accuracy. For example, she added that the cruise would take two weeks. In checking her notes, Pamla also discovered that she had not quoted Mr. Gundersen accurately, so she made the appropriate corrections. When you edit a news story, make sure that the most important questions are answered first and that all of your information is accurate.

Practice

A. 1. Copy Pamla's news story, making the changes she marked.

B. 2. Study the corrected news story, and then close your book and take out a sheet of paper. Write the news story as your teacher reads it aloud.

C. These sentences contain inaccurate information. Rewrite them so that they will be accurate.

3. The telegram was delivered on Tuesday morning.
4. Caesar Gundersen weighs almost 500 pounds.
5. Cyrel and Gerte consider themselves "parents" to the prize-winning sow.
6. The cruise will take the Gundersens to three islands.
7. The Gundersen farm is located at the intersection of Thorndyke Lane and Route 502.

Apply

D. 8. Reread the news story that you wrote in Lesson 8. Are the most important questions answered at the beginning of the story? Is all of your information accurate? Edit your news story, and then rewrite it.

Using Apostrophes

- Use an apostrophe for possessive nouns but not for possessive pronouns.

    Olivia's   Cass's   women's   hers   his   theirs

- Use an apostrophe to form contractions of pronouns and verbs and to form contractions of verbs and the adverb *not.*

    we'd   they'll   you've   weren't   hasn't   shouldn't

- Use underlining and an apostrophe to form the plurals of letters.

    <u>c</u>'s   <u>h</u>'s   <u>m</u>'s   <u>u</u>'s

A. Write the contractions for these verbs and adverbs.

1. could not   **2.** she is   **3.** have not
4. they are   **5.** will not   **6.** he has

B. Copy these sentences, adding apostrophes and underlining where necessary.

7. Chris was learning to type. Valerie, Chriss sister, was teaching her.
8. "Its easy," she told her. "Youll be typing like a pro in no time."
9. Before long, Chris decided that her sisters words had come too soon.
10. After all, Valerie found typing easy; in fact, she made money by typing many of her friends papers.
11. The principal of Valeries school had even given her an award for her typing ability.
12. Chris found that her fingers slipped and that she was typing rs instead of ts and ms instead of js.
13. "Whats the use?" she complained. "My typing will never be as good as Valeries." She looked at the sentence that she had been typing and noted that she had spelled *Mississippi* with ds instead of ss.
14. Because of Valerie's and her parents encouragement, Chris kept trying.
15. Years later, she said, "Thats why Ive been so successful. My familys message was to stick with a task, and Im glad to say that Ive followed that message all my life."

LITERATURE

Lesson 10: Understanding the Characteristics of a Novel

Theme, plot, and characters are important features of many kinds of literature. The narrative poem, the one-act play, the short story, and the novel all share these characteristics. In what way is the novel different from other kinds of literature?

Think and Discuss

A **novel** is a long, complex story that follows several *characters* over an extended period of time. During this time the characters change and the *plot* evolves. Because of the great length of most novels, the plot can undergo many shifts and strange twists that allow the characters to grow and mature. A novel, for example, can show the good qualities in a character who would ordinarily be considered a villain. A short story, because of its space limitations, rarely can reveal such depth of personality. The change in the characters as a result of plot development helps to illustrate the main idea, or *theme*, of the novel.

Another advantage of a novel's length is that the plot can be developed gradually and in a more complex way. There can be many minor characters and themes, and greater detail can be used to develop the major theme, characters, and setting. In a novel it is not unusual to have the action occur in several widely separated countries or to show the lives of family members over many generations.

Here is part of a chapter from Ray Bradbury's *Dandelion Wine*. In this novel a 12-year-old boy from Illinois, Douglas Spaulding, experiences a summer of ordinary and extraordinary events that make him a more mature person. If the action seems slower in this selection than in the others you have read so far, remember that this is only a small part of the entire book. Since the selection is taken from the *body* of the novel, you must understand that the characters and setting have already been established. You are like an unexpected visitor who suddenly comes in on a situation that has been in progress for some time.

She was a woman with a broom or dustpan or washrag or mixing spoon in her hand. You saw her cutting piecrust in the morning, humming to it, or you saw her setting out the baked pies at noon or taking them in, cool, at dusk. She rang porcelain cups like a Swiss bell ringer, to their place. She glided through the halls as steadily as a vacuum machine, seeking, finding, and setting to rights. She made mirrors of every window, to catch the sun. She strolled twice through any garden, trowel in hand, and flowers raised their quivering fires upon the warm air in her wake. She slept quietly and turned no more than three times in a night, as relaxed as a white glove to which, at dawn, a brisk hand will return. Waking, she touched people like pictures, to set their names straight.

But, now . . .?

"Grandma," said everyone. "Great-grandma."

Now it was as if a huge sum in arithmetic were finally drawing to an end. She had stuffed turkeys, chickens, squabs, gentlemen, and boys. She had washed ceilings, walls, invalids, and children. She had laid linoleum, repaired bicycles, wound clocks, stoked furnaces, swabbed iodine on ten thousand grievous wounds. Her hands had flown all around about and down, gentling this, holding that, throwing baseballs, shining bright croquet mallets, seeding black earth, or fixing covers over dumplings, ragoûts, and children wildly strewn by slumber. She had pulled down shades, pinched out candles, turned switches, and — grown old. Looking back on thirty billions of things started, carried, finished, and done, it all summed up, totaled out; the last decimal was placed, the final zero swung slowly into line. Now, chalk in hand, she stood back from life a silent hour before reaching for the eraser.

The family surrounded her bed.

"Just let me lie," she whispered.

Her ailment could not be seen in any microscope; it was a mild but ever-deepening tiredness, a dim weighting of her sparrow body; sleepy, sleepier, sleepiest.

As for her children and her children's children — it seemed impossible that with such a simple act, the most leisurely act in the world, she could cause such apprehension.

"Great-grandma, now listen—what you're doing is no better than breaking a lease. This house will fall down without you. You must give us at least a year's notice."

Great-grandma opened one eye. Ninety years gazed calmly out at her physicians like a dust-ghost from a high cupola window in a fast-emptying house. "Tom . . .?"

The boy was sent alone to her whispering bed.

"Tom," she said, faintly, far away, "in the Southern Seas there's a day in each man's life when he knows it's time to shake hands with all his friends and say goodbye and sail away, and he does, and it's natural—it's just his time. That's how it is today. I'm so like you sometimes, sitting through Saturday matinees until nine at night when we sent your Dad to bring you home. . . . I'm leaving while I'm happy and still entertained."

Douglas was summoned next to her side.

"Grandma, who'll shingle the roof next spring?"

Every April as far back as there were calendars, you thought you heard woodpeckers tapping the housetop. But no, it was Great-grandma somehow transported, singing, pounding nails, replacing shingles, high in the sky!

"Douglas, don't let anyone do the shingles unless it's fun for them. . . . Because up on that roof you can see the whole town going toward the country and the country going toward the edge of the earth and the river shining, and the morning lake, and birds on the trees down under you, and the best of the wind all around above. Any one of those should be enough to make a person climb a weather vane some spring sunrise. It's a powerful hour, if you give it half a chance . . ."

Her voice sank to a soft flutter.

Douglas was crying.

She roused herself again. "Now, why are you doing that?"

"Because," he said, "you won't be here tomorrow."

She turned a small hand mirror from herself to the boy. He looked at her face and himself in the mirror and then at her face again as she said, "Tomorrow morning I'll get up at seven and wash behind my ears; I'll run to church with Charlie Woodman; I'll picnic at Electric Park; I'll swim, run barefoot, fall out of trees, chew spearmint gum. . . . Douglas, Douglas, for shame! You cut your fingernails, don't you?"

"Yes'm."

"And you don't yell when your body makes itself over every seven years or so, old cells dead and new ones added to your fingers and your heart. You don't mind that, do you?" . . . .

What single event takes place in this novel excerpt? What will the remainder of the novel show?

Practice

A. Answer these questions in complete sentences.

1. How is the plot of a novel different from the plot of a short story?
2. This excerpt deals with a minor theme of the novel. What is it?
3. Which character dominates this part of the novel?
4. What qualities of this character emerge in the excerpt?
5. What characteristics does Douglas reveal?

B. 6. Write a paragraph about Douglas, explaining how you think he reacted to his great-grandmother's death. Base your ideas on the information about him supplied in the excerpt.

Apply

C. 7. Write a short selection of several paragraphs in which you present Great-grandmother as she must have been during her early married life. Portray her doing some of the things mentioned in the excerpt.

A BOOK TO READ

Title: **A Day of Pleasure**
Author: Isaac Bashevis Singer
Publisher: Farrar, Straus and Giroux

In this collection of stories the author writes of his early days in Poland, from 1908 to 1918, when life was always hard but always a wonder to a boy of his imagination. Isaac Bashevis Singer tells of a world rich in comedy and tragedy, wisdom, foolishness, wildness, and goodness.

⑨ UNIT TEST

● **Clauses**   pages 314–315

Number your paper 1–8. Next to each number write the letter that tells you what the underlined group of words is. Use this code.

    a. verb phrase   **b.** independent clause   **c.** prepositional phrase

1. In earlier times, people believed in all kinds <u>of supernatural beings.</u>
2. <u>Some of these beings were kind and even friendly</u>; others, however, were to be feared.
3. Still others were happy if people stayed away <u>from them</u>.
4. Asrai, water sprites, <u>would evaporate</u> if kept from their watery home.
5. The aughisky were water-horses that made excellent mounts when caught, but <u>they had to be kept away from the sea.</u>
6. If they saw the sea, they <u>would run</u> into it.
7. <u>Do you believe these tales</u>, or do you think that I am all wet?
8. <u>The giants</u>, who were the largest group of supernatural beings, <u>were often quite fearsome.</u>

● **Adverb Clauses**   pages 316–317

Copy these sentences. Underline each adverb clause and draw an arrow to the verb it modifies.

9. The Foawr, when they were feeling unfriendly, often threw stones at people and cattle.
10. Although he was not a Foawr, Jimmy Squarefoot was a stone-throwing giant who could take the form of a giant pig.
11. Because she could take the form of a giant bird, Caillagh ny Groamagh might have been a good match for Jimmy Squarefoot.
12. If you are not eager to meet a Foawr, you would certainly not like an ogre.
13. People of earlier times would shudder when tales of horrible ogres were told around the camp fire.

340   TEST: Unit 9

Adjective Clauses pages 318–319

Copy these sentences. Underline each adjective clause and draw an arrow to the word it modifies.

14. Many supernatural creatures were animals or humanlike creatures that could become animals.
15. The Selkies, who lived both on land and in the water, could become seals.
16. The Roane were gentle folk who wore sealskins and could travel in the sea.
17. Swan maidens, who often appeared as swans, could also appear as doves.

Noun Clauses pages 320–321

Underline each noun clause and tell how it is used.

18. Did you know that the Phouka could become a man, a horse, a bull, an eagle, or a bat?
19. That it was a creature of varied talents is quite evident.
20. The stories of what these creatures did were passed on by word of mouth to each succeeding generation.
21. It seems that the stories improved with each telling.

Misplaced Modifiers pages 322–323

Rewrite these sentences so that they are correct.

22. I saw an elf walking to the store to buy my lunch.
23. He was carrying tour books in his hands that were dog-eared with use.
24. I asked him if he needed any help clearing my throat.
25. "Yes," he answered. "The map says that I am near the Brooklyn Bridge that I bought. How far is it from here?"

Skimming and Scanning pages 326–327

Read this list of questions, and then read the paragraph that comes after it. Answer the questions and write whether you used *skimming* or *scanning* to get the answer.

1. What is the main idea of the paragraph?
2. With what do you attach the fabric to the stretcher bars?
3. Name two key words or phrases that appear in this paragraph.
4. What piece of equipment is optional?

Preparing a piece of fabric for framing and hanging is not a difficult task. You will need a length of fabric, four stretcher bars, a wood stapler, and a plant mister (optional). Buy stretcher bars that are 6 inches (15.2 cm) shorter than the fabric. Assemble the stretcher bars into a frame. Mist or sprinkle water lightly on the reverse side of the fabric, and then center the fabric over the stretcher bars. Next, staple the centers of two sides of the fabric to the bars, stretching the fabric firmly. Work up and down the stretcher bars to the corners, stretching the fabric firmly and stapling neatly. Finally, fold the fabric neatly at the corners and repeat the steps on the opposite sides of the fabric. Your wall hanging is now ready to display and enjoy.

Taking Tests   pages 328–329

5.–8. Suppose the paragraph in the previous exercise contained material on which you would later be tested. Write four questions that might appear on the test. (Do not use the questions in the exercise.)

Writing a News Story   pages 330–332

1. Write a news story based on the information in these notes.

Who?   Maria Ortega, an eighth-grader at Tyler Intermediate School
What?   Received a silver trophy and was interviewed on TV
Where?   At the track at Montgomery High School
When?   Saturday, June 18
Why?   Set a school record for the mile run: 5 minutes, 10 seconds
How?   By putting on a dazzling burst of speed in the final turn

Editing a News Story   pages 333–334

2. Reread the news story about Maria Ortega, which you wrote for the previous exercise. Does the information in your story match your notes? Does the most important information come first? Edit your story to make any changes that you feel are necessary; then rewrite it.

Mechanics Practice   page 335

Write the contractions for these verbs and adverbs.

3. who is   4. is not   5. must not   6. they have

Copy these sentences, adding apostrophes and underlining.
7. Hasnt anyone seen my baby sisters alphabet blocks?
8. They are Tinas favorite toys, and shes sure to throw a fit if theyre lost.
9. Here are two ks and two ns, but I cant seem to find the rest.
10. Tina, youve hidden the other blocks under your bed!

Read this passage from *Tuck Everlasting,* a novel by Natalie Babbitt, and then answer the questions that come after it. In this scene, Mae Tuck, the mother in a family who have become immortal after drinking from a secret spring, has been jailed. Winnie Foster, a girl who has discovered their secret, wants to help but does not know what to do. She is considering the problem when Jesse Tuck, the eternally 17-year-old son, arrives.

"Oh, Jesse!" Her eyes flew open and she reached through the fence to grasp his hand. "I'm so glad to see you! What can we do? We have to get her out!"

"Miles's got a plan," said Jesse, speaking quickly, his voice almost a whisper. "He knows a lot about carpentering. He says he can take Ma's window frame right straight out of the wall, bars and all, and she can climb through. We're going to try it tonight when it gets dark. Anyhow, I come to say goodbye. We won't be able to come back here for a long, long time, Winnie, if we get away. I mean, they'll be looking for Ma. Winnie, listen—I won't see you again, not for ages. Look now—here's a bottle of water from the spring. You keep it. And then, no matter where you are, when you're seventeen, Winnie, you can drink it, and then come find us. We'll leave directions somehow. Winnie, please say you will!"

He pressed the little bottle into her hands and Winnie took it, closing her fingers over it. "Jesse, wait!" she whispered breathlessly, for all at once she had the answer. "I can help! When your mother climbs out the window, I'll climb in and take her place. That would give you time to get away! You'd have at least till morning!"

"Then—at midnight, Winnie. I'll be waiting for you right here at midnight."

"Winifred!" an anxious voice called from the cottage. "Who's that you're talking to?"

Winnie stood up and turned to answer. "It's just a boy, Granny. I'll be in in a minute." When she turned around again, Jesse was gone. Winnie clutched the little bottle in her hands and tried to control the rising excitement that made her breath catch. At midnight she would make a difference in the world.

1. Up to this point in the story, Winnie and the Tucks had been together most of the time. In this scene, how does that situation change?
2. Name two of Winnie's characteristics.
3. What lesser plot do you think centers on Jesse?
4. How does what happens in this scene change Winnie?
5. What do you think is one of the themes of this novel?

Monday

Dear James,
    We had a 20 inch
snowfall over the week-
end, so we will not be
able to attend the opening
of your exhibit on Wednesday. However, if road
conditions improve by
Friday, we shall drive
over for the weekend. I
will call you on Fri-
to let you
our pla

LANGUAGE
Learning
About Verbals

COMPOSITION
Writing Letters

STUDY SKILLS
Evaluating
Information

LITERATURE
Enjoying Letters

Have you ever heard someone ask, "Any mail for me?" or watched someone open a long-expected letter? If you have, then you understand something about the enjoyment that comes from receiving and reading letters. Knowing how to write a good letter is a valuable skill, and in this unit you will write several different kinds of letters. You will also learn about some famous letter writers by reading their work.

During this year you have seen that an important part of any kind of communication is knowing how words fit together to form sentences. Part of this knowledge is understanding the functions of words, phrases, and clauses. In this unit you will learn about verbals and how they function in sentences. You will also see how evaluating information can help you to communicate your thoughts and understand the thoughts of others.

Study the pictures on the opposite page. What pictures show subjects that would be appropriate for a letter to a friend? What pictures show subjects that would be appropriate for a letter to a business or organization?

LANGUAGE

Lesson 1: Understanding Participles and Participial Phrases

Read these sentences.

1. <u>Speaking clearly</u>, the mayor read his proclamation.
2. <u>Finished at last</u>, he looked out over the crowd.

Name the simple subject and predicate of each sentence. To which word in each sentence does each underlined phrase refer?

Think and Discuss

Forms of verbs that are used as other parts of speech are called **verbals.** The words *speaking* and *finished* in sentences 1 and 2 are verbals called **participles.** You have used participles before in learning the principal parts of verbs. The present participle is formed from the first principal part plus *ing*. The past participle is the third principal part of the verb. Used as they are in sentences 1 and 2, the underlined participles and their accompanying words form **participial phrases** that are used as adjectives.

Do not confuse participial phrases with verb phrases made of helping verbs and main verbs. When a present or past participle with a helping verb expresses the action of the subject, the phrase is a verb phrase. A present or past participle that is used as an *adjective* functions as a true participle.

3. The speech <u>had been delivered</u> enthusiastically.
4. <u>Delighted</u> at the crowd's response, the mayor smiled.

In sentence 3 the word *delivered* is used with the helping verbs *had been.* Together they make a verb phrase. In sentence 4 *delighted* has no helping verb, and it refers to or modifies the noun *mayor. Delighted* is a participle.

Participial phrases are formed from a participle plus another word or a word group, such as a prepositional phrase. Participles may also be used alone. Either way, they will always modify nouns or pronouns in a sentence.

5. Cheering loudly, the crowd expressed approval.
6. Announcing the project, the mayor had won votes.

- A **verbal** is a word that is formed from a verb but does the work of another part of speech in a sentence.
- A **participle** is a verbal that functions as an *adjective*.
- A **participial phrase** is a group of words that contains a participle and its modifiers or objects. The entire phrase functions as an adjective.

Practice

A. Copy these sentences. Underline the participles or participial phrases and draw arrows to the words they modify.

1. Many ruined neighborhoods have been renovated.
2. In the past, these decaying neighborhoods would have been torn down.
3. Today such deteriorating areas are being rebuilt one house at a time.
4. Many people, lured back to the city by renovated buildings, are forming new neighborhoods.
5. Located near theaters, museums, and shops, these new neighborhoods are inviting places to live.
6. Some areas, long abandoned, have been rebuilt.
7. Others, well preserved, have simply been modernized.
8. Renovated by experts, some buildings have been restored to their former splendor.
9. These restored buildings are now historical landmarks.
10. Protected by law, these buildings are open to the public.

Apply

B. 11.–20. Write ten sentences about a project in your city that has been successful or about a project you would like to see carried out. Use a participle or a participial phrase in each sentence that you write.

Lesson 2: Correcting Dangling Participles

What is wrong with these sentences?

1. Jogging along the path, the roses smelled good.
2. Made of rubber, children cannot break these toys.
3. Eating our ice cream, the cake looked delicious.

Think and Discuss

One of the easiest mistakes to make when you are writing is to use **dangling participles.** Participles and participial phrases dangle when they do not really modify the word the writer intends. In sentence 1, for example, *jogging along the path* seems to indicate that the *roses* are doing the jogging. There is no other noun for the participial phrase to modify, hence the reader forms a mental picture of roses huffing and puffing down the walk. In sentence 2 the writer obviously meant the participial phrase to modify *toys.* Since a participial phrase modifies the noun that is closest to it, the reader must deduce that the *children* are made of rubber. According to sentence 3, who or what is *eating our ice cream?*

You can avoid writing dangling participles by being specific about the nouns your participles modify and by writing the nouns and participles next to one another.

Practice

A. Copy only the sentences in which the participles and participial phrases do not dangle. Underline each participle or phrase in the correct sentences and draw an arrow from it to the noun it modifies.

1. Unfastening my sweater, a button popped.
2. Although ringing loudly, Oki did not hear the alarm.
3. Sitting quietly on the beach, Evella watched the waves.
4. Nobu did not see the loose board jutting up from the floor.
5. Hovering over the flower, the hummingbird sipped nectar from its depths.
6. Exhausted by my long ordeal, the path was finally cleared of snow.

7. Filled with children, the adults could not find room in the crowded theater.
8. The St. Louis Arch came into view landing at Lambert Airport.
9. Last week Mrs. Itaka bought the shawl displayed in Macy's window.
10. Nori bounced the ball against the house whistling happily.

B. 11.–16. Correctly write the sentences from Practice A that have dangling participles.

C. Add to these sentences participial phrases that do not dangle.

17. The boys sang loudly.
18. All eight girls successfully completed the Jog-a-Thon.
19. Andrea once rescued a child from drowning.
20. Mrs. Marsh rocked her infant daughter to sleep.

Apply

D. 21.–30. Write ten sentences about a good time you once had with your family or friends. Be sure to use participial phrases correctly in the sentences.

HOW OUR LANGUAGE GROWS

Have you heard of the "star sailors" in the sky? Where are the "little mice" in your body? Who is the "daugher of the wind?" The words *astronaut, muscle,* and *anemone* have something special in common. Their original meanings are poetic. They are metaphors that make pictures out of words.

Ralph Waldo Emerson once said that "language is fossil poetry." The etymology, or study of the origins of words, unearths these fossils for us. A *dandelion* is "the tooth of a lion." An artist's *easel* is a "donkey." If you have *spirit,* you have "breath." When you *brood,* you are "sitting on eggs." A *clue* is a "thread," and something *electric* has "sun glare." The meanings of these words reveal their hidden poetry.

Use a dictionary that contains references to etymology to find the original meanings of the words *anthology, perplexed,* and *reflect.*

Lesson 3: Understanding Gerunds and Gerund Phrases

Read these sentences.

1. Leah had been exercising all afternoon.
2. Exercising on the parallel bars, she looked like a winner.
3. That kind of exercising requires balance and stamina.

How is the word *exercising* used in sentences 1 and 2?

Think and Discuss

You have seen that a word may be used in a sentence in many different ways. In sentence 3 the word *exercising* is used as the object of the preposition *of,* making its function that of a noun. *Exercising,* however, is a verb form called a **gerund.** A gerund is a verbal ending in *ing* that is used as a noun.

Nouns can be used as subjects, direct and indirect objects, and as objects of prepositions. They may also be used as predicate nouns and as appositives. The gerund, too, can perform all of these functions. In addition, it can be used in phrases with other words. Study these sentences.

4. Tumbling is an exhausting sport.
5. Another sport that requires stamina is jogging.
6. Adesina lists ice skating as her favorite sport.
7. A recent survey gave jogging first place in popularity.
8. Another sport, horseback riding, is also popular.

Name the gerunds in sentences 4–8. How is each used?

> - A **gerund** is a verbal that ends in *ing* and functions as a *noun.*
> - A **gerund phrase** is a group of words that contains a gerund and its modifiers or objects. The entire phrase functions as a noun.

Gerund phrases are composed of gerunds and many combinations of other words. Because gerunds are verb forms, they may be modified by adverbs. Because they function as nouns, they may be modified by adjectives. When a person's name is used with a gerund, the possessive form of the name must appear. Likewise, the possessive form of a pronoun must be used in the same situation. Study these sentences.

9. Practicing exercises daily brings success.
10. Leah's faithful practicing will make her a champion.

Name the gerund phrases in sentences 9 and 10. Tell how the words that are not verb forms function in the phrases.

Practice

A. Copy these sentences. Draw two lines under each gerund and one line under any other words in a gerund phrase.

1. The results of exercising are a trim body and resistance to illness.
2. Concentrating intently often aids one's exercising.
3. Walking suits some people better than more heavy exercise.
4. A person can benefit as much from walking as from jogging.
5. Maintaining a vigorous pace for a half hour every day activates one's sluggish breathing and circulation.

B. 6.–10. Write the function of each of the gerunds in Practice A.

C. Copy these sentences, completing each with gerunds and gerund phrases.

11. Leah's _____ keeps her in excellent shape.
12. She stretches all her muscles by _____.
13. _____, another good conditioning sport, is quite popular.
14. Leah jogs occasionally, but she enjoys _____ more.
15. A recent study gave _____ high marks for its excellent conditioning qualities.

Apply

D. 16. Write a paragraph about one of these topics: skating, sailing, horseback riding, surfing, snorkeling, running, skiing, jumping (on a trampoline), dancing, skipping rope, or fencing. Describe how the sport or occupation is performed, or tell how you or someone you know has enjoyed it. Use gerunds and gerund phrases in your paragraph.

Lesson 4: Understanding Infinitives and Infinitive Phrases

The underlined phrases in these sentences are verbals.

1. The Itois wanted <u>to move</u>.
2. They had a great deal of luggage <u>to carry</u>.
3. Mr. Itoi went <u>to buy the tickets</u>.

How do these verbals differ from partciples and gerunds?

Think and Discuss

A verbal that consists of a present tense verb form with the word *to* before it is called an **infinitive.** These are examples of infinitives.

to go	to believe	to sell	to understand
to see	to combine	to refuse	to accomplish

The word *to* in an infinitive is not a preposition but part of the verbal. If a prepositional phrase begins with *to,* it is followed by a noun or a pronoun, not by a verb.

Infinitives can be used as several different parts of speech. In sentence 1, for example, the infinitive *to move* functions as a noun, the direct object of that sentence. In sentence 2 the infinitive *to carry* is an adjective modifying the noun *luggage.* You can see in sentence 3 that infinitives, like the other verbals, can take objects and modifiers. The infinitive phrase *to buy the tickets* is an adverb modifying the verb *went. Tickets* is the direct object of the infinitive *to buy.*

Now study the infinitive phrases in these sentences. Tell what part of speech each one is and how it is used.

4. The Itois wanted <u>to travel west</u>.
5. The family was ready <u>to leave the East Coast</u>.
6. Mr. Itoi's ambition was <u>to publish a newspaper</u>.

Sometimes the word *to* is omitted in an infinitive. This is especially true after forms of verbs like *help, make, see,* and *dare.* Read these sentences.

7. The Itois didn't dare <u>lose their tickets</u>.
8. Kuni helped her father <u>carry the luggage</u>.

You can determine whether or not a word or phrase is an infinitive by its present tense verb form and by its function as a noun, an adjective, or an adverb.

> - An **infinitive** is a verbal that usually begins with the word *to* and is used as a *noun*, as an *adjective*, or as an *adverb*.
> - An **infinitive phrase** is a group of words that contains an infinitive and its modifiers or objects. The entire phrase functions as a noun, as an adjective, or as an adverb.

Practice

A. Copy these sentences and underline the infinitives or infinitive phrases.

1. The passengers started to collect their things.
2. Many people traveled west to visit relatives.
3. To travel west by train in 1880 was an adventure.
4. Strength was needed to undertake such a journey.
5. If you liked to ride in comfort, this was not the way to travel.
6. Wooden benches were not long enough to lie on.
7. When it was time to sleep, the travelers bought boards and cushions to lay across the seats.
8. People bought books and newspapers to read on the trip.
9. A stove stood in each car to heat the train.
10. The practice at mealtimes was to use the stoves for cooking.

B. **11.–20.** Write the function of each of the infinitives or infinitive phrases in Practice A.

C. Use each of these infinitives in a sentence. After each sentence write *noun, adjective,* or *adverb,* depending on how you used the infinitive in the sentence.

21. to complain	22. to locate	23. to enjoy
24. to find	25. to offer	26. to report

Apply

D. **27.–36.** Write ten sentences about a trip to the West in the 1880's. Use an infinitive or an infinitive phrase in each sentence. Identify the function of each infinitive.

LANGUAGE REVIEW

Understanding Participles and Participial Phrases   pages 346–347

Copy these sentences and underline the participles and participial phrases. Then draw an arrow from the participle or phrase to the noun or pronoun it modifies.

1. Masika scurried over the broken fence in her family's orchard.
2. The apples hanging on the tree were ripe.
3. Having noticed them, Masika eagerly climbed the tree.
4. The shining sun made Masika squint.
5. The swaying branches moved in the gentle breeze.
6. Each branch, swaying back and forth, held its prizes away from Masika's reach.
7. From a lower branch Masika reached the apples hanging above.
8. A bent twig snapped in her hand.
9. Finally, carrying two large apples, Masika dropped to the ground with a thud.
10. Sitting under the tree and feeling somewhat dazed, she decided that grapes, growing nearer to the ground, were better for her health.

Correcting Dangling Participles   pages 348–349

Each of these sentences contains a dangling participle. Beginning with the same participial phrase, revise the rest of the sentence so that the subject is the word modified by the phrase. Do not change the participial phrase to a verb phrase.

11. Having seen Bo's bicycle, the wheel needed repair.
12. Knowing of my repair service, Bo's idea was to ask for my assistance.
13. Talking about the job, a price was decided upon.
14. Planning for a trip, the bike had to be ready by Friday.
15. Thinking of Bo's first trip, my first task was to repair the wheel.
16. Working on the tire, my mother's advice returned to my thoughts.
17. Hoping to encourage me, my work should be done accurately.
18. Having finished with the wheel, the painting was begun.
19. Waiting for the paint to dry, the trip was discussed.
20. Being in no hurry, a few hours' wait was all right with her.

Understanding Gerunds and Gerund Phrases   pages 350–351

Copy these sentences, Underline the gerunds or gerund phrases. After each sentence indicate how each verbal was used.

21. Hiking is an excellent sport for springtime.
22. Jane and Alison enjoy hiking every spring.
23. Their favorite part of a hike is climbing steep mountain paths.
24. Afterward they enjoy eating the lunch they brought with them.
25. Chen prefers the joys of camping in springtime.
26. His idea of fun is putting up a tent on a riverbank.
27. Sleeping under the stars is the best part of Russ's trip.
28. Most of our class enjoys swimming in the summer.
29. My classmates like playing tennis in the spring.
30. By June, sailing on Indian Lake is their favorite pastime.

Understanding Infinitives and Infinitive Phrases   pages 352–353

Copy these sentences and underline the infinitives and infinitive phrases. After each sentence tell how the infinitive or infinitive phrase is used in the sentence.

31. To work with Shiro and Isabel has been a pleasure.
32. We want to thank each of them.
33. We have also planned a party to surprise them.
34. Unfortunately, we have no money to spare.
35. Our plan is to prepare all the food ourselves.
36. To plan a surprise party is not easy.
37. We just want to do the best job possible.
38. Our plan was to surprise them completely.
39. We called Isabel to discuss our plans.
40. She had no advice to offer.

Applying Verbals

41.–50. Write ten sentences about characters in your favorite myths or legends. Use at least three participles, three gerunds, and three infinitives in your sentences. Then proofread to be sure that capitalization, punctuation, subject-verb and pronoun-antecedent agreement are correct.

STUDY SKILLS

Lesson 5: Distinguishing Fact from Opinion

Read these two comments about the same book.

1. *Ben's Trumpet,* written and illustrated by Rachel Isadora, was selected as a Caldecott Honor Book.
2. *Ben's Trumpet* is a wonderful book with an original story and beautifully drawn pictures.

Think and Discuss

A **fact** is a statement that can be proved true or false. Here is an example of a statement of fact: *Fort Peck Dam in Montana was completed in 1940.* You can go to the reference section of the library and check that statement. You will find that it is true.

Here is another statement of fact: *Fort Peck Dam in Montana was completed in 1935.* You can check that statement in the same way. You will find that it is false. But even though it is false, it is still a statement of fact. A statement of fact doesn't have to be true; it just has to be something you can prove to be either true or false.

An **opinion** expresses someone's personal feelings. There is no way to prove whether an opinion is right or wrong. Here is a statement of opinion: *Michelangelo was the greatest sculptor and painter of all time.* The speaker may have many factual reasons for this opinion, but there is no way to prove that it is true. Even if all the art historians and art critics in the country agreed on Michelangelo's supremacy, they could not prove it.

It is not always easy to tell facts from opinions. In advertising and promotional writing, the two are often deliberately confused in order to persuade you. Fact and opinion may even be combined in the same sentence. To tell the difference between them, ask yourself this key question: Is it possible to prove this statement to be either true or false?

Practice

A. Copy each of the following statements. Write whether each is a statement of *fact* or a statement of *opinion.*

1. Boston is the capital of Massachusetts.
2. It is an interesting city to explore on foot.
3. The Freedom Trail is a marked path that leads to many historic landmarks.
4. Faneuil Hall is one of the landmarks on the Freedom Trail.
5. Paul Revere's House has the best exhibits.
6. Boston Common is pleasant on a summer afternoon.
7. Everyone enjoys a visit to the U.S.S. *Constitution.*
8. The *Constitution,* nicknamed "Old Ironsides," is the oldest commissioned ship in the U.S. Navy.
9. It is thrilling to be on a ship that fought in the War of 1812.
10. A short distance from the *Constitution* is a monument commemorating the Battle of Bunker Hill.

B. 11. Copy the following paragraph on your paper. Underline every sentence that is a statement of opinion.

Dorothea Todd married James Madison on a September morning at his plantation in Virginia. It was surely the most fortunate day of his life. Madison was the smallest American President, and his bride was at least 5 inches taller and 30 pounds heavier. There was also a big difference in their ages, because she was 24 and he was 43. It is likely that Dolley married James Madison for his money and position, but she grew to love him more than she could have loved anyone else. And Madison loved her just as much in return. He mentioned her name often, even in his official letters. When he left the White House after two terms as President, they retired to Virginia. Dolley continued to care for James and to try to keep him from working too hard. When he died, she was heartbroken.

Apply

C. 12. From a current issue of a newspaper or magazine, select an advertisement that contains at least a paragraph of text. Mark each statement in the ad as either *fact* or *opinion* or a *combination* of both.

Lesson 6: Drawing Logical Conclusions

"I don't feel very well," Lamont exclaimed to his friend George one day. "It must have been something I ate at Sally's party last night."

"I feel queasy myself," answered George. "Maybe we got food poisoning from the potato salad!"

What conclusion was George drawing about Sally's party? Was his conclusion logical?

Think and Discuss

Logic is the science of reasoning correctly. You would probably feel foolish if you knew that you had been tricked by something that had appealed to your emotions rather than to your mind. Such frustration can be avoided, however, if you learn to think logically.

The fact that Lamont and George had both attended the party the night before and that both felt ill on the following day was no reason for them to blame Sally or her food for their problems. Either one of them could be coming down with a cold or the flu. Either one could have eaten *too much* at the party. In that case gluttony, not bad food, was probably responsible for the illness. To reason that they got food poisoning from the potato salad proves that George was not thinking logically. The conclusion he reached is an example of the false idea that "if event B took place *after* event A, then event B was *caused* by event A." This error in reasoning is called **false cause.**

Another illogical argument might have arisen if Sally had served a number of spicy dishes at the party. Regardless of any other factors that might have made him ill, George might have drawn the conclusion that he cannot eat spicy foods. If the refreshments at Sally's party were the only basis for his belief, he would have fallen prey to **hasty generalization.** In reality, George did not have enough evidence to make a logical conclusion. It would have been just as unreasonable to say, "Sally lives in a red house. I felt ill after eating there. Therefore I cannot eat any food served in a red house."

George might really have caused some problems with his faulty conclusions if, after feeling sick, he accused Sally of serving bad food on purpose. George probably wouldn't go this far unless he harbored a grudge against Sally. By suggesting that Sally had wanted to make him sick, George might hope to discredit her and to keep other friends from attending her parties. Only a very independent-minded person could refuse to be influenced, even a little, by George's remark about food poisoning. This kind of bad reasoning is called **argument by attack** against the person.

Practice

A. Copy these patterns of reasoning. After each indicate whether the conclusion was *logical* or *illogical.*

1. Yesterday I saw two eighth-graders from Bradley School, and neither one smiled or said hello to me. I guess all the students at Bradley are snobs.
2. Pigs are actually very clean creatures. I know that Jim bought a new pig last week, and I can imagine that he has no trouble at all keeping it clean.
3. I haven't liked Tomi since the day he beat me at chess. The only way he could beat me is by cheating. I wouldn't be surprised if he's the biggest cheater in the history of chess!
4. The dress I tried on yesterday was blue, and it looked terrible on me. I guess blue is just not my color!
5. Mary went skateboarding yesterday. This morning she came to school with bruises on her arms and legs. She must have fallen off her skateboard.

B. 6.–10. Copy the patterns of reasoning from Practice A. Then label those that are illogical with the type of faulty reasoning used.

Apply

C. 11. Use newspapers, magazines, or books to find an example of each of the types of faulty reasoning presented in this lesson. Copy the faulty reasoning. Then, under each, write a similar sentence that is logical.

COMPOSITION

Lesson 7: Writing Friendly Letters and Social Notes

Read this letter.

> 187 Pine Street
> Florissant, Missouri 63031
> May 12, 19—
>
> Dear Jenny,
>
> Here are the pictures of our spring party. I can't believe it took two months to get them developed!
>
> My classes are fine at school this quarter. Mrs. Ellis has added some humanities field trips to our Language Arts curriculum. So far we have visited the St. Louis Art Museum and Powell Hall.
>
> Everyone at home is well. The only problem is that Randy is keeping four white mice for his science project. He plays loud music to them at certain hours, and there has been some static from Gramps and Elena.
>
> I hope you got your next year's schedule straightened out. We haven't even begun to plan for ninth grade yet! Write soon if you have time, or even if you don't.
>
> Love,
> Dolores

What makes this friendly letter interesting?

Think and Discuss

A **friendly letter** is a way of communicating with relatives and friends. Friendly letters generally give news and express interest in the life of the receiver. They refer to shared interests and experiences. In most cases friendly letters are written to people with whom one cannot speak or visit regularly.

A friendly letter has five parts: the *heading,* the *salutation* or greeting, the *body,* the *closing,* and the *signature.* Think about the letters you write to friends and relatives. They should resemble the sample letter in this lesson.

A **social note** is a specific type of friendly letter. It usually expresses appreciation for a social favor such as a birthday gift or a short stay at a friend's house. A social note is usually brief. It should be sent promptly—that is, upon receipt of the gift or return from a visit. It should mention the gift by name and say specifically what pleases you about it. After a visit you should refer to specific activities that you enjoyed during that time. In all other respects the social note is written in the same way as an ordinary friendly letter. Study this example of a social note.

```
                                    104 Center Street
                                    Haywarden, Iowa 51023
                                    May 5, 19--

Dear Grandma,
   Today I came home to find your card and generous
check. Was I surprised! I have been saving to buy a
new guitar; your check puts me way ahead on this. I
will start browsing through music stores this weekend.
   I am glad to be shopping for my birthday gift
this year. I'm sorry to hear that shopping and other
trips have become more difficult for you. You are
right to stay put during the icy weather.
   I'll talk to you soon. I want to find out how
you are--and to report my progress with the guitar!

                                    Love,
                                    Mary
```

Compare this letter to the letter that Dolores wrote to her friend Jenny. Are the two letters similar in form? Do they observe the same rules of punctuation and capitalization? Do they seem to have been written for similar purposes?

Practice

A. The following sentences are taken from typical social notes. Improve upon them by making them more specific. Use your experience and imagination for the details.

1. Thank you for the check. I am sure that it will be useful.
2. The book arrived today. It's on a subject I like.
3. Thank you for the magazine subscription. I'm looking forward to receiving the first issue.
4. Thanks for the gift. It fits just fine.
5. I had a pleasant time at your house for the holiday.

B. 6. Make a draft of the body of a friendly letter. Include references to these topics.

something interesting that is happening in your life
experiences, interests, or acquaintances you share with your friend or relative
something you would like to know about your friend or relative; a way in which you feel involved in his or her life (Be sure that you ask at least one question that encourages your friend or relative to write back.)

Apply

C. 7. Write a friendly letter describing the annual eighth-grade play at your school. Be sure to mention your role in the production as a cast member or as a behind-the-scenes person. If there is no eighth-grade play, invent one!

To Memorize

Mistakes are a fact of life;
It is the response to error that counts.

Nikki Giovanni

Can you think of another saying that echoes the thought of "mistakes are a fact of life?" If you believe that mistakes truly *are* a fact of life, how will you probably respond to error?

Lesson 8: Writing Business Letters

Read this letter.

> 408 Elm Avenue
> Pittsburgh, Pennsylvania 15318
> May 1, 19—
>
> Ms. B. Jones, General Manager
> Palisades Interstate Park Commission
> Bear Mountain, New York 10911
>
> Dear Ms. Jones:
>
> My family is planning a vacation in late May. We would like to include Bear Mountain in our itinerary.
> Can you send us information on the lodging facilities that are open at this time of year? We are interested in staying in a housekeeping cabin or an inn.
> Please include information on rates and regulations. (For example, we need to know if pets are welcome.) Thank you for your help.
>
> Sincerely,
>
> *Layla Garcia*

How is the tone of this letter different from the tone of the friendly letter?

Think and Discuss

The writing in friendly letters is conversational and personal; it reflects the personality of the sender. The **business letter,** however, must be impersonal in tone and clear and concise in wording. Letters in which people order goods or request information are examples of business letters. Everything must be spelled out in appropriate detail. For example, Layla's friends may know that her family prefers cabins to tents and travels with a large dog. Ms. Jones does not know that, so Layla must remember to ask for information on cabins and pet policy.

Look at the business letter that Layla wrote to Ms. Jones. How many parts does it have? What part appears in the business letter that does not appear in a friendly letter? What other differences do you see in the salutation and closing?

This is how the envelope for Layla Garcia's letter probably looked.

Ms. Layla Garcia
408 Elm Avenue
Pittsburgh, PA 15318

Ms. B. Jones, General Manager
Palisades Interstate Park Commission
Bear Mountain, NY 10911

What element of the heading in Layla's letter is omitted from the return address?

Practice

A. Write the business letter described below. Make up any names and facts needed for a complete letter. Sign your name.

You ordered a holiday fruit basket for your uncle. It was never sent. Write to The Fruit Basket, 78 Water Street, Lauderhill, Florida 33319. Be sure to include a description of the order and the address to which it was to be sent.

Apply

B. Look through the travel or airline advertisements in your local newspaper. Choose a travel destination that interests you. Write to the company or organization that placed the advertisement and ask for additional informtion.

A Challenge

Choose one of these situations and write an appropriate letter. Imagine yourself as the main character in the situation and try to express yourself as this character would.

★ You are a cantaloupe that has just won first prize at the state fair. Write to Washington, D.C., requesting official recognition of this high honor from the White House.

★ You are an oak tree in one of our national forests. Write a friendly letter to an elm you know in another forest.

Lesson 9: Editing Letters

Study the editing that was done on this letter.

236 140th Street
Cleveland, Ohio
May 8, 19--

The Western Reserve Historical Society
10825 East Boulevard
Cleveland, Ohio 44106

Dear Sir or Madam,

eighth-grade
Our history class is producing a scrapbook on the
history of our *the Woodland* neighborhood. We hope to include
photographs of our *the Woodland* residential and commercial streets
in the early days *late 1800's and early 1900's.*
Can you tell us if you have photographs from this
If you have some photographs we would appreciate
period? If so, how might we acquire some prints for our project?
being able to include them in our class project.

Thank you for your help.

Sincerely Yours,

Elijah Fox

Think and Discuss

Elijah's letter is a business letter that makes a request. When Elijah checked his letter against the sample business letter, he found several errors. He had omitted the ZIP code in both the heading and the inside address. He used the caret (∧) to show where the ZIP codes should be added. Elijah also noticed that he had made error in the closing of his letter. Elijah used the slash (/) to show that the *Y* should be a lowercase letter.

A bigger problem was that Elijah did not give the society the specific information it needs in order to respond to his request. Elijah corrected one such omission by writing in the name of his neighborhood. What other corrections made his request more specific?

Another problem with Elijah's letter was wordiness. Words that are unnecessary, repetitious, or vague distract the reader and can make the writer's meaning unclear. Elijah realized that the clause *where the homes and businesses were* simply repeated the idea expressed by *residential and commercial streets*. By removing this clause, Elijah made his letter more concise.

Practice

A. Copy Elijah's letter showing all corrections.

B. Edit this letter. Correct punctuation and capitalization errors, and make the letter more specific about the action that the writer expects the recipient to take.

```
                              14 Joshop Road
                              Fort Worth, Texas 76129
                              May 16, 19--
Station WVN
135 Revere Plaza
Forth Worth Texas 76129

Dear Sir
   I am interested in being a member of the studio
audience of "It's All Right" sometime during
January. In fact, I have often thought that I
would like to appear on the show.
   I look forward to hearing from you.

                         yours truly,
                         Jan Lim
```

Apply

C. Choose one of the letters you wrote in Lessons 7 or 8. Use editing marks to make necessary changes. Rewrite the letter, and give both copies to your teacher.

Using Hyphens and Underscoring

- Underscore numbers used out of context.

    My telephone number has only one 7 in it.

- Use a hyphen to divide words at the end of a line.

    The first bridge across the Mississippi River con-
    nected Davenport, Iowa, to Rock Island, Illinois.

- Underscore names of ships and aircraft.

    Stephen H. Long's ship, the Western Engineer, sailed to Council
    Bluffs, Iowa, in 1819.

- Underscore all words in a foreign language.

    An Oktoberfest is held in Middle Amana, Iowa, every fall.

Copy these sentences. Add underscores and hyphens wherever necessary.

1. You said that the summer temperature in Des Moines, Iowa, averaged 170 degrees Fahrenheit; I think you had better take the 1 out.
2. The Native American words maquoketa and wapsipinicon became the names of two Iowa rivers.
3. The steamship DeWitt Clinton once sailed the Mississippi River.
4. The name of the city Des Moines comes from the French words des, which means "of the," and moins, which means "least."
5. The President flew over Iowa in Air Force One.
6. The status of the town of Carter Lake, Iowa, was changed by a geo graphical fluke.
7. At one point, when the Missouri River changed course, Car ter Lake became part of Nebraska.
8. Although technically part of Nebraska, Carter Lake's area code is that of Iowa—702. No, change the 0 to a 1.
9. The name of Bellevue, Iowa, comes from the French word belle, meaning "beautiful," and vue, meaning "view."
10. Iowa is sometimes called the Corn State, but the Hawk eye State is its famous nickname.

LITERATURE

Lesson 10: Reading Letters

John Donne, an English poet, once said, "Our letters are ourselves." Read this part of a letter by American poet Emily Dickinson.

Dear Friend,

A letter always feels to me like immortality because it is the mind alone without corporeal friend. Indebted in our talk to pose and accent, there seems a power in thought that walks alone.

You speak kindly of seeing me. Could it please your convenience to come as far as Amherst I should be very glad, but I do not cross my Father's ground to any house or town.

What does this letter tell you about Emily Dickinson?

Think and Discuss

The letters written by famous people are fascinating to study. They can tell much about a person's thoughts and feelings. For that reason people interested in biography find them especially helpful. You do not have to be a biographer, however, to enjoy reading letters. You can enjoy reading letters merely because they are interesting. You may even find that the inner thoughts and feelings of famous people are not very different from your own.

Emily Dickinson carried on an extraordinary friendship through letters. For 24 years she exchanged letters with someone she had met only once. The letter you have just read is part of that correspondence. In that letter Emily Dickinson makes it clear that she prefers letter writing to a face-to-face encounter. She was not just shy: she preferred to live in isolation. If you did not know that she was a poet, you might guess that her letter has a poet's touch.

Famous people are often more open in their letters than they are in a conversation or in other forms of writing. Through their letters you may find that their public image does not give a complete picture of their personality. For example, C. S. Lewis, the author of *The Chronicles of Narnia* and many other books, was thought of as a rather stuffy, bookish professor who loved nothing better than to spend his time in the libraries of the university town of Oxford, England. Read this part of a letter he wrote to his brother about a hiking trip he took. How does the letter contradict his public image?

. . . No one can describe the delight of coming to a sudden drop and looking down into a rich wooded valley where you see the roofs of the place where you're going to have supper and bed; especially if the sunset lies on the ridge beyond the valley. There is so much mixed in it; the mere physical anticipation, as of a horse nearing its stable, the sense of accomplishment and the feeling of "one more town," one further away into the country you don't know, and the old, never hackneyed romance of travelling.

The letters of famous people can also have historic importance; they can shed an interesting light on a major event in history. For example, a letter that Albert Einstein wrote in 1948 to the World Congress of Intellectuals deals with the question of the responsibilities of the scientists who invented atomic weapons. Read this part of the letter.

By painful experience we have learned that rational thinking does not solve the problems of our social life. We scientists, whose tragic destiny it has been to help make the methods of annihilation ever more gruesome and more effective, must consider it our solemn duty to do all in our power in preventing these weapons from being used for the brutal purpose for which they were invented. What task could possibly be more important to us?

How does this letter show Einstein's inner thoughts and feelings?

A brief glance at the biography section of your library shows that there are many collections of modern letters that are well worth reading.

Practice

A. Read this letter that was written by E. B. White, the author of *Stuart Little* and *Charlotte's Web*. Write a brief paragraph to describe what this letter tells you about its author.

North Brooklin, Maine
30 March 1973

Dear Mr. Nadeau:

As long as there is one upright man, as long as there is one compassionate woman, the contagion may spread and the scene is not desolate. Hope is the thing that is left to us, in a bad time. I shall get up Sunday morning and wind the clock, as a contribution to order and steadfastness.

Sailors have an expression about the weather: they say, the weather is a great bluffer. I guess the same is true of our human society — things can look dark, then a break shows in the clouds, and all is changed, sometimes rather suddenly. It is quite obvious that the human race has made a mess of life on this planet. But as a people we probably harbor seeds of goodness that have lain for a long time, waiting to sprout when the conditions are right. Man's curiosity, his relentlessness, his inventiveness, his ingenuity have led him into deep trouble. We can only hope that these same traits will enable him to claw his way out.

Hang onto your hat. Hang onto your hope. And wind the clock, for tomorrow is another day.

Sincerely,
E. B. White

B. Read this part of a letter that Benjamin Franklin wrote to Sir Joseph Banks, president of the Royal Society of London, at the end of the Revolutionary War. Write a brief paragraph to describe how this letter contradicts Franklin's public image.

I hope soon to have more leisure, and to spend a part of it in those studies, that are much more agreeable to me than political operations.

I join with you most cordially in rejoicing at the return of peace. I hope it will be lasting, and that mankind will at length, as they call themselves reasonable creatures, have reason and sense enough to settle their differences without cutting throats; for, in my opinion, *there never was a good war, or a bad peace.* What vast additions to the conveniences and comforts of living might mankind have acquired, if the money spent in wars had been employed in works of public utility!

Apply

C. Find a collection of letters in the biography section of your school or local public library. Choose a letter that you find interesting. Write a paragraph about the personality of the writer, based on the letter.

A BOOK TO READ

Title: **Dragonwings**
Author: Laurence Yep
Publisher: Harper & Row

In 1909, when Moon Shadow was just eight years old, he left his mother in China and journeyed to San Francisco to live with his father, whom Moon Shadow had never seen. Windrider, his father, worked in a laundry to earn money in hopes that his family could soon be together once again.

As he got to know Windrider, Moon Shadow saw that he was a man with special talents and one very special dream: he wanted to fly!

In the early years of the twentieth century, Windrider's dream of flying seemed both fabulous and crazy. Living in poverty and working with a single-minded purpose, Windrider and Moon Shadow built their flying machine. They compared notes with the Wright Brothers, whose airplane was in experimental stages at this time.

Dragonwings is based upon an actual account of an immigrant from China who made a flying machine. In this "historical fantasy," Laurence Yep has tried to be faithful to this period of history and to the lives of the Chinese who came to America at this time.

● **Participles and Participial Phrases**   pages 346–347

Read this paragraph. Then answer the questions that follow.

Springtime is beautiful in French Canada. Freshening breezes stir daffodils and hyacinths out of the once frozen ground. Throughout Quebec returning birds fly southward, pausing in the countryside for food and drink. The quaint French villages awake after their slumbering winter to find life once again renewed.

1. There are   **a.** four   **b.** five   **c.** six   participles in the paragraph.
2. There are   **a.** one   **b.** two   **c.** three   past participles in the paragraph.
3. The participle *pausing* modifies   **a.** countryside   **b.** food and drink   **c.** birds.
4. The longest participial phrase in the paragraph has more than   **a.** seven   **b.** eight   **c.** nine words in it.
5. The word *life* is modified by the participle   **a.** *slumbering*   **b.** *renewed*   **c.** *find*

● **Dangling Participles**   pages 348–349

Rewrite these sentences, correcting the dangling participles.

6. Flying to and fro, Micheline watched a bird as it built its nest in a tree.
7. Its mate was seen by her brother Emile dangling a worm in his beak.
8. The dead underbrush of winter was burned off by the villagers gathered into heaps.
9. Built into the stone faces of mountains and hills, French women baked crusty loaves of bread in their ovens.
10. Men, women, and children needing repairs after the long winter met to clean the village church.

● **Gerunds and Gerund Phrases**   pages 350–351

Copy these sentences. Underline all the gerunds and gerund phrases. After each sentence indicate the function of the gerund or gerund phrase.

11. The farmer's first task in springtime was plowing the fields.

12. Fields extending to the bottoms of hillsides make plowing difficult.
13. In Quebec the seeding of fields is often done in April.
14. Great care is taken to feed and water the seeds after planting.
15. Much farming is done along the banks of the St. Lawrence River.

● **Infinitives and Infinitive Phrases**   pages 352–353

Copy these sentences. Underline all the infinitives and infinitive phrases. After each sentence indicate the part of speech and the function of each verbal.

16. The Brown family traveled from Arkansas to Maine to live.
17. To earn a living in New England was not difficult for them.
18. Mr. Fred Brown had begun to learn metalworking when he was only a boy.
19. His new job, to manage an entire metalworking shop, was found immediately.
20. Within a week his wife Pearl had been offered an architectural job to suit her talents.

● **Fact and Opinion**   pages 356–357

Copy these sentences, writing *fact* after those that state facts and *opinion* after those that offer opinions.

1. The American flag is red, white, and blue.
2. October has 31 days.
3. Pancakes are delicious.
4. Cats and dogs are the best pets to have.
5. Today's snarled traffic was due to the parade in midtown.

● **Drawing Logical Conclusions**   pages 358–359

Copy these patterns of reasoning. Next to each write *logical* or *illogical* according to your assessment of each conclusion.

6. Tara likes to go swimming. Tara's face and arms are very red. Therefore Tara is sunburned.
7. Before I entered the room, everyone looked serious. As I entered the room, everyone laughed. Therefore they were laughing at me.
8. Unselfish people share with others. Carla did not share her test answers with me. Therefore Carla is selfish.
9. My shirt was clean before that taxi went by. Now my shirt has mud on it. Therefore that taxi splashed me.
10. Most of my friends live on Johnson Street. Ellen does not live on Johnson Street. Therefore Ellen is not my friend.

● Friendly Letters and Social Notes   pages 360–362

1. Choose one of these situations, and write an appropriate letter for it.

   a. Your favorite relative is in the hospital. Write a letter that will amuse and entertain him or her. Wish your relative a speedy recovery.

   b. A friend of yours in another state has just won an important national award. Congratulate your friend, and since you are writing anyway, give him or her some news of your own.

   c. A cousin from a faraway state will be touring the country this summer with a student orchestra. Invite him or her to spend a week with you when the schedule permits. Mention some of the things you want to do during the visit.

● Business Letters   pages 363–364

2. Choose one of these situations, and write an appropriate letter for it.

   a. A pair of binoculars you ordered eight weeks ago from a reputable store has not yet arrived. Write a letter requesting the binoculars or your money by return mail.

   b. You are preparing a report on geothermal energy for your science class. Write to Alternative Energy Resources, Inc., for information on locations and descriptions of geysers and hot springs throughout the country. Ask how geothermal energy might be put to work in your area.

   c. One of your duties as secretary of your math club is to help set up field trips for the coming year. Write to a nearby computer factory, asking whether the club might tour the plant in October.

3. Draw a rectangle for the business letter you wrote and address the "envelope" correctly.

● Editing Letters   pages 365–366

4. Edit either the friendly letter or the business letter you just wrote. Be sure that all the parts of the letter are correctly placed. Check spelling, capitalization, and punctuation as well.

● Mechanics Practice

Copy these sentences. Use hyphens and underscores correctly.

5. When England conquered Canada, many French Cana dians called Acadians were forced to leave their homeland.

6. The word Acadian is a French word that refers to the territory inhabited by the French Canadians.

7. There are three as in the word Acadian; the second a is a long vowel.

8. Most of the dispossessed French Canadians made their way to Louisi ana, which had just been purchased by Louis XIV of France.

9. In Louisiana the French Canadians came to be known as Cajuns, which is a French-Spanish-Indian word.

10. Many Cajun families have lived in Louisiana since the 7100's; no, change the position of that 1 and that 7.

● **Reading Letters**   pages 368–371

Read this letter from Helen Keller to her mother. Then answer the questions that follow.

South Boston, April 13, 1893.

Dear Mother,

    Mr. Westervelt gave us a reception one afternoon. A great many people came. Some of them asked odd questions. A lady seemed surprised that I loved flowers when I could not see their beautiful colors, and when I assured her I did love them, she said, "no doubt you feel the colors with your fingers." But of course, it is not alone for their bright colors that we love the flowers. . . . A gentleman asked me what beauty meant to my mind. I must confess I was puzzled at first. But after a minute I answered that beauty was a form of goodness—and he went away.

    When the reception was over, we went back to the hotel and teacher slept, quite unconscious of the surprise which was in store for her. Mr. Bell and I planned it together, and Mr. Bell made all the arrangements before we told teacher anything about it. This was the surprise—I was to have the pleasure of taking my dear teacher to see Niagara Falls!

    You can never imagine how I felt when I stood in the presence of Niagara until you have the same mysterious sensations yourself. I could hardly realize that it was water that I felt rushing and plunging with impetuous fury at my feet. One feels helpless and overwhelmed in the presence of such a vast force. I had the same feeling once before when I first stood by the great ocean and felt its waves beating against the shore. I suppose you feel so, too, when you gaze up to the stars in the stillness of the night, do you not?

Love,
Helen

1. What new experience does Helen Keller share in this letter?
2. What does Helen reveal about herself in the incident about the flowers?
3. What feelings for her teacher does Helen reveal?
4. Is Helen a child or an adult when she writes this letter? How can you tell?
5. How does Helen feel toward her mother? What element of the friendly letter helps you to understand this?

11

DEPOSIT LITTER
IN
BASKETS

LANGUAGE
Listening and
Speaking

COMPOSITION
Writing a Speech

STUDY SKILLS
Applying
for a Job

LITERATURE
Enjoying Speeches

You have probably heard the expression "in one ear and out the other." Unfortunately, that expression describes the way that some people listen to others. There is a great difference between truly listening and just hearing, as you will see in this unit as you study proper ways of listening and speaking in different situations. You will then have the opportunity to put that knowledge to use as you prepare and deliver a speech and as you read a well-known speech. You will also see how these skills have a very practical use when it comes to finding a job.

Study the pictures on the opposite page. As they suggest, you are involved in listening and speaking situations each day. As you study this unit, think about how the things that you are learning could make you a better listener and speaker.

LANGUAGE

Lesson 1: Listening Critically

Read these parts of advertisements for an imaginary shoe. Do any of them sound like advertisements that you have heard elsewhere?

1. "March with the crowd—wear Treadlites."
2. "Your feet will feel 20 percent more comfortable in Treadlites."
3. "Treadlites—the glamour shoe"
4. "Hi, folks. I'm Bunt Horsehide, star pitcher for the Portland Puffins, and I'm here today to tell you about those great Treadlite shoes."
5. "If you don't wear Treadlites, you might as well go barefoot."

Think and Discuss

Every day you are surrounded by people who wish to persuade you to do something or to share their point of view. You can find examples of many persuasive techniques in advertisements.

One of the most popular techniques is that of the **bandwagon.** This technique tries to convince you that you will be different from everyone else if you do not do as the advertisement says. People who use this technique hope that you will not want to be considered "different" and will therefore "get on the bandwagon" and follow their advice. Which of the advertisements for Treadlites uses the bandwagon technique?

A technique that is similar to the bandwagon is that of the **testimonial.** A company or organization has a well-known figure—someone who may or may not be an expert on the subject—talk about the product or service. The hope is that you will want to be like the celebrity and buy the product or support the organization that he or she does. Which of the advertisements for Treadlites uses a testimonial?

The **this-or-nothing** appeal tries to convince you that there is really only one sensible choice—the particular company's choice—and that if you don't choose it, you are better off with nothing at all. Which Treadlites advertisement is based on a this-or-nothing appeal?

Loaded words—words that imply more than is actually stated—are used in many advertisements. Advertisement 3 uses loaded words by calling Treadlites "the glamour shoe." *Glamour* is a loaded word, for it brings to mind pictures to convince you that you will be famous, rich, and attractive if you wear Treadlites; yet it does not actually make that promise. Notice that the four techniques discussed thus far depend to different extents on *snob appeal;* they want you to buy the product or use the service so that you will feel more important than other people.

A final persuasive technique is one that uses **meaningless statistics.** It makes you think that abstract qualities can be measured and that a product that has more of a certain quality than a competitor's product has is the better one. Which advertisement for Treadlites quotes a meaningless statistic? Be sure to listen carefully and critically when someone tries to persuade you, especially when one of these techniques is used.

Practice

A. Copy these advertisements for an imaginary soap. Write the name of the persuasive technique used in each one.

1. "Kleen will get you twice as clean as any other soap."
2. "Join the Kleen people."
3. "Get luxuriously Kleen."
4. "This is Lola Linguine. If you saw me in *Encounter at the Equator*, you will know why I use Kleen. It's the only soap that could keep me fresh on those jungle locations."
5. "Why be dirty when you can be Kleen?"

Apply

B. 6. Using a magazine or newspaper, find and clip an advertisement that uses one of the five persuasive techniques discussed in this lesson. Write a short paragraph to explain why the advertisement says what it does.

Lesson 2: Giving Explanations and Directions

Minnie asked Uncle Franklin how to make country sausage. He said it was easy to do using a sausage grinder. "Just use that twisting thing and mount it on the edge of the table. Then put the grinding thing in right way around, and put the whole thing together Then you stick the turning thing in the little dingus so it won't fall out. Take all the stuff you make it with and push it into the place where it goes in, and turn the gizmo, and catch it when it comes out Don't forget to clean it really well when you're finished.

"You'd better just let me watch you next time you make it. said Minnie What could Uncle Franklin have done to make his explanation better?

Think and Discuss

It is easy to forget that not everyone is familiar with the things you know well When you give directions, think about how much the person you are instructing already knows. For instance, when you give strangers directions to your home, you might ask if they know how to get to the corner of Sixth and Lamar, and start the directions there. Study these other guidelines for giving explanations and directions

> **How to Give Explanations or Directions**
> 1. **Organize your material into logical steps.**
> 2. **Present the steps in the order in which they should be followed.**
> 3. **Keep your information simple and clear; make sure that it is accurate and complete.**
> 4. **Stay on the subject.**
> 5. **Explain any difficult or unfamiliar terms.**
> 6. **Use models, diagrams, pictures, maps, or charts if they help to make your meaning clear.**

When might you need to give directions? What visual aids could you use?

The best directions are useless unless they are followed. Read or listen to each step carefully. If you do not understand a step, stop and ask questions. When oral directions are complicated, take notes if possible, and then read your notes back to the speaker to be sure that neither of you has made a mistake.

Practice

A. Aunt Daisy explained how they used to do the wash when she was a girl in the East Texas piney woods. Write her sentences in logical order.

1. Dip the clothes in the creek and rub in soft soap.
2. Once a week, put the dirty clothes in a big basket and carry them down to the creek.
3. You can wash your cottons, but don't wash buckskin, as it will shrink away to nothing.
4. Wring the clothes and lay them out to dry over some bushes.
5. Battling sticks are those flat, smooth paddles you use to beat the wash.
6. Lay the wet clothes on top of big pine stumps and beat them with your battling sticks.
7. You should beat the wash until you are plumb worn out, but not until the clothes are!
8. Delicate Sunday dresses you just beat for a few minutes, but dirty overalls take a very long time.
9. Rinse the clothes in the fast-running creek.
10. White clothes put in the direct sun to dry will bleach nicely.

B. 11. On a separate sheet of paper, write the sentences that your teacher will dictate. Then follow the directions that you will be given.

Apply

C. 12. Choose a task you know well and write instructions on how to do it, as you would explain it to a person your own age. Then rewrite the instructions as you would explain the task to a five-year-old child. Remember that the instructions and the language in which you write them will have to be simplified.

Lesson 3: Making Announcements and Introductions

Violet put this announcement in the local newspaper:

Tryouts for the Alamance County Women's Bowling League will be held on Saturday, November 4. Interested teams and individuals are urged to attend.

Only one new person showed up at the League meeting. "Did you read the announcement in the paper?" asked Violet. "No," replied the newcomer. "The hostess at a party introduced me to Gwen and mentioned that we were both bowlers. Then Gwen invited me to the tryouts."

What was the matter with Violet's announcement?

Think and Discuss

Announcements may be printed or spoken. A good announcement will give clear, complete information.

How to Make an Announcement

1. Tell *what* the event is.
2. Tell the *purpose* of the event.
3. Tell *when* and *where* the event will take place.
4. Tell *who* is expected to respond to the announcement.

"Gwen, meet Eunice; Eunice, meet Gwen," said the hostess. "It is time you two fabulous bowlers got together."

Gwen, Eunice, and their hostess were all about the same age, so the introduction was an informal one. The introduction of a younger person to an older person should be more formal:

"Grandpa, this is my classmate Amal Haj. She is from Lebanon. Amal, meet my grandfather, J. M. Mercer. He manufactures bowling balls."

Introducing yourself to someone you would like to meet is permissible in informal situations: "Hi, I'm Peter Jones, the class secretary. I enjoyed your talk on Lebanon, and I wondered if you would give me some information for the class newsletter."

> **How to Make Introductions**
>
> 1. If a person is being introduced to a group, mention the name of the group first.
> 2. If two people are being introduced, mention the older person's name first.
> 3. If the person being introduced is standing, you should stand as well.
> 4. It is not necessary to shake hands, but if one person extends a hand, the other should do likewise.
> 5. Appropriate responses to introductions include "How do you do?" and "I am pleased to meet you."

Practice

A. Write announcements for these events. Invent the necessary details.

1. a field trip to a bowling ball factory for which the parents of all the students must give permission
2. a dance performance for which admission will be charged

B. Write what you would say in introducing these people to each other. Invent the necessary details.

3. a classmate and a friend you met last summer
4. your little sister and your basketball coach
5. your health class and a speaker who is a nutrition expert
6. yourself and your new next-door neighbor

Apply

C. 7. Imagine that a well-known person will speak at a school assembly. Write a three-paragraph introduction, giving a brief biography, telling how you met this person, and announcing the subject of his or her speech.

A Challenge

You are the head chipmunk in your part of the forest. Write an announcement (in chipmunk, of course) of a meeting that will take place in your tree. The topic will be an advanced method for collecting acorns. Provide an English translation.

Lesson 4: Conducting a Meeting

Have you ever attended a meeting in which matters got out of hand? What could have been done to avoid such a situation?

Think and Discuss

If the people participating in a formal meeting follow the rules of **parliamentary procedure,** they should have a meeting that runs smoothly and efficiently. The purpose of such rules (which are explained in *Robert's Rules of Order*) is to bring a group, after orderly discussion, to a majority decision.

Formal meetings are presided over by a **chairperson,** who follows an **agenda,** or list of items to be covered, in running the meeting. Notes of the meeting, called **minutes,** are taken by a **secretary.** At most meetings the secretary will also read the minutes from the previous meeting.

Old business—items from an earlier agenda that were not discussed or decided upon at the previous meeting—is raised and settled before moving on to **new business.** In matters of discussion people must ask to be **recognized,** or given permission to speak, by the chairperson. Unrecognized discussion can cause a lot of confusion. It may bring about a **point of order,** or objection to the way that the meeting is proceeding, which the chairperson must settle before returning to the matter under discussion. A **motion,** or suggestion for discussion or action, must be **seconded,** or agreed to by a second person, before it can be discussed. During the discussion the motion may be **amended,** or revised.

People in a meeting **nominate,** or name, candidates when officers are to be elected. At the close of the nominations, the chairperson calls for a vote, usually by handing out **secret ballots**—slips of paper on which each person writes the name of his or her choice without fear of that choice being revealed. The officers must usually receive a **majority** (more than half) of the votes to win. When other business is voted upon, a **quorum** (usually a majority, but always the number of people necessary to decide on business matters) is needed.

When all business has been discussed by the participants in the meeting and all voting has been completed, the chairperson **adjourns,** or closes, the meeting.

Practice

A. Write the definition of these terms.

1. adjourn
2. agenda
3. amend
4. chairperson
5. minutes
6. motion
7. nominate
8. old business
9. point of order
10. quorum
11. recognize
12. second
13. secretary
14. secret ballot

Apply

B. 15. Write a script for a meeting that has been called to decide on the destination for a class trip. Be sure to follow the rules of parliamentary procedure in your meeting.

HOW OUR LANGUAGE GROWS

Have you ever been to *Utopia* or to *Camelot*? Where and what is *Shangri-La*? Literature has given us a great many interesting places to visit by way of the written word. Although none of them exist in real life, they have all become symbols for situations or states of mind. *Utopia,* for example, is the name of a land in which everything is perfect. *Camelot,* as you probably already know, was the headquarters of King Arthur's Round Table, a group of the greatest and best knights of Europe in the Middle Ages. *Shangri-La* from the novel *Lost Horizon* is a place of peace, security, and agelessness somewhere high in the Himalayas.

Never-Never Land, from the book *Peter Pan*, is a state of eternal youth where children never grow up. *Oz,* that strange city down the yellow brick road, is a land of magic, strange and wonderful on the outside but false and empty within.

Each of the places already mentioned is not so much a material or bodily kingdom as a state of mind. Using a *Dictionary of Classical Mythology* or some similar reference source, find out what these places signify:

a. the river Lethe
b. the river Styx
c. El Dorado
d. Scylla and Charybdis
e. the land of the Lotos-Eaters

LANGUAGE REVIEW

Critical Listening   pages 378–379

Copy these parts of advertisements for Fountain of Youth, an imaginary bottled water. Write the name of the technique on which the advertisement's appeal is based.

1. "Next to Fountain of Youth, all other bottled waters fall flat."
2. "Fountain of Youth—the sparkling alternative"
3. "This is Ponce de Léon. Almost 500 years ago I searched for the Fountain of Youth, but I never found it. You can find it today, though, at your nearest supermarket."
4. "Other sparkling waters are only half as bubbly as Fountain of Youth."
5. "Fountain of Youth—the champagne of bottled waters"
6. "You will feel 40 percent more refreshed when you drink Fountain of Youth."
7. "Quench your thirst the way your neighbors do—with Fountain of Youth."
8. "If you were drinking Fountain of Youth, you wouldn't still be thirsty."
9. "Hi. I'm Dirk Benchwarmer, quarterback for the Bloomington Blockers. When that gridiron heats up, nothing cools me off more quickly than Fountain of Youth."
10. "Be a part of the Fountain of Youth crowd."

Explanations and Directions   pages 380–381

11. Copy the beginning of this explanation, and then invent details to explain the device mentioned. Make sure that your explanation is simple and clear, even though the device may be imaginary.

    Last year my sister was in a very serious accident and remained in the hospital for days. Her recovery would have taken longer if it had not been for one of the most unusual devices I have ever seen. Here is how it works.

12. Write a brief set of directions for one of these topics.

    How to Pack a Suitcase   How to Wash Your Dog
    How to Iron a Shirt   How to Make Lemonade
    How to Find the Public Library from Your House

Announcements and Introductions pages 382–383

Rewrite these announcements so that the information that they give will be complete.

13.   Here's a bulletin for all theater fans. This Friday the senior class at Hawkins Intermediate will present a three-act comedy, <u>The Rise and Fall of Danny Garth</u>, in the school auditorium. Tickets are 50¢ and on sale today in Room 312.

14.   The Laurel Avenue Block Association will be holding a spring Rummage Sale on Saturday, April 3. There will also be baked goods for sale. The money is for a good cause, so come!

Study these introductions. Copy the ones that are correct and rewrite the ones that are incorrect.

15. "Kern Ho, stand up and say hi to my dad. Dad, Kern Ho is the new president of the Chess Club."

16. "Mrs. Burke, I would like to introduce Ada Halstad. Ada, this is Mrs. Burke, our school nurse."

17. "Ms. Ochoa? You don't know me, but I loved your piano concert."

18. "Hey, Pam! Shake hands with Maria Pérez, my new neighbor."

Conducting a Meeting pages 384–385

Copy the terms from column A. Next to each term write the proper definition from column B.

A	B
19. chairperson	**a.** person who records the minutes
20. adjourn	**b.** list of items to be covered
21. agenda	**c.** to revise a motion
22. nominate	**d.** to close a meeting
23. secretary	**e.** to name a candidate
24. amend	**f.** person who runs the meeting

Applying Listening and Speaking Skills

25. Imagine that you are conducting a tour of a new ocean liner. Write an introduction that you would use to make yourself known to the people on the tour, and then write a set of directions you would give them so that they could find the dining room.

STUDY SKILLS

Lesson 5: Completing a Job Application

Wenona was applying for a summer job in a bicycle shop. Her older brother offered advice on filling out the application.

"Even though you have never held a full-time job, you do have work experience. Mention that you repaired bikes for individuals, and give their names as references. Include the fact that you fixed toys for the holiday bazaar too."

"Shall I mention baby-sitting?"

"That doesn't have much to do with bikes. Do list someone you sat for as a character reference, though."

"I think I'll add that I sold pep decals for the school band. After all, at the bicycle shop I'll have to meet the public and handle money."

Think and Discuss

Your application is the first thing an employer will see, so it should make a good impression. Write it neatly, and include as much information as possible that is relevant to the job you want. Often, you will be expected to fill out the application at the employer's office. Before you leave home, make a list of all the data you will need:

Kind of job you are applying for and salary you expect Ask for a job that might be offered to a person of your age and experience.

How can you find out the kinds of jobs (and their rate of pay) that an employer might have available?

Hours you can work If you have to be in by 9 P.M., or if you have football practice every morning, that may restrict the jobs available to you.

Work history If you have held other jobs, you will need the titles, names, addresses, and telephone numbers of your previous employers; the dates you worked there; your reasons for leaving; and the salaries you were paid. List volunteer experience too, if it is relevant.

Specialty skills Do you speak a second language? Can you type or take shorthand—and how fast? Can you run machines or repair them? Think of skills that might be useful to your employer.

Education List all the schools you attended and the years you went there, as well as any special training you have had. You may have a chance to mention awards and extracurricular activities.

Health Be aware of any physical ailments which could affect your ability to work under certain conditions. Some employers may ask for a list of major illnesses and operations you have had.

References List the titles, names, addresses, and telephone numbers of several people who know you well enough to give a good recommendation. They may be teachers, friends of the family, leaders of groups to which you belong—anyone who is respected in your community. It is courteous to ask these people if you may give their names as references.

Official records You will need to know your Social Security number. Some states require that you show proof of age or working papers in order to get a job.

How do you think the information in each category will help an employer decide whether to hire you?

Practice

A. Suppose you were applying for an after-school job at a local restaurant. How would you answer these questions on a job application?

1. What position are you applying for, and what salary do you expect?
2. What hours are you available to work?
3. Give your employment record.
4. What is your educational background?
5. List four personal references.
6. Do you have any skills or experiences that make you especially qualified for this job?

Apply

B. 7. Pick up an application form from a company that hires young people. Make a list of all the data you would need to fill it out. Compare the form with those brought in by other class members.

Lesson 6: Preparing for a Job Interview

Wenona and her friend Jacy compared notes on their first job interviews. At the end of his interview, Jacy had been offered the job he wanted, helping to care for patients in a nursing home.

"Did you get your job?" he asked Wenona.

"I don't know yet. The owner said she admired my initiative but that she had a lot of highly qualified applicants."

"Don't give up. After she checks your references, I'm sure she'll hire you. You're a good bike mechanic."

"True, but other people are good too. I'll call Monday and see what she says, but I can't put all my hopes on just one possibility. I'll apply at some other shops in the meantime."

Think and Discuss

Often the first impression in an interview is based on how you look. Prepare in advance to have clothes that are clean and well pressed; they should also be comfortable so that you can be relaxed. Wear a style similar to what people wear in the kind of work you want. How do you think Wenona and Jacy dressed for their interviews?

The second impression is made by your general manner. Be courteous. Ask questions about how the business is run, but convey that you respect the owner and the business.

There are two things every employer looks for in a beginning worker. One is the desire to work. The other is reliability. Before you go in for your interview, think about why you want this job. Also think of things you have done that demonstrate your reliability, such as responsibilities you have held at home or for an organization.

Concentrating on your successes and knowing what you want will give you an air of self-confidence. If you should be asked about your weaknesses, answer honestly; but you do not have to volunteer unfavorable information, such as a poor grade in math.

Plan in advance what you want to find out about the job, such as the hours, the wages, and whether you will have to buy a uniform. Even if you do not get one job, things you learn in one interview can help you prepare for the next one.

Practice

A. Wenona and Jacy were both hired for the types of jobs for which they applied. Copy these statements about their interviews, inserting the correct descriptions of their behavior.

1. They were (late, on time, a half hour early) for their interviews.
2. When Jacy entered the office, the first thing he did was (sit down, shake hands, ask "When do I start?").
3. Wenona asked (if she could work full time during the summer, if she would be permitted to ride the bicycles, how much money the owner was making).
4. Jacy wore (neatly pressed shorts, a business suit, clean, pressed slacks and a sport coat).
5. Wenona wore (high heels, rubber shower sandals, sensible shoes).
6. Jacy said, ("I used to help my elderly grandmother when she lived with us.", "How much money does this nursing home take in each year?", "We took better care of Grandma than any nursing home!")

Apply

B. 7. Choose a job you might like to apply for and do some research to find out the qualifications you would need, something about the working conditions, and the usual starting salary. Sources of information might include the library, people who have similar jobs, and the employer.

To Memorize

You have to sniff out joy, keep your nose to the joy-trail.

Buffy Sainte-Marie

According to Buffy Sainte-Marie, does joy come along naturally, or do you have to look for it? What does it mean to "keep your nose to the joy-trail"?

COMPOSITION

Lesson 7: Writing and Delivering a Speech

In the course of a year, most people hear a variety of speeches. These may include graduation speeches, political speeches, special school reports, informative presentations at assemblies, and entertaining speeches at social events. What kind of speech have you heard most recently?

Think and Discuss

At some point in your life, you probably will be called upon to give a speech. Knowing how to prepare a speech and how to present it well will make you a confident, effective speaker.

The first step in preparing a speech is to choose an *appropriate topic*. Unless you are an experienced speaker, you should plan to speak about a topic that you know well, rather than a topic that would require you to master a large amount of new information. Your topic should be one that you can cover in an interesting, meaningful way in the amount of time you have been given.

You also need to determine who your *audience* will be. A speech given to a group of senior citizens, for example, would probably be different from a speech given to a group of exchange students. You will need to take into account the special characteristics of your audience and develop your topic to meet the interests and needs of that audience. Keep the *occasion* of the speech—its time and place—in mind as well. A speech given in the school auditorium on graduation day will be different from a speech you might give in the gymnasium to introduce the winner of an athletic award.

One final consideration is the *purpose* of your speech. Speeches can inform, persuade, or entertain. The occasion of the speech will often determine its purpose and its length. Name an example of an informative speech that would be given on a certain occasion.

Once you have determined your topic, audience, occasion, and purpose, you are ready to begin writing. Jot down your ideas or record your research on note cards, as you would do to prepare a research report. Use your notes to prepare an outline. Study this outline for a speech that Barbara King, the president of her school's Student Council, is preparing for the presentation of an award at the final school assembly program.

   I. Introduction
      A. School Citizenship Award created five years ago
      B. Given by PTA to student who has served the community
  II. Body
      A. Eighth-grader who has served the elderly
      B. Founder of the Adopt-a-Grandparent program at the Natrona County Retirement Home
         1. Running errands
         2. Assisting with shopping
         3. Reading and writing letters
         4. Conducting "Saturday Singalong"
      C. Recipient of commendation from the AARP
 III. Conclusion
      A. Introduction of Diego Ramirez
      B. Request for applause

Using this outline, Barbara will prepare the complete text of her speech. (For the edited version of that complete text, see page 395.) She will practice that speech several times to learn it as well as possible. When she presents her speech at the school assembly, however, she will refer only to a set of note cards that contain its key points.

After you have gone through these same steps of planning, preparing, and practicing your speech, you will be ready to present it. Keep these points in mind as you deliver your speech.

How to Deliver a Speech

1. Speak clearly and carefully.
2. Avoid saying *er* and *uh*.
3. Make sure that you can be heard easily by all.
4. Look at your audience.
5. Stand naturally, neither stiffly nor too informally.
6. Make sure that your gestures and body movements are appropriate to the speech.

Practice

A. Put these steps in preparing a speech in the correct order, and then copy them in that order.

1. Prepare the complete text of the speech.
2. Record your thoughts or research on note cards.
3. Record the key points of your speech on note cards.
4. Prepare an outline.
5. Practice the text of the speech until you know it well.
6. Determine your topic, audience, occasion, and purpose.

B. Copy these speech titles. Write whether the purpose of each speech would be to *inform*, to *persuade*, or to *entertain*.

7. TV Commercials — Are They Bad for Your Health?
8. How a Successful TV Commercial Is Produced
9. 101 Things to Do During a TV Commercial Break
10. First Aid Procedures for Baby-Sitters
11. The Real-Life Disasters of Baby-Sitting
12. Fair Pay for Baby-Sitters

C. 13.–14. Write down two ideas for topics that you might treat in an informative speech, a persuasive speech, or an entertaining speech. Write down at least two reasons why each topic would be of interest to the audience.

Apply

D. 15. From Practice C select a topic for your speech. Jot down your ideas on note cards, prepare an outline and a complete text, and then practice the speech until you need only your second set of note cards. Present your speech in class.

Lesson 8: Editing a Speech

Read the edited version of Barbara's speech.

Editing Marks

The School Citizenship Award was created here at Laramie Junior High five years ago. Each spring the Parent-Teacher Association presents that award to one student who has served the community.

This year the award is being given to an eighth-grader who has *made a special effort to* served the elderly in our area. Last fall he founded the Adopt-a-Grandparent program at the Natrona County Retirement Home. This program provides many services for the residents there. The students run errands, assist the residents with shopping, ~~and~~ help the residents with correspondence, *and hold a monthly* ~~Every month the students have a~~ "Saturday Singalong" at the home~~as well.~~ The Adopt-a-Grandparent program has been very successful--so successful, *in fact,* that the recipient of the School Citizenship Award ~~was~~ recently *received a commendation from* ~~congratulated by~~ the American Association of Retired *Persons* ~~People~~ for his work.

By now I *am sure* ~~guess~~ you know the winner of the School Citizenship Award--Diego Ramirez. *Let's all give him a big hand.*

¶ The Russian novelist Leo Tolstoy once said, "The vocation of every man and woman is to serve others." It was with that thought in mind that

, in which 22 students are now involved,

Does Barbara's edited speech match the outline she prepared?

Editing Marks

- ≡ capitalize
- ⊙ make a period
- ∧ add something
- ⌄, add a comma
- ⌄" add quotation marks
- ℮ take something away
- ◯ spell correctly
- ¶ indent the paragraph
- / make a lowercase letter
- ∾ tr transpose

Think and Discuss

The changes that Barbara made in her speech improve that speech in four ways. First, by adding the request for applause at the end, she made sure that her speech matched her outline. She also kept the parallel structure that she had used in her outline by revising a sentence in the middle of the second paragraph.

After rereading her first draft, Barbara decided that she needed to introduce her speech in a more interesting way. She searched through some books of quotations and found an appropriate quotation for her speech. Quotations are often a good way to add interest to a speech.

Finally, Barbara made several changes that made the language of her speech more formal. The occasion, after all, was a formal one, and she wanted the speech to fit the occasion. That is why she changed *worked* to *made a special effort* and *I guess* to *I am sure*. Name one other place where Barbara made the language of her speech more formal.

Practice

A. Copy Barbara's speech, making the changes she has indicated.

B. Study the edited version of the speech that you have just copied. Close your book and take out a sheet of paper. Copy the speech as your teacher reads it aloud.

Apply

C. Reread the speech you wrote in Lesson 7. Is the language of the speech appropriate to the occasion on which it will be given? Have you used parallel structure to express parallel ideas? Would an appropriate quotation make your speech more interesting? Edit your speech and mark any corrections that you wish to make; then rewrite it.

MECHANICS PRACTICE

Using Colons, Dashes, and Parentheses

- Use a colon before a list or series of items, especially when the list follows expressions such as *the following* and *as follows.*

  Example: The city of Houston, Texas, could be given several titles: the largest city in Texas, the leading trade center of the Southwest, one of the fastest-growing cities in the country, and the fifth most populous city in American today.

- Use a dash to show a sudden break in thought or to mean *namely* or *in other words* before an explanation.

  Example: In the early 1900's an important discovery — petroleum — resulted in the building of oil refineries at Houston.

- Use parentheses ( ) around material that adds an incidental explanation to a sentence but is not of major importance.

  Example: World War I (1914–18) and World War II (1939–45) created a demand for Houston's petroleum products and caused the city to grow.

Add colons, dashes, or parentheses ( ) where needed in these sentences.

1. Houston is located in southeast Texas, about 50 miles 80 kilometers from the Gulf of Mexico.
2. The Houston Ship Channel connects this important port to the Gulf of Mexico; in fact, only two other American ports New Orleans and New York City handle more cargo than Houston does.
3. Houston is the home of two daily newspapers the *Chronicle* and the *Post.*
4. It is also home to the following universities Rice University, Texas Southern University, and the University of Houston.
5. In southeastern Houston sits the Lyndon B. Johnson Space Center known as the Manned Spacecraft Center from 1962–1973.
6. The world's first stadium with a roof the Astrodome was built in Houston. It is the home of two professional teams the Astros of the NBL and the Rockets of the NBA.
7. The Houston Symphony Orchestra which usually performs at the Jesse H. Jones Hall for the Performing Arts gives summertime concerts at the Miller Outdoor Theatre in Hermann Park.
8. There is only one more thing I can say Houston, I love you!

LITERATURE

Lesson 9: Reading a Speech

In 1971 William Wayne Keeler was elected chief of the Cherokee nation—the first chief chosen by the people instead of appointed by the government in many years. Read this part of his inaugural address.

This is a historic moment for all Cherokees, Delawares, and Shawnees. It marks the return of the management of their tribal affairs into the hands of the people. We have not had this responsibility for more than threescore years. I am proud and happy
5 to see this day. I am honored to be your elected leader.

The Cherokees were a free and independent nation, with a constitutional government elected by the people, almost a century and a half ago. In the years between then and now, our forebears and we suffered internal strife, removal to an alien land, a civil war
10 that was not of our making, loss of our land without fair compensation, discrimination because of our color, and indignity because we were few in number.

But we are a dauntless people. Our fathers would not bow to a stronger force. Neither have we ever bowed to it. Not when we were
15 penniless; nor when we were without food to fill our children's stomachs. Not when we were without clothing to shield us against bitter winds that howl in the forgotten hollows between these hills; nor when these hallowed grounds on which we stand were a place of mockery and contempt for those who had herded us onto them.
20 We were dauntless in our defeat. We remembered the hardships of those who gave us our heritage. We took courage from their example. We would not be overcome. The blood of our fathers beats strongly in our veins; and we can still hear the distant drums that echo against the mountainsides of the lost and lonely memories that
25 whisper along the byways of our hallowed heritage.

Today we see the beginning of the realization of everything that was only a dream during the lifetime of most of us here today.

The Cherokee nation was never dead; only asleep. Today it stirs
and begins to awaken. Today our children see the dream that you
and I have had for so many bleak years.

We are again entrusted with the management of our own affairs.
We are now free to elect our own leaders. We are free to train our
people for jobs; to improve the educational opportunities of our
children; to provide adequate medical care for all who need it; to
record and promote our noble heritage.

We must be united if we are to accomplish the heavy work that
lies ahead. We must join hands with all of our brothers as never
before in the history of our people.

Past mistakes and animosity must be laid aside. All of us have
been mistaken at some time in the past. We must learn from those
mistakes. If we fail in this, the opportunity of this moment will be
lost—perhaps beyond recall. We must think of the work to be done
in the future; not of what we should have done in the past.

I pledge to you today, in this historic setting, my time and the
best of whatever talents I have.

I thank you for your support in years past; and for your
confidence in me to lead the tribe for the next four years.

I humbly and sincerely ask for your support and for your best
advice in the years ahead.

Together, we can accomplish even greater things than have been
accomplished in the past. With God's help, we can bring about
miracles even greater than the accomplishment of this day.

Cherokees! Give me your trust and your united support. Thank
you.

Think and Discuss

Memorable speeches have covered many topics and have
been delivered by many people. What usually makes some
speeches memorable are some literary devices that they share.

One such device is **repetition.** A speaker will repeat certain words and phrases to impress key ideas upon his or her listeners. The word *dauntless* is repeated in the third and fourth paragraphs of this speech. The key idea that Mr. Keeler wants to impress upon his listeners is that the Cherokees must face the challenges of the future with the same courage as they faced hardships of the past. He then repeats the word *heritage* to remind his people of their past. Key ideas may also be repeated through the use of synonyms. Mr. Keeler uses *forebears, example,* and *blood of our fathers* as synonyms for the same ideas expressed in the word *heritage.*

Variety is another device that effective speech writers use. Longer, more involved sentences or paragraphs are mixed with shorter, more simple ones. This mixing gives the speech an interesting, unpredictable rhythm and so keeps the listeners' attention. Where do you first see a mixing of longer and shorter paragraphs in this speech?

To help make a point, many speech writers depend on the **poetic devices** that you have studied. In the third paragraph of Mr. Keeler's speech, for example, the words *howl, hollows, hill,* and *hallowed* all appear in the same sentence. What devices of sound do they use? Such use of language gives a speech a poetic, inspiring air.

Perhaps the most important literary device in a speech is **parallelism,** the expression of related ideas through similar wording. One example of parallelism can be found in the second paragraph of Mr. Keeler's speech. There he lists related ideas—the hardships his people have faced—in groups of words beginning with a noun that is a direct object of *suffered.* Besides suffering internal strife, he says, the Cherokees have suffered "removal . . . civil war . . . loss . . . discrimination . . . and indignity." Another example of parallelism occurs in the seventh paragraph. What things does Mr. Keeler say that his people are now free to do?

Finally, notice that this speech, like most memorable speeches, concentrates on only **a few key ideas.** When the information in a speech is presented simply, clearly, and vividly, the speech will be effective and easy to remember. The next time you listen to a speech, see if you can remember the key ideas after the speaker has finished.

Practice

A. Reread William Wayne Keeler's speech. Answer the questions.

1. Name two key ideas of this speech.
2. What words does Mr. Keeler use to express unity?
3. Why do you think there are three one-sentence paragraphs near the end of the speech?
4. In lines 20–25 how does Mr. Keeler poetically express the thought that the past is remembered?
5. What poetic device appears twice in the phrase "the mountainsides of the lost and lonely memories"?
6. Study the paragraph that appears on lines 13–19. What words introduce related ideas and make them parallel?
7. What example of parallelism appears on lines 39–43?

Apply

B. 8. Use a magazine, a newspaper, or a book from the library to locate a short speech that interests you. Write a paragraph to explain the literary devices that it uses.

A BOOK TO READ

Title: **Words by Heart**
Author: Ouida Sebastyen
Publisher: Atlantic—Little, Brown

Lena Sills and her family have traveled from the deep South to the wide-open spaces of America's West in search of freedom and room to grow. Expecting friendliness and acceptance from the townspeople in Bethel Springs, Lena is shocked to find them close-minded, prejudiced, even deliberately cruel and violent. Her parents, who are resigned to the situation, face the town's coldness with their own strength of spirit. Lena, however, wants more—she wants equality and respect, and she is determined to make a place for herself in the all-white community.

Ouida Sebastyen has written a compelling novel that shows Lena's growth beyond her fear to new strength and hope. It is the story of a girl trying to live up to age-old ideals in a new and confusing world.

● **Listening Critically**   pages 378–379

Read these parts of advertisements. Then write the letter that correctly identifies the persuasive technique used. Follow this code:

a *bandwagon*   **b** *testimonial*   **c** *this-or-nothing*   **d** *loaded words*
e *meaningless statistics.*

1. If you are one of the very fussy few who deserve the very best in stereo equipment, ConcertSound is the best sound around!
2. ConcertSound is 75 percent better than the next brand of stereo equipment.
3. Those who don't own a ConcertSound don't own a stereo!
4. ConcertSound is the best-selling stereo in the state! Join your neighbors in owning the sound equipment that *everyone* prefers!
5. This is Stix Snaredrum of the Down-at-Heels Band saying that ConcertSound is your best bet for hi-fi stereo equipment!

● **Explanations and Directions**   pages 380–381

6. Using this map of Ariel III, explain to Bian how to get from her house to Space Suits, Inc.

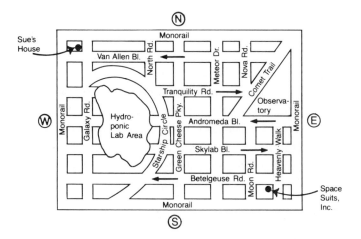

NOTE: Ariel III is a government colony on the moon. Only government employees on government business are allowed to use the Monorail. One-way streets are marked. There are no traffic lights.

Announcements and Introductions   pages 382–383

Copy these sentences, completing each one correctly.

7. When introducing a younger person and an older person, the _____ person should be introduced to the _____ person first.
8. A formal introduction should include, besides the guest's name, his or her _____, _____, and possibly _____.
9. It is permissible to introduce yourself to someone else when _____.
10. A good announcement should contain these five kinds of information: _____, _____, _____, _____, and _____.

Conducting a Meeting   pages 384–385

Match each person or thing connected with a meeting to its proper definition. Copy column A, and add the correct match from column B.

A	B
11. chairperson	a. a person who takes and reads the minutes of the meeting
12. secretary	b. a suggestion for discussion or action
13. adjourn	c. the person who presides over the meeting
14. recognize	d. to close a meeting
15. motion	e. to give someone permission to speak

Job Applications   pages 388–389

Beatrice is 14 years old. She wants to apply for a summer volunteer job at her city's museum of natural history. What answers would she give to these questions to show her suitability for the job? You may invent Beatrice's credentials as long as they are reasonable for a person of 14.

1. What special skills or interests do you have that have led you to apply for this job?
2. In this job you will work with exhibits of all kinds, including fossils, animal habitats, maps of the stars, and the skeletons of extinct animals. What experience have you had that will enable you to handle a variety of materials?
3. You may be asked to talk to museum visitors from time to time. What skills do you have that involve working with people?
4. List your educational background, mentioning any special honors or awards you have received. What grades do you usually receive in science?
5. List three references we might want to contact. Tell why you are using each of these people as a reference.

● **Job Interviews** pages 390–391

Bob applied for a job as dog walker in an apartment house where many business people lived. The apartment dwellers were very concerned about the honesty and reliability of the person who would be hired. Answer these items as if you were Bob.

6. How would you be dressed for the interview?
7. This is your first job. How can you present yourself as a reliable person if you have never worked before?
8. You know a lot about handling dogs from contact with your own pets and those of your friends. How can you mention this in a way that will not make the interviewer think you are a know-it-all who will not take instructions?
9. How can you present yourself as an honest person?
10. Tell the interviewer why you are interested in this particular job.

● **Speech Writing** pages 392–394

1. Write a three-paragraph speech for one of these occasions.

   a. to commend the members of the school sports teams at the annual Sports Banquet;
   b. to introduce your aunt Alice to your classmates on Career Day. Your aunt is a specialist in medical technology, and she will speak to the class about the requirements and the advantages of careers in her field;
   c. to honor a deaf classmate who has worked for several years to help found a Theater of the Deaf in your state.

2. Condense your speech into a set of notes from which you would be able to deliver it.

● **Editing a Speech** pages 395–396

3. Edit the speech you wrote for Exercise 1. Give particular attention to the effectiveness of the introduction and closing. Edit for formal word choice and for parallel structure as well. Finally, check for correct spelling, capitalization, and punctuation.

● **Mechanics Practice** page 397

Copy these sentences. Add colons, dashes, and parentheses ( ) wherever needed.

4. The six New England states Maine, New Hampshire, Vermont, Massachusetts, Rhode Island, and Connecticut were all part of the thirteen colonies.

404 TEST: Unit 11

5. Three of the New England states have extensive industrial areas Massachusetts, Rhode Island, and Connecticut.
6. One of these states Connecticut is part of the New York metropolitan area.
7. Yale University founded in 1636 is the second oldest university in the United States.

● **Reading a Speech**   pages 398–401

Read this portion of a speech that was given by Jawaharlal Nehru of India on the death of Mahatma Gandhi. Then answer the questions that follow.

Friends and comrades, the light has gone out of our lives and there is darkness everywhere. I do not know what to tell you and how to say it. Our beloved leader, Bapu as we called him, the father of the nation, is no more. Perhaps I am wrong to say that. Nevertheless, we will not see him again as we have seen him for these many years. We will not run to him for advice and seek solace from him, and that is a terrible blow, not to me only, but to millions and millions in this country, and it is a little difficult to soften the blow by any other advice that I or anyone else can give you.

The light has gone out, I said, and yet I was wrong. For the light that shone in this country was no ordinary light. The light that has illumined this country for these many years will illumine this country for many more years, and a thousand years later that light will still be seen in this country and the world will see it and it will give solace to innumerable hearts. For that light represented the living truth . . . the eternal truths, reminding us of the right path, drawing us from error, taking this ancient country to freedom.

1. The word *light* appears in this brief excerpt seven times. What literary device does this indicate?
2. Who or what is this light that has gone out? What figure of speech has Nehru used here?
3. The sentence in paragraph 1 that begins, "We will not run to him. . . ." is very long. How does it compare to the other sentences in the same paragraph? What device of good speech writing does this indicate?
4. Show how the device of parallelism was used in the sentence from paragraph 2 that begins, "For that light represented. . . ."
5. By the end of the second paragraph it is evident that Jawaharlal Nehru has given an *additional* meaning to the word *light*. What is this new meaning?

MAINTENANCE and REVIEW

Read and then copy this part of the first chapter of *Dune,* a science fiction novel by Frank Herbert.

In the week before their departure to Arrakis, when all the final scurrying about had reached a nearly unbearable frenzy, an old crone came to visit the mother of the boy, Paul.

It was a warm night at Castle Caladan, and the ancient pile of stone
5 that had served the Atreides family as home for twenty-six generations bore that cooled-sweat feeling it acquired before a change in the weather.

The old woman was let in by the side door down the vaulted passage by Paul's room and she was allowed a moment to peer in at him where
10 he lay in his bed.

By the half-light of a suspensor lamp, dimmed and hanging near the floor, the awakened boy could see a bulky female shape at his door, standing one step ahead of his mother. The old woman was a witch shadow — hair like matted spiderwebs, eyes like glittering jewels.

15   Is he not small for his age, Jessica?'' the old woman asked.

Paul's mother answered in her soft contralto: ''The Atreides are known to start late getting their growth, Your Reverence.''

''He's awake and listening to us,'' said the old woman. ''Sly little rascal.'' She chuckled. ''But royalty has need of slyness. And if he's
20 really the Kwisatz Haderach . . . well . . .''

Within the shadows of his bed, Paul held his eyes to mere slits. Two bird-bright ovals — the eyes of the old woman — seemed to expand and glow as they stared into his.

''Sleep well, you sly little rascal,'' said the old woman. ''Tomorrow
25 you'll need all your faculties to meet my gom jabbar.''

And she was gone, pushing his mother out, closing the door with a solid thump.

Paul lay awake wondering: *What's a gom jabbar?*

In all the upset during this time of change, the old woman was the
30 strangest thing he had seen.

Sentences and Paragraphs   pages 2–3, 12–13, 47–49

1.–2. Copy one interrogative sentence and one imperative sentence that appear in lines 15–24.

3. The paragraph that begins on line 11 consists of two sentences. Is each sentence *simple* or *compound*? How do you know?

4. Which paragraph expresses the main idea of the selection?

Nouns and Verbs   pages 80–81, 90–91, 120–123, 126–131

5.–16. Using lines 1–10, copy and label six common concrete nouns, one common abstract noun, three proper nouns, and one appositive.

17.–24. Using lines 4–24, copy and label three transitive action verbs, three intransitive action verbs, and two linking verbs.

25.–30. Write the principal parts of these verbs: *reach, come, answer, know, seem,* and *go.* Which of these verbs are irregular?

Adjectives, Adverbs, and Complements   pages 162–163, 166–167, 200–207

31.–37. Copy seven adjectives (not counting articles) in lines 1–14.

38.–40. What three adverbs might describe how the woman watched Paul?

41.–46. Using this entire selection, copy and label three direct objects, two predicate nominatives, and one predicate adjective.

Pronouns   pages 239–241

47.–54. Using lines 8–24, copy two subject pronouns and two object pronouns.

Prepositions, Interjections, and Conjunctions   pages 272–273, 276–279

55.–64. Copy ten prepositional phrases that appear in the selection.

65.–69. Copy and label two coordinating conjunctions, two subordinating conjunctions, and one interjection from this selection.

Clauses and Verbals   pages 314–321, 346–347, 350–353

70.–74. The first three paragraphs each consist of one sentence. Which sentences are *complex,* and which are *compound complex*?

75.–79. Copy one gerund, two participles, and two infinitives in lines 1–17.

Listening and Speaking   pages 382–383

80. What might Jessica say to introduce Paul to the old woman?

SENTENCE DIAGRAMING

A sentence diagram is a line picture that shows the relationship between words and groups of words in a sentence.

The Simple Subject and Predicate

To diagram a sentence, first pick out the simple predicate, the verb, and write in on the right hand half of a base line. Then pick out the simple subject and put it on the left half of the base line. Use a vertical line to separate the simple subject from the simple predicate.

Many tourists visited the mall.

tourists	visited

Inverted Word Order

When the predicate precedes the subject in the sentence, that sentence is in inverted word order. Inverted word order does not show up in a sentence diagram. Notice that all capitalized words remain capitalized in a sentence diagram.

Compare these sentences and their diagrams.

People surged into the mall.

People	surged

Into the mall surged the people.

people	surged

The Four Types of Sentences

The four types of sentences are diagramed here. The simple subject and simple predicate of each sentence are shown in the diagram.

Declarative: Shoppers carried many packages.

Shoppers	carried

Interrogative: Did the shoppers carry many packages?

shoppers	Did carry

Imperative: Carry these packages.

(you)	carry

Exclamatory: How many packages the shoppers carried!

shoppers	carried

Notice that in an interrogative sentence the subject often comes between two parts of a verb phrase. In the imperative sentence there is no expressed subject; the subject is *you* understood.

Practice

Diagram the simple subjects and predicates in these sentences.

1. How many shoppers visited this store?
2. We bought three packages.
3. The clerk packed our souvenirs.
4. How nice they looked!
5. Down the escalator rode the family.
6. Take your time.
7. Everyone is in a hurry.
8. We can wait over here.
9. How comfortable are the benches?
10. Did you buy something for me?

Direct and Indirect Objects

A direct object follows an action verb and receives the action of the verb. It is diagramed like this:

Joan wrote a story.

Joan	wrote	story

Notice that the vertical line that separates the subject from the predicate crosses the base line. The line that separates the verb from the direct object stops at the base line.

An indirect object usually tells to whom or for whom the action of a verb is done. An indirect object comes before a direct object in a sentence. In a sentence diagram, the indirect object is written beneath the verb and joined to the verb with an angled line.

Manny read us his story.

Manny	read	story

us

Possessives and Articles

Possessive nouns and pronouns often precede nouns to show ownership. The articles *a, an,* and *the* always signal a noun. The relationship between possessives, articles, and nouns is shown in a diagram. The possessives and articles are written on slanting lines beneath the nouns they modify.

Practice

Diagram the simple subjects, simple predicates, direct objects, indirect objects, possessive nouns and pronouns, and articles in these sentences.

1. Send them your entry.
2. Tina read us her story.
3. Tina's story won a prize.
4. Her friends congratulated Tina.
5. They gave Tina a party.
6. Did you see Tina's prize?

Adjectives and Adverbs

Adjectives modify nouns and pronouns. Adjectives are written on slanted lines beneath the nouns they modify.

A noisy crowd arrived.

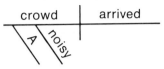

Adverbs modify verbs. In a sentence diagram, adverbs are placed beneath the verbs they modify.

A noisy crowd arrived early.

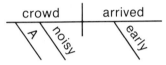

An adverb is placed beneath the verb it modifies even if the two words are separated in the sentence. The word *not* is diagramed like other adverbs.

Today the home team will not lose.

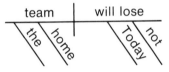

Adverbs also modify other adverbs and adjectives, answering such questions as *How much?* and *To what degree?* A sentence diagram shows the relationship of the adverb to the adjective or adverb it modifies.

Unusually loyal fans always support our team.

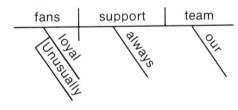

Practice

Diagram these sentences.

1. The cheerleaders enthusiastically led the cheers.
2. The coach praised the very talented players.
3. The game clock steadily ticked.
4. Crowds did not leave the stadium.
5. Nobody predicted the game's outcome.
6. A desperate throw tied the game.

Predicate Nominatives, Appositives, and Predicate Adjectives

Predicate nominatives follow linking verbs. They occur in the predicate part of a sentence, but they rename the subject. When you diagram predicate nominatives, place them on the base line after the verb.

Annie Oakley was a sharpshooter.

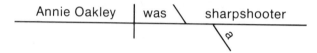

Notice that the line separating the predicate nominative from the verb is slanted toward the subject of the sentence.

An appositive is written in parentheses next to the word it modifies.

Annie, a sharpshooter, outshot Frank Butler.

| Annie (sharpshooter) | outshot | Frank Butler |

A predicate adjective follows the linking verb and describes the subject. The predicate adjective is diagramed in the same way as the predicate nominative.

She became immensely popular.

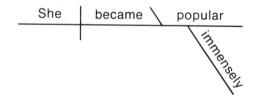

Practice

Diagram these sentences.

1. Annie Oakley became America's sweetheart.
2. She remains an American legend.
3. Davy Crockett was a frontier scout.
4. He became Kentucky's congressional representative.
5. Crockett, the Coonskin Congressman, was often outspoken.
6. He quickly became a folk hero.

Prepositional Phrases

A prepositional phrase is composed of a preposition, its object, and any words that modify the object. Such phrases can modify nouns or pronouns (adjective phrases) or verbs, adjectives, and adverbs (adverb phrases). Here is how they are diagramed.

Adjective Phrase

rosin *for the bow*

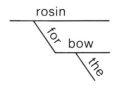

Adverbial Phrase

was kept *on the fiddle*

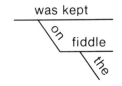

In a diagram the prepositional phrases are connected to the words they modify. Words that modify the object of the preposition are connected to the nouns they modify.

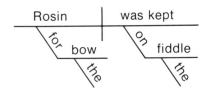

Practice

Diagram these sentences, paying close attention to the prepositional phrases.

1. The fiddle was the dance band of the frontier.
2. Many dances centered around it.
3. The other popular instrument of the West was the banjo.
4. It accompanied the songs of the cowhands.
5. Both instruments were good for dances.
6. Many cowhands came from the South.
7. Their songs were often adaptations of old ballads.
8. Many songs had a personal point of view.
9. Singers sang ballads for camp entertainment.
10. Herders' songs quieted the cattle at night.

Coordinating Conjunctions

The connecting words *and, but,* and *or* are coordinating conjunctions. They join words, phrases, or sentences. Here are diagrams of different parts of a sentence joined by conjunctions.

Compound Subject and Compound Direct Object:
Swans and geese have narrow wings and webbed feet.

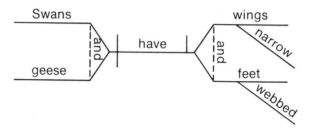

Compound Predicate: Geese fly and swim.

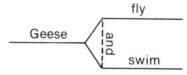

Compound Sentence:
Swans are clumsy on land, but they are graceful in water.

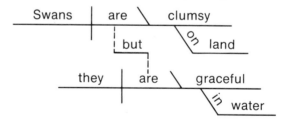

Notice that a compound sentence is diagramed as two single sentences joined at their verbs.

Practice

Diagram these sentences.

1. Ducks feed on the surface or swim under water for food.
2. The ostrich and the penguin are flightless birds.
3. Ostriches run swiftly, and penguins swim expertly.
4. The powerful sea eagles hunt fish and ducks.
5. Some kingfishers eat insects, but others catch fish.

Complex Sentences

A complex sentence contains an independent clause and a dependent clause. Dependent clauses can act like adverbs, adjectives or nouns. A sentence diagram shows the relationship of the dependent clause to the independent clause.

Adverb Clauses

Adverb clauses tell when, where, why, or how, or they state conditions. Adverb clauses can modify verbs, adjectives, or adverbs. Subordinating conjunctions, such as *when, if, because, although, wherever*, and *whenever*, introduce adverb clauses.

When our school plans a show, everyone becomes involved.

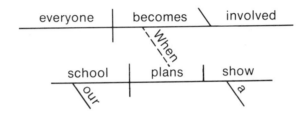

Notice that the main clause appears first in the diagram and that a dotted line connects the *verbs* in the clauses.

Adjective Clauses

Adjective clauses tell how many, which one, or what kind. Adjective clauses modify nouns and pronouns. Relative pronouns, such as *who, whom, which*, and *that* introduce adjective clauses. A dotted line shows which word the clause modifies.

Mr. Bates has chosen the play that we will perform.

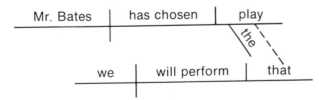

The relative pronoun *who (whom, whose), which*, or *that* is a sentence element in its own clause. It may be the subject, the object, or a modifier.

Noun Clauses

Noun clauses tell who or what. They are used in place of nouns as subjects, objects, or objects of the preposition. Noun clauses may be introduced by subordinating conjunctions or relative pronouns.

I know that you will like our show.

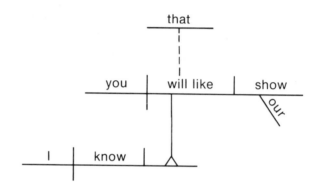

A noun clause is connected by a vertical line to the base line of a diagram where a single noun would appear. The conjunction *that* is placed on a separate line in the sentence, since it is not a basic sentence part of either the main or the subordinate clause.

Practice

Diagram these sentences.

1. Whoever is interested in the play should report to the auditorium.
2. Tryouts will begin when Mr. Bates arrives.
3. Dancers will report to the gymnasium, which has more room.
4. Tryouts will determine who plays the roles.
5. If you can design scenery, report to room 101.
6. Marge will see everyone who will be on the stage crew.
7. The play requires elaborate scenery, which we will build.
8. Everyone who enjoys a show can participate.
9. The director says that rehearsals have gone well.
10. We owe thanks to everyone who helped.

Participles, Gerunds, and Infinitives

A participle is a verb form used as an adjective. A participle is diagramed beneath the word it modifies. Unlike an adjective, however, a participle is written on an angle.

Evaluating the suggested courses, we made our plans.

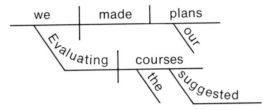

A gerund is a verb form used as a noun. A gerund is diagramed in the same manner as a noun.

Career planning is difficult.

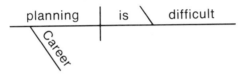

An infinitive is the first principal part of the verb used with *to*. An infinitive or an infinitive phrase can function like a noun, an adjective, or an adverb.

To choose a career is to find a path to follow.

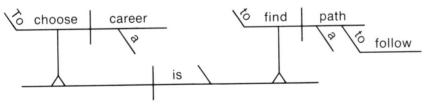

Practice

Diagram these sentences.

1. To select the right job is very important.
2. Many people seek challenging jobs.
3. We saw Edwin reading economics books.
4. Perhaps he plans a career in banking.
5. Do you like caring for the sick?
6. Nursing is an rewarding profession.

REVIEW HANDBOOK

Sentences

GRAMMAR

sentence

- A **sentence** is a group of words that expresses a complete thought. Every sentence begins with a capital letter and ends with a mark of punctuation. *(page 3)*

declarative sentence

- A **declarative sentence** makes a statement. It ends with a period (.). *(page 3)*

    This airport is a busy place.

interrogative sentence

- An **interrogative sentence** asks a question and ends with a question mark (**?**). *(page 3)*

    Is my flight on time?

imperative sentence

- An **imperative sentence** gives a command or makes a request. It ends with a period (.). *(page 3)*

    Please give me a window seat.

exclamatory sentence

- An **exclamatory sentence** expresses strong feeling or surprise. It ends with an exclamation point (!). *(page 3)*

    How nervous I am!

fragment

- A **fragment** is an incomplete sentence. It is missing either a subject or a predicate or both. *(page 14)*

    Fragment: The airplane on the runway.
    Sentence: The airplane on the runway is a jet.

run-on sentence

- A **run-on sentence** is two sentences that have been run together without proper punctuation between them. *(page 14)*

    Run-on sentence: I'm flying on a 747 it is a large jet.
    Correct: I'm flying on a 747. It is a large jet.

Practice

Add capital letters and end punctuation to write each group of words as a sentence. Correct fragments and run-ons. Then write which of the four sentence types each sentence is.

1. we are ready to board
2. do you have your ticket
3. the flight attendant
4. we're late it's my fault
5. is this your first flight
6. please bring me a pillow
7. travel in a jet plane
8. what a view this is

Clauses

- A **clause** is a group of words that contains a subject and a verb. *(page 315)*

  clause

  <u>The factory polluted the river</u>, and <u>soon it was closed</u>.

- An **independent clause** contains a subject and a verb and can stand by itself as a sentence. *(page 315)*

  independent clause

  <u>People were upset</u> because the fish were dying.

- A **dependent clause** contains a subject and a verb but cannot stand alone because it does not express a complete thought. *(page 315)*

  dependent clause

  People were upset <u>because the fish were dying</u>.

- An **adverb clause** is a dependent clause that begins with a subordinating conjunction and modifies a verb, adjective, or adverb. *(page 317)*

  adverb clause

  We laughed <u>when Tom climbed out of the water</u>.

- An **adjective clause** is a dependent clause that begins with a relative pronoun and modifies a noun or a pronoun. *(page 319)*

  adjective clause

  Near the pool is the lifeguard <u>whom we hired</u>.

- A **noun clause** is a dependent clause that is used in the same way that a noun is used in a sentence. *(page 320)*

  noun clause

  Everyone knew <u>that we needed a new lifeguard</u>.

Practice

Copy these sentences. Then underline the dependent clause in each sentence and identify it as an *adverb, adjective,* or *noun clause.*

1. The lifeguards give swim caps to whoever needs one.
2. When I dived into the water, I lost my contact lens.
3. The lens that I lost was found near the drain.
4. I thanked the guard who found it.
5. Sam didn't think that he could dive well.
6. When he tried it, he did a flop.
7. That board, which is not high for beginners, is quite high
8. Sam practiced diving from a deck that was lower.

Sentence Types

simple sentence
- A **simple sentence** has only one complete subject and one complete predicate. *(page 12)*

  The water is polluted.

compound sentence
- A **compound sentence** is made up of two simple sentences joined by a comma and a coordinating conjunction or by a semicolon. *(page 12)*

  Some vegetation died, and the trout have disappeared.

complex sentence
- A **complex sentence** contains one independent clause and one or more dependent clauses. *(page 315)*

  After repairs have been made, the factory can be reopened.

compound-complex sentence
- A **compound-complex sentence** has more than one independent clause and at least one dependent clause. *(page 315)*

  The owners want to keep the river clean, and they will hire consultants who will show them proper ways of disposing of wastes.

Practice

Copy these sentences. Draw one line under each independent clause and two lines under each dependent clause. Label each sentence *simple, compound, complex,* or *compound-complex.*

1. The river is shallow, and it is full of rapids.
2. The river flows quickly, and its pure, clear water sparkles when the ice thaws in the spring.
3. Unless polluting is stopped, the river will become ugly, and its fish will die.
4. We must stop pollution before it is too late.
5. Please help us save the river for the benefit of our children and our children's children.
6. Because pollution affects everyone, we must try to stop it.
7. Our air is polluted, and our water is polluted too.
8. If we all work together, we can stop pollution, and then we will be able to breathe clean air again.

Subjects and Predicates

- The **subject** of a sentence is the part about which something is being said. All the words that make up the subject are called the **complete subject.** *(page 4)*

  <u>Everyone in the club</u> stopped at the drugstore.

  subject

  complete subject

- The **predicate** of a sentence is the part that contains the verb and that says something about the subject. All the words that make up the predicate are called the **complete predicate.** *(page 4)*

  We <u>ordered ice cream sodas and shakes.</u>

  predicate

  complete predicate

- The **simple subject** is the key word or group of words in the subject. *(page 6)*

  The <u>boy</u> in the plaid jacket borrowed a quarter.

  simple subject

- The **simple predicate** is the key word or group of words in the predicate. The simple predicate is always a *verb.* *(page 6)*

  Then he <u>paid</u> the cashier.

  simple predicate

- A **compound subject** consists of two or more simple subjects that are joined by a coordinating conjunction such as *and, but, or,* or by a correlative conjunction such as *either . . . or.* Compound subjects have the same predicate. *(page 10)*

  Both <u>Carla</u> and <u>Mitch</u> played records.

  compound subject

- A **compound predicate** consists of two or more simple predicates joined by a coordinating conjunction. Compound predicates have the same subject. *(page 10)*

  They <u>sang</u> or <u>danced</u> to the music.

  compound predicate

- *You* **(understood)** is the subject of an imperative sentence. *(page 8)*

  <u>(You)</u> Come with us tomorrow.

  you (understood)

Practice

Copy each sentence. Draw one line under the complete subjects and two lines under the complete predicates.

1. Mr. Lee owns the drugstore.
2. Jan and Sam work there.
3. They dust and polish.
4. The whole Lee family helps.

Complements

complement
- A **complement** completes the meaning begun by the subject and the verb. *(page 200)*

direct object
- A **direct object** receives the action of a transitive verb or shows the result of the action. *(page 200)*

    My friend Paul <u>built</u> a <u>rowboat</u> in his spare time.

indirect object
- An **indirect object** tells to whom or for whom the action of the sentence is done. *(page 200)*

    His father <u>gave</u> <u>him</u> two oars.

predicate nominative
- A **predicate nominative** is a noun or pronoun that refers to the same person or thing as the subject of the sentence. The subject noun or pronoun and the predicate nominative are joined by a linking verb. *(page 204)*

    Boating <u>is</u> Paul's <u>hobby</u>.

predicate adjective
- A **predicate adjective** is an adjective that follows a linking verb and modifies the subject of the sentence. *(page 206)*

    His new boat <u>looked</u> <u>trim</u>.

Practice

A. Copy these sentences. Underline the action verbs twice and the direct objects once. Circle the indirect objects.

1. I bought Joan a can of waterproof paint for her boat.
2. Then I gave her the paint.
3. She handed me a brush.
4. Joan brought us two seat cushions.
5. When the paint was dry, she gave me a ride.

B. Copy these sentences. Underline the linking verbs twice and the predicate nominatives once. Circle the predicate adjectives.

6. The boat ride was fun.
7. The river looked calm.
8. The seat cushions were comfortable.
9. Joan is a natural navigator.
10. This channel is her favorite place to row.

Nouns

- A **noun** is a word that names a person, place, thing, or idea. *(page 80)* — **noun**
- A **common noun** names any person, place, thing, or idea. Common nouns are not capitalized unless they come at the beginning of a sentence. *(page 80)* — **common noun**

  girl   city   boat

- A **proper noun** names a particular person, place, thing, or idea. Proper nouns are always capitalized. *(page 80)* — **proper noun**

  Hank Aaron   San Francisco   August

- A **concrete noun** names an object that can be recognized by at least one of the senses. *(page 80)* — **concrete noun**

  cough   cloud   heat

- An **abstract noun** names a quality or an idea that cannot be recognized by the senses. *(page 80)* — **abstract noun**

  liberty   happiness   justice

Practice

A. Copy these sentences and underline the nouns. Above each noun write *C* if it is a concrete noun or *A* if it is an abstract noun.

1. Margaret and her friend own a sailboat.
2. Their sailboat is called the *Mermaid*.
3. The *Mermaid* is kept at a dock in San Francisco.
4. Margaret enjoys the freedom of sailing.
5. She and her friend usually sail in the bay.
6. Once they sailed under a bridge to the Pacific Ocean.
7. Her heart pounded with excitement as the sailboat glided over the waves.

B. Write a proper noun for each common noun.

9. holiday
10. city
11. musician
12. nationality
13. man
14. friend
15. boat
16. business
17. country
18. street
19. doctor
20. planet

Noun Plurals

plural nouns

- Form the plurals of most nouns by adding *s*. *(page 82)*

  comet/comets   germ/germs   vaccine/vaccines

- Add *es* to nouns ending in *s, ss, zz, x, sh,* or *ch*. *(page 82)*

  actress/actresses   eyelash/eyelashes   hatch/hatches

- When the final *y* in a noun is preceded by a consonant, change the *y* to *i* and add *es*. *(page 82)*

  tributary/tributaries   quantity/quantities

- If the final *y* is preceded by a vowel, add only *s*. *(page 82)*

  stingray/stingrays   monkey/monkeys   joy/joys

- Add *s* to some nouns ending in *o;* for others, add *es*. *(page 82)*

  solo/solos   hero/heroes

- To form the plurals of some nouns ending in *f* or *fe,* change the *f* to *v* and add *s* or *es*. *(page 82)*

  life/lives   half/halves

- The plurals of some nouns are formed by a vowel change within the singular form or by an addition to the singular form. *(page 83)*

  goose/geese   child/children   ox/oxen

- Some nouns have the same form for singular and plural. *(page 83)*

  moose   deer   sheep

- To form the plural of a compound noun, make only the most important word plural. *(page 83)*

  father-in-law/fathers-in-law

- A few nouns have only a plural form. Some of these nouns require a plural verb. Others are singular in meaning and require a singular verb. *(page 83)*

  scissors   politics   slacks   news

Practice

Copy these singular nouns. Then write the plural of each.

1. dragonfly
2. toy
3. city
4. mouse
5. eclipse
6. jack-o'-lantern
7. elk
8. zero

Verbals

- A **verbal** is a word that is formed from a verb but does the work of another part of speech in a sentence. *(page 347)*

  verbal

- A **participle** is a verbal that functions as an adjective. *(page 347)*

  participle

  Boiling water spilled onto the buttered muffins.

- A **participial phrase** is a group of words that contains a participle and its modifiers or objects. The entire phrase functions as an adjective. *(page 347)*

  participial phrase

  The chef cooking the dinner was upset.

- A **gerund** is a verbal that ends in *ing* and functions as a noun. *(page 350)*

  gerund

  Cooking requires a great deal of training.

- A **gerund phrase** is a group of words that contains a gerund and its modifiers or objects. The entire phrase functions as a noun. *(page 350)*

  gerund phrase

  The training of a pastry chef is long and difficult.

- An **infinitive** is a verbal that usually begins with the word *to* and is used as a noun, as an adjective, or as an adverb. *(page 353)*

  infinitive

  The chef likes to cook. (noun — direct object)
  The restaurant has many customers to serve. (adjective)
  The customers come to eat. (adverb)

- An **infinitive phrase** is a group of words that contains an infinitive and its modifiers or objects. The entire phrase functions as a noun, as an adjective, or as an adverb. *(page 353)*

  infinitive phrase

  To tip the waiter is customary. (noun — subject)
  We have a large bill to pay. (adjective)
  We paused to compliment the chef. (adverb)

Practice

Copy these sentences and underline the verbal phrases. Then identify each and tell how it is used.

1. The busboy hated clearing the tables.
2. Muttering under his breath, he did the job.
3. To become a waiter was his ambition.

Verbs

verb
- A **verb** expresses action or a state of being. *(page 121)*

action verb
- An **action verb** expresses physical or mental action. *(page 121)*

  wrote   dreamed   fell   thought

transitive verb
- A **transitive verb** expresses action that is carried to a receiver of the action. *(page 121)*

  The wind <u>blows</u> the seeds away.

intransitive verb
- An **intransitive verb** does not have a receiver of the action. *(page 121)*

  The wind <u>blows</u> from the ocean.

linking verb
- A **linking verb** connects the subject of a sentence to a noun, a pronoun, or an adjective in the predicate. It does not show action. *(page 122)*

  is   are   was   were   seems   feels   sounds

verb phrase
- A **verb phrase** is a verb that consists of more than one word. *(page 124)*

  was blowing   had been played   are going

main verb
- The **main verb** is the verb in a verb phrase that expresses action or being. *(page 124)*

  was <u>blowing</u>   had been <u>played</u>   are <u>going</u>

helping verb
- A **helping verb** is used with the main verb to express tense, person, or number. *(page 124)*

  <u>was</u> blowing   <u>had been</u> played   <u>are</u> going

subject/verb agreement
- The subject and verb in a sentence must agree in number. *(page 136)*

  The <u>wind</u> <u>is</u> strong.   The <u>winds</u> <u>are</u> strong.

Practice

Copy these sentences. Draw two lines under each verb or verb phrase. Label each verb *transitive* or *intransitive*.

1. The wind has been blowing since the storm.
2. It blew some branches down.
3. The branches are scattered all over the yard.

Verb Tenses

- The time expressed by a verb is its **tense.** *(page 133)*   **tense**
- The **present tense** expresses action that is taking place   **present tense**
  now. *(page 133)*

     Martha <u>plays</u> chess.   Chess <u>requires</u> patience and skill.

- The **past tense** expresses action that took place at some *definite*   **past tense**
  time in the past. *(page 133)*

     Joe and I <u>played</u> chess last night.

- The **future tense** expresses action that will take place at some   **future tense**
  time in the *future.* *(page 133)*

     Lynne <u>will play</u> in the tournament tomorrow.

- The **present perfect tense** expresses action that took place at   **present perfect tense**
  some *indefinite time* in the past or that began in the past and *is*
  still going on. *(page 133)*

     Jed <u>has watched</u> the tournament all morning.

- The **past perfect tense** expresses action that took place in the   **past perfect tense**
  past *before some other past action.* *(page 133)*

     Joe and I <u>had finished</u> our game before we ate dinner.

- The **future perfect tense** expresses action that will take place in   **future perfect tense**
  the future, but that will be over *before some other future*
  action. *(page 133)*

     The tournament <u>will have ended</u> by this time tomorrow.

Practice

Copy the verb from each sentence and identify its tense.

1. All the players will concentrate on each move.
2. The winner will have earned the trophy.
3. The players have studied each other's strategies.
4. Some bought books about chess.
5. One book outlined maneuvers used by professional players.
6. A chess board always has 64 squares.
7. By the year 1400 chess had been played all over Europe.
8. Modern chess evolved in the fifteenth century.
9. The word *chess* comes from the Persian word for *king.*
10. Many chess champions have come from the U.S.S.R.

Regular and Irregular Verbs

principal parts
- The three basic forms of a verb are its **principal parts.** These principal parts are the **present,** the **past,** and the **past participle.** *(page 127)*

regular verbs
- The past and past participle of **regular verbs** are formed by adding *d* or *ed* to the present form. The past and past participle of regular verbs ending in a consonant followed by *y* are formed by changing the *y* to *i* and adding *ed.* *(pages 128–131)*

Present	Past	Past Participle
lock(s)	locked	(has, have, had) locked
carry(ies)	carried	(has, have, had) carried
chase(s)	chased	(has, have, had) chased

irregular verbs
- The past and past participle forms of **irregular verbs** are not formed by adding *d* or *ed* to their present forms. Their past and past participles are formed in a variety of ways, as shown on this chart. *(pages 130–133)*

Present	Past	Past Participle (has, have, had)	Present	Past	Past Participle (has, have, had)
come(s)	came	come	do(es)	did	done
go(es)	went	gone	eat(s)	ate	eaten
run(s)	ran	run	fly(ies)	flew	flown
begin(s)	began	begun	give(s)	gave	given
drink(s)	drank	drunk	grow(s)	grew	grown
ring(s)	rang	rung	know(s)	knew	known
sing(s)	sang	sung	ride(s)	rode	ridden
swim(s)	swam	swum	take(s)	took	taken
bring(s)	brought	brought	write(s)	wrote	written
catch(es)	caught	caught	break(s)	broke	broken
say(s)	said	said	choose(s)	chose	chosen
sell(s)	sold	sold	freeze(s)	froze	frozen
think(s)	thought	thought	speak(s)	spoke	spoken
burst(s)	burst	burst	tear(s)	tore	torn
hit(s)	hit	hit	wear(s)	wore	worn

Practice

A. Copy and complete this verb chart by filling in the missing principal parts.

Present Tense	Past Tense	Past Participle (has, have, had)
1. _____	_____	interfered
2. _____	relied	_____
3. assume	_____	_____
4. transport	_____	_____
5. _____	despised	_____
6. _____	_____	sponsored
7. share	_____	_____
8. _____	_____	denied

B. Copy these sentences and complete each one with the correct verb in parentheses ( ).

9. I (wrote, written) a letter to my cousin.
10. I (knew, known) she would want to hear the news.
11. My puppy has (began, begun) his chewing stage.
12. He has even (ate, eaten) my bedroom slippers.
13. He has (grew, grown) to the size of a small pony!
14. He (sank, sunk) my little rowboat.
15. We both (swam, swum) to shore.

C. Rewrite these sentences, using the correct form of the verb in parentheses ( ).

16. My cousin (answer) my letter immediately.
17. She asked what had (become) of the boat.
18. Then she (tell) me about her baseball team.
19. She had (hit) a home run in the last game.
20. Later, she (catch) a fly ball.
21. The pitcher had (throw) a fast ball.
22. She has never (think) of being anything but an athlete.

Adjectives

adjective

- An **adjective** is a word that modifies a noun or a pronoun. *(page 163)*

  <u>That</u> train is on the <u>express</u> track.

article

- **Articles** are the most common adjectives. They are definite *(the)* or indefinite *(a, an)*. *(page 163)*

  <u>A</u> clerk is in <u>the</u> ticket booth.

common adjective

- **Common adjectives** are not capitalized unless they come at the beginning of a sentence. *(page 163)*

  The clerk returned the <u>brown</u> hat to Mr. Murphy.

proper adjective

- **Proper adjectives** are made from proper nouns and must always be capitalized. *(page 163)*

  Mr. Murphy ate some <u>Danish</u> pastry in the station.

positive degree

- The **positive degree** of an adjective is used to describe only one thing. *(page 164)*

  The first bite of the pastry was <u>good</u>.

comparative degree

- The **comparative degree** of an adjective is used to compare two things. *(page 164)*

  The second bite tasted even <u>better</u>.

superlative degree

- The **superlative degree** of an adjective is used to compare three or more things. *(page 164)*

  The third bite was <u>best</u> of all.

Practice

Copy these sentences and underline each adjective.

1. Mr. Murphy makes several trips each year.
2. The longest trip he ever took was to the Oregon Coast.
3. He traveled three days by passenger train.
4. He thinks trains are more comfortable than airplanes.
5. Of course, jet travel is the speediest of all.
6. Some European trains are very modern and luxurious.
7. The better trains are like fine hotels on wheels.

Adverbs

- An **adverb** is a word used to modify a verb, an adjective, or another adverb. Adverbs often answer the questions *where, when, how, how often*, and *to what extent.*   *(page 167)*

    <u>Yesterday</u> I ran in the track meet.

    adverb

- The **positive degree** of an adverb is used to describe only one action.   *(page 168)*

    Valerie ran <u>quickly</u>.

    positive degree

- The **comparative degree** of an adverb is used to compare two actions.   *(page 168)*

    Jan ran <u>more quickly</u> than Andrew.

    comparative degree

- The **superlative degree** of an adverb is used to compare three or more actions.   *(page 168)*

    I ran <u>most quickly</u> of all!

    superlative degree

Practice

A. Copy these sentences. Underline each adverb and draw an arrow from it to the word it modifies.

1. We always practice early.
2. Sometimes we stay rather late.
3. Charles frequently leaves his track shoes at home.
4. He is somewhat forgetful.
5. We learn to jump the hurdles carefully.
6. Each time we use our strength more efficiently.
7. Today I carelessly tripped.
8. I was so embarrassed!
9. I will not do that again.
10. Tomorrow I will practice harder.

B. Rewrite each adverb, changing it to the degree of comparison shown in parentheses ( ).

11. more fiercely (positive)
12. well (superlative)
13. carelessly (comparative)
14. later (superlative)
15. quietly (comparative)
16. most gently (positive)

Pronouns

pronoun
- A **pronoun** is a word that is used in place of one or more nouns. *(page 237)*

  Marsha is running for president. <u>She</u> hopes to win.

antecedent
- The **antecedent** of a pronoun is the word to which a pronoun refers. Pronouns must agree with the noun they replace in number, in gender, and in person. *(page 237)*

  I dropped my keys. Have you seen <u>them</u>?

subject pronoun
- A **subject pronoun** acts as the subject of a sentence or as a predicate nominative. The words *I, you, he, she, it, we,* and *they* are subject pronouns. *(page 239)*

object pronoun
- An **object pronoun** acts as a direct object, as an indirect object, or as the object of the preposition. The words *me, him, her, us, them,* and sometimes *you* and *it* are object pronouns. *(page 240)*

possessive pronoun
- A **possessive pronoun** takes the place of a possessive noun or a possessive noun phrase. Possessive pronouns never have apostrophes. The words *my, mine, your, yours, his, her, hers, its, our, ours, their,* and *theirs* are possessive pronouns. *(page 242)*

reflexive pronoun
- A **reflexive pronoun** is a compound personal pronoun made with *self* that is used as a direct object, an indirect object, or an object of a preposition. The words *myself, yourself, himself, herself, itself, ourselves, yourselves,* and *themselves* can be reflexive pronouns. *(page 245)*

intensive pronoun
- An **intensive pronoun** is a compound personal pronoun made with *self* that is used for emphasis to intensify a noun or a pronoun. *(page 245)*

  I myself do not object.

demonstrative pronoun
- A **demonstrative pronoun** points out a particular person, place, or thing. The demonstrative pronouns are *this, that, these,* and *those.* *(page 245)*

indefinite pronoun
- An **indefinite pronoun** refers to any one or any number of people or things. It does not specify a particular person or thing. The words *all, each, everyone, most, none, several,* and *some* are among the words that can be indefinite pronouns. *(page 247)*

- An **interrogative pronoun** introduces a question. The words *who*, *whom*, *whose*, *what*, and *which* can be used as interrogative pronouns. *(page 247)*
- A **relative pronoun** introduces an adjective clause and relates it to the noun that the clause modifies. The words *who*, *whom*, *whose*, *which*, and *that* can be used as relative pronouns. *(page 255)*

interrogative
pronoun

relative
pronoun

Practice

A. Rewrite these sentences, using a pronoun in place of the underlined words. Then label each pronoun *subject pronoun* or *object pronoun.*

1. <u>Marsha</u> will make several speeches before the election.
2. <u>The election</u> is next week.
3. Marsha wants <u>Evan and me</u> to listen to her new speech.
4. <u>Evan and I</u> should try to help <u>Marsha</u>.
5. She depends on <u>Evan and me</u>, her campaign managers.
6. Let's put up posters for <u>the students</u> to read.
7. <u>All the students</u> must decide on a candidate soon.
8. <u>The candidates</u> will speak about <u>school government</u>.
9. <u>Marsha</u> and <u>Hal</u> are running against each other.
10. Are you voting for <u>Marsha</u> or <u>Hal</u>?

B. Complete these sentences, choosing the correct pronoun in parentheses ( ). After each sentence write *possessive, reflexive, intensive, demonstrative, indefinite, interrogative,* or *relative pronoun.*

11. Who put up (these, that, them) campaign posters?
12. That poster is (my, myself, mine).
13. I made it (yourself, myself, itself).
14. It describes the candidate (whom, who, which) I support.
15. (Whom, Who, Whose) speech did you like best?
16. (Everyone, Which, Themselves) listened to the speeches.
17. All (this, that, these) candidates are qualified.
18. They prepared (them, themselves, they) well.
19. (All, Nobody, Anyone) of them know the issues.
20. This is the best campaign (what, that, whom) I have ever seen.

Prepositions

preposition

- A **preposition** is a word that shows the relationship between the noun or the pronoun that follows it and another word in the sentence. *(page 272)*

  Look at that house <u>across</u> the street.

  Some common prepositions are: *about, above, around, at, beside, between, by, for, from, in, into, next to, of, off, on, on top of, out, over, through, to, under, until, up, with.*

prepositional phrase

object of preposition

- A **prepositional phrase** is a group of words that begins with a preposition and ends with a noun or a pronoun called the **object of the preposition.** *(page 272)*

  It has been abandoned <u>for many years</u>.

modifiers

- Prepositional phrases can modify nouns or pronouns, as adjectives do. They can also modify verbs, adjectives, or adverbs, as adverbs do. *(page 274)*

  The old house <u>on the corner</u> was sold.   (modifies noun)

  Nils stumbled <u>up the dark stairs</u>.   (modifies verb)

  It was frightening <u>in the moonlight</u>.   (modifies adjective)

  I walked next <u>to Nils</u>.   (modifies adverb)

Practice

A. Copy these sentences. Then underline each prepositional phrase and draw an arrow from it to the word it modifies.

1. The windows in the house were boarded up.
2. We stood on the porch wondering what to do.
3. Nils reached for the door.
4. It opened with a rusty squeak.

B. Make up a prepositional phrase for each of these prepositions and use the phrase in a sentence. Underline each phrase and identify it as an *adjective* or an *adverb phrase*.

5. between	6. across	7. against	8. around
9. behind	10. beside	11. from	12. inside
13. on	14. out	15. over	16. under

Interjections and Conjunctions

- An **interjection** is a word or a brief expression that is used to express feeling. *(page 276)*

    <u>Wow</u>! Did you see that bronco rider?

- A **conjunction** is a word that joins words or groups of words. *(page 279)*
- A **coordinating conjunction** joins words or groups of words of equal importance in a sentence. *(page 279)*

    The bronco kicked, <u>and</u> the rider was thrown off.

- **Correlative conjunctions** are used in pairs to join words or groups of words in a sentence. *(page 279)*

    <u>Either</u> Tex <u>or</u> Millie will ride in the next event.

- A **subordinating conjunction** is a conjunction used to introduce some type of dependent clause. It becomes part of the clause and makes it a dependent clause. *(page 315)*

    <u>If</u> we hurry, we can get good seats.
    I come to the rodeo <u>whenever</u> it is in town.

interjection

conjunction

coordinating conjunction

subordinating conjunction

Practice

A. Copy these sentences. Underline each interjection and its punctuation.

1. Whew! It's hot in the sun.
2. Ah, our seats are in the shade.
3. Oh dear, I've torn my program.
4. Hurrah! Here come the riders!

B. Complete these sentences with conjunctions. Write whether the conjunctions are *coordinating, correlative,* or *subordinating.*

5. I love rodeos _____ they are so exciting.
6. _____ Mom _____ Dad like to go with me.
7. The clown will ride the bronco _____ make faces at it.
8. _____ bronco riding is my favorite event, I like roping, too.
9. I admire the clowns _____ they are so brave.
10. They distract the bull _____ a rider falls off.

Paragraphs

paragraph
main idea

topic sentence

detail sentence

first sentence
indented

- A **paragraph** is a group of sentences that develop a single topic. The single topic is the **main idea** of the paragraph. *(page 42)*
- The **topic sentence** expresses the main idea of a paragraph. *(page 44)*
- **Detail sentences** support, explain, or expand the topic sentence. *(page 48)*
- The first sentence in a paragraph is indented. *(page 105)*

> Before you decide upon a certain career, you should consider a number of factors.

Practice

A. Read the paragraph that follows. Then answer these questions about it.

1. What is the topic sentence? Write it.
2. What three sentences support the topic sentence? Write those sentences.

   The spotted skunk of the desert has developed a mysterious defense mechanism against its enemies. Like striped skunks, the spotted skunk can spray a powerful offensive-smelling liquid to discourage attackers. But this technique is used only in extreme emergencies. For some unknown reason, the spotted skunk does a handstand on its front paws when it is faced with everyday threats. Evidently, a skunk doing a handstand is a less attractive prospect for a meal than is a skunk with four feet on the ground. The reason why this is so, however, remains one of Nature's mysteries.

B. Write a paragraph on one of the following topics or on a topic of your choice. Draw two lines under your topic sentence and one line under each supporting sentence.

   My favorite film (book, play, and so on)
   Why I like/dislike . . . (name of sport)
   Fads come and go

Friendly Letters and Social Notes

428 Penn Avenue
Macon, Georgia 31204
February 16, 19–

Dear Christy,

   I have just finished reading <u>The Case of the Missing Lynx</u>. You were right; it's a real thriller!

   I'm sending you a copy of one of my favorites, <u>The Disappearance of the Thin Heir</u>. Let me know how you like it. By the way, how is your first mystery novel coming along? Have you finished your plot outline?

   Write soon, if you have a chance.

                Fondly,

                Jennifer

- The **friendly letter** or **social note** has five parts. *(page 361)*
- The **heading** is in the upper right-hand corner. It contains the letter writer's address and the date. A comma is used between the city and the state and between the day and the year. *(page 361)*
- The **salutation** is next to the left margin. It begins with a capital letter and is followed by a comma. *(page 361)*
- The **body** of the letter is organized into paragraphs determined by subject. Each paragraph is indented. *(page 361)*
- The **closing** at the end of the letter lines up with the heading. The first word of the closing is capitalized. A comma follows the closing. *(page 361)*
- The **signature** lines up with the closing. *(page 361)*

                    heading

                    salutation

                    body

                    closing

                    signature

Practice

Write a friendly letter to a real or made-up individual, or write a social note thanking someone for a gift or for his or her hospitality or accepting (or declining) an invitation.

Business Letters

Heading

239 Henry Street
Torrance, California 93111
October 1, 19—

Inside Address

Ms. Marsha King
Head, Customer Services
Pure Health Foods, Inc.
1244 Stony Creek Road
Allen, Texas 75002

Salutation

Dear Ms. King:

Body

On December 1 of this year I will be opening a health food store in Torrance, California. I am interested in carrying your line of health food products. Would you please send me your catalog as well as a wholesale pricing list and information about any special discounts you offer.

Closing Signature

Yours truly,
Alice Smith

- A **business letter** has six parts.

heading
- The **heading** is in the upper right-hand corner. A comma is used between the city and the state and between the day and the year. *(page 362)*

inside address
- The **inside address** starts at the left margin. It shows the name and address of the person or business receiving the letter. *(page 363)*

salutation
- The **salutation** begins at the left margin. It begins with a capital letter and is followed by a colon. *(page 363)*

body
- The **body** tells why you are writing the letter. It should give briefly and clearly all the facts that the receiver will need to answer your letter or fill your order. *(page 363)*

closing
- The **closing** at the end of the letter lines up with the heading. The first word of the closing is capitalized. A comma follows the closing. *(page 363)*

signature
- The **signature** is in a line with the closing. The signature includes the writer's full name. *(page 363)*

Envelopes

Jim Barlow
321 Wayne Ave.
Castile, NY 14427

Mrs. Laura Gibson
30 South Drive
Burlington, KS 66025

Return
Address

Mailing
Address

return
address

mailing
address

- An addressed envelope has two parts. The **return address** is in the upper left-hand corner of the envelope. *(page 364)*
- The receiver's name and address—the **mailing address**—is written in the middle of the envelope. Postal abbreviations of states' names are written with two capital letters and no periods. Use a ZIP code in all addresses. *(page 364)*

Practice

A. 1. Write a business letter to a company that you invent to request a catalog or order merchandise; or, write a complaint or a commendation of the company's product or service.

B. Draw three sample envelopes on your paper. Using the information below, address the envelopes correctly.

2. To: Mrs. Grace McDonald
124 Chalet drive
Cortland, New york
ZIP 13045

From: Ann Cray
Pineville LA
ZIP 71360
19 king st.

3. To: P.O. Box 44
Ms. E. Frieland
President, E.F. Imports
Mayville, N.D. 58257

From: G.S. Ingram
Kent T.X. 78732
413 LaSalle st.

4. To: Mr. Louis DeAngelo
Conway, A.Z.
ZIP 85719
13 james court

From: dr N.P. Andersen
31 Westside rd.
ZIP 30032
Jonesville, G.A.

Editing

Editing Marks

≡ capitalize

⊙ make a period

∧ add something

⋏ add a comma

⋎⋎ add quotation marks

ჸ take something away

○ spell correctly

⋔ indent the paragraph

/ make a lowercase letter

∿ / tr transpose

Editing Checklist

1. Did I express a complete thought in each sentence?
2. Did I write a good topic sentence for each paragraph?
3. Did I write detail sentences that support the main idea?
4. Did I write detail sentences that keep to the topic?
5. Did I begin each sentence with a capital letter?
6. Did I end each sentence with the correct punctuation mark?
7. Did I use other punctuation marks correctly?
8. Did I indent the first line of each paragraph?
9. Did I spell correctly?
10. Did I write neatly?

Practice

Copy the following letter. Make all the changes and corrections shown.

123 Wayward Place

Holmes, Maine⋏ 04240

July 5⋏ 19—

dear aunt jane⋏

your Birthday present arrived⋏and its just great! I have always wanted a genueen army swiss knif. Dad says I can use it wen we go camping.

Thank you for remembering my Birthday.

Sincerely yours⋏

Fred

Names and Titles of People, Places, and Organizations

- Capitalize names of people, including initials, titles, and abbreviations of titles. *(page 69)*

    Dr. Jonathan D. Samuels   Ms. Elena J. Matthews

- Always capitalize the pronoun *I*. *(page 239)*

    My brother and I are planning a trip.

- Capitalize geographical names and names of monuments, buildings, and organizations, as well as their abbreviations. *(page 107)*

    Burlington, Iowa   Mason St.   American Express
    Blvd. (Boulevard)   Ct. (Court)   Flatiron Building

- Use a comma between the city and the state in an address; use a period after most abbreviations. *(page 107)*

    Sumter, S.C.   Sen. Dirksen

- Capitalize names of nationalities. *(page 187)*

    Irish   Chinese   Polish   Canadian

person's names and titles

pronoun I

geographical names and abbreviations

nationalities

Practice

A. Rewrite these names, titles, and addresses correctly.

1. mrs. a.r. reynolds
2. dusseldorf, germany
3. atlantic ocean
4. park avenue, n.y., n.y.
5. mount everest
6. 70 frog hollow road
7. mr. paul choy
8. sherwood forest
9. manchester, n.h.
10. rev. hector r. perez
11. dr. m.c. evans
12. mt. st. helens

B. Rewrite these sentences. Use capital letters as needed.

13. My brother casey and i went to the library on emerson street in teaneck, new jersey.
14. In preparation for our trip to the british isles, we checked out several books on england and scotland.
15. As we were leaving, we met dr. ian fraser, who was born in scotland.

Names of Days, Months, and Holidays

days, months

- Capitalize all proper nouns and adjectives, including the names of days and months and their abbreviations. *(page 187)*

    Wednesday/Wed.   January/Jan.

holidays

- Capitalize each important word in the name of a holiday. *(page 187)*

    Fourth of July   Valentine's Day

Practice

A. Write the following days, months, and holidays correctly.

1. june 14, flag day
2. washington's birthday
3. oct. 31, halloween
4. sun., father's day
5. october 12, columbus day
6. sat., april 11
7. mon., november 1
8. labor day
9. may 25, memorial day
10. tuesday, dec. 31
11. thursday, september 16
12. martin luther king day
13. february 2, groundhog day
14. thurs., feb. 10
15. tues., nov. 3
16. election day

B. Rewrite these sentences. Add capital letters where needed.

17. The year's first holiday is january 1, new year's day.
18. In february we celebrate lincoln's birthday and also washington's birthday.
19. We celebrate valentine's day on february 14.
20. On march 17 we go to the st. patrick's day parade.
21. I love to play tricks on april fools' day.
22. The second sunday in may is mother's day.
23. Dad receives his recognition on the third sunday in june.
24. The fourth of july is also called independence day.
25. The first monday in september is labor day.
26. My favorite holiday, thanksgiving, comes on the fourth thursday in november.
27. The holiday armistice day was renamed veterans day.
28. In Vermont the first tuesday in march is set aside as town meeting day.
29. In Oklahoma april 22 is oklahoma day, a state holiday.

Titles, Historical Events, and Languages

- Capitalize the first word, the last word, and all other important words in a title. *(page 261)* — **titles**

    The Last of the Mohicans   Catcher in the Rye

- Capitalize historical and special events and periods. *(page 187)*

    Industrial Revolution   the Middle Ages

- Capitalize names of languages. *(page 187)*

    Italian   Japanese   English   Swahili

historical events and periods languages

Practice

A. Write the following titles correctly.

1. "the tree on the corner" (poem)
2. only earth and sky last forever (book)
3. "working on the railroad" (song)
4. the empire strikes back (film)
5. dial m for murder (play)

B. Rewrite these sentences. Add capital letters where they are needed.

6. Mario is reading the brothers karamazov by Dostoevski.
7. Since the novel was originally written in russian, Mario is reading an english translation of it.
8. Have you read this article about the russian revolution?
9. It is called "the February revolution" and appears in this month's issue of times past.
10. The event occurred during world war I.
11. Perhaps you have seen the long film war and peace.
12. It is a dramatization of an epic novel in russian about the napoleonic wars.
13. Many of the classics are translations from such languages as french, italian, spanish, greek, and german.
14. a tale of two cities, a novel written in english, is about the french revolution.
15. a doll's house was written in norwegian by Henrik Ibsen.

Periods

to end sentences

- Place a period at the end of a declarative or an imperative sentence. *(page 31)*

  The wind is chilly. Wear a sweater.

in abbreviations

- Place a period after most abbreviations. *(page 69)*

  Sept.   U.S.A.   Tues.   Prof.   M.D.   St.

- Do not place a period after abbreviations of organizations or agencies or after postal service abbreviations of state names. *(pages 69, 87)*

  NATO   IRS   IL   MN   NY

after an initial

- Place a period after an initial. *(page 69)*

  John F. Kennedy   A.R. Lofft

in outlines

- Place a period after a numeral or a letter in an outline. *(pages 284–285)*

  I. Sources of Energy
    A. The sun
      1. Fission

Practice

Write these items correctly. Use periods where needed.

1. Dr Jane L Kerr of Boston, MA
2. Wiseman Blvd in Bowman, PA
3. Mt Hood in Oregon
4. Prof Montrose from St Louis
5. Pablo L Riviera, D V M
6. Sen J Edward Howes, Jr
7. Holmes Rd in Abilene, TX
8. Pres Ulysses S Grant of Point Pleasant, OH
9. Tell me how to get to Peoria, Ill, from Chicago
10. Jim R Tibbs, Sr, gave me these directions.
11. IV Hardships of pioneers
      A Travel
        1 Few roads
        2 Few maps
      B Dangers

Commas

- Place a comma between the day and the year in a date. If the year is followed by more words in the sentence, place a comma after the year. Do not place a comma between the month and the day. *(page 223)*

  On April 6, 1975, I made my first plane trip.

  in dates

- Use a comma between the city and the state in an address. If the address or place name is in a sentence, put commas after the street address, between the city and state, and at the end of the address. *(page 107)*

  We live at 752 Carrol Drive, Fulton, Maine.
  Is 416 Dale Road, Durham, North Carolina, his address?

  in letters

- Place a comma after the salutation of a friendly letter or a social note and after the closing of any letter. *(pages 361–362)*

  Dear Helen,   Very truly yours,   Your friend,

- Place commas after every element but the last in a series. *(page 297)*

  We ordered hot dogs, hamburgers, and milk.

  in a series

- Place a comma before the coordinating conjunctions *or*, *and*, or *but* in a compound sentence.

  Farmers in that country could grow wheat, but they need years of agricultural assistance.

  in compound sentences

- Use commas to set off a noun in direct address.

  Horace, add more oregano to the pizza.

  in direct address

- Place a comma after the words *yes* and *no*, after mild interjections, after most dependent clauses, and after long prepositional phrases or participial phrases that introduce a sentence. *(pages 276, 297, 317)*

  Yes, I made the soup.   Ouch, it's hot.
  Because my parents were late, I made supper.
  Having eaten supper, we washed the dishes.

  with introductory elements

- Use a comma to set off quoted words from the rest of a sentence unless a question mark or exclamation point is needed. *(page 150)*

  "I wonder," said Cory, "if I can learn to ski."

  with direct quotations

with interrupting expressions
- Use commas to set off transitional expressions and other "interrupters" in a sentence. *(page 297)*

   Woolens, however, are not practical in a warm climate.

in a bibliography
- Place commas in parts of a bibliography. *(pages 288–289)*

   Decker, Daniel J. "The Beaver: New York's Empire
      Builder," *The Conservationist*, Nov./Dec. 1980, pp. 1–17.

with appositives
- Use commas after two introductory prepositional phrases and to set off most appositives. *(page 297)*

   In the center of town, there stands a clock.
   We visited Laura Adams, a neighbor of mine.

Practice

Copy these sentences, adding commas where needed.

1. Today Jerry we are going to learn about bats.
2. Bats the only flying mammals are fascinating creatures.
3. I saw a bat at a picnic on July 4 1982.
4. The picnic was in Orange New Jersey.
5. No I've seen only one in my life.
6. Margarita however discovered a whole cave of bats.
7. She has read a great deal about them too.
8. For example she told me that the free-tailed bat is probably the fastest bat in the world.
9. "Bats can hear better than any other animal" said Marta.
10. "The fruit bat" she added "has the best hearing and the largest wing span of all bats."
11. Although it is hard to be sure at least three species of bats can fly 48 kilometers an hour.
12. Fruit bats vampire bats and little brown bats are some of the many species of bats living today.
13. The pipistrelle which is the smallest species has a wing span of about 15 centimeters.
14. Flying in the dark bats are guided by sound waves.
15. Indeed there really is such a thing as a vampire bat, and they are a serious problem in some parts of the world.
16. A bat at least 24 years old was found in a cave in East Dorset Vermont.

Question Marks and Exclamation Points

- Place a **question mark** at the end of an interrogative sentence. *(page 31)*

  Have you heard the weather report?

- Place an **exclamation point** at the end of an exclamatory sentence. *(page 31)*

  How frightened I am of tornadoes!

- Place an exclamation point after a strong interjection. *(page 276)*

  Oh no! Let's find shelter!

- NOTE: Do not overuse the exclamation point. Never use more than one after a word.

question mark

exclamation point

Practice

Copy these sentences, adding question marks, exclamation points, and capital letters where necessary.

1. Who saw the tornado
2. Where is the safest place to be
3. Go downstairs to the basement
4. Has anyone seen Melanie
5. Oh dear I think she was in the orchard.
6. Who will go and get her
7. Hurrah here she comes.
8. Is there a flashlight in the basement
9. Aha here are some candles.
10. Do we have matches
11. Ouch I stubbed my toe on the stairs.
12. Stay calm, everybody
13. What station shall I turn to
14. Wow do you hear that wind
15. It sounds pretty strong
16. You said it
17. How long will we have to stay here
18. My goodness I'm getting hungry.
19. Shall I go to the kitchen for some food
20. Is it safe in here

Underlining/Quotation Marks and Dialog

major titles

- Underline titles of books, plays, newspapers, magazines, movies, records, works of art, musical compositions, and long poems. *(page 261)*

  The Adventures of Tom Sawyer (book)
  The News Chronicle (newspaper)
  Romeo and Juliet (play)

- Place quotation marks around titles of songs, articles, short stories, TV shows, chapters in books, and short poems. *(page 261)*

  "Battle Hymn of the Republic" (song)
  "Crafts for Fun and Profit" (article)

direct quotation

- Place quotation marks around the exact words of a direct quotation. If the quotation is divided into two parts by other words, place quotation marks around the quoted words only. *(page 150)*

  Mr. Bailey said, "The corn is ready to be harvested."
  "I must have my tractor repaired," he continued, "or we will not finish harvesting in time."

end punctuation for quotations

- If there are several sentences in a direct quotation, do not close the quotation until after the last sentence. *(page 150)*

  "I'll buy the part I need today. It shouldn't be too expensive. Then I can repair the tractor," he said.

- Always place commas and periods inside the closing quotation marks. Place questions marks and exclamation points inside the closing quotation marks if the quotation itself is a question or an exclamation. *(page 150)*

  Mr. Bailey said, "We'll begin harvesting next week."
  "Wow! It's going to be hot!" his daughter exclaimed.
  "Will the tractor be ready in time?" Betty asked.
  Did Mr. Clark say, "I have the part you need"?

- When you write dialog, begin a new paragraph every time the dialog speaker changes. *(page 150)*

  "Can we repair the tractor ourselves?" asked Betty.
  "I think so," answered Mr. Bailey. "We had the same problem about two years ago."

Practice

A. Copy these sentences. Add quotation marks and end punctuation marks where they are needed.

1. Here is the part you ordered said Mr. Clark
2. Mr. Bailey replied How much do I owe you
3. That will be $75.98 answered Mr. Clark The fencing wire you ordered came in. Would you like that today
4. Yes said Mr. Bailey Wasn't that about $35
5. It will be $30.98. I was able to get a discount on my last order said Mr. Clark.
6. Mr. Bailey said I'll write you a check for $106.96, and then we can be on our way
7. Isn't that awfully expensive inquired Betty
8. Nothing is inexpensive anymore replied her father
9. Now I understand said Betty why you want to repair the tractor yourself
10. That's right laughed her father We've got to save money somewhere
11. Betty, will you carry the roll of wire out to the truck asked Mr. Bailey
12. Hey you're getting the wrong roll said Mr. Clark
13. Betty asked Isn't this the one we bought
14. No, it's that roll over there Mr. Clark replied.

B. Rewrite the following dialog. Indent where necessary, and add punctuation and underlines where needed.

Are you helping Dad with the tractor repair asked Mrs. Bailey. Certainly replied Betty. He needs my help I know he does Mrs. Bailey said and it's too bad your brother can't lend a hand What is Mark doing asked Betty. By Monday Mrs Bailey replied he has to finish a book report on The Sea of Grass by Conrad Richter Betty asked Isn't that the book about the settling of Texas Yes, it is replied her mother. There was an article about the settling of the Southwest in a recent issue of Newsweek. Perhaps Mark might enjoy reading that as well said Betty.

Parentheses and Apostrophes

parentheses
- Use parentheses around material that adds an incidental explanation to a sentence but is not of major importance. *(page 397)*

    Two of my friends (Fred knows them) are contestants.

apostrophe in possessive nouns
- Use an apostrophe for possessive nouns but not for possessive pronouns. *(page 335)*

Lewis's	Fluffy's	girls'	people's
his	its	theirs	yours

apostrophe in contractions
- Use an apostrophe to form contractions of pronouns and verbs and to form contractions of verbs and the adverb *not*. *(page 335)*

    I'm   she'd   shouldn't   won't

apostrophe in plurals
- Use an apostrophe and underlining to form the plurals of letters. *(page 335)*

    Lydia got two A's, three B's, and a C.

Practice

A. Write the possessive form of each noun below.

1. Tony
2. watches
3. conductor
4. Phyllis
5. children
6. editors
7. Charles
8. geese

B. Copy these sentences. Add parentheses and apostrophes where they are needed.

9. Didnt Claudia send in Shellys entry blank?
10. The winner Curtis hopes it will be Shelly wont get a prize until next month.
11. Wasnt the contestants big challenge the crossword puzzle?
12. There were no es in the puzzle.
13. The girls efforts were rewarded with success.
14. I wouldnt have left if Id known that Shelly had won.
15. Shellys prize is a trip to San Francisco.

Semicolons, Colons, Hyphens, and Dashes

- Use semicolons to separate items in a series in which commas have already been used. *(page 299)*

  I visited London, England; Paris, France; and Lima, Peru.

  semicolon in a series

- A semicolon can also be used to take the place of the comma and coordinating conjunction in a compound sentence. *(page 31)*

  Ned likes watercolors; I prefer oil paints.

  semicolon in compound sentence

- Use a colon after the salutation of a business letter. *(page 363)*

  Dear Mr. Iversen: Dear Senator Forbes:

  colon in salutation

- Place a colon between the hour and the minute in the time of day. *(page 223)*

  6:05 A.M.   9:30 P.M.

  colon in time of day

- Use a colon before a list or series of items, especially when the list follows expressions such as *the following* or *as follows*. *(page 397)*

  We must order the following: brushes, canvas, paint.

  colon used to introduce lists

- Use a dash to show a sudden break in thought or to mean *namely* or *in other words* before an explanation. *(page 397)*

  Ned's cat—you remember Tabby—ate his toothpaste.

  dash

- Use a hyphen to divide a word at the end of a line. *(page 367)*

  Tabby evidently was attracted by the smell of spearmint toothpaste.

  hyphen

- A hyphenated compound is a compound word connected by hyphens. *(page 216)*

  a three-way tie   one-third full

Practice

Copy these sentences. Add punctuation marks where needed.

1. I've lived in Cleveland, Ohio Miami, Florida and here.
2. Our train leaves at 10 30 A.M. but you know that!
3. My brother in law got us first class accommodations.
4. The letter ended as follows "Travel by train you will see our great nation."

Troublesome Words

a, an
- Use the article *a* before a word that begins with a consonant sound. Use the article *an* before a word that begins with a vowel sound. *(page 163)*

   a dog   <u>an</u> Old English sheepdog

among, between
- The preposition *among* refers to three or more things. The preposition *between* refers to two things only. *(page 273)*

   <u>Among</u> my family there is a friendly feeling.
   This secret will be <u>between</u> you and me.

at, to
- The preposition *at* shows that someone or something is already in a place. The preposition *to* shows movement toward someone or something. *(page 273)*

   Shaggy is <u>at</u> home.
   She will be going <u>to</u> the veterinarian soon.

beside, besides
- Use the preposition *beside* to mean "at the side of." Use the preposition *besides* to mean "in addition to" or "except." *(page 273)*

   Shaggy lay <u>beside</u> the hearth.
   <u>Besides</u> her, we own two other dogs.

I, me, myself
- Always use the pronoun *I* as a subject pronoun. Always use the pronoun *me* as an object pronoun. *(page 239)*

   <u>I</u> love my pet dog.
   She is very special to <u>me</u>.

in, into
- The preposition *in* means "within" or "inside." The preposition *into* shows movement from the outside to the inside. *(page 273)*

   Shaggy is <u>in</u> her bed.
   Earlier, she crawled <u>into</u> the bed.

its, it's
- Use the possessive pronoun *its* when you mean "belonging to it." *It's* is a contraction for *it is.* *(page 242)*

   That dog took <u>its</u> time eating.
   <u>It's</u> hungry.

- Use the possessive pronoun *their* when you mean "belonging to them." Use the adverb *there* when you mean "in that place."

There is also a way of starting a sentence. *They're* is a contraction for *they are.*   *(page 242)*

their, there, they're

> Their puppies are playing over there.
> There is no way I could have another dog.
> They're cute, but Shaggy is the dog for me.

● Use the possessive pronoun *your* when you mean "belonging to you." *You're* is a contraction for *you are.*   *(page 242)*

your, you're

> You're going to love your new puppy.

Practice

Write each sentence, using the correct word in parentheses.

1. Sylvia went (at, to) the pet shop.
2. (At, To) the shop she read about the dog show.
3. She ran home to tell (I, me, myself) about it.
4. Shaggy had never been (in, into) a dog show before.
5. (I, Me, Myself) sent it (a, an) entry blank.
6. (Their, There, They're) was a large crowd at the show.
7. We went (at, to) the registration table.
8. Shaggy stood (among, between) Sylvia and (I, me).
9. I think that (their, there, they're) the judges.
10. (Its, It's) not easy to judge a dog show.
11. There are three women (among, between) the judges.
12. Which dog is (your, you're) favorite?
13. (Their, There, They're) is the refreshment stand.
14. (Beside, Besides) food, I need something to drink.
15. That dog made (its, it's) way through the crowd.
16. (Its, It's) our turn!
17. Shaggy walks (in, into) the ring like (a, an) pro.
18. (Your, You're) really something, Shag!
19. The announcer is standing (at, to) the microphone.
20. One judge is standing (beside, besides) the announcer.
21. (Their, There, They're) going to announce the winners.
22. I wonder what (their, there, they're) decision will be.
23. I told (I, me, myself) not to worry.
24. (A, An) Airedale wins best-of-class.
25. Shaggy, (your, you're) best-of-show!

Agreement

subject/verb
agreement

- The subject and verb in a sentence must agree in number. A singular subject takes a singular verb; a plural subject takes a plural verb. *(page 136)*

    <u>Doris</u> <u>runs</u> rapidly.   The <u>others</u> <u>run</u> slowly.

- A compound subject takes a plural form of the verb except when singular words are joined by *or, either . . . or,* or *neither . . . nor.* When one part of a compound subject that is joined by these conjunctions is singular and the other part is plural, the verb agrees with the part that is nearer. *(pages 136–137)*

    The <u>teacher</u> and the <u>coach</u> <u>know</u> the new principal.
    Neither the <u>teacher</u> nor the <u>coach</u> <u>knows</u> the principal.
    Either <u>Lois</u> or my <u>sisters</u> <u>are</u> using the dictionary.
    Either my <u>sisters</u> or <u>Lois</u> <u>is</u> using the dictionary.

- Collective nouns name groups. A singular verb is used to show that the members of a group are acting as a unit. A plural verb is used to show individual action within the group.

    The <u>team</u> <u>has won</u> a trophy.
    The <u>team</u> <u>have been arguing</u> about where to display it.

pronoun/
antecedent
agreement

- Always use a singular form of a verb after a singular subject pronoun. These indefinite pronouns are singular. *(page 246)*

each	one	anybody	neither
either	everyone	somebody	none

- Pronouns must agree with the nouns they replace in number, gender, and person. *(page 236)*

    A <u>girl</u> cut the grass. <u>She</u> stopped to rest.

Practice

Write each sentence, choosing the correct word in the parentheses ( ).

1. Everyone in school (is, are) excited about the trophy.
2. Liz Jones (think, thinks) that (it, they) should be in the showcase in the hall.
3. Ed (say, says) that (he, him) disagrees with (she, her).
4. Neither Liz nor Ed (is, are) going to give in.
5. If (they, them) can't agree, shall we (vote, votes)?

Dangling Participles

- A **dangling participle** is a participial phrase that does not modify the word the writer intends. *(page 348)*

dangling participle

Dangling: Taking a break, refreshments were served.
Correct: <u>Taking a break</u>, everyone ate refreshments.

Practice

A. Rewrite the sentences that are incorrect.

1. Having made several mistakes, the letter was rewritten by Jeri.
2. Buried in a dresser drawer, Jeri finally found the postage stamps.
3. Hurrying, she put the stamp on the envelope.
4. Licking the envelope, her fingers became sticky.
5. Having written a thank you note, her appreciation of the gift was shown.
6. Jeri thought of the gift her grandmother had sent her smiling happily.
7. It was a beautiful box filled with writing paper.
8. Making use of the stationery, the note had been written promptly.
9. Running to the corner, the letter was mailed.
10. Feeling carefree, the bus came along, and Jeri went downtown.

B. Using these participles, write complete sentences. Be sure that the participle is placed correctly.

11. riding on the subway train
12. standing on the platform
13. missing the Spring Street station
14. waiting for a long time
15. carrying a briefcase and some bags
16. struggling to stay upright in the speeding train
17. clutching a pole with a mittened hand
18. giving a seat to an elderly person
19. reaching his stop with a minute to spare
20. calling his cousin from the station

MORE PRACTICE

UNIT 1
Kinds of Sentences   pages 1–3

Decide which of these word groups are sentences. Write only the sentences, adding capital letters and end punctuation.

1. those fish over there
2. are swimming very slowly
3. they are looking for food
4. is the river muddy

Rewrite these sentences. Add capital letters and end punctuation where needed. After each sentence write *declarative, interrogative, imperative,* or *exclamatory.*

5. tornadoes often occur during the spring months
6. what damage did they say was done by that tornado
7. a tornado is heading towards our house
8. write a report on the causes of tornadoes

Complete Subjects and Predicates   pages 4–5

Copy these sentences. Draw one line under the complete subjects and two lines under the complete predicates.

1. The boy in the red jacket stands at the bus stop.
2. The bus is ten minutes late.
3. It arrived five minutes late yesterday.
4. The boy paces back and forth.
5. A woman with a briefcase looks at her watch.
6. The boy sees a bus turning the corner.
7. All the people at the bus stop breathe a sigh of relief.

Simple Subjects and Predicates   pages 6–7

1.–7. Reread the complete subjects and complete predicates you underlined for the sentences in Complete Subjects and Predicates. Go back and circle the simple subject and simple predicate in each of those sentences.

Word Order in Sentences   pages 8–9

Copy these sentences. Draw one line under the simple subject and two lines under the simple predicate. After imperative sentences, write *you* (understood). After each sentence, write *natural word order* or *inverted word order*.

1. Eliseo behaved rather well.
2. Down the steps rolled his bicycle.
3. What did he do then?
4. Be quiet for a minute.
5. I will tell you the rest of the story right away.
6. On the ground lay the wreckage of the bicycle.
7. Take that heap of metal to the town dump.

Compound Subjects and Predicates   pages 10–11

Copy these sentences. Underline any compound subjects once and any compound verbs twice. Circle coordinating conjunctions.

1. Cotton and wool are used for sweaters but are obtained through different methods.
2. Both must be cleaned and processed.
3. Then yarn is made and sold in stores.
4. Mother knits or sews.
5. Jack or Dad will get this homemade sweater.
6. Shall I knit or crochet the sweater?
7. Jack washes and irons his own clothes.
8. I make some of my clothes and buy the rest.

Compound Sentences   pages 12–13

Copy these sentences. Underline each complete subject once and each complete predicate twice. After each sentence, write *simple sentence* or *compound sentence*.

1. The lawyers and the witnesses walked into the courtroom.
2. The trial began two weeks ago, and it is still going on.
3. The jury seems sympathetic, but the judge is impartial.
4. The jurors may not go home or see their families.
5. They may talk to each other, but they may not read any newspapers or magazines.

Correcting Fragments and Run-on Sentences page 14

1.–8. Rewrite this paragraph. Correct all sentence fragments and run-on sentences.

Did you ever wonder who invented the zipper two people worked on it. Whitcomb L. Judson was an engineer he developed a hook-and-eye gadget with a handle. It was sold as "The C-Curity Placket Fastener" unfortunately the fasteners popped open. Gideon Sundback worked. For the makers of C-Curity. He decided to interlock metal teeth. Which would hold together. Better than wiggly hooks and eyes.

Dictionary pages 18–19

These three word pairs are dictionary guide words and page numbers: **leafage—leathery,** *page 102;* **leave—left wing,** *page 103;* **leg—Leibnitz,** *page 104.* Write 1–12 in alphabetical order. After each write the page number on which it would appear.

1. legislative
2. lei
3. lease
4. leeway
5. legato
6. leaflet
7. leech
8. legally
9. leavings
10. lean-to
11. legalize
12. legation

Sentence Combining pages 24–25

Combine these sentences using the words *or, but, and,* or *therefore.* Use correct punctuation in the new sentences.

1. It started to rain. The ball game was not cancelled.
2. The batter hit a fly ball. The center fielder caught it.
3. We wanted the Dodgers to win. They lost.
4. The pitcher sprained his wrist. He will not pitch today.

Mechanics Practice page 31

Copy the sentences. Add capitalization and end punctuation.

1. are you a football fan
2. yes, I enjoy the game
3. what a fantastic catch
4. that's the game, and we won

Devices of Sound in Poetry page 34

1.–4. Write one sentence illustrating each of these devices: alliteration, assonance, consonance, and onomatopoeia.

UNIT 2

Paragraph Structure   pages 42–43

Rewrite these sentences to form a paragraph. Put the sentence that gives the main idea first, sentences that give details next, and a concluding sentence last. Indent the first sentence.

1. The planets' intensely cold temperatures, powerful gravity, and poisonous atmospheres forbid human exploration.
2. Astronauts could, however, land on any of the giants' numerous satellites.
3. Astronauts will probably never land on these huge worlds.
4. Jupiter has at least fourteen satellites, and Saturn at least twelve; Uranus has five, and Neptune has two.
5. The four biggest planets of our solar system are Jupiter, Saturn, Uranus, and Neptune.
6. By observing the four distant planets from their moons, scientists could gather valuable new information.

Topic Sentences/Main Idea   pages 44–49

Copy these sentences. Write *topic* after the topic sentence. Write *detail* after each sentence that supports the topic. Draw a line through any sentences that do not support the topic, or main idea.

1. Earth orbits the sun at 67,000 miles per hour.
2. Earth is unique in the solar system for three reasons.
3. Earth's nearest neighbor is Venus.
4. Earth is the only known planet that has intelligent life.
5. Mercury and Venus do not have moons.
6. Earth is the only planet that has a single large moon.
7. Only Earth has large amounts of water on its surface.

The Card Catalog   page 55–57

For each book, write whether you would use the *title, author,* or *subject card* to find it in the library.

1. A Bell for Adano
2. a book by Arthur Hailey
3. a book on clipper ships
4. Wuthering Heights
5. poems of Emily Dickinson
6. a book on etiquette
7. Fantastic Voyage
8. a book by Isaac Asimov
9. a book on Saturn's rings
10. a novel by Jack London

Developing Paragraphs by Comparison and Contrast and with Time Order and Space Order   pages 62–65

Copy these sentences. After each, write *comparison, contrast, space order,* or *time order,* depending on how the sentence would be best developed in a paragraph.

1. My schedule on Mondays is very hectic.
2. The oboe and the English horn are very similar.
3. The police inspector examined the room in which the robbery had been committed.
4. Follow these directions to make delicious chicken soup.
5. How can you tell a mushroom from a toadstool?
6. Here is one plan for laying out a small vegetable garden.

Mechanics Practice   page 69

Rewrite these sentences, using correct capitalization. Correctly abbreviate names of agencies and of titles that precede names.

1. My mother is working toward her ph.d degree at harvard.
2. Didn't president John f kennedy graduate from harvard?
3. In 1952 he ran against senator Henry cabot lodge, jr., and won a seat in Congress.
4. Was the national aeronautics and space administration begun under president dwight d eisenhower?
5. The federal communications commission was established under the administration of F.D.R. — a President greatly admired by both uncle mike and my grandfather.

Figurative Language in Poetry   pages 70–71

Copy these lines by Shakespeare. Identify each as a *simile* or a *metaphor.*

1. All the world's a stage, and all the men and women merely players.
2. O! he's as tedious as a tired horse. . . .
3. I am as viligant as a cat to steal cream.
4. I am as poor as Job, my lord, but not so patient.
5. Trust none; for oaths are straws, men's faiths are wafer-cakes. . . .
6. Life is as tedious as a twice-told tale, vexing the dull ear of a drowsy man.

UNIT 3

Common and Proper Nouns   pages 80–81

Rewrite these sentences, capitalizing the proper nouns.
Underline all nouns. Write *concrete* above each concrete noun
and *abstract* above each abstract noun.

1. The first woman to be granted a medical degree in the
   united states was elizabeth blackwell.
2. Her family held strong beliefs in equality for women.
3. Her brother married antoinette brown, the first woman to
   be ordained as a preacher in america.
4. Another brother married lucy stone, who worked for
   women's suffrage.
5. Because she was not allowed to practice in existing
   hospitals, elizabeth blackwell helped found the new york
   infirmary and college for women.

Singular and Plural Nouns   pages 82–83

Copy these singular nouns. Next to each write its plural form.

1. shrimp	2. luggage	3. hunch
4. belief	5. sheep	6. fox
7. brigadier general	8. winner	9. piano
10. country	11. monkey	12. precaution

Collective Nouns   pages 84–85

Copy these sentences. Underline each collective noun. Write
singular above the noun if it is used as singular and *plural* if it is
used as a plural.

1. A trio was asked to sing at my brother's wedding.
2. Now the couple has walked down the aisle.
3. A large crowd of well-wishers waits outside.
4. An orchestra has been hired to play at the reception.
5. The family were the first to offer their congratulations.
6. A firm of caterers has prepared the food.

Abbreviating Nouns   pages 86–87

Copy these proper nouns. Next to each, write its abbreviation.

1. January	2. Mister Ed Blaine	3. Friday
4. New Mexico	5. Farber Boulevard	6. Senator Morris

Possessive Nouns   pages 88–89

Write the possessive form of each of these nouns. Then use each possessive noun in a sentence.

1. girl
2. boys
3. child
4. children
5. Dolores
6. Mrs. Jones
7. woman
8. men
9. people
10. teachers
11. babies
12. Eskimos

Appositives   pages 90–91

Rewrite these sentences, adding commas where necessary. Underline the appositives.

1. Mia lives in New York City the twelfth-largest city in the world.
2. She takes the subway an underground train to school.
3. Her sister Hara goes with her.
4. Their father works on Wall Street a financial district.
5. A famous landmark Trinity Church is opposite his office.

Encyclopedias and Almanacs and *The Readers' Guide to Periodical Literature*   pages 94–97

Write whether you would use an encyclopedia, an almanac, or *The Readers' Guide to Periodical Literature* to locate these items.

1. the most important current events of the past year
2. the history of photography
3. listings of winners of Oscar and Tony awards
4. a listing of current magazine articles on new tax laws
5. how synthetic fabrics are made
6. the author of a current article, "How Sun Spots Affect us"

Writing Explanations   pages 100–101

Put these steps in order. Then make up a topic sentence, and rewrite the material as a paragraph.

1. Then assemble any materials or supplies you will need.
2. Follow each step of the directions in order.
3. Picture yourself carrying out each step as you read it.
4. First, read the entire set of directions and study any accompanying diagram or illustration.
5. After you carry out a step, reread the next step.

Developing Cause-and-Effect Paragraphs   pages 102–104

Copy these sentence fragments. Complete each one in such a way that the sentence expresses a cause-and-effect relationship.

1. Because it rained on Saturday _____.
2. I was late for school today because _____.
3. The hurricane resulted in _____.
4. Since he was a terrible driver, _____.
5. Eating candy before meals _____.
6. If I do not study for the test, _____.
7. The reason I have one brown and one black shoe on _____.
8. If he ever dares to show his face in here again, _____.

Choose one of the sentences you completed in the exercise above to be used as a basis for a cause-and-effect paragraph. Write a cause-and-effect paragraph of at least five sentences. You may begin the paragraph with the sentence from the preceding exercise or use new wording.

Mechanics Practice   page 107

Rewrite these sentences. Add capital letters and punctuation marks where needed.

1. When in Chicago Illinois try to see the museum of science and industry on lake shore drive.
2. The national baseball hall of fame on Main Street Cooperstown New York is a must for baseball lovers.
3. The museum of new mexico at 113 lincoln street Santa fe New Mexico has fine Native American displays.
4. I enjoyed visiting carnegie institute on forbes avenue pittsburgh pennsylvania

Myths   pages 108–111

Answer the following questions about myths.

1. How were myths originally transmitted?
2. What are nature myths and behavioral myths, and how are those two categories of myths different?
3. Why are behavioral myths sometimes called moral myths?
4. Why were nature myths invented?

UNIT 4

Transitive and Intransitive Verbs   pages 120–121

Copy these sentences. Underline the action verbs twice. Then write *transitive* or *intransitive* after each sentence. For the transitive verbs, circle the receiver of the verb's action.

1. For almost a million years, great sheets of ice buried most of Europe, Asia, and North America.
2. Sometimes the ice moved very far south.
3. At other times, the ice retreated.
4. Prehistoric peoples often lived in caves.
5. The cave people mastered the art of hunting.
6. They drew pictures of animals on the cave walls.
7. When the ice retreated, people developed agriculture.
8. Farming provided a different kind of food.

Understanding Linking Verbs   pages 122–123

Copy these sentences. Underline each verb twice. After the sentence write *action verb* or *linking verb*.

1. Margaret visits me every weekend.
2. She is a good friend of mine.
3. Margaret's new coat looks terrific.
4. We saw it in a department store window.
5. The coat feels very warm.
6. We felt the cold wind against our faces.
7. We smelled smoke from burning leaves.
8. The burning leaves smell pungent.

Main Verbs and Helping Verbs   pages 124–125

Draw two lines under each verb phrase in these sentences. Circle the helping verb or verbs in each verb phrase.

1. The wind is blowing.
2. Mark will raise the sail on his boat.
3. He must hold the rope.
4. The rope could have been lost.
5. Mark might sail across the bay.
6. The wind had dropped.
7. We have been watching Mark for a half hour.
8. He should be going home soon.

Principal Parts of Regular and Irregular Verbs   pages 126–131

Rewrite these sentences using the correct principal part of the verb in parentheses. After each sentence write *regular verb* or *irregular verb*.

1. Greta (*decide,* past) to have a Halloween party.
2. All her friends (*is,* past) invited.
3. Everyone (*wear,* past) silly costumes.
4. Kent (*work,* past participle) on his costume for two days.
5. At first, no one (*know,* past) who anyone was.
6. It (*is,* past participle) difficult to keep the costumes a secret.
7. Finally, everyone (*guess,* past participle) who was who.
8. Greta (*think,* present) she'll have a party next year.

Verb Tenses   pages 132–135

Copy these sentences. Underline each verb or verb phrase twice. After each sentence, write the tense of the verb.

1. Amanda recently bought a bike.
2. She has ridden her new bike to school all week.
3. Until yesterday, she had parked it in the bike stand.
4. The custodian had painted the stand early in the morning.
5. Will everyone notice the new paint?
6. They all will have moved their bikes by noon.
7. The bikes usually stand in the yard all day.
8. The paint will have dried by tomorrow morning.
9. Amanda had bought a lock for her bike.
10. She locked it securely to a pole.

Subject and Verb Agreement   pages 136–137

Copy these sentences, choosing the correct word in parentheses.

1. The monkeys and chimps (is, are) in their cages.
2. Both the trainer and her assistant (was, were) there.
3. Either a pair or monkeys or a chimp (is, are) going to perform first.
4. (Hasn't, Haven't) you and your friends seen the show yet?
5. (Is, Are) monkeys or chimps more easily trained?
6. (Does, Do) monkeys or chimps ever bite?

Homophones and Homographs pages 140–141

Copy these sentences. Underline the two words that are homophones or homographs. Write *homophone* or *homograph* after the sentence to identify the word pair.

1. Please permit me to see your driving permit.
2. Let's not have a row over who is going to row!
3. The carpenter bored a hole in the board.
4. The striking sanitation workers refuse to collect refuse.

Synonyms and Antonyms pages 142–143

Copy each word and write a synonym and an antonym for each.

1. huge   2. prosper   3. dull
4. command   5. wide   6. uncommon

Narrative Paragraphs pages 146–147

Write a personal anecdote about one of the topics listed. Underline your introductory sentence once and your concluding sentence twice. Include at least three sentences in the body.

— mistakenly taking home the wrong package from a store
— having an unexpected bit of good luck

Mechanics Practice pages 150–151

Rewrite these sentences correctly.

1. Do you prefer Italian food asked Roger or Greek food
2. This pizza is super exclaimed Jeannette where did you buy it
3. The crust commented Dave is especially good
4. What writer said waste not, want not asked george
5. I don't he continued intend to waste the last piece

Autobiographies page 152

Answer these questions about autobiographies.

1. How are biographies and autobiographies similar?
2. How are biographies and autobiographies different?
3. Why does the author of an autobiography have more freedom than the author of a biography?

UNIT 5

Common and Proper Adjectives   pages 162–163

Rewrite these sentences, capitalizing the proper adjectives. Then underline each adjective and draw an arrow to the noun or pronoun it modifies. Do not underline articles.

1. I think that swiss cheese and danish pastry are among the choicest of european foods.
2. However, french cooking is the type of cooking I prefer.
3. It contains richer sauces than american cooking, but the taste is perfect.
4. Of course, asian food is interesting, too.
5. The japanese and chinese people have fine cuisines.
6. You don't have to leave America to enjoy exotic foods.
7. A new york or san francisco resident can choose from a wide variety of foreign restaurants.
8. In fact, throughout our country you can find fine restaurants that serve foods from many lands.

Comparing with Adjectives   pages 164–165

Write the comparative and superlative degrees for these adjectives. Use *er* and *est, more* and *most,* or *less* and *least.* Then use one word from each set in a sentence. Underline the adjective and draw an arrow from it to the word it modifies.

1. slow	2. cold
3. attractive	4. happy
5. brave	6. serious
7. much	8. good
9. delicious	10. clever
11. simple	12. far

Rewrite these sentences using the correct degree of comparison for each adjective in parentheses ( ).

1. This is the (friendly) puppy in the litter.
2. He was the (small) at first, but now he is getting (big).
3. The brown puppy is the (funny) one of all.
4. The black one is definitely the (smart).
5. Puppies are (difficult) to train than slightly (old) dogs.

Adverbs   pages 166–167

Use each word or phrase in a sentence. Underline each adverb and draw an arrow from it to the word it modifies.

1. here
2. rather rapidly
3. safely
4. tomorrow
5. less expensive
6. thoroughly
7. quite small
8. more careful
9. utterly quiet

Comparing with Adverbs   pages 168–169

Write the comparative and superlative degrees for each adverb.

1. cautiously
2. loudly
3. unhappily
4. carefully
5. soon
6. willingly
7. brightly
8. close

Using Adjectives and Adverbs Correctly   pages 170–171

Rewrite these sentences, choosing the correct word from the modifiers in parentheses ( ).

1. I am not feeling (good, well) today.
2. A head cold is (really, real) unpleasant.
3. I (most, almost) always catch cold when I get too little sleep.
4. Staying up late is a (bad, badly) idea.

Classifying Information   pages 174–175

Copy the three items in each list that belong to the same category. Then name the category.

1. biology, music, chemistry, botany
2. Shanghai, Leningrad, Austria, Cairo
3. meter, centimeter, foot, kilometer
4. wood, furnace, oil, gas
5. handball, tennis, weight lifting, soccer

Verbal Analogies   pages 176–177

Make an analogy with the words in each list.

1. mammal, snake, whale, reptile
2. grape, prune, plum, raisin
3. English, mathematics, calculus, language
4. noun, adverb, verb, adjective

Descriptive Paragraphs   pages 180–184

1. Write a paragraph in which you describe someone's living room or office. Include sensory words and underline them. Try to indicate something about the room's occupant by the details you choose to include.

2. Write a character sketch of the person whose room you just described. Remember to include both physical characteristics and personality traits. Try to help the reader visualize the person.

Mechanics Practice   page 187

Rewrite these sentences. Add capital letters and punctuation where needed.

1. The english, dutch, swedes, and germans were some of the groups who colonized America in the 17th century.

2. In the first major battle of the revolutionary war, the continental army retreated from the british on Long Island.

3. However, the colonists defeated the hessians at Trenton.

4. During the 1700s the british had conflicts with the french.

5. Washington did not live to see the 1800s.

6. The victorious american general of the war of independence died on sunday, december 14, 1799, at the very close of the 18th century.

7. On thursday, december 20, 1860, South Carolina seceded.

8. The civil war, or the war between the states, took place during the latter half of the 19th century, 1861–1865.

9. independence day and Washington's birthday are national american holidays.

10. Americans commemorate events of the 20th century as well.

Narrative Poems   pages 188–191

Answer these questions about narrative poems.

1. How is a narrative poem different from other types of poetry?

2. What are some of the characteristics of a narrative poem?

3. Give an example of a story or a theme that would be suitable for a narrative poem.

UNIT 6

Direct Objects   pages 200–201

Copy these sentences. Underline each verb twice and identify it by writing *transitive* or *intransitive* after each sentence. Underline each direct object once. Not every sentence has a direct object. Some sentences have more than one.

1. Naomi wrote a letter to her grandparents.
2. She put a stamp on it and mailed it.
3. She had invited her grandparents for a visit.
4. Her grandparents lived in Detroit.
5. Soon Naomi received an answer and some good news.
6. They would be arriving by train next Tuesday.
7. That Tuesday Naomi's whole family went to the station.
8. The train station was busy.
9. Finally Naomi saw her grandparents.
10. She hugged them and welcomed them to the city.

Indirect Objects   pages 202–203

Copy these sentences. Underline the action verbs twice and the direct objects once. Circle the indirect objects. Not every sentence has an indirect object.

1. Mr. Steiner, our teacher, assigned the class a report.
2. He allowed us a week to do the work.
3. Jerry asked Marie a question about the assignment.
4. Marie gave him advice.
5. Jerry accompanied Marie on the trip to the library.
6. They gave themselves sufficient time for research.

Predicate Nominatives   pages 204–205

Copy these sentences. Underline the subjects and the predicate nominatives once and the linking verbs twice.

1. Ann became class president this year.
2. The president is the leader on the class trip.
3. I hope to be a class officer next year.
4. My brother Justin is treasurer of the science club.
5. He will not become a class officer.

Predicate Adjectives   pages 206–207

Copy these sentences. Underline each subject and predicate adjective once and each linking verb twice.

1. The evening is perfect for a party.
2. The sky is cloudless and starry.
3. The punch tastes delicious, and the pizza is spicy.
4. We are glad the party is successful.
5. The yard looks messy now.
6. The cleanup crew seems weary.

Prefixes and Suffixes   pages 210–213

Copy these words. Underline the prefix or suffix. Then write a definition of each word.

1. greenish
2. government
3. predict
4. antifreeze
5. merciful
6. interaction
7. semiliquid
8. destructive
9. hasten
10. tripod
11. happiness
12. submarine

Roots   pages 214–215

Copy these words and circle each root. Next to each word, write another word containing each root. Some words contain two roots.

1. autograph
2. audiometer
3. microscope
4. television
5. kilowatt
6. portage
7. inspect
8. multiple
9. convocation

Compound Words   pages 216–217

Combine each word of group 1–8 with a word from group a–h to form a compound word. Write the compounds and use each one in a sentence.

1. eye
2. ship
3. snow
4. some
5. ginger
6. gang
7. news
8. earth

a. quake
b. paper
c. wreck
d. lash
e. flake
f. body
g. plank
h. bread

Persuasive Paragraphs   pages 218–219

Write a persuasive paragraph on a topic of your choice, or choose one of the topics below. Give at least three reasons to support your opinion. When you have finished, edit your work.

The legal driving age should/should not be lowered.
Students would learn more/less if grades were abolished.
(Name of singer) is the greatest/worst popular singer.

Mechanics Practice   page 223

Rewrite these dates and times correctly.

1. 1049 am
2. 329 pm
3. may 2 1948
4. december 9 1701
5. 1201 am
6. august 11 1896

Rewrite these sentences. Use capital letters, commas, and colons where needed.

7. On friday february 9 2063 the citizens of the planet Zanze were awakened at 301 am by strange rumblings.
8. The last rumblings had occurred over a century before on thursday may 10 1951 at exactly 1212 pm.
9. The rumblings continued off and on until saturday february 10 at precisely 101 am.
10. Nothing further occurred until 409 pm on thursday march 7 2064, when a great crack appeared in Mt. Gooz.
11. The crack continued to widen until 1109 pm.
12. At 1111 pm the first giant bamwhat crawled from the crack.
13. The monstrous bamwhat was thought extinct since wednesday july 18 1984, when the last known bamwhat had died of indigestion at 204 am.

Short Story   page 224

Write an outline of a plot for a short story, using the three steps described. You may invent a plot or use the plot from a short story that you have read.

Write *Introduction.* Describe briefly what it includes.
Write *Complications,* and briefly describe them.
Write *Resolution.* Tell how the story problem is resolved.

UNIT 7
Pronouns   pages 236–237

On your paper, list each personal pronoun and its antecedent in this passage.

1.–4.   The lumberjacks in the story of Paul Bunyan had a difficult time keeping warm. They grew long beards and covered themselves with blankets. When the lumberjacks began tripping over their beards all day, Paul declared a new camp rule. Here it is: A man with a beard over two meters long must keep it tucked inside his boots.

Subject and Object Pronouns   pages 239–240

Rewrite these sentences. Use pronouns to replace the underlined nouns. If the noun replaced is the subject, write *subject* after the sentence. If it is a predicate nominative, write *predicate nominative* after the sentence.

1. <u>Astrid</u> baked a cake.
2. <u>Astrid's brother</u> frosted the cake.
3. <u>The cake</u> was lemon flavored.
4. <u>Astrid and her family</u> love lemon cakes.
5. <u>Astrid</u> and <u>her brother</u> served the cake to their guest.

Rewrite these sentences. Use pronouns to replace the underlined nouns. Then underline direct objects once and indirect objects twice, and circle objects of prepositions.

1. Sol tossed <u>Ned</u> the <u>newspaper</u>.
2. Ned called <u>Sandy</u>.
3. He showed <u>Sandy</u> <u>an article</u>.
4. The article was about <u>Sandy and her scout troop</u>.
5. Sandy took <u>Michelle</u> <u>a copy</u>.

Possessive Pronouns   pages 242–243

Complete these sentences with possessive pronouns. Do not use the same pronoun more than twice. Above each pronoun write *adjective, subject,* or *subject complement.*

1. Gwen said, "Let's help them pack _____ camping gear."
2. "These are _____ boots. _____ are on the hall table."

3. "With _____ tent and _____ stove, we should be comfortable."
4. "This sleeping bag is _____, and that one is _____."
5. "When _____ trip is over, let's go to _____ house."

Reflexive and Demonstrative Pronouns   pages 244–245

Rewrite these sentences, completing each with the correct reflexive pronoun. After each sentence, identify the reflexive pronoun by writing *direct object, indirect object,* or *objective of a preposition.*

1. We decided to make _____ a garden.
2. The neighbors enjoyed _____ watching us.
3. Don't cut _____ with those garden shears.
4. Juan and I made _____ some lemonade.
5. A bird made a nest for _____ in the new garden.

Rewrite these sentences, choosing the correct demonstrative pronoun.

6. (This, This here, These) is my best friend.
7. (This, That, That there) is his brother standing there.
8. (Those, That, That there) are their parents.
9. (Those, This, This here) are your friends.

Indefinite and Interrogative Pronouns   pages 246–247

Rewrite these sentences, choosing the correct words.

1. All the cyclists (is, are) ready for the bike tour.
2. Everyone has checked (his or her, their) tire pressure.
3. Each of the leaders (is, are) wearing a bright shirt.
4. Several boys and girls are carrying (his or her, their) repair kits.

Rewrite these sentences, choosing the correct pronouns.

5. (Who, Whom) lost Mary's watch?
6. To (who, whom) did she lend it?
7. (Whose, Who's) going to tell her?
8. (Whose, Who's) responsibility is it?

Front and Back Matter of a Book   pages 250–251

Write the part of a book in which you would look for the answer to each of these questions. Choose from these book parts: *title page, copyright page, preface, table of contents, index,* or *glossary.*

1. What is the Library of Congress Catalog number?
2. How is *tracheitis* pronounced?
3. How many major divisions are in the book?
4. Why did the author write the book?
5. Where was the book published and by whom?
6. Is the book likely to have current information?
7. How many times has the book been revised?
8. On what page is there an illustration of a pipefish?

Book Reports   pages 256–258

Write a TV commercial for a book. Include all the information that would appear in a book report. Also tell the price of the book and where to buy it.

Mechanics   page 261

Rewrite these titles correctly.

1. the spy who came in from the cold   (book)
2. hold fast your dreams   (poem)
3. the atlantic monthly   (magazine)
4. nouns and pronouns   (book chapter)
5. the mouse that roared   (movie)
6. the night watch   (painting)
7. up in central park   (record album)
8. in the shade of the old apple tree   (song)
9. journal herald   (newspaper)
10. fiddler on the roof   (play)

Essay of Opinion   page 262

Choose one of the "To Memorize" selections from this book. Think about how you could expand it into an essay of opinion. Write the "To Memorize" quotation and its page number. Then write three examples or statements that could be included in the essay that would help persuade the reader to agree with the writer's opinion.

UNIT 8

Prepositions and Prepositional Phrases   pages 272–273

Copy the prepositional phrase from each sentence. Underline each preposition and draw an arrow from it to its object.

1. Jan and Ilse climbed up the trail.
2. They scrambled over some rocks.
3. At noon they rested beneath a pine tree.
4. Ilse dipped cold water from a mountain stream.
5. She splashed it on her face.
6. Jan walked to the edge of the water.
7. He slipped on some mossy stones.
8. Into the stream he tumbled.
9. He came out of the water and sat in the sun.
10. Ilse gave him a towel for his dripping face.

Rewrite each sentence, choosing the correct preposition. Draw an arrow from the preposition to its object.

11. A group of us were sitting (at, to) the soda fountain.
12. An argument began (between, among) John and Hector.
13. They were sitting (beside, besides) each other.
14. John jumped up angrily and went (in, into) a phone booth.
15. Hector looked (at, to) us, somewhat embarrassed.

Prepositional Phrases as Adjectives and Adverbs   pages 274–275

Copy these sentences. Underline each prepositional phrase and draw an arrow from it to the word it modifies. After the sentence write *adjective* or *adverb* to show how the phrase is used.

1. The fans on the bench cheered wildly.
2. The football sailed over the goalpost.
3. The applause from the crowd was deafening.
4. The coach from the other team stormed back and forth.
5. The numbers changed on the scoreboard.
6. The fans watched the next play with mounting excitement.
7. The quarterback threw a pass with unerring skill.
8. It was caught by Gary in the end zone.

Interjections page 276

Rewrite these sentences, using commas, exclamation points, and capital letters where needed.

1. My it's hot today
2. Wow look at the temperature
3. Hey let's make limeade.
4. Oops we're out of limes.
5. Aha we have some lemons.
6. Ah lemonade will be fine.
7. Goodness that's sour.
8. Oh put some sugar in it.

Conjunctions page 278

Write these sentences, completing each with a correct coordinating conjunction. Circle words or phrases and underline simple sentences joined by a conjunction.

1. Tip _____ Top are nice pets, _____ sometimes they make life difficult for me.
2. One _____ the other is always getting into something.
3. The other day, _____ Tip _____ Top got into a grocery bag on the kitchen chair.
4. _____ Tip _____ Top had jumped up to investigate the bag _____ had spilled the contents.
5. The bag contained _____ a sack of flour _____ a box of rice.
6. They were already in trouble, _____ they decided to have fun.
7. _____ the rice _____ the flour were an important part of their entertainment.
8. The house was a mess, _____ I spent hours cleaning up.
9. Of course, _____ Tip _____ Top means to be bad, _____ perhaps I expect too much of them.
10. I must be patient, _____ they are only puppies.

Choosing and Limiting a Topic pages 282–283

Each of these topics is too broad for a research report. For each one write a suitably narrowed topic on that subject.

1. history of baseball
2. storms
3. Florida
4. dogs of the world
5. money
6. cars
7. science fiction films
8. World War II
9. reptiles
10. the American Revolution
11. energy
12. education

Preparing a Bibliography   pages 288–289

Write a bibliography entry for each of the publications described below. You may invent titles, names, page numbers, and other information as needed.

1. a book
3. a book with an editor instead of an author
5. an article in a newspaper
2. an encyclopedia article
4. an article in a magazine
6. a book with two authors

Research Reports   pages 292–295

Suppose that you will be writing a research report on how to write a research report. Think about the main points you would cover and what you would say in the introduction. You may refer to the lessons on writing a research report on pages 292–295 if you wish. Then follow steps 1 and 2.

1. Write an outline of the information you would include. Write your title for the research report as the title of your outline.
2. Write an introductory paragraph to interest the reader in your topic. Give an overview of what he or she will learn from your report.

Mechanics Practice   page 299

Rewrite these sentences. Add commas and semicolons where they are needed.

1. Is it true Dan that you toured the South by bus?
2. Yes I started Jean by going to Washington D.C. Richmond Virginia Raleigh North Carolina and Charleston South Carolina the home of the dance "the Charleston."
3. Jean you have heard of course of Blackbeard a hated pirate.
4. Along South Carolina's coast in Colonial times Blackbeard his henchmen and other pirates preyed on American ships.

One-Act Play   pages 300–305

In one or two paragraphs, define a one-act play and explain the construction of a play's plot. Be sure to include these terms: *introduction, body, resolution, protagonist, antagonist, dialog, climax,* and *dénouement.*

UNIT 9

Clauses   pages 314–315

Copy these sentences. Draw one line under every independent clause and two lines under every dependent clause. Then label each sentence *compound, complex,* or *compound-complex.*

1. Joe's brother Sid played the flute, but all Joe wanted to play was basketball.
2. Because he loved music, Sid talked to Joe about the band, and he tried to persuade Joe to play a band instrument.
3. Joe thought about it, and he decided to try it.
4. Joe said nothing about his decision since he wanted it to be a surprise.

Adverb Clauses   pages 316–317

Copy these sentences. Underline each adverb clause, and draw an arrow to the word or words it modifies.

1. Juanita runs to school whenever the weather is nice.
2. Since it is raining today, she will take the bus.
3. While she waits for the bus, she reads a book.
4. She will chat with friends before she goes to class.
5. Juanita can't read her book until the lunch bell rings.

Adjective Clauses   pages 318–319

Copy these sentences. Underline each adjective clause, and draw an arrow to its antecedent.

1. The puppy that Pat bought is not pure-bred.
2. I know the people who owned the puppy's mother.
3. The puppy's dish, which I filled this morning, is now under the bed in the spare room.
4. The socks that Pat folded are on the floor.
5. Pat, who is always so neat, should have chosen a puppy that was better trained.

Noun Clauses   pages 320–321

Copy these sentences. Underline the noun clauses that are used as subjects. Circle the noun clauses that are used as direct objects.

1. What I like about Mr. Barnes is his unfailing sense of humor.
2. I understand that he was once a professional comedian.
3. What I cannot understand is his becoming an English teacher.
4. I wonder if he will return to the world of the theater.
5. Do you suppose that Mr. Barnes prefers teaching to acting?

Misplaced Modifiers   pages 322–323

Rewrite these sentences. Correct the misplaced modifiers.

1. The traffic officer stopped the car whistling loudly.
2. We saw a skyscraper walking down the street.
3. My wallet was found by a merchant with all my money.
4. Sleeping under a park bench I finally found my dog.
5. I saw a child fall from my seat on the park bench.
6. The child was picked up by his parent with a sticky face.

Skimming and Scanning   pages 326–327

Read the list of questions. Then read the paragraph that comes after it. Answer the questions and write whether you used *skimming* or *scanning* to get the answer.

1. What discovery was made?
2. On what date was the discovery made?
3. What was the importance of the discovery?
4. Who reported the discovery?
5. How is antimatter different from matter?
6. How much did the research program cost?
7. What government organization sponsored the research program?
8. What are positrons?

A NASA-sponsored research project has resulted in an important discovery concerning antimatter. (Antimatter is the counterpart of ordinary matter. For example, it is composed of antiprotons instead of protons and positrons instead of electrons.) On October 16, 1979, a high-altitude balloon carrying sensitive measuring instruments detected streams of antimatter that came from interstellar space. Previous to this discovery, antimatter had only been produced in the laboratory. Its existence in nature had not been proven. The discovery was announced by Dr. Robert L. Golden and his colleagues at New Mexico University, Albuquerque, New Mexico. They were working under a $5-million NASA program.

News Story   pages 330–331

Write a news story about the discovery of antimatter described in the paragraph in the preceding exercise. Be sure to answer the questions *who, what, where, when, how,* and *why.*

Mechanics Practice   page 335

Rewrite these sentences correctly. Add punctuation where needed.

1. Johns research report hasnt been written yet.
2. 'Ive been putting it off, but now Ill have to start it, wont I?" he asked himself.
3. The students spelling wasnt the best.
4. "Wheres <u>banana</u>?" he wondered, looking through the <u>b</u>'s in his <u>Websters Unabridged Dictionary</u>.
5. "I cant find it, but its got to be here somewhere doesnt it?" he thought.

Novels   pages 336–339

Answer these questions about the novel.

1. How are narrative poems, one-act plays, short stories, and novels similar?
2. How is the novel different from other kinds of literature?
3. What advantage does the novelist have over the short story writer in developing the characters?
4. What advantage does the novelist have in developing plot?
5. What is meant by the *theme* of a novel?

UNIT 10

Participles and Participial Phrases   pages 346–347

Copy these sentences. Underline the participles or participial phrases. Draw an arrow to the word each one modifies.

1. A sparkling brook splashed over the rocks.
2. Stepping carefully, I crossed the rickety bridge.
3. The meadows bordering the brook were wet.
4. Slowly trudging up the hill, I headed home.
5. When I reached the top of the hill, I saw plowed fields.

Dangling Participles   pages 348–349

Rewrite these sentences, correcting the dangling participles.

1. Opening the mailbox, a package was found by Juana.
2. Wrapped inside the box, Juana discovered a gift.
3. Thrilled with her gift, Juana's eyes sparkled.
4. Wanting to wear it, the scarf was arranged on her neck.
5. Smiling happily, the mirror showed Juana how she looked.

Gerunds and Gerund Phrases   pages 350–351

Copy these sentences. Underline each gerund or gerund phrase. After each sentence, indicate how the verbal was used.

1. Dancing helps develop grace and self-assurance.
2. Dancers practice their dancing conscientiously every day.
3. Writing a novel requires conscientious work too.
4. The first step, planning the novel, takes much time.

Infinitives and Infinitive Phrases   pages 352–353

Copy these sentences. Underline the infinitives and infinitive phrases. After each sentence indicate how the infinitive or infinitive phrase was used.

1. Don't forget to start dinner this afternoon.
2. To have Jan for dinner is the plan for tonight.
3. The object of the dinner is to present a gift.
4. It is two opera tickets to be used this Friday.
5. To see an opera has been a secret wish for Jan.

Fact and Opinion   pages 356–357

Copy these sentences. Draw one line under the part of each sentence that gives a statement of fact. Draw two lines under the part that expresses an opinion.

1. The state bird of Utah is the sea gull, which must find Utah's Great Salt Lake almost too salty.
2. Texas has fabulous farms and the largest ranch in the U.S.
3. The Annual Hobo Convention, held in Iowa, is fascinating.
4. You will love touring Alaska, America's biggest state.
5. The inspiring song "America the Beautiful" was written by Katherine Lee Bates after her trip to Colorado.

Friendly and Business Letters   pages 360–364

1. Write a social note to a friend or relative in which you express your appreciation for a gift. Be sure to follow the correct form for a friendly letter.
2. Write a business letter in which you thank the personnel director of a company for granting you a job interview. Ask if there is any more information the company needs that was not asked at the interview.

Mechanics Practice   page 367

Rewrite these sentences, using exactly the same line divisions you see here. Add underscores and hyphens.

1. How many s's are there in the name Mississippi?
2. Vermont's name comes from the French vert, the transla tion of which is "green," and mont, meaning "mountain."
3. The motto of Arkansas is the Latin Regnant populus, mean ing "The people rule."
4. Colorado, the state with three o's in its name, has a Lat in motto, Nil sine Numine, "Nothing without Providence."

Reading Letters   pages 368–371

Famous literary figures and celebrities may take special pains with their letters, knowing that someday they may be published. Write a short composition in support of this opinion.

UNIT 11

Listening Critically pages 378–379

Read these parts of advertisements for dog clothes. For each one write the name of the technique on which the advertisement's appeal is based.

1. Your dog will reflect your good taste in an outfit by Rudolfo.
2. Picture your pooch in a chic Rudolfo handmade sweater or a dazzling Rudolfo disco outfit.
3. Actress Rita Starr says, "My Peaches is crazy about her denim Rudolfo cape—and so am I!"
4. Join the growing numbers who have discovered Rudolfo.
5. Why be seen with an unfashionable pet when you can walk a dog dressed by Rudolfo?

Explanations and Directions/Announcements and Introductions pages 380–383

1. Write a set of directions on how to make introductions. Tell how to introduce a person to a group, how to introduce two people to each other, and how to behave when you are seated and the person being introduced to you is standing.
2. Write an announcement that gives an explanation of an event. For example, it could be an explanation of why a sporting event or a space flight was postponed. It could be an announcement made on an alien planet about the arrival of strange-looking "Earthlings" and the supposed purpose of their visit.

Conducting a Meeting pages 384–385

Answer these questions about conducting a meeting.

1. What is the purpose of rules of parliamentary procedure?
2. What does the secretary do at a meeting?
3. What is discussed first at a meeting before new topics are introduced?
4. What does a person do to speak to the group?
5. What may happen if people speak out of turn?
6. What must happen before a topic can be discussed or an action taken?

Applying for a Job   pages 388–391

1. Write an application in response to this help-wanted ad. Assume that you have the necessary qualifications. Feel free to invent names, places, and companies.

   AUTO SALESPERSON: M/F Aggressive, experienced pro with good sales record. Salary + commission to right person.

Imagine that you have been asked these questions on a job interview. Write your answers.

2. Why do you want this job? 3. What are your career plans?
4. Why should we hire you?   5. What questions do you have?

Writing a Speech   pages 392–394

Write the opening paragraph and the concluding sentence of a speech on one of these topics.

   How To/How Not To Apply for a Job
   What to Say/What Not To Say in a Job Interview

Mechanics Practice   page 397

Rewrite these sentences. Add punctuation where it is needed.

1. Typical topics in an almanac are as follows current events, awards, maps, taxes, space, and science.
2. According to the almanac, third-class mail under 16 ounces is used for the following circulars, books, and other printed matter.
3. My favorite almanac category "The Best of This Year's Trivia" contains both silly and startling facts.
4. The almanac gives the birthplace of Lucille Ball stage name of Dianne Belmont as Celoran, New York.

Reading a Speech   pages 398–401

Find Lincoln's Gettysburg Address in your workbook or some other source. Write two paragraphs explaining the purpose of the speech, how it was suited to the occasion, and why it was memorable. Use quotations to illustrate your points.

INDEX

Commas, *continued*
    in letter parts, 437–438, 445
    with quotation marks, 150, 445–446, 448–449
    in a series of items, 297, 445, 478
    with transitional expressions, 297, 446
Common adjectives, 162–163, 192, 467
    defined, 163, 430
Common nouns, 80–81, 92, 112, 117, 197, 407, 461
    defined, 80, 423
Comparative degree, 164–165, 168–169, 172–173, 197, 430–431, 467–468
Comparison/contrast paragraphs. *See* Paragraphs
Comparison
    of adjectives, 164–165, 172, 192, 197, 430, 467
    of adverbs, 168–169, 173, 192–193, 197, 431, 468
    with analogies, 176–177, 193, 468
    in poetry. *See* Metaphors; Similes
Complements, defined, 200, 422. *See also* Direct objects; Indirect objects; Predicate adjectives; Predicate nominatives
Complete predicates, 4–5, 16, 36, 116, 196, 456
    defined, 4, 421
Complete subjects, 4–5, 16, 36, 116, 196, 456
    defined, 4, 421
Complex sentences, 314–315, 407, 479
    defined, 315, 415, 420
    diagraming, 415
Compound-complex sentences, 314–315, 407, 420, 479
Compound direct objects, diagraming, 414
Compound predicates, 10–11, 17, 116, 196, 457
    defined, 10, 421
    diagraming, 414
Compound sentences, 12–13, 17, 37, 116, 196, 457, 479
    complex, 314–315, 407, 420, 479
    defined, 12, 420
    diagraming, 414
    punctuation of, 12, 24, 25, 31, 38, 420, 445–446, 451
Compound subjects, 10–11, 17, 116, 457
    defined, 10, 421
    diagraming, 414
    with pronouns, 240
    verb agreement with, 136–137, 454
Compound words, 216–217, 232, 451, 471
    plural forms, 83, 424
Concrete nouns. *See* Nouns
Conjugations of verbs, defined, 134
Conjunctions, 24–25, 31, 278–281, 306, 477

coordinating. *See* Coordinating conjunctions
correlative, 278–279, 280–281, 421, 435
    defined, 279, 435
    diagraming, 414
subordinating, 314–317, 407, 415–416, 435
Consonance, 34–35, 39, 458
Contractions, 335, 342, 450, 481
    pronouns in, 240, 247
Coordinating conjunctions, 278–279, 280–281, 407, 477
    with compound predicates, 10, 421
    in compound sentences, 12, 38, 420, 458, 477
    with compound subjects, 10, 136–137, 421
    defined, 279, 414, 435
    diagraming, 414
Copyright page, using a, 250–251, 267, 475
Correlative conjunctions, 278–279, 281, 421
    defined, 279, 435
Critical listening, 378–379, 386, 402, 484
Cross-references, 94, 96–97, 145

Dangling participles, 348–349, 354, 372, 482
Dashes, 397, 404–405, 451
Dates, 223, 233, 437–438, 445–446, 469, 472
Days of the week
    abbreviations, 86–87, 93, 113, 117
    capitalization of, 187, 442, 469, 472
Declarative sentences, 2–3, 16, 36, 116, 456
    defined, 3, 418
    diagraming, 409
    punctuation of, 2–3, 31, 39, 418, 444
Definite articles, defined, 162–163, 430
Definitions, 20–21
    homographic, 22–23, 38, 140–141, 466
    multiple, 22–23
Degrees of comparison, 164–165, 168–169, 172–173, 197, 430–431
Delete, editing mark for, 29, 440
Demonstrative pronouns. *See* Pronouns
Dénouement. *See* Resolution
Dependent clauses, 314–321, 324–325, 419
    adjective, 254, 318–319, 324–325, 415, 419, 479
    adverb, 316–317, 324, 415, 419, 479
    defined, 315, 419
    diagraming, 415
    noun, 320–321, 325, 341, 416, 419, 480
Descriptive paragraphs. *See* Paragraphs
Detail sentences, 42–43, 45, 436, 459
    supporting the main idea with, 47–49, 51, 75, 116–117, 196, 459

Hyphens
        in compound words, 216, 451
        end-of-line word divisions, 20–21, 367,
        374–375, 451, 483

I
        capitalization of, 441
        and *me,* 239–241, 452–453
Idioms, 145
Imperative sentences, 2–3, 16, 36, 116, 407,
        456
        defined, 2–3, 418
        diagraming, 409
        punctuation of, 2–3, 31, 39, 418, 444
        understood subject in, 2, 8, 16, 409, 421,
        457
In and *into,* 273, 452–453
Indefinite articles, defined, 162–163, 430
Indefinite pronouns. *See* Pronouns
Indenting
        editing mark for, 105, 149, 440
        in outlines, 286–287
        of paragraphs, 42, 105, 149, 436
Independent clauses, 314–315, 324, 340
        defined, 315, 419
Index
        almanac, 95
        book, 252–253, 268, 475
        encyclopedia, 94
Indirect objects, 202–203, 208, 230, 470, 473
        defined, 202, 410, 422
        diagraming, 410
Infinitive phrases, 352–353, 355, 373, 482
        defined, 353, 425
        diagraming, 417
Infinitives, 352–353, 355, 373, 407, 482
        defined, 353, 417, 425
        diagraming, 417
Information, classification of, 174–175, 193,
        468
Initialisms, 169
Initials, 69, 441, 444
Intensive pronouns. *See* Pronouns
Interjections, 276–277, 280–281, 306, 407
        defined, 276, 435
        punctuation of, 276, 447, 477
Interrogative pronouns. *See* Pronouns
Interrogative sentences, 2–3, 16, 36, 116, 407,
        456
        defined, 2–3, 418
        diagraming, 409
        punctuation of, 2–3, 31, 418, 447
        word order in, 8
Interrupting expressions, punctuation of,
        297, 446, 478
Interviews
        for jobs, 390–391, 404, 485

of people, 98–99
Intransitive verbs. *See* Verbs
Introductions, of people, 382–383, 387, 403,
        407, 484
Introductory words and expressions, punctu-
        ation of, 297, 445–446, 478
Inverted word order, in sentences, 8, 16, 26,
        36, 136, 457
        diagraming, 408
Irregular verbs. *See* Verbs
Its and *it's,* 242, 452–453

Job hunting
        applications, 388–389, 403, 485
        interviews, 390–391, 404, 485
Joining words. *See* Conjunctions

Language Review, 16–17, 50–51, 92–93, 138–
        139, 172–173, 208–209, 248–249, 280–
        281, 324–325, 354–355, 386–387
Languages, capitalization of, 187, 443
Latin expressions, abbreviations of, 87
Letters
        business, 363–366, 374, 438, 440, 451,
        483
        editing, 365–366, 374, 440
        envelope, addressing an, 86–87, 364, 439
        of famous people, 368–371, 375
        friendly, 360–362, 374, 437, 445, 483
        parts of, 361, 437–438
        social notes, 361–362, 374, 437, 445, 483
        writing, 360–364, 374, 483
Letters of the alphabet, plural forms, 335, 342,
        374, 450, 481, 483
Library, 52–59, 75–76, 459
        card catalog, 55–57, 76, 459
        Dewey Decimal System, 56, 58–59, 76
        organization of, 52–54, 75
Library of Congress System, 56
Linking verbs, 122–123, 138, 156, 197, 407,
        464
        defined, 122, 426
        with predicate adjectives, 206, 209, 412,
        422, 471
        with predicate nominatives, 204, 209,
        412, 422, 470
Listening
        critically, 378–379, 386, 402, 484
        to directions and explanations, 380–381,
        386
List of items, punctuation of a. *See* Series
        of items, punctuation of a
Literature, words originating from, 323, 385
Loaded words, 379, 386, 402
Logical conclusions, 358–359, 373
Lowercase, editing mark for, 29, 365, 440

Macron marks, 20, 37
Magazines
    as reference sources, 96–97
    titles of, 261, 288–289, 448, 475
Main idea, in paragraphs. *See* Paragraphs
Main verbs. *See* Verbs
Maintenance and Review, 116–117, 196–197, 310–311, 406–407
Me and *I*, 239–241, 452–453
Meaningless statistics, in advertising, 379, 386, 402
Mechanics Practice, 31, 69, 107, 150–151, 187, 223, 261, 297, 335, 367, 397, 458, 460, 463, 466, 469, 472, 475, 478, 481, 483, 485
Media, nonprint, 98–99
Meeting, conducting a, 384–385, 387, 403, 484
Metaphors, 70–73, 183, 349, 460
Meter, in poetry, 33
Microfiche, 53, 98
Microfilm, 53, 98, 114
Minutes, of meetings, 384–385
Modifiers
    defined, 322
    misplaced, 322–323, 325, 341, 480
Months
    abbreviations, 86–87, 93, 113, 117
    capitalization of, 187, 194, 223, 442, 472
Monuments, capitalization of, 107, 441
Moral myths, 108–110, 463
More Practice, 456–485
Most and *almost*, 171, 173, 193, 468
Motions, at meetings, 384–385, 403
Movies, titles of, 261, 443, 448, 475
Musical compositions, titles of, 261, 448
Myths, 108–111, 115, 463

Names of people, 69, 77, 441, 460–461
Narrative paragraphs. *See* Paragraphs
Narrative poetry, 188–191, 195, 469
    "Casey at the Bat," 189–190
    "Lochinvar" (excerpt), 188
Nationalities, 187, 441, 469
Natural word order, in sentences, 8, 16, 26, 36, 457
Nature myths, 108, 111, 115, 463
News articles
    bibliography listings, 288–289
    editing, 333–334, 342
    editorials, 221–222
    titles of, 288
    writing, 330–332, 342, 481
Newspapers
    in libraries, 53–54
    titles of, 261, 448, 475
Nonfiction, in libraries, 52–54, 56
Nonprint media, 98–99

Nonrestrictive adjective clauses, 318–319, 324–325
Note taking, 284–285, 307
Noun clauses, 320–321, 325, 341, 419, 480
    defined, 320, 416
    diagraming, 416
Nouns, 80–93, 117, 423–424, 461–462
    abbreviations of. *See* Abbreviations
    abstract, 80–81, 92, 112, 407, 423, 461
    appositive. *See* Appositives
    clauses, 320–321, 325, 341, 416, 419, 480
    collective, 84–85, 92–93, 112, 117, 137, 197, 454, 461
    common, 80–81, 92, 112, 117, 197, 407, 423, 461
    concrete, 80–81, 92, 112, 407, 423, 461
    defined, 80, 423
    gerunds. *See* Gerunds
    infinitives as, 352–353, 355, 373, 425, 482
    plural, 82–83, 92, 112, 117, 197, 424, 461
    possessive, 88–89, 93, 113, 117, 197, 335, 450, 462, 481
    proper, 80–81, 112, 117, 197, 407, 461
    singular, 82–83, 92, 112, 117, 461
Novels, 336–339, 343, 406, 481
    characteristics of, 336–337
    Dandelion Wine (excerpt), 336–339
    Dune (excerpt), 406
    Tuck Everlasting (excerpt), 343
Number, defined, 136, 236
Numbers
    plural forms, 187, 194
    underlining of, 367, 375

Objects
    diagraming, 410, 414
    direct. *See* Direct objects
    indirect. *See* Indirect objects
    of prepositions, 240, 272–273, 320–321, 434, 473, 476
    pronouns as, 240–241, 248, 266–267, 272, 407, 432–433, 473
Onomatopoeia, 34–35, 39, 458
Open compound words, 216–217
Opinion
    essays of. *See* Essays of opinion
    fact and, distinguishing between, 159, 356–357, 373, 483
Organizations, names of, 69, 77, 87, 113, 441, 460
    acronyms for, 169
Origins of words, 9, 89, 129, 238, 323, 349, 385
Outlines
    preparation of, 286–287, 308, 393, 444
    for research reports, 286–287, 290–291, 308

Positive degree, of comparison, 164–165, 168–169, 172–173, 197, 430–431
Possessive nouns, 88–89, 93, 113, 117, 197, 335, 450, 462, 481
Possessive pronouns. *See* Pronouns
Postal abbreviations, 86–87, 439
Predicate adjectives, 206–207, 209, 231, 471
    defined, 206, 407, 412, 422
    diagraming, 412
Predicate nominatives, 204–205, 209, 230–231, 407, 470, 473
    compound, 204, 240
    defined, 204, 412, 422
    diagraming, 412
    noun clauses as, 320–321, 325
Predicates
    complete, 4–5, 16, 36, 116, 196, 421, 456
    compound, 10–11, 17, 116, 196, 414, 421, 457
    defined, 4, 421
    simple, 6–7, 16, 36, 116, 124, 196, 408, 421, 456
    verb phrases, 124
Prefaces, in books, 250–251, 475
Prefixes, 210–211, 231, 471
Prepositional phrases, 272–275, 280–281, 306, 340, 407, 476
    as adjectives and adverbs, 274–275, 280, 413, 434, 476
    defined, 272, 413, 434
    diagraming, 413
Prepositions, 272–273, 280, 306, 476
    defined, 272, 434
    objects of, 240, 272–273, 320–321, 434, 473, 476
    phrases. *See* Prepositional phrases
    troublesome, 273
Present perfect tense, 132–135, 427
Present tense, 132–135, 427
Principal parts of verbs
    irregular verbs, 128–131, 139, 157, 197, 407, 428–429, 465
    regular verbs, 126–127, 138, 156–157, 197, 407, 428–429, 465
Pronouns, 236–249, 266–267, 432–433, 473–474
    antecedents of, 236–238, 246–248, 432, 454, 473
    combining sentences with, 254–255, 268
    compound personal, 244–245
    in contractions, 240, 247
    defined, 237, 432
    demonstrative, 244–245, 249, 267, 432–433, 474
    indefinite, 246–247, 249, 267, 432–433, 454, 474
    intensive, 244–245, 432–433

interrogative, 247, 249, 267, 433, 474
object, 240–241, 248, 266–267, 272, 407, 432–433, 473
possessive, 84–85, 162, 242–243, 248, 267, 432–433, 473–474
reflexive, 244–245, 249, 267, 432–433, 474
relative, 254–255, 268, 318–319, 415, 433
subject, 239–241, 248, 267, 407, 432–433, 473
troublesome, 452–453
Pronunciation of words, in dictionaries, 20–21, 37
Proper adjectives, 162–163, 187, 192, 194, 442, 467
    defined, 163, 430
Proper nouns, 80–81, 112, 117, 197, 407, 461
    abbreviations of. *See* Abbreviations
    capitalization of, 69, 80–81, 92, 187, 194, 423, 442, 461
    defined, 81, 423
Protagonists, in plays, 298, 305, 309, 478
Punctuation, 444–451. *See also* Apostrophes; Colons; Commas; Dashes; Exclamation points; Hyphens; Parentheses; Periods; Question marks; Quotation marks; Semicolons; Underlining

Question marks, 2–3, 31, 418, 447
    with quotation marks, 150, 448–449
Questions. *See* Interrogative sentences
Quorum, 384–385
Quotation marks, 150–151, 448–449
    editing mark for, 259–260, 440
    with end punctuation, 150–151, 445–446, 448–449, 466
    with titles of written works, 261, 268–269, 448, 475
Quotations
    punctuation of, 150–151, 159, 445–446, 448–449, 466
    in speeches, 396

Readers' Guide to Periodical Literature, 96–97, 114, 462
Real and *really,* 170, 173, 193, 468
Reasoning correctly, 358–359, 373
Records
    as reference sources, 98–99, 114
    titles of, 261, 448, 475
Reference section, in libraries, 53–54
Reflexive pronouns. *See* Pronouns
Relative pronouns, 254–255, 268, 318–319
    defined, 255, 319, 433
    diagraming, 415
Repetition, in speeches, 400

A 2
B 3
C 4
D 5
E 6
F 7
G 8
H 9
I 0
J 1